Local Action
Global Change

Local Action ——— Global Change

A Handbook on Women's Human Rights

Julie A. Mertus and Nancy Flowers

Paradigm Publishers
Boulder • London

Paradigm Publishers is committed to preserving ancient forests and natural resources. We elected to print *Local Action/ Global Change* on 30% post consumer recycled paper, processed chlorine free. As a result, for this printing, we have saved:

11 Trees (40' tall and 6-8" diameter)
4,814 Gallons of Wastewater
1,936 Kilowatt Hours of Electricity
531 Pounds of Solid Waste
1,042 Pounds of Greenhouse Gases

Paradigm Publishers made this paper choice because our printer, Thomson-Shore, Inc., is a member of Green Press Initiative, a nonprofit program dedicated to supporting authors, publishers, and suppliers in their efforts to reduce their use of fiber obtained from endangered forests.

For more information, visit www.greenpressinitiative.org

Published in the United States by Paradigm Publishers, 3360 Mitchell Lane Suite E, Boulder, CO 80301 USA.

Paradigm Publishers is the trade name of Birkenkamp & Company, LLC, Dean Birkenkamp, President and Publisher.

Library of Congress Cataloging-in-Publication Data
Mertus, Julie A., 1963–
    Local action/global change : a handbook on women's human rights / Julie A. Mertus and Nancy Flowers.
        p. cm.
    Includes bibliographical references and index.
    ISBN 978-1-59451-514-9 (hardcover : alk. paper)
    1. Women's rights—Handbooks, manuals, etc.   I. Flowers, Nancy.   II. Title.
    HQ1236.M428 2008
    323.3'4—dc22
                                    2007045739

Printed and bound in the United States of America on acid-free paper that meets the standards of the American National Standard for Permanence of Paper for Printed Library Materials.

Designed and typeset by Mulberry Tree Enterprises.

12   11   10   09   08   1   2   3   4   5

Contents

Acknowledgments   ix
Foreword   xi
Prologue   xv

Chapter 1: Introduction to Women's Human Rights   1

Learning Activity 1: From Human Needs to Human Rights   9
Learning Activity 2: The Body of Human Rights   11
Learning Activity 3: Sex or Gender?   16
Learning Activity 4: Exploring Gender Stereotypes   17
Learning Activity 5: Women's Experience with Discrimination   18
Learning Activity 6: Standing Up for Yourself   19
Learning Activity 7: What Are Women's Human Rights?   23
Learning Activity 8: The Roots of Our Activism   24
Learning Activity 9: Victim, Abuser, Bystander, Helper   26

Chapter 2: Women's Human Rights to Equality and Nondiscrimination   28

Learning Activity 1: Identity and Interconnectedness   29
Learning Activity 2: The Complex Nature of Discrimination   35
Learning Activity 3: Examples of Discrimination   36
Learning Activity 4: Defining and Analyzing Racism   39
Learning Activity 5: Analyzing Culture and Religion   45
Learning Activity 6: Myths and Stereotypes about Disability   49
Learning Activity 7: Examining Women's Intimate Relationships   52
Learning Activity 8: Acknowledging Class   53
Learning Activity 9: Responding to Concerns of Older Women   56
Learning Activity 10: Speaking Out Against Discrimination   56

Chapter 3: Women's Human Rights in the Family   62

Learning Activity 1: Decision-Making Power in the Family   65
Learning Activity 2: Indivisibility and Interdependence of Rights   69
Learning Activity 3: Religion, Culture, and the Family   71

Learning Activity 4: When Private Is Public   74
Learning Activity 5: Marriage Customs   76
Learning Activity 6: Nationality Laws   78
Learning Activity 7: Responding to Women Who Live Apart from Men   81
*Learning Activity 8: Speaking Out for Women's Human Rights
    in the Family   84*

Chapter 4: The Human Rights of Young Women and Girls   87

Learning Activity 1: Childhood Myths   89
Learning Activity 2: Traditional Practices   95
*Learning Activity 3: Taking Action Against Sexual Harassment
    and Violence   100*
Learning Activity 4: A Girl Laborer's Story   103
*Learning Activity 5: Speaking Out for the Human Rights of Young
    Women and Girls   106*

Chapter 5: Women's Human Right to Health   112

Learning Activity 1: Defining Women's Health   114
Learning Activity 2: Health Needs at the Community Level   116
Learning Activity 3: Impact of a Woman's Health on Her Life Cycle   120
Learning Activity 4: Speaking Out for Women's Health   123

Chapter 6: Women's Human Rights to Reproduction and Sexuality   127

Learning Activity 1: Discussion Circle on Reproductive Rights   128
Learning Activity 2: Decisions About Reproduction and Sexuality   130
Learning Activity 3: Taking Action for Reproductive Rights   133
Learning Activity 4: Conflicting Messages About Reproduction   136
Learning Activity 5: Blaming the Poor   139
Learning Activity 6: Sex Education for Whom?   141
*Learning Activity 7: Speaking Out for Women's Reproductive and
    Sexual Rights   143*

Chapter 7: Women's Human Right to Freedom from Violence   147

Learning Activity 1: Defining Violence Against Women   151
Learning Activity 2: The Cycle of Recognition and Enforcement of Rights   157
Learning Activity 3: Myths and Facts About Domestic Violence   160
Learning Activity 4: Violence and Inability to Flee   163
Learning Activity 5: Human Rights and Violence Against Women   164
Learning Activity 6: Speaking Out on Violence Against Women   168

Chapter 8: Women's Human Right to an Adequate Standard of Living   172

Learning Activity 1: Identifying Basic Needs   173
Learning Activity 2: Impact of Poverty on Women   175
Learning Activity 3: Last in Line for Food   180
*Learning Activity 4: Thinking About Adequate Housing as
    a Human Right   186*
*Learning Activity 5: Speaking Out for Women's Human Right to an
    Adequate Standard of Living   188*

Chapter 9: Women's Human Rights and Globalization

Learning Activity 1: The Global Marketplace   194
*Learning Activity 2: Weighing the Positive and Negative Effects of
   Globalization on Women   196*
Learning Activity 3: Trafficking and Gender Bias   198
Learning Activity 4: Women and Poverty Reduction   204
Learning Activity 5: Gender and Development—Taking a Stand   207
Learning Activity 6: Making Women's Economic Rights a Reality   210

Chapter 10: Women's Human Rights and Work

Learning Activity 1: The 24-Hour Day   216
Learning Activity 2: Informal Work   219
Learning Activity 3: Women Wage Earners in Your Community   220
Learning Activity 4: Discrimination on the Job   223
Learning Activity 5: Affirmative Action—Should Mano Be Hired?   225
Learning Activity 6: Is This Sexual Harassment?   227
Learning Activity 7: Unsuitable Work for a Woman   229
Learning Activity 8: Speaking Out for Women at Work   232

Chapter 11: Women's Human Right to Education

Learning Activity 1: Why We Learn   236
Learning Activity 2: Education Makes a Difference   238
Learning Activity 3: I Can't Read It!   240
Learning Activity 4: Bringing Education to All Women   243
Learning Activity 5: Gender-Role Stereotyping in Education   245
Learning Activity 6: Nko's Story   248
*Learning Activity 7: The Role of Government Versus the
   Role of Tradition   249*
*Learning Activity 8: Speaking Out for Women's Human
   Right to Education   252*

Chapter 12: Women's Human Rights in Politics, Public Life, and the Media

Learning Activity 1: A Recipe for Political Success   260
Learning Activity 2: Obstacles to Public Participation   262
Learning Activity 3: Political Persecution of Women   264
Learning Activity 4: Becoming a Public Person, Taking a Public Stand   268
Learning Activity 5: Portrayal of Women in the Media   272
Learning Activity 6: Alternative Media for Women   274
*Learning Activity 7: Speaking Out for Women's Human Rights in
   Politics, Public Life, and the Media   276*

Chapter 13: Human Rights of Refugee, Displaced, and War-Affected Women

Learning Activity 1: The Impact of Armed Conflict on Women's Lives   284
Learning Activity 2: Political Flight   286
Learning Activity 3: Possible Intervention for Women Refugees   289
Learning Activity 4: The Right to Asylum—Refugees at the Border   292
Learning Activity 5: The Right to Asylum—Refugees Before a Tribunal   294

Learning Activity 6: Women as Agents for Peace?　300
Learning Activity 7: Speaking Out for the Human Rights of
　　Women in Wartime　302

Chapter 14: The Road Ahead: Local Action and Global Change　309

Appendix I　Analytical Tables: Analyzing Human Rights Problems,
　　　　　　Implementing Human Rights Strategies　311
Appendix II　Participatory Methodologies for Educators
　　　　　　and Facilitators　313
Appendix III　Using Human Rights Systems and Mechanisms　325
Glossary　329
Bibliography　336
Index　342
About the Authors　350

Acknowledgments

Local Action/Global Change reflects the efforts and voices of many people around the world. We are very grateful for the generous support the book has received through the several years and drafts that have led to this publication.

Had not Roxanna Carrillo of the United Nations Development Fund for Women (UNIFEM) and Charlotte Bunch of the Center for Women's Global Leadership (CWGL) believed in this project, it would never have come to fruition. We also thank UNIFEM consultants Daniella van Gennep and Jane Summer and CWGL staff members Deevy Holcomb, Shona Chakravartty, Surabhi Kukke, Lisa Clarke, and Lucy Vidal for their support.

We would especially like to acknowledge the work of Janet Lord, who wrote most of Chapter 8, "Women's Human Right to an Adequate Standard of Living," and, with Kathy Guernsey, improved the content on women with disabilities. Beyond these contributions, Janet and Kathy warrant special appreciation for their continued support of us, the book, and human rights education.

We also give our warm thanks to:

- Inspiring leaders in human rights education Mahnaz Akhfani, Loretta Ross, Margaret Schuler, and Krsiti Rudelius-Palmer
- Krishanti Dharmaraj and Mallika Dutt
- Shulamith Koenig and the People's Decade for Human Rights Education
- Sonja Licht and the Soros Yugoslavia Foundation
- Larry Cox, Helen Neuborne, and the Ford Foundation
- Sevdie Ahmet, the International Working Group on Refugee Women, Tara Krause, Katrine Kremmler, Mobility International USA, Zorica Mrsevic, the Older Women's Network of London, Hitha Prabhakar, Judy Persky, Debra Robbins, and Rachel Wareham
- Stephanie Urdang, Liz Fisher, Sofia Gruskin, Lucie Lamarche, Lyn Reece, and Daniel Ravindran
- Susan Fried, Leila Hessini, Janine Hicks, Vesna Kesic, Saraphina Maboso, Ali Miller, Betty Powell, Beth Richie, Ruth Selwyn, Olena Suslova, Dorothy Thomas, Mariama Williams, and Felice Yaban
- Jennifer Forrence, Kathy Forrence, and Shirley Steele
- Jelica Todosijevic, Ted Andersson, and Daniel Sumit Ghosal

- Student researchers at American University's Ethics, Peace, and Global Affairs Program Alison Long, Laura K. Ritter, and Laurie Rosenberger
- Jane Gindin, Paula Kentworthy, Martha Moses, Samantha Parsons, Mary Hill Rojas, Anita Sachariah, and Kelly Scott Vaena.

We dedicate this book to Julie's children Lynne and Daniel and to Nancy's granddaughter Emmeline, who remind us daily why we work for a better world.

Foreword

"Women's rights are human rights" has become an important rallying cry for women around the world over the past two decades. It expresses both women's determination to claim their full birthright as one-half of humanity and their exasperation that such an obvious assertion has taken so long to gain international acceptance. As the recognition of women's and girl's human rights has grown, so too has the need for more works that explore and expound upon their meaning.

Local Action/Global Change speaks to this need through human rights educational materials that explain and give examples of issues in women's human rights, while also providing learning activities that allow for exploration of the ways in which these questions affect the lives of all people—not just women and girls but men and boys as well.

The idea that women's rights are human rights is at once both simple and complex. Its power lies in the fact that it is simultaneously ordinary and revolutionary. On the one hand, it is common sense to declare that as human beings, women and girls have human rights. On the other hand, it is a radical reclamation of women's humanity and right to equality—a reclamation that has transformative potential. The full incorporation of women's and girls' lives into human rights concepts and practices exposes the failure of countries worldwide to accord females the human dignity and respect they deserve simply as human beings.

Denial of human rights means denial of the fundamental components of being human. It means the dehumanization of women, which fosters discrimination and violence against women and girls—from rape during wartime to economic exploitation and culturally rationalized restrictions on basic freedoms. Human rights principles demand an end to practices that treat women and girls as less than full human beings. Thus, the language of human rights assists in the task of identifying not just the violators, who must then be held accountable, but also the appropriate remedies for such abuses.

Women's peripheral status has been exacerbated, and sometimes rationalized, by the division of life into public and private spheres that prevails in so many societies. Since the public sphere is seen as the arena of interaction between state actors and citizens, abuses of that relationship have been the focus of human rights advocacy. However, much of the abuse of women and girls is carried out by individual male partners or family members and is often overlooked by governments even when there are laws against it. Thus, many violations of women's human rights that are committed in the name of family, religion, and culture have been hidden by the sanctity of the so-called private sphere, and the perpetrators have enjoyed immunity from accountability for their actions.

The status of citizen, too, has often been exclusionary, entailing gender, racial, and socioeconomic bias and privileges that marginalize women. Indeed, as public and governmental realms are populated predominantly by men, the human rights issues given the most attention have tended to be those to which men are most vulnerable—arbitrary detention, political imprisonment, torture, and abuses of civil and political rights, such as the rights to freedom of speech, religion, and assembly.

A human rights perspective helps to illuminate the complicated relationship that exists between gender and other aspects of identity, such as race, class, religion, age, sexual orientation, disability, culture, and refugee or migrant status. From this perspective, discrimination and violence against women and girls can be understood as having been shaped by the ways in which gender interfaces with such factors. An example of human rights violations that entail discrimination on the basis of class and race as well as gender—one example among many—is the forced sterilization of poor women in certain countries.

Taking action for women's and girl's human rights involves a shift both in thinking about human rights and in talking about female lives. Current human rights practices have failed to account for many of the ways in which human rights abuses affect females differently than males. The approach detailed in this book calls for more gender sensitivity in human rights practices in the interests of fully including the experiences of the female half of the population.

Viewing women's and girls' human rights through a human rights framework has brought new clarity and powerful tools to bear on women's issues. For example, the movement to draw attention to violence against women as a human rights issue has built on the Universal Declaration's fundamental premise that "[n]o one shall be subject to torture or to cruel, inhuman or degrading treatment or punishment." Human rights vocabulary has helped to define and articulate women's and girls' experiences of violations such as rape, female genital cutting, and domestic violence in ways that raise the level of expectations about what can and should be done about them. Understanding such violence in terms of human rights establishes unequivocally that states are responsible for such abuse, whether committed in public or in private. It raises questions about how to hold governments accountable when they are indifferent to such abuses and about what sorts of mechanisms are needed to expedite the process of redress for violations of women.

The concept of women's human rights has opened the way for hard questions to be posed about the official inattention and indifference to the widespread discrimination and violence that women and girls experience. Whether used in political lobbying in legal cases, in grassroots mobilization, or in broad-based educational efforts, the idea of women's human rights has been taken up by women across many boundaries and has facilitated international networking and the creation of collaborative strategies.

A global movement has emerged to challenge limited notions that have deemed the lives of women secondary to other human rights issues. The United Nations World Conference on Human Rights held in Vienna in 1993 became a natural vehicle to highlight new visions of human rights thinking and practice. Its initial call did not mention women, nor were any gender-specific aspects of human rights recognized in its proposed agenda. Yet since the conference represented a historic reassessment of the state of human rights, it became the unifying public focus of a worldwide Global Campaign for Women's Human Rights—a collaborative effort that sought to integrate women into the conference agenda. Indeed, the concept of women's human rights provides a common framework for collaboration around broad and similar concerns about the status of women, while also providing a way to articulate the diverse pressing human rights issues specific to particular political, geographic, economic, and cultural contexts.

The Vienna Declaration and Program of Action, signed by 171 governments present at the 1993 conference, is intended to indicate the agreement of the international community on various aspects of human rights. It states unequivocally that

> [t]he human rights of women and of the girl-child are an inalienable, integral, and indivisible part of universal human rights. The full and equal participation of women in the political, civil, economic, social and cultural life, at the national, regional and international levels, and the eradication of all forms of discrimination on grounds of sex, are priority objectives of the international community.

Another achievement of women growing out of the Vienna conference was the appointment by the UN Commission on Human Rights of a Special Rapporteur on Violence Against Women, whose job it is to report each year to the Commission on such violence and to specify what the United Nations and governments should be doing about it as a human rights issue. Women have also continued to lobby for and gain wider recognition of women's human rights at subsequent United Nations conferences. For example, at the International Conference on Population and Development in Cairo in 1994, women's reproductive rights were explicitly recognized as human rights. The Platform for Action at the Fourth World Conference in Beijing in 1995 became an agenda outlining the human rights of women and what it will take to achieve them. And in 1998, advocates for women's human rights succeeded in getting rape, forced pregnancy, and sexual slavery recognized as crimes against humanity in the statute for the creation of an International Criminal Court at its founding in Rome.

The human rights framework creates a space in which the possibility for a different account of women's lives can be developed. What is so useful about this framework is that it provides principles by which to develop alternative visions of women's and girls' lives without suggesting the substance of those visions. The fundamental principles of human rights that accord to each and every person the entitlement to human dignity give women a vocabulary for describing both violations and impediments to the exercise of their human rights. The large body of international covenants, agreements, and commitments about human rights gives women political leverage and a tenable point of reference. And, finally, the idea of women's human rights enables women to define and articulate experiences in their lives at the same time that it provides a vocabulary to share the experiences of other women around the world and work collaboratively for a change.

Human rights systems provide a way to hold governments, communities, and international institutions accountable to some basic ethical standards—a crucial part of which is human rights education and the recognition of one's rights. This book aims to help advocates to identify and recognize such claims. The next step is moving from rights recognition to rights empowerment. Each chapter of this book provides ideas for organizing for action at the community, state, regional, and international levels. When advocates for the human rights of women and girls are challenged at home, regional and international documents can help prevent one from feeling isolated and be used to demonstrate that governments have already undertaken obligations to recognize and respect these human rights. We must ensure that such documents amount to more than words on paper. Together, we must find ways to turn the vision of human rights into action, leading to meaningful change in our lives and in the world. As this book seeks to demonstrate, through local action, we can bring global change.

—Charlotte Bunch,
Center for Women's Global Studies, Rutgers University

Prologue

From the Kitchen Table
to the Burmese Border

Like the human rights movement itself, the development of this book was non-linear and multidimensional. Its complex genesis and development was propelled by four historic moments: (1) the meetings of the Belgrade kitchen tablers during 1994–1995; (2) Amnesty International's early support of human rights education; (3) sponsorship by the People's Decade for Human Rights Education of human rights education projects at the 1995 World Conference on Women in Beijing; and (4) sponsorship by the Center for Global Leadership's and the United Nations Development Fund for Women (UNIFEM). While the Belgrade developments were crucial for one author, the entry of Amnesty International into educational endeavors was a decisive factor for the other. The last two moments were vital for bringing the authors together and for making this project real.

Kitchen Tablers in Belgrade

Sometime during the long, cold winter of 1994, a group of women sat around a kitchen table in Belgrade and dreamed of a better world. An incredibly diverse collection of anti-war activists, domestic violence hotline volunteers, women's studies professors, journalists, therapists, and artists, the women hailed from such faraway places as Jerusalem, New York, London, Frankfurt, and Moscow, folding in multiple nationalities, religions, and ages. They were united by one common goal: the need to promote peace and justice throughout the Balkans.

Optimism was hard to come by, and when the young American lawyer suggested improving the world through human rights education, the group erupted in snickers. "No, I'm serious," she insisted. "We could start here."

Here? Belgrade seemed like a strange place for human rights.

"We could have two language versions of the text to start," the lawyer explained, "one in Serbian and the other in Albanian" (referring to the ethnic Albanians in Kosovo). The idea was to make the book available for other language groups to translate and adapt, but to not offer any funding for translations. "That way, if the translations happen," the supporters of the book suggested, "[it is] because they are seen by local activists as fulfilling their needs." In other words, the phenomenon of books being printed or training being offered just because the money exists would be eliminated. Language editions would exist only if local groups were willing to make their own investment in their creation.

Because a number of the "kitchen tablers" had participated in the 1993 World Conference on Human Rights in Vienna, they had already begun to think in terms of using human rights to improve women's daily lives. The promise of human rights was both a source of optimism and a good in itself.

Workshops in Berkeley, Birmingham, Bratislava, and Bucharest

Be careful how you time your trips to the Ladies' Room! An English teacher excused herself from a meeting and returned to find herself named Amnesty International USA's national coordinator for human rights education. The endeavor was new not only to Amnesty but, to the United States, with no precedents to break but also, no support staff, established resources, or networks. The early years involved learning how to make the human rights framework accessible to a wide range of Americans, finding allies and collaborators, building a network of human rights educators, and creating materials. And lots and lots of workshops, from Bloomington and Burlington and Washington to Disneyland and Dallas.

New opportunities for human rights education burgeoned. In the early 1990s, as former Soviet-bloc countries began to change regimes, rewrite their constitutions, and revamp their legal and educational system, Amnesty's International Secretariat took up the challenge with major educational initiatives in central and eastern Europe. The old Marxist-required courses in "civics" went out of the curriculum to be replaced by "democracy and human rights," but the shift involved retraining everyone from professors of education and Ministry of Education officials to classroom teachers and NGO activists in the fundamentals of human rights and the interactive methodologies of human rights education. Just the kind of assignment for someone with both human rights knowledge and pedagogic skills and experience.

Inspiration in Beijing

In the early 1990s, the People's Decade for Human Rights Education was the only organization working exclusively in the field. By dint of determination and chutzpah, its dynamic founder, Shulamith Koenig, managed to put human rights education on the United Nations agenda. It is largely due to her efforts that the UN declared 1994–2005 the Decade for Human Rights Education.

It is also due to Shula that the authors met and, with Mallika Dutt, entered into collaboration on what would become a decade-long human rights education program. "Da-link," she said, "you must meet Julie Mertus. She's writing the same book you are." And indeed she was.

The People's Decade underwrote the development of some of the core exercises that would find their way into this book. A quickly photocopied version of the text was distributed for review in English, Spanish, and Russian at the 1995 Fourth World Conference on Women in Beijing. As part of an international collective of women human rights educators brought together by the People's Decade, the authors had the opportunity in Beijing to work through many of the exercises in the book with women from around the world, to hear their stories, and to learn from their experiences. Philomena from South Africa could entice even shy Asian women to sing and dance together, Megna from Bangladesh had the gift of storytelling, and the women from the United States took a back seat and listened and learned.

A Refugee Camp in Burma

"This you, this you?" A middle-aged Thai woman ran up to us and pointed to a dog-eared bundle of pages. The writing on the cover sheet looked like squiggles to us, but we had come to recognize it as our names in Burmese.

It was mid-day and the refugee camp on the Thai-Burmese border had begun to come to life. The woman clutching the pages had translated the refugee chapter of *Local Action/Global Change* to teach tribal women who had fled the Burmese regime's forced labor on the oil pipeline.

"This us," we thought, as we examined the tattered photocopy of the booklet she was waving, "is human rights education."

We were amazed at how fast the photocopies had got around, and how far. Almost immediately after the text was released in 1999 during the annual meeting of the UN Committee on the Status of Women, it began emerging in different languages. Because the original text was copyright free for educational purposes, an accurate number of translations is not possible, but the authors have received copies of all or part of the project in these languages: Albanian, Arabic, Burmese, Chinese (two versions, one for Hong Kong and one for Mainland China), Croatian, English, Hungarian, Romanian (two versions, one for Moldova and one for Romania), Russian (two versions), Serbian, Spanish, Thai, and Ukrainian. (Undoubtedly, other language versions have yet to reach our desks.) In addition to these separate language versions, exercises and entire sections from the project have found their way into numerous training manuals throughout the world. The whole point behind the project was to get the news of human rights education "out there"—as long as it was needed and desired. There is no question: It is out! And now, with the help of Chemonics and Paradigm Publishers, it will have even further reach.

It is indeed high time for the official publication of *Local Action/Global Change*. The women's human rights movement has made great strides since 1999. The Office of the High Commissioner for Human Rights has devoted significant resources to promoting women's human rights worldwide, in both wartime and peacetime. Thanks to the UN Special Rapporteur on Violence Against Women, states can no longer claim ignorance of states' responsibilities to address violence against women and girls. In many places, women have benefited from the National Action Plans emerging as part of states' commitments to the 1995 World Conference on Women Declaration and Platform for Action. And more and more states have signed onto the Optional Protocol to Convention on the Elimination of All Forms of Discrimination Against Women

(CEDAW), which permits individuals to bring complaints about violations to the committee monitoring CEDAW. Granted, women face new challenges to their human rights resulting from the negative effects of globalization, economic-based migration, and forms of warfare that incorporate human rights abuses as a part of war strategy. But the explosion of Internet communications in the last decade has radically changed human rights education, making information and learning materials readily accessible to millions.

This official publication of *Local Action/Global Change* has the same fundamental intention as the earlier version: to help women learn about their human rights and take action to promote and defend them. It uses the same format, combining information on each rights issue with interactive learning activities. Along with the text itself, resource lists, statistics, and information about women's activism have been updated. Also new to this book are a chapter on women's right to an adequate standard of living, sections on the new Convention on the Rights of Persons with Disabilities, and greater coverage of issues impacting girls.

As the authors of this book, we have learned perhaps more than anyone else from writing and using it. The book has brought us into the lives and activism of hundreds of women, who in turn have been our teachers and inspiration. It has also fostered a decade of warm friendship among us and our families. For all this we are sincerely grateful.

Let us know how you use this book and make it your own.

—*Julie Mertus (mertus@american.edu)*
—*Nancy Flowers (nflowers@sbcglobal.net)*

1

Introduction to Women's Human Rights

Why Was This Book Written?

All human beings, female and male alike, are entitled to the same human rights. Historically, however, violations based on biological and gender differences have not been recognized as human rights violations. Even organizations dedicated to the protection of human rights have often failed to devote attention to abuses against women or to develop effective methods to investigate gender-based violations. Most women and girls themselves remain unaware of their human rights and of the documents and mechanisms that define and protect them.

We use the phrase *human rights* to emphasize that we are talking about fundamental, indivisible claims that governments must protect. Advocacy groups increasingly express their demands in human rights terms because experience has shown that doing so is an effective way for having their concerns met. At the same time, we stress *women's human rights* to underscore that the practice of human rights is not gender-neutral. Just as women and girls often experience human rights violations in a manner different from men and boys, so the resources women and girls bring to addressing human rights issues differ as well. Hence the solutions for bias and abuse against women and girls must reflect their specific needs.

A worldwide movement is working toward recognition and protection of the human rights of women and girls. Central to that effort is education. Only women and girls who know about their human rights can take effective action to exercise and advocate for them. *Local Action/Global Change* was written to be a flexible, practical tool in the service of this movement—to share information about women's human rights with women, men, and organizations everywhere and to initiate and develop strategies for translating these rights into action for positive social change.

Who Can Use This Book?

An earlier version of this book[1] was translated into more than a dozen languages and used around the world in countries ranging from Romania to Thailand to

Egypt. The book's audience, like the power of human rights for social change, has proven to be vast and diverse. Factory workers on their lunch break, schoolteachers enrolled in advanced training, judges and police officers considering mandatory reforms, staff of international development and human rights organizations searching for advanced training skills, university students preparing papers, and seminarians polishing sermons have all used *Local Action/Global Change* in their work.

This current version gives greater attention to training possibilities and includes new sections on globalization, development, and adequate standards of living, while retaining the clear language, practical learning activities, and extensive examples and data that made the earlier book so popular. Its new and updated material also better meets the needs of professional staff with international development organizations and government agencies at all levels.

As an overview of the field of women's human rights, *Local Action/Global Change* does not aspire to be a human rights primer or an introduction to gender: Excellent resources for both are readily available elsewhere.[2] Because everyone needs to learn about the human rights of women and girls, *Local Action/ Global Change* was designed for the broadest possible audience. It combines information on the principal topics of women's human rights with learning activities for making them meaningful and strategies for taking action to realize them. The activities require no special materials or resources, only time to meet and talk. Every effort has been made to allow for wide differences in culture, age, religion, geography, economics, and politics.

How Is This Book Organized?

Each chapter addresses topical issues on women's human rights. Even readers interested in just a single topic are encouraged to read the present chapter, on general human rights principles and techniques, as well as Chapter 2, on women's human rights to equality and nondiscrimination, as these provide an overview that can facilitate a full understanding of any issue.

Local Action/Global Change contains principles and methods of human rights education, more than eighty learning activities, a guide to facilitating learning, and a variety of complementary resources: notes at the end of each chapter that include web addresses for a wealth of dynamic websites with updated information and new links, appendices with analytical charts to serve as workshop tools, guidelines for facilitating a workshop, explanations of how to seek redress for human rights violations through the proper channels, a glossary of key terms, a bibliography for further research, and an index of topics discussed in the book.

Each chapter beyond the present one uses the following general framework to address specific issues in women's human rights:

- Objectives for the chapter
- A "Getting Started" section introducing and defining the chapter topic
- Learning activities focusing on the principal issues of this topic
- Boxes within the text offering statistics, special information, and examples

- Strategies for taking action on the issues under discussion
- An examination of international human rights law on this topic
- A "Remembering Core Concepts" section.

What Methodology Does This Book Employ?

Local Action/Global Change invites readers to engage fully in learning about the human rights of women and girls. To this end, it provides both factual information and participatory exercises. Some people will read *Local Action/ Global Change* on their own; others will experience the book collectively with the aid of a facilitator. Some will use all of the chapters; others might focus on a single chapter. In all cases, however, women's human rights need to be seen in a holistic context.

The Conceptual Context

Every woman's human rights issue needs to be understood in both its theoretical and concrete particulars. The concepts of human dignity and equality inform all discussion of women's human rights. Chapter 2, "Women's Human Rights to Equality and Nondiscrimination," sets forth these and other fundamental human rights concepts such as universality, interdependence, and indivisibility. Even the most pragmatic activist would want to be grounded in this framework, with its principles woven into every educational effort.

Furthermore, because all human rights are interconnected and interdependent, no issue can be considered in isolation. A woman's right to education, for example, cannot be separated from her rights with respect to the family, the workplace, the economy, or public life. For this reason, *Local Action/Global Change* provides frequent cross-references among chapters. For example, in Chapter 3, "Women's Human Rights in the Family," the discussion of the "public-private split" directs readers to a related section in Chapter 7, "Women's Human Right to Freedom from Violence." Facilitators should emphasize this interrelatedness among human rights whenever they use the book.

The Personal Context

Human rights begin, as Eleanor Roosevelt, chair of the UN commission on human rights from 1946 to 1951, observed, "in small places ... close to home." Each subsequent chapter of *Local Action/Global Change* also begins close to home, with a "Getting Started" section that draws on individual experience with a human rights topic and provides opportunities to tell personal stories and include local culture and history. The focus shifts continually between the objective and the subjective, with background information and data on specific subtopics followed by exercises that elicit personal reflection and discussion. To create an empowering learning environment, facilitators need to establish a similar balance between introducing external, "expert" information and honoring the first-hand knowledge of the participants.

The Factual Context

Each chapter of *Local Action/Global Change* provides substantive information, including background, statistics, and illustrative examples of both human rights abuses and victories. Although not intended as a resource documenting human rights abuses, *Local Action/Global Change* includes factual illustrations in order to delineate the issues that are especially relevant and to identify their principal subtopics. Both kinds of material serve to inform the individual reader as well as provide facilitators with a basis for mini-lectures or handouts.

Where possible, factual information is drawn from United Nations sources, as these are widely available and accepted. In addition, the text draws extensively from the Beijing Platform for Action, the final document of the Fourth World Conference on Women (1995). Although the Platform for Action is not a legally binding document, it does provide an indication of worldwide understanding of the human rights of women and girls; moreover, it may impact the future development of international treaties or international customary law. Thousands of advocates for women's human rights played a role in drafting the Platform for Action, and thousands more are contributing to its interpretation and implementation.

The Legal Context

Learning about women's human rights also requires grounding in local, regional, and international law. Every woman, even those with little education and no experience of the law, is empowered by knowing how her human rights are recognized and protected by such documents.

Seven Principles for Women's Human Rights[3]

Principle 1: Dignity. The core basis of human rights is the protection and promotion of human dignity.

Principle 2: Universality. The universal nature of rights does not mean that they are experienced in the same manner for all people. Universality means that governments and communities should uphold certain moral and ethical values that cut across all regions of the world.

Principle 3: Equality and Non-Discrimination. The United Nations (UN) *Universal Declaration of Human Rights* (UDHR) and other international human rights documents affords the same rights and responsibilities equally to all women and men, all girls and boys, by virtue of their humanity, regardless of any role or relationship they may have. When violations against women are not recognized as human rights abuses, women are collectively diminished as human beings and denied their inherent personhood.

Principle 4: Indivisibility. Women's rights should be addressed as an indivisible body, including political, social, economic, cultural and collective rights. These cannot be "prioritized" or divided into "generations" of rights, some of which should be achieved before others.

Seven Principles for Women's Human Rights continued

Principle 5: Interconnectedness. Human rights concerns appear in all spheres of life—homes, schools, workplace, elections, courts, etc. Violations of human rights are interconnected; loss of human rights in one area may mean loss in another. At the same time, promotion of human rights in one area supports other human rights.

Principle 6: Government Responsibility. Human rights are not gifts bestowed at the pleasure of governments. Nor should governments withhold them or apply them to some people but not to others. When governments do so, they must be held accountable.

Principle 7: Private Responsibility. Governments are not the only perpetrators of human rights violations against women. Corporations and private individuals should also be held accountable; cultural mores and social traditions that subordinate women should be challenged.

The Action Context

Each topical section in the book concludes with a Learning Activity that explores ways of making a particular human right a reality in the local community. The aim is to directly reinforce the ultimate goal of all human rights education: understanding and accepting individual responsibility for the human rights of all people. Each chapter supplies inspiring examples of action strategies that women around the world have used to establish and protect their rights. Participants are asked to reflect on how government, culture, traditions, families, and their own decisions limit or support a specific human right in their community. They are also encouraged to consider what actions they can reasonably take to foster positive change. Exercising critical analysis and strategizing how to effect a better human rights environment are, in themselves, steps toward improving women's human rights.

The Goals of Human Rights Education

Learning about one's human rights also means learning about the responsibilities that accompany all rights. Just as human rights belong both to individuals and to society as a whole, so the responsibility to respect, defend, and promote human rights is both individual and collective. Human rights education teaches not just *about* human rights but also *for* and *in* human rights. Its goals are to help people understand human rights, value human rights, take responsibility for respecting, defending, and promoting human rights—and, ultimately, bring about human rights, justice, and dignity for *all* people. A related, but no less important, outcome of human rights education is empowerment—the process through which people and communities increase their control of their own lives and the decisions that affect them.

Education About Human Rights

Education *about* human rights provides people with *information* about human rights. It includes learning:

- about human rights principles, such as the universality, indivisibility, and interdependence of human rights
- about how human rights promote participation in decision making and the peaceful resolution of conflicts
- about the history and continuing development of human rights
- about international laws, such as the UDHR or the Convention on the Rights of the Child (CRC)
- about regional, national, state, and local laws that reinforce international human rights laws
- about using human rights laws to protect human rights and to call violators to account for their actions
- about human rights violations such as torture, genocide, or violence against women and the social, economic, political, ethnic, and gender forces that cause them
- about the persons and agencies that are responsible for the promotion of, protection of, and respect for human rights.

Education for Human Rights

Education *for* human rights helps us feel the importance of human rights and make them part of the way we live. In this sense, we can speak of human rights *values and attitudes.* These include:

- "strengthening respect for human rights and fundamental freedoms" (UDHR Article 30.2)
- nurturing compassion, self-esteem, and hope
- understanding the nature of human dignity and respecting the dignity of others
- relating to individuals whose rights are violated and feeling a sense of solidarity with them
- recognizing that the enjoyment of human rights by all citizens is necessary for a just and humane society
- understanding the human rights dimension to social, political, and domestic issues and conflicts
- valuing peace and believing that cooperation is better than conflict.

Education *for* human rights also gives people a sense of responsibility for respecting and defending human rights and empowers them through skills to take appropriate action. These *skills for action* include:

- recognizing that human rights may be promoted and defended on an individual, collective, and institutional level
- developing critical understanding of life situations
- realizing that unjust situations can be improved
- recognizing a personal and social stake in the defense of human rights
- analyzing factors that cause human rights violations
- knowing about and being able to use global, regional, national, and local law for the protection of human rights

- strategizing appropriate responses to injustice
- acting to promote and defend human rights.

Education in Human Rights

In education *in* human rights, *example* is the strongest practice. Both the environment and the process in which human rights is learned should reflect human rights principles of dignity, equality, and nondiscrimination and model a culture of human rights in all its aspects. In this connection, the reader is referred to the participatory methodologies recommended in Appendix II. These methodologies should be complemented by a spirit of open-minded inquiry and respect for the opinions and experiences of all participants, however much they may disagree.

The Bottom Line: Education for Action

Because most women experience some form of gender discrimination from an early age, diminished self-worth often becomes integral to their identity. When society treats a woman as less than fully human, learning and claiming her human rights may be either powerfully transformative or deeply threatening. Some women will embrace human rights education as a long-awaited affirmation. Others will reject it vehemently, claiming that it is destructive of their religious or cultural values. Still others will welcome ideas that broaden their views but initially retreat from action to change society. But the hope is that, over time, most if not all of these participants in human rights education will begin to reexamine their own lives, to identify violations of human rights, and to construct strategies for their own communities. Every woman must proceed at her own pace, with adequate time to process new information and attitudes and overcome the debilitating sense of victimization.

All human rights educators must appreciate the charged nature of the human rights vision and honor the differences among individual women's needs and responses. Without such sensitivity, human rights education could become yet another form of manipulation or oppression of women.

Yet educators and students do not start with a blank slate. Just as each individual's own feelings and opinions about human rights must be acknowledged and valued, so the international, regional, and local agreements that frame the current range of possibilities for action need to be taken into account. Women's advocates have worked diligently to ensure the adoption of specific laws and declarations pertaining to women and girls; in addition, they have striven to include women and girls in existing human rights documents. Therefore, when a participant in a training session denies the existence of a human right that has been recognized nationally, regionally, and/or internationally, the facilitator has a responsibility to point out such agreements.

This book is called *Local Action/Global Change* to emphasize that women and men need to discuss what steps have to be taken in their own communities to advance human rights for all. No "recipe" exists for community-level change because no two communities are alike. But changes that reflect human rights norms will assuredly improve all of our lives. Through local action, then, we see global change.

What Are Women's Human Rights?

Human rights are those rights that every human being possesses and is entitled to enjoy simply by virtue of being human. Human rights are based on the fundamental principle that all persons possess an inherent human dignity and that they are equally entitled to enjoy these rights regardless of sex, race, color, language, national origin, age, class, or religious or political beliefs. Human rights therefore apply to both men and women equally and are found in general human rights documents, such as the UN International Covenant on Civil and Political Rights (ICCPR) and the UN International Covenant on Economic, Social and Cultural Rights (ICESCR), both of which articulate rights applicable to all without discrimination.

There are also rights that are specific to women or that need to be amplified for women's situations. Thus, women's human rights include those rights that apply specifically to women and are found in specialized instruments such as the UN Convention on the Elimination of All Forms of Discrimination Against Women (CEDAW).

Finally, some women's human rights are still evolving; they are yet to be defined or to be included in a human rights instrument. Among these are the human rights related to a safe environment, to indigenous peoples, and to people with disabilities.

The concept of "women's human rights" can lead to confusion because such rights are found in various instruments and, in some cases, have not yet been recognized in international laws. Each of these situations creates a different challenge for advocates of women's human rights.

- *Rights found in specialized instruments*, such as CEDAW. Some people may not regard these rights as being equal in seriousness to general human rights or to those that apply to men. In this case, the challenge for advocates is to ensure that they are given equal importance.
- *Rights not yet defined and protected* in any human rights document. Here the challenge for advocates is to work to have these rights defined and recognized.

Discussion Questions

1. What are women's human rights?
2. Why do we make a distinction between human rights and women's human rights if human rights apply to all persons?
3. Why is there a special convention covering women's rights?
4. Is CEDAW sufficient to cover women's rights? Why or why not?
5. In cases where rights are not yet found in any instrument, why do we still call them rights?

6. Name some of the instruments that define general human rights. How do women advocate for these rights?
7. What is the challenge to women's rights advocates with regard to those rights found in the general instruments?
8. What are some of the specialized instruments that define rights specific to women? How do women advocate for these woman-specific rights?
9. What is the challenge to women's human rights advocates with regard to those rights found in specialized instruments?
10. Name some areas of concern to women that are not yet defined as rights. How do women advocate for still-evolving rights?
11. What is the challenge to women's human rights advocates with regard to those rights not found in any instruments?

Learning Activities[4] for Introducing Human Rights

Note: The activities in this section can be adapted for use with any chapter. They are selected for their effectiveness and representative use of a variety of participatory methodologies.

✠ Learning Activity 1: From Human Needs to Human Rights ✠

Objective   To identify human needs at every stage of life and to relate these to human rights

Time   1 hour

Materials   Chart paper and an even number of "identity cards."

Table 1.1   Human Needs and Human Rights

	Physical Needs	Emotional and Spiritual Needs	Intellectual or Mental Needs
Necessary for Survival			
Necessary for Full Development			
Wanted			

1. Explore an Identity

Have each participant draw a card on which is written his or her "identity" for this activity. There will be two people for each identity (e.g., newborn girl/boy; elementary-school child; adolescent girl/boy; woman/man in her or his 20s, 40s, or 60s; woman/man over 80).

Ask everyone to find her or his partner of the same age and to sit together. Give each pair a chart similar to the one shown in Table 1.1. This is their task:

continues

✠ Learning Activity 1 Continued ✠

- Have each pair discuss what a person at this age needs to stay alive and to write it on their chart.
- Explain that such needs might be (a) physical, spiritual, and emotional or (b) intellectual and mental. Ask the pair to note these in the appropriate column.
- Ask: "What needs are specific to this age of life?" Make those with a star.
- Ask: "What needs are specific to women and men?" Mark those with a female or male symbol.

2. Report

Ask: "Who is the oldest here?" Then ask the over-80 pair to summarize their chart. Encourage them to role-play their parts, speaking in the voices of an old man and an old woman. Repeat the same questions for each age pair, emphasizing which needs are age-specific and which are sex-specific.

Alternative: Hang the charts in chronological order and ask participants to do a "gallery walk," noticing especially age- and sex-specific needs.

3. Analyze/Discuss

Ask participants for their observations about the charts:

- What needs were sex-specific?
- What needs were age-specific? (For example, mature men and women may need advice on family planning and HIV-AIDS prevention; girls and women may need protection from sexual violence; older people may need special care such as reading glasses and protection in cases of emergency.)
- What needs were both age- and sex-specific? (For example, women in their childbearing years may need special protection and provision, such as gynecological and obstetric services and improved nutrition.)
- What were some principal examples of physical, spiritual, and emotional needs versus intellectual and mental needs?
- Are most of these needs being met for people in your community? Which ones are most frequently unmet? Does age or sex play a role in determining which needs are being met?

4. Discuss

Go back to each age-group pair, in turn, and ask: "What more do you need to be happy and become the best person you can be?" or "What else do you need for full human development that goes beyond just staying alive?" Ask each pair to list their answers in the chart under "Necessary for Full Development."

5. Imagine

Ask: "Besides these things that you must have to live and need to develop fully, are there some other things you would like to have just to make you happy?" List these in the chart under "Wanted."

Learning Activity 1 Continued

Note to Facilitator: Typical answers are toys, smart clothes, beer, cigarettes, bicycle, radio, cosmetics, jewelry, and travel. Mark each category for sex differences. This step can be made quite funny and lively, especially when age groups are role-played. (For example, the 60-year-old man may want a young wife but the 60-year-old woman may want to be left alone.) Encourage creativity.

6. Conclude

Ask participants to look back at their charts and reflect on which needs should be guaranteed to people as a human right. Mark their responses by circling or highlighting the needs mentioned. Ask for reasons underlying these opinions.

Conclude by defining *human rights* and explaining how human rights are directly related to human needs.

Note to Facilitator: You may wish to read a definition of *human rights* and/or clarify that human rights include social, economic, and cultural rights as well as civil and political rights.

Learning Activity 2: The Body of Human Rights

Overview To relate articles of the Universal Declaration of Human Rights (UDHR) to parts of the body

Time 30 minutes

Materials Large sheets of paper, markers, copies of the UDHR

1. Draw/Delineate

- Working in small groups, participants draw the outline of a person (or outline a group member) on the paper.
- Next, they try to locate each article of the UDHR on a particular part of the body, writing the number of the article or a symbol in the appropriate place (e.g., Article 26, Right to Education, might be written on the head).

Alternative: Ask participants to work together on one large figure. Each person is assigned a specific article to include on the group drawing, and the figure is then drawn in chalk on the pavement, floor, or wall.

2. Discuss

Ask participants to walk around, compare notations, and discuss.
Source: Demonstrated by Professor David Shiman, University of Vermont.

Development of the Women's Human Rights Movement

The women's human rights movement is to be distinguished from the women's rights movement of the nineteenth and early twentieth centuries in Europe and the United States, which was essentially a Western and middle-class movement. The women's rights movement offers many examples of nineteenth-century women in the Western world struggling to enter universities, practice in new professions, obtain rights to own property, and vote and take part in government.

Unlike the earlier women's right movement, the contemporary women's human rights movement is rooted in both developing and developed countries and is shaped by global factors of the late twentieth century.

The Emergence of the UN Human Rights System

The UN human rights system emerged at the very foundation of the United Nations in 1945 with human rights principles enunciated in the UN Charter and further articulated in the International Bill of Rights, which includes the UDHR (1948), the International Covenant on Civil and Political Rights (1976), and the International Covenant on Economic, Social and Cultural Rights (1976).

Because these foundations of the UN human rights system were laid well before the emergence of the women's human rights movement, women were essentially excluded from the process of defining the rights and creating the evolving structures for monitoring and enforcing them. In its first decades, the evolving human rights system focused principally on:

- curtailing powers of the state rather than on demanding accountability for positive actions to ensure women's human rights
- civil and political rights rather than on social, economic, and cultural rights, within which many of the rights most central to women's experiences are located.

The "Public-Private Split"

This emphasis on civil and political rights in the early years of the UN human rights system had a particular impact on women. Most women in the world were excluded from public activities including commerce, government, law, and political activities, which were most affected by civil and political rights. Most women's lives centered on the home and family, where social, economic, and cultural rights were much more relevant. So long as the UN human rights system gave greater importance to civil and political rights, women's human rights concerns would remain at a disadvantage.

Thus, part of the impetus for the women's human rights movement has been the struggle to seek inclusion in the system, both through separate institutions and through integration into the mainstream of the UN human rights system. Despite the system's limitations, its very existence gave later generations of women's rights advocates new tools to use in their struggle.

Economic Development and Underdevelopment

Economic development and underdevelopment first became common concepts and major concerns after World War II. Factors included in this growing awareness were:

- poverty in the developing world
- inequality between social classes
- growing economic disparity between the developed world and the underdeveloped world.

The "development decades" of the UN—the 1960s and 1970s—addressed agriculture and food production while failing to acknowledge that, in most parts of the world, women were the primary producers of food. These decades offered new technologies but excluded women from access and training; they initiated land reforms but failed to recognize that women were usually restricted from ownership of land. Women became displaced from many of their traditional roles and were disempowered as a result. However, later development projects emphasized employment and income generation, and recognized the importance of the informal sector and women's critical roles. It was this initial real understanding of the social role of women that laid the foundations for women's activism. (For more on these development decades, see Chapter 9, "Women's Human Rights and Globalization.")

Political Struggles and Human Rights Activism

Political repression throughout the world after World War II—dictatorships, disappearances, extra-judicial killings, and totalitarianism—led not only to armed conflict but also to new awareness and new forms of activism. Struggles to oust dictatorships and gain independence from colonial rule engaged women in a new way and developed their skills as activists.

At the same time, colonial nations intensified their struggles to overthrow their imperial masters and to achieve independence and control over their own national resources and institutions. Independence movements were inspired by the UDHR and its recognition of the equality and dignity of all people. The rise of human rights activism ran parallel to the demise of colonial empires and the emergence of new sovereign states around the globe.

A new form of activism emerged that used human rights as its basis for bringing about social change. Activists began to employ the newly developing human rights framework in their efforts not only to oppose oppression but also to press for international recognition and support.

After World War II, particularly in the 1960s and 1970s, many international human rights organizations were founded. Among them were Amnesty International[5] (1961), Human Rights Watch[6] (reestablished as a Helsinki Watch in 1978), and the Helsinki committees (initially Helsinki Watch groups, founded in 1976),[7] as well as regional and national groups both large and small.

Ordinary citizens in grassroots groups around the world began to monitor human rights violations, develop new skills in advocacy, and forge links with international human rights groups. As part of this process, women gained both awareness and capacity.

The Development of Gender Theories

As women became more active in the world of development, the women in development (WID) framework emerged in the 1970s as a response to women's unequal status in the developing world. The WID framework recognized the differences between men and women in needs, skills, and access to resources. It also upheld equality in gender roles as essential to equality in development.

In the 1980s, the gender and development framework advanced the WID framework by moving from addressing women's issues in isolation to considering how the roles of women and men were socially determined because of their sex, and how these social definitions played a role in women's unequal status.

The new thinking of the twenty-first century requires understanding that women's situation cannot improve without including men—hence the movement toward inclusion of male gender issues in development work, which is "likely to be the third major evolution of the gender paradigm."[8]

Evolving alongside these development theories was feminist theory, principally a product of academic women whose analysis of the systematic subordination of women energized efforts to emancipate women around the world. Among its results were:

- research on women in all sectors (e.g., sociology, medicine, literature, economics)
- recognition of the pervasive effects of violence against women and the inadequate response of both society and the law
- the development of gender theory (now institutionalized at most universities), along with highly dynamic debate, which analyzed how consciousness and societal position created differing constructs of social concepts and institutions.

Key Concepts for Women's Human Rights

Sex vs. Gender

Sex refers to the biological characteristics of women and men and the experiences related to them. Sexual characteristics of women include, for example, menstruation, menopause, childbirth, and lactation.

Gender refers to how men's and women's roles are constructed in a society. Gendered roles vary from one culture to another and are often influenced by religious texts and practices and traditional customs and conventions. Gender expectations may include physical appearance, talents, attitudes, and appropriate behaviors for men and women. Many gendered characteristics are institutionalized in society, for example, the belief that women are born timid, dependent, and passive.

Key Concepts for Women's Human Rights Continued

Private Sphere vs. Public Sphere

Private sphere is used to describe the areas of human life centered on familial and other close relationships. Work in the private sphere is often called "reproductive work," which involves care and maintenance of the household and family, and is usually performed by women.

Public sphere is used to describe the area of human life focused on economic and social production, especially business, public policy, and governance. Traditionally men control the public sphere.

The Public-Private Split

The main focus of human rights practices has been on what governments should or should not do. However, individuals can also be challenged to meet human rights standards.

Sometimes governments and political authorities try to create a difference between public and private life, claiming that human rights standards apply to everything within the public sphere (such as in a public place, court, or official office) while for everything in the private sphere (including the home and family) human rights standards do not apply.

Human rights advocates and scholars challenge this distinction between public and private spheres, arguing that the two are interrelated. For instance, women's lower status in the family often furthers their lower position in public life. Furthermore, political authorities influence private life through laws and regulations; thus, for example, women may need the assistance of authorities to stop violence and discrimination in the family.

Discussion Questions

1. In what ways do women in your country experience the "public-private split"?
2. What influences and obstacles have affected women in your country (e.g., economic development, political struggles, women-in-development framework, feminist theory)? Which influences and obstacles have they *not* experienced?
3. How has the presence or absence of these influences impacted women's activism in your country?
4. What other factors have influenced the development of the women's rights movement in your country or region?

Learning Activities for Gender and Women's Human Rights

✠ Learning Activity 3: Sex or Gender? ✠

Objective To clarify the difference between sex and gender
Time 15 minutes
Materials A pair of *Sex* and *Gender* signs for each panel member

1. Define
Define the word *stereotype*.

> **Stereotype:** An oversimplified or generalized conception or idea of a person or thing. Stereotypes might apply to people belonging to a particular group or category, such as a country, tribe, age, class, or sex.

Explain that many stereotypes are based on the difference between *sex* and *gender*. Referring to the box titled "Key Concepts for Women's Human Rights," define these terms and ask for examples of each concept.
Also explain that gender determines:

- what behavior is expected of females and males
- what responsibilities are given to females and males
- what rights are given to females and males
- what is valued in females and males

2. Organize
Select a panel consisting of an equal number of men and women. Give each group a large sign with the word *Sex* and an agreed-upon symbol for sex indicated on one side and the word *Gender* and an agreed-upon symbol of gender on the other.
Explain that you will read out a list of statements and that each member of the panel will decide whether that statement relates to sex or gender and then hold up the appropriate sign.

3. Decide
Start with easy statements and go on to more complex ones. When panelists disagree, ask them to state their reasons and invite the audience to express their opinions.
Avoid arguments. Explain that some statements may not be classified under *Sex* or *Gender* alone, and that scientific evidence regarding what is determined by sex and what is determined by gender is often inconclusive.
Some sample statements follow:

- Women give birth to babies. (*Sex*)
- Men are more courageous and adventuresome. (*Gender*)
- Boys' voices "break" and deepen at puberty; girls' do not. (*Sex*)
- Women are in charge of cooking. (*Gender*)
- Almost all soldiers are men. (*Gender*)

continues

✠ Learning Activity 3 Continued ✠

- Most men are taller and have stronger muscles than women. (*Sex*)
- Carrying water is women's work. (*Gender*)
- Women can breastfeed babies. (*Sex*)
- Women naturally enjoy caring for children. (*Gender*)
- Women are in charge of raising children. (*Gender*)
- Little boys are more aggressive and adventuresome. (*Gender? Sex?*)
- Women enjoy cooking. (*Gender*)
- As they grow older, women lose the ability to have children. (*Sex*)
- Men are better musicians and composers of songs. (*Gender*)
- Men are decision makers. (*Gender*)
- Men are more rational, women are more emotional. (*Gender?*)
- In Ancient Egypt, men stayed at home and did weaving. Women handled family business. Women inherited property and men did not. (*Gender*)
- Women do 67 percent of the world's work, yet their earnings amount to only 10 percent of the world's income.[9] (*Gender*)

Note to Facilitator: Adapt these statements to local circumstances and culture.

✠ Learning Activity 4: Exploring Gender Stereotypes ✠

Objective To explore gender stereotypes and their effects on women
Time 30 minutes
Materials Paper and pens

1. List
Ask participants to think of two answers to each of these questions:

- What activities do I do and enjoy that are considered acceptable for my sex?
- What activities do I do *but don't enjoy* that are considered acceptable for my sex?
- What activities do I do that are considered appropriate activities for the opposite sex, whether I enjoy them or not?
- What activities would I prefer to do *but don't participate in,* as they are considered activities appropriate for the opposite sex?

2. Report
Go around the group asking participants how they would respond to each of the four categories noted in the preceding list. Record their responses on a chart similar to the one shown in Table 1.2.

continues

✠ Learning Activity 4 Continued ✠

Then discuss some of these questions:

Table 1.2   Exploring Gender Stereotypes

Women's Activities Enjoyed	Women's Activities Disliked	Men's Activities Enjoyed	Men's Activities Disliked

- What generalizations about men and women can you make from this list?
- To what extent are gender roles unconscious?
- How do these roles lead to discrimination against women?
- How have sex roles influenced your personal history?
- Can you give examples of people who did not retain their sex role?
- What is needed to improve the roles assigned to women?

✠ Learning Activity 5: Women's Experience with Discrimination ✠

Objective   To identify discrimination experienced by women
Time   30 minutes
Materials   Cards or slips of paper that can be used for selecting male or female roles randomly, sheets of paper for making lists

1. Discuss/Describe

Divide participants into small groups. Ask half of each group to think of as many advantages and disadvantages of being a woman as they can, and to list these on a sheet of paper. Ask the other half of each group to do the same with respect to men.

Next, ask all participants to rate on a scale of one to five how important each advantage and disadvantage is to the life of an individual. For example, something trivial like "wearing a certain kind of attractive clothing" might be given a one while "having less food" might receive a five.

2. Explain

Draw a line on the floor with chalk or outside on the ground. Explain that this is the starting line and ask everyone to put his or her toes on the line.

continues

✠ **Learning Activity 5 Continued** ✠

Explain that all the participants are babies born on the same day and that, according to the UDHR, they are "born free and equal in dignity andrights."

Then explain that, unfortunately, some members of the community are not really "equal in rights and dignity." Ask each participant to randomly select a card or piece of paper on which is drawn a male or female sign to indicate the role they will play.

3. Enact
Using the lists that participants have prepared, alternately read a male and female advantage and/or disadvantage. The rating given each indicates how many steps forward or backward the "males" or "females" may take. For example, if "having less food" was rated as a five and a disadvantage, the "females" would take five steps backward.

4. Discuss
In almost every case, the "males" will rapidly get far ahead of the "females." When a large gap has developed, ask the two groups to turn and face each other. Ask several individuals from each group:

- How do you feel about your "position"?
- What do you want to say to those in the other group?
- How would you feel if you were in the other group?

Conclude the activity with a discussion of the effects of both sex and gender roles:

- Which of these disadvantages cannot be changed?
- Which could be changed? How?
- Which disadvantages would be the most important to seek to change?

✠ **Learning Activity 6: Standing Up for Yourself** ✠

Objective   To relate personal experience to human rights concepts and articles of the UDHR and/or CEDAW
Time   90 minutes total; 30 minutes for each part
Materials   Blackboard or chart paper, chalk or markers

1. Remember
After gathering participants into small groups, ask each woman in each group to remember a time in her life when she asserted her human rights or stood up for herself as a person entitled to dignity and fairness. Have her tell her story to the group, taking about five minutes total.

continues

20

✠ **Learning Activity 6 Continued** ✠

2. Analyze

After everyone has told her story, each small group should take up each story again and analyze the conditions that made each woman's act of assertion possible.

Choose someone in the group to act as recorder to write down the different responses to these questions:

- Who or what helped me to stand up for myself?"
- What was the driving motive?
- What were the sources of strength?
- What conditions are necessary for women to recognize their needs and stand up for themselves?

Many women find that self-determination is possible only in the context of social and economic conditions that allow them to say "yes" to their needs. For example, financial security often is a big factor in the ability to assert their rights (e.g., "I couldn't tell him 'no' until I could afford to have my own place to live"). For some, the support of other women is crucial (e.g., "I knew my mother was behind me all the way" or "I don't know what would have happened if there hadn't been a battered women's shelter in town"). For others, education and/or the freedom to express themselves is the key (e.g., "Writing about my feelings gave me strength" or "I didn't realize I had a choice until I began to read articles about other women").

3. Plan/Retell

Each small group should select one story to retell or dramatize for the whole group. A woman might retell her own story, or someone else might tell it for her. Group members might also act out the central events of the story. Alternatively, the small group may wish to create a composite story that contains elements of each woman's personal story.

Each small group then presents one story told in that group. While the stories are being told or reenacted, the facilitator represents each graphically as a wheel with spokes. On the spokes themselves are written acts of assertion (e.g., "demanding equal pay," "challenged harassment"), whereas the areas between the spokes are taken up with "supports" that helped enable the woman or girl to stand up for herself (e.g., "self-worth," "mother," "colleague").

4. Analyze/Connect

After all the stories have been shared, the whole group examines the various "spokes" and "supports" on this wheel and derives from them the basic human rights or needs that the stories represent (e.g., "Education," "Economic Equality," "Freedom from Violence"). These rights or needs are written on the rim of the wheel. (Note that we say *rights or needs* at this point, as some of the items identified may not be legally enforceable rights.)

continues

✠ Learning Activity 6 Continued ✠

Breaking again into small groups, participants use the copies of the UDHR (or CEDAW) to match the rights and needs on the wheel to particular articles.

Alternative: Each group takes a different document or the facilitator presents a simplified version of the UDHR, CEDAW, or some other document as the basis for discussion.

Each group reports its findings and notes the relevant article(s) next to each need written on the rim of the wheel.

The activity concludes with a brief discussion of the relationship of human rights to human needs in real life situations.

Note to Facilitator: If the group wishes to pursue this topic further, the following additional steps can be taken:

1. Discuss

Often when a woman or girl first asserts her human rights, she is challenging the role determined for her by society.

- Was this the case for you?
- What are the roles expected of you in society?
- How do you feel about these expectations?
- Are they fair or unfair? Do they have a positive or negative effect on women?

2. Discuss

Often when a woman or girl first asserts her rights, she is daring to say "no" to others and "yes" to her own needs.

- Was this the case for you?
- How do you feel about asserting your needs?

3. Discuss

As noted in the first part of this Learning Activity, many women find that self-determination is possible only when certain social and economic conditions permit them to say "yes" to their needs. Review this earlier passage, and then ask participants the following questions:

- What made self-determination possible in your life?
- What social and economic conditions do most women in your community need in order to stand up for their human rights?
- What can be done to help more women achieve those social and economic conditions?

Achievements of Women's Human Rights Activism

In the 1980s and 1990s, due to the advocacy of women within the UN system and to the efforts of nongovernmental organizations (NGOs), progress was made in the form of the development of women-specific instruments and institutions. These included the following:

- The Convention on the Elimination of All Forms of Discrimination Against Women (CEDAW)—entered into force in 1981—is the first legally binding international instrument prohibiting discrimination against women and obligating governments to take affirmative steps to advance the equality of women.
- The Declaration on the Elimination of Violence against Women, adopted by the General Assembly in 1993, recognizes the right of women to be free from violence and obligates governments to take steps to eliminate violence against women.
- The Special Rapporteur on Violence Against Women, established in 1994, has the responsibility to investigate and make reports on cases of violence against women worldwide.
- The Optional Protocol to CEDAW, adopted by the General Assembly in 1998, permits individual complaints to be made to the CEDAW Committee by people in those states that have ratified the protocol.

As these instruments and institutions became operative, however, women realized that exclusive recourse to separate, women-specific institutions contributed to the marginalization of women's concerns within the system. Accordingly, women began to push for full integration of women into the mainstream of the human rights system.

The strategic use of UN conferences to further women's human rights by putting them on the international agenda was a powerful and empowering approach, resulting in many advances. Some highlights follow.

The 1992 World Conference on Environment and Development in Rio de Janeiro:

- recognized women's role in environmental management
- improved status of women necessary for sustainable development.

The 1993 World Conference on Human Rights in Vienna:

- resulted in the Vienna Declaration, which contains the first official recognition of violence against women as incompatible with human dignity and, as such, violates human rights; examples include violence in armed conflict, murder, systematic rape, sexual slavery, forced pregnancy, gender-based sexual harassment, and trafficking.

The 1994 International Conference on Population and Development in Cairo:

- resulted in agreement among 180 countries, for the first time, that population growth can be stabilized and development efforts enhanced by the advancement of women
- led to the Beijing Program for Action, which recognizes the need of women and men to be informed about and have access to safe, effective, and affordable means of contraception and other health care services
- condemned harmful practices such as prenatal sex selection, female infanticide, female genital cutting (FGC), trafficking of girl children, and use of girls in prostitution and pornography.

The 1995 Fourth World Conference on Women in Beijing:

- was the largest-ever intergovernmental conference to address women's issues as well as the most-attended NGO Forum (with 30,000 participants)
- resulted in a Program for Action that contextualized women's concerns within the framework of human rights and called on the United Nations to integrate gender perspectives into all policies and programs—a clear advance from Vienna.

The Beijing+5 (2000) and Beijing+10 (2005) Conferences:

- generated follow-up meetings to monitor how states have complied with obligations to which they voluntarily agreed at the 1995 World Conference in Beijing.

Learning Activities for Women's Human Rights Activism

> ### ✠ Learning Activity 7: What Are Women's Human Rights? ✠
>
> **Objective** To develop a working definition of *women's human rights*
> **Time** 20 minutes
> **Materials** Chart paper and markers
>
> **1. Define**
> Ask participants what they mean when they use these terms: *women's movement*, *women's rights*, and *women's human rights*. Record their suggestions on a chart like the one shown in Table 1.3. Circle the key words mentioned.
>
> **Table 1.3 What Are Women's Human Rights?**
>
> | Women's Movement | Women's Rights | Women's Human Rights |
> |---|---|---|
> | | | |
>
> *continues*

✠ Learning Activity 7 Continued ✠

Note to Facilitator: You might also include other words that cause confusion, such as *feminist, feminism, women's studies,* and *women's liberation.*

2. Discuss
Do these terms have the same meanings? If not, how do they differ?

3. Explain
Provide a clear definition of *women's human rights* for use in this course. Write this definition on chart paper and post at the front of the group.

✠ Learning Activity 8: The Roots of Our Activism ✠

Objective   To relate the women's human rights movement to female participants' personal and professional experiences
Time   45 minutes
Materials   Copies of the discussion topics in Step 2 below (optional)

1. Organize
Divide participants into small groups. Give each group these instructions in written and/or oral form.

Discuss the factors that have influenced your own awareness of, understanding of, and activism for women's human rights:

- personally, in your private and family life
- professionally, in your work and public life
- nationally, in the women's human rights movement in your country.

Ask someone to take notes during the discussion and summarize each small groups' experiences for the whole group.

2. Discuss
Compare the small groups' summaries.

Discuss the following, listing positive and negative influences in separate columns:

- What are the main factors that have influenced our awareness, understanding, and activism for women's human rights?
- How can we encourage and/or create these factors for other women?

Recognition of Women's Human Rights

The interactive quality of the human rights process permits new ideas and needs to challenge current thinking and approaches and to articulate new theory and practice. Indeed, the vision of women's rights advocates and their engagement with the human rights system have confronted the world's inadequate view of women's human rights and led to significant change.

Violence against women provides an excellent example of how women's advocacy has led to change. Violence against women is not mentioned in any human rights document—including even CEDAW, the most women-specific rights document. Only in 1993 in the Vienna Declaration, as the result of intense pressure from women's human rights advocates, was violence against women either by the state or by private actors recognized as a human rights violation.

Obstacles to Women's Human Rights

Yet, as women and women's interests are still not totally integrated into the human rights arena, continued action is needed. The women's human rights movement faces these obstacles in particular:

- *Failure to recognize the universality of human rights:* Despite progress, many women still enjoy far fewer human rights than do men.
- *The "public-private split":* In many parts of the world human rights stop at the door of the family home, where many of the most serious violations against women occur.
- *Neglect of social and economic rights:* Whereas civil and political rights restrain governments, the more weakly defined social and economic rights require governments to take action and thus are more difficult to enforce. Yet these are often the rights most significant to women's lives.
- *Weak human rights monitoring and enforcement.*

Challenges

Women's activism aims primarily to:

- expand the definition of rights to include new interpretations
- expand the scope of government responsibility for the defense and protection of women's rights.

Developing each human right entails three processes:

- naming the right
- gaining acceptance of the right by the public and within the private sphere
- ensuring that the right is enforced.

Advocacy is essentially a process of

- identifying a policy issue or interest (problem) and proposing a policy change (solution)

- gaining public recognition of the problem and support for the solution
- ensuring correct implementation or enforcement through vigilant action.

Discussion Questions

1. In what ways are women's human rights being integrated into the general field of human rights?
2. What are some of the benefits of such integration?
3. Can you give examples from your country or region of women's issues that have been marginalized through segregation into special legislatures, administrative departments, or agencies?
4. Can you give examples of women's issues that have been neglected as a result of not getting special focus?
5. Name some of the ways in which women in your country experience the conflict between the universality of human rights, on the one hand, and cultural and religious traditions, on the other.
6. Name some of the ways in which women in your country experience the inadequacy of definitions and enforcement of social and economic rights.
7. What, if anything, can women do to confront these challenges?
8. Can you give examples of attempts to mainstream gender issues nationally? Regionally? Internationally? Have they been successful? Why or why not?

Remembering Core Concepts

✠ Learning Activity 9: Victim, Abuser, Bystander, Helper ✠

Objective To recognize that everyone can be, and has been, both an abuser and a defender of human rights

Time About 30 minutes, depending on the size of the groups

Materials Sheets of paper, each divided into four quadrants

1. Remember/Discuss

Divide participants into small groups and give each a sheet of paper on which the four quadrants are headed "Abuser," "Victim," "Bystander," and "Helper."

Ask participants, one by one, to give an example of having played one of these roles:

- when they violated someone's rights
- when their own rights were violated
- when they stood by and did nothing
- when they witnessed someone's rights being violated and took action to help or prevent the violation.

continues

✠ Learning Activity 9 Continued ✠

2. Discuss

Gather the whole group together and discuss the activity, as follows:

- Ask volunteers to give examples from each of the four categories listed above.
- Ask some follow-up questions of the whole group: (a) When you violated someone's rights, when did you realize what you had done? (b) When your own rights were violated, what did/could you do? (c) When you did nothing, what did/do you wish you had done? (d) When you took action, what motivated you to do so? What qualities does a person need to take action?
- Ask what feelings and new understanding the activity elicited.

3. Conclude

Emphasize in conclusion that everyone plays all these roles at one time or another. Remind participants of the human right principle of responsibility, not only of governments but also of individuals to protect the human rights of others.

Source: Kristi Rudelius-Palmer, University of Minnesota Human Rights Resource Center.

Notes

1. J. Mertus, N. Flowers, and M. Dutt, *Local Action, Global Change: Learning About the Human Rights of Women and Girls* (UNIFEM and the Center for Women's Global Leadership, 1999).

2. On human rights, see *Women's Human Rights Step by Step: Women, Law and Development International* (2007), available online at http://www.unhchr.ch/hredu.nsf/; and Nancy Flowers, *Human Rights Here and Now: Celebrating the Universal Declaration of Human Rights* (Human Rights Resource Center, 1998), available online at http://www.hrusa.org. On gender, see Suzanne Williams, Janet Seet, and Adelina Mwau, *Oxfam Gender Training Manual* (Oxfam, 1995).

3. Mertus, Flowers, and Dutt, *Local Action, Global Change*, p. v.

4. Adapted from Nancy Flowers, *The Human Rights Education Handbook: Effective Practices for Learning, Action, and Change* (Human Rights Resource Center, 2000); and *Index of Methods, Techniques, and Activities* (University of Minnesota Human Rights Library, available online at http://www1.umn.edu/humanrts/edumat/hreduseries/hrhandbook/aboutseries.html.

5. The website address for Amnesty International is http://www.amnesty.org/.

6. The website address for Human Rights Watch is http://www.hrw.org/.

7. The website address for the Helsinki committees is http://www.hrw.org/reports/1989/WR89/Helsinki.htm.

8. Ian Bannon and Maria C. Correia, eds., *The Other Half of Gender: Men's Issues in Development* (World Bank, 2006), pp. xvii–xviii.

9. Charles Dokmo, "Loans to the World's Poor Can Enrich Everyone," August 4, 1999, International Herald Tribune; Neuilly Cedex (France), available online at http://www.iht.com/articles/1999/08/04/eddokmo.2.t.php.

2

Women's Human Rights to Equality and Nondiscrimination

The human rights of women and of the girl-child are an inalienable, integral and indivisible part of universal human rights. The full and equal participation of women in political, civil, economic, social and cultural life, at the national, regional and international levels, and the eradication of all forms of discrimination on the grounds of sex are priority objectives of the international community.

—Vienna Declaration and Program of Action (part I, paragraph 18), adopted by the World Conference on Human Rights, Vienna, June 25, 1993 (A/CONF. 157/24)

Objectives

The learning activities and background information in this chapter will enable participants to work toward the following objectives:

- Understand that all human beings are entitled to human rights without discrimination.
- Examine the complex way in which all human rights are interconnected and interrelated.
- Discuss how women and girls can experience discrimination in different ways based on the following factors: race, class, ethnicity, religion, culture, disability, sexuality, and age.
- Acknowledge that these differences can become the basis for discrimination or prejudice.
- Construct an understanding of human rights that attempts to take into account all groups in a society.
- Recognize the ways in which women challenge discriminatory practices in creative and effective ways.
- Remember core concepts.

Getting Started: Thinking About Equality and Nondiscrimination

Equality and nondiscrimination form the cornerstone upon which all human rights are constructed. At its core, recognition of human rights means accepting the notion that all human beings have equal worth and are entitled to respect for their human dignity. This principle is violated all too often.

The ways in which women and girls experience discrimination vary greatly, based not only on their status in their own society but also on factors that exacerbate the unfair opportunities and discriminatory treatment they face. For example, a poor, indigenous woman may be treated unfairly because of her gender as well as because of her ethnicity and socioeconomic status. This chapter explores the interconnected nature of discriminatory factors, first examining human rights concepts as general guiding principles and then focusing on specific categories of discrimination.

✠ Learning Activity 1: Identity and Connectedness ✠

Objective   To develop awareness of shared identity and differences among participants
Time   30 minutes for each part
Materials   Paper and pens, chart paper and markers or blackboard and chalk

1. Draw
Ask participants to work individually, following these instructions:

- Draw a circle and write your name inside.
- Draw five to ten "petals" around the circle, as if drawing a flower.
- In each petal write the name of a group with which you personally identify. It might be a group made up of individuals known by you (e.g., members of a family, clan, town, place of worship, school). Or it might be a group with more generalized membership, including people you do not know personally (e.g., teachers, widows, activists, single mothers, left-handed people).

2. Compare
Ask the participants to work in pairs, comparing their drawings and identifying the circles they have in common. They should write each other's name in these common circles.

Then ask each pair to combine with another pair and do the same thing within this group of four.

3. Draw/Discuss
Discuss the common features of the "flowers." Was race included? Class? Religion? Sexual orientation? Nationality? Family or refugee status?

continues

✠ Learning Activity 1 Continued ✠

Construct a web with the whole group. Write "us" in the central circle, and ask participants to call out the groups with which many people identified. Place these groups close to the center of the web.

Ask for the names of groups with which only one or a few identified. Place these further away from the center of the web.

4. Discuss

- What are the major areas of commonality? Of difference?
- To which circles do only one or two persons belong?
- Ask: "How did it feel to find others who shared an area of identify with you? To find that no one shared an area of identity with you?"
- Ask: "What does this web show us about our commonalities? Our differences?"

Note to Facilitator: For additional learning activities on human rights, see Chapter 1, "Introduction to Women's Human Rights."

Nondiscrimination as a Core Human Right

The starting point for thinking about equality, nondiscrimination, and human rights is the Universal Declaration of Human Rights (UDHR). The UN General Assembly unanimously adopted this document in 1948, soon after the end of World War II. Although the UDHR was not legally binding at the time of its adoption, most, if not all, of its provisions have since attained the status of customary international law and set the standards that all UN Member States are legally obligated to uphold. The UDHR approaches the protection of human rights based on the following four principles: universality, equality, nondiscrimination, and indivisibility and interconnectedness.

Universality

Article 1 of the UDHR proclaims the principle that "all human beings are born free and equal in dignity and rights." We call human rights *universal* because each and every one of us, wherever we are placed, has human rights that are grounded in a moral order. This is not to imply that human rights can never change or that all people experience them in the same manner; nor does *universality* denote a unified worldwide culture. Rather, it means that governments and communities should uphold certain moral and ethical values that cut across all regions of the world. One example of a universally held moral belief is the condemnation of genocide—the intent to destroy, in whole or in part, a national, ethnic, racial, or religious group. Another is the belief that slavery—property ownership over a human being—is wrong. And yet both of these practices continue to this day.

Trafficking in human beings for profit is a modern-day form of slavery. It is prohibited in the Protocol to Prevent, Suppress and Punish Trafficking in Persons, a supplement to the United Nations Convention Against Transnational Organized Crime. This Protocol was adopted in 2000 as a tool to help prevent and combat trafficking.[1] Numbers of persons trafficked are not well documented, but thanks to a strong outcry from the activist community this practice is considered a growing human rights issue around the world.

As noted, genocide is universally held as immoral, yet it continues. In September 2004, then U.S. Secretary of State Colin Powell declared that genocide was taking place in Sudan.[2] But three years later, despite international attention drawn to this area of the world, Human Rights Watch reported that Sudanese government forces and Janjaweed militias had killed or caused the deaths of at least 200,000 people in the Darfur area, and had raped and assaulted thousands of women and girls.[3] For further information on the Darfur situation, see Chapter 13, "Human Rights of Refugee, Displaced, and War-Affected Women."

While many of us understand women's lack of power in relation to men, we are often insensitive to the differences in power and privilege that result from a woman's membership in a particular class, ethnic group, religion, geographic location, race, or sexual orientation. Such imbalances of power do not occur simply at the individual level; at times they are systematically maintained by society, government, religious institutions, and other social and economic forces. Access to resources, work, housing, education, protection by the government, and many other advantages can be determined by the power an individual has in society. Thus, in recognizing that human rights are universal we must also acknowledge how differences in power among and between groups can result in discrimination and inequality.

The principle of the universality of human rights is complicated by the fact that human rights standards are unevenly applied throughout the world. In particular, governments of some industrialized nations have denounced violations of human rights in other countries while ignoring human rights abuses within their own borders. For example, although the Convention on the Elimination of All Forms of Discrimination Against Women (CEDAW) was ratified by 182 states as of April 2006, the nations ratifying the document have human rights standards as dissimilar as Canada's and Saudi Arabia's. In addition, nations can place a reservation on their signature in cases where "national law, tradition, religion or culture are not congruent with Convention principles." Fifty-seven countries have done so.[4]

Still other governments have attempted to justify violating their citizens' human rights by challenging the notion that human rights belong to all people and claiming that their own cultures, moral codes, or level of economic development allow certain human rights to be violated. While such debates on the universal nature of human rights are important to understand, women throughout the world share many common experiences of violations of their rights. Therefore, even as these debates continue, women everywhere must know that they can invoke the same international human rights standards to advocate for change in their own communities.

Challenges to Universality

The universal nature of human rights is often questioned:

- *by oppressed communities attempting to assert their own identity against the domination of a more powerful group.* Many dominant communities assume that their own definitions of human rights are the only valid definitions and impose these values on the religious and cultural practices of minority communities. Of course, the practices and belief systems of various groups around the world differ greatly. Human rights, therefore, it is argued, must be understood in the particular context within which these communities exist.
- *by governments to justify political and/or economic repression against the general population or particular groups of people.* Some governments argue that human rights cannot be universally applied because of the differing histories, cultures, and religions of various regions. While it is true that human rights should be understood in the context of people's lives, governments that contest the universal nature of human rights in the name of culture or religion almost always use such arguments to limit people's fundamental rights, not to expand them.
- *by governments and other authorities to justify acts of discrimination and violence against women.* When women assert their human rights, governments often raise the argument against their universality. Women demanding equal inheritance laws, changes in family law, access to political arenas, and a range of other rights often face opposition in the name of culture and religion.

Equality

The notion that human rights are universal and belong to all people is centrally connected to the principle of equality. All people everywhere are born with the same human rights, although they may not have the same ability to enjoy those rights. Article 2 of the UDHR states that "everyone is entitled to all the rights and freedoms set forth in this Declaration, without distinction of any kind, such as race, color, sex, language, religion, political or other opinion, national or social origin, property, birth or other status." One cannot embrace the idea of human rights and also hold that these rights apply only to some individuals, or that only some states have a responsibility to respect human rights. At the same time, one cannot believe in the idea of human rights and also believe that they are earned, or that some individuals may be more worthy of human rights than others.

Two approaches to equality can be identified in both domestic and international law. The first—formal or "juridical" equality—refers to the notion that individuals in like situations should be treated in like manner. Hence formal equality focuses on achieving equal treatment based on the assumption that individuals are similarly situated. It does not take into account broader contexts within which individuals are placed in society. For example, structural factors can ensure that, regardless of equal treatment or prohibition of direct discrimination, certain groups fall behind the rest of society; thus formal equality, if applied on its own without taking into account differences as well as similarities, may achieve inconsistencies in treatment and fail to ensure the broader aims of equality. The second approach to equality—"substantive" equality—refers to the notion that individuals in different situations should be treated differently. It encompasses two distinct ideas—equality of results and equality of opportunity.

- "Equality of results" requires that the outcome as well as the purpose of a particular measure must be taken into account and that the actual results of a particular measure must be equal. For example, although there may be the same number of women as men in a particular educational program, equality of results recognizes that the identical treatment both groups receive may nevertheless reinforce inequality because of past or ongoing discrimination or differences in access to power or resources.
- "Equality of opportunity" aims to ensure that all individuals have an equal chance to access a particular benefit and takes into account the fact that different people may have different starting points—for example, in education and employment. In short, women and men must have equal chances, even if the results are not the same. The concept of equal opportunity is reflected in many modern legislative models. For example, this more difficult standard would give men and women equal chances to succeed once they have been accepted into an education program. This might mean offering women and men flexible scheduling, child care, or more time to graduate for people with family responsibilities.

In the human rights context, equality does not necessarily mean treating everyone in the same manner. When people are in unequal situations, treating them in the same way invariably perpetuates, rather than eradicates, injustices. Women often require different treatment than men to enjoy the same rights. For example, to enjoy the right to work, women may require help with child care and/or official recognition of the unpaid work that women traditionally do in the home. In addition, particular groups of women may require accommodations to enjoy their right to nondiscrimination and equality. Promoting equality means taking steps to address institutionalized power imbalances and, ultimately, to create a truly just society. This is the context in which we emphasize that human rights are not gender-neutral. Violation of rights and their solutions cannot be addressed without recognizing the unequal positions of women in society.

Nondiscrimination

Just as Article 2 of the UDHR requires rights without distinction of any kind, Article 7 states that "[a]ll are equal before the law and are entitled without any discrimination to equal protection of the law." The principle underlying this article is that every individual has a right to live with dignity and freedom, and that no person or government may make an arbitrary distinction between peoples when protecting such a right.

The nondiscrimination principle under international human rights law addresses five types of conduct:

- *Direct discrimination* is based on the idea of formal equality. It may be defined as less favorable or detrimental treatment of an individual or group of individuals on the basis of a prohibited characteristic or on grounds such as sex, race, or disability.

- *Indirect discrimination* occurs when a practice, rule, requirement, or condition appears to be neutral but in actuality disproportionately impacts particular groups, unless that practice, rule, requirement, or condition is justified. Prohibitions of indirect discrimination require a state to take account of relevant differences between groups.
- *Harassment* refers to unwanted conduct that has the purpose or effect of violating the dignity of a person and of creating an intimidating, hostile, degrading, humiliating, or offensive environment. An example is sexual harassment in the workplace.
- *Positive-action* or *affirmative measures* (also known as *special measures*) are proactive measures taken by a government or private institution to address the effects of past and present discrimination by giving reverse preferences that favor the previously disadvantaged group. Such preferential treatment runs counter to the strictly formal notion of equality. Many international instruments explicitly permit positive action without imposing an obligation on states to take such measures.
- *Reasonable accommodation* (as applied in the employment context) is any modification of or adjustment to a job, an employment practice, the work environment, or the manner or circumstances under which a position is held or customarily performed in order to make it possible for a qualified individual to apply for, perform the essential functions of, and enjoy the equal benefits and privileges of employment. The requirement to accommodate difference has arisen most frequently in the context of disability.

Not all differences of treatment are perceived as prohibited discrimination under human rights law. There may be good reasons for differential treatment, such as achieving substantive equality in the case of positive action. To be justified under international law, an instance of differential treatment must have an "objective and reasonable justification." Specifically, (a) it must pursue a legitimate aim, and (b) there must be a reasonable relationship of proportionality between the aim sought to be realized and the means employed. In other words, the means of achieving the legitimate aim must be appropriate and necessary, and the reasons given must be relevant to the difference that is sought to be made in the way people are treated.

Some of the more pervasive forms of discrimination have been further elaborated in specialized human rights treaties, including CEDAW, which elaborates on discrimination based on sex. Article 1 of CEDAW defines *discrimination against women* as "any distinction, exclusion or restriction made on the basis of sex which has the effect or purpose of impairing or nullifying the recognition, enjoyment or exercise by women, irrespective of their marital status, on the basis of equality of men and women, of human rights and fundamental freedoms in the political, economic, social, cultural, civil or any other field."

The Convention on the Elimination of All Forms of Racial Discrimination (CERD), adopted and opened for signature and ratification by the UN General Assembly in 1965, addresses the discrimination experienced by many communities on the basis of color or "race." On December 13, 2006, the General Assembly adopted the Convention on the Rights of Persons with Disabilities (CRPD) and its Optional Protocol. And on March 30, 2007, the Convention and Optional Protocol were opened for signature. As of February 2008, 125 countries have signed the CRPD and seventy countries have signed the Optional Protocol.[5] This Convention obtained a higher number of signatories on its first day than any other Convention in the history of the UN. Article 6 of the Convention on the Rights of Persons with Disabilities specifically concerns women: "States Parties recognize that women and girls with disabilities are subject to multiple discrimination, and in this regard shall take measures to ensure the full and equal enjoyment by them of all human rights and fundamental freedoms."[6]

🞧 Learning Activity 2: The Complex Nature of Discrimination 🞧

Objective To elicit discussion about aspects of shared identity and differences among participants

Time 30 minutes

Materials None

1. Read/Imagine

Read to the group the following story titled "Elena Wants a Job":

> Elena is a disabled mother who is part of an ethnic minority group in Borfilia. This country has no laws protecting disabled people, and although Borfilia has laws that protect minorities, these laws are rarely enforced. On the contrary, the best jobs are routinely given first to the dominant ethnic majority group, even in areas of the country where ethnic minorities outnumber the dominant majority, Borfilia sends in members of the majority group to fill top posts in nearly all workplaces. Borfilia is also a patriarchal country; and although women work, they hold the lowest-paid positions. Elena applies for a job at Factrex, for which she is superbly qualified, but a less-qualified male is hired. He is a member of the majority group and is not disabled.

2. Discuss

Lead the group through a discussion based on the following points:

- On what grounds did Factrex discriminate against Elena? Because of her gender? Her disability? Her national group? Or the complex interaction of all three factors?
- Do you think Elena's prospects for a job were hampered by the fact that she is also a mother?

3. Analyze/Discuss

Read aloud the following comments.

> Some people think of discrimination as "additive." According to this thinking, Elena was discriminated against because she is a woman, plus a disabled person, plus a member of a national minority. However, other people argue that discrimination is much more complex. It is not simply a matter of adding up all discriminatory factors or even of multiplying them together. On the contrary, discriminatory factors work together in a manner that makes them inseparable. Just as Elena cannot separate out the disabled part of herself, people who discriminate against her are not able to do so, either consciously or subconsciously.

continues

✠ **Learning Activity 2 Continued** ✠

Discuss these questions:

- Could this story have taken place in your community? Explain.
- If such a case of discrimination occurred in your community, would women respond? Which women? Why or why not?

Indivisibility and Interdependence

Human rights are also considered to be indivisible and interdependent. All human rights are part of a mutually reinforcing framework. Denial of one type of human right has an impact on the ability to exercise other human rights. For example, the right to work is connected to the right to get an education, and the right to vote is connected to the right to have access to a voting booth. At the same time, promoting one type of human right promotes all other rights. For example, promoting women's economic rights has a direct impact on women's ability to be free from violence, since financial dependence is one of the primary reasons women do not leave a violent situation.

The indivisibility and interdependence of human rights have important implications for the implementation and interpretation of human rights law and documents. Just as human rights do not exist in isolation, neither should human rights documents be interpreted in isolation from one another. Through an ongoing process, they reinforce each other. For example, the cultural rights mentioned in the UDHR (1948) and the International Covenant on Economic, Social, and Cultural Rights (1976) are elaborated further in the Convention on the Rights of the Child (1989) in relation not only to nondiscrimination but also to the child's right to participate in the culture of his or her family and community and to receive an education that respects their culture.

✠ **Learning Activity 3: Examples of Discrimination** ✠

Objective To connect nondiscrimination principles with local examples
Time 30 minutes
Materials Chart paper and copies of the list of types of conduct from the earlier section headed "Nondiscrimination"

1. Discuss

Remind participants that the nondiscrimination principle under international human rights law addresses many types of conduct. Divide participants into small groups. Give each group a copy of the list of actions related to nondiscrimination:

- Direct discrimination
- Indirect discrimination
- Harassment
- Positive-action or affirmative measures
- Reasonable accommodation.

continues

✠ Learning Activity 3 Continued ✠

Ask participants to give examples of each action, both from world and national history and from their own experience.

Alternative: Write examples on individual pieces of paper and attach them to the chart described in Step 2.

2. Discuss/Analyze

Go over these terms with the whole group and ask them for examples. When the group offers an example of direct discrimination, ask which aspects of the person's identity were the basis for this discrimination. Enter the results on a chart like the one shown in Table 2.1.

Table 2.1   Examples of Discrimination

	Direct Discrimination	Indirect Discrimination	Harassment	Victimization
Sex				
Race/Ethnicity				
Culture				
Disability				
Family Status				
Sexuality				
Religion				
Class				
Age				
Other				

Note to Facilitator: Save this chart for use in the concluding "Learning Activity 10: Speaking Out Against Discrimination."

Ask the participants what conclusions they can draw from these examples.

- Were historical examples of discrimination based on a dominant cause? Were personal or local examples of discrimination based on a dominant cause?
- Did most examples have a single basis or several bases?
- What seems to be the most common bases for discrimination in this community?

For positive examples, ask the group about who benefits from affirmative measures or reasonable accommodation. List their responses.

- What people or institutions were responsible for the positive measures taken to end or address discrimination?
- Which measures seemed most successful? Least successful? Why?

Types of Discrimination

Discrimination Based on Race and Ethnicity

As one of the most fundamental freedoms, human rights law supports the principle that all human beings are born free and equal in dignity and rights. Discrimination and persecution on the grounds of race and ethnicity are clear violations of this principle. Racial and ethnic discrimination occurs in many forms. Among the most brutal and well-documented forms of discrimination are *genocide*, the deliberate and systematic destruction of a racial, political, or cultural group, and *apartheid*, racial segregation. Less well documented are examples of racial and ethnic discrimination that prevents individuals and groups from enjoying the same civil, political, economic, social, and cultural rights as those enjoyed by other groups in society. Statistics and other social indicators often can help identify such discrimination.

For example, in Central and Eastern Europe, the Roma (gypsy) population, which now exceeds 5 million, continues to exist on the margins of society and is subject to widespread and often institutionalized racism. This group is systematically deprived of basic communal infrastructure (i.e., a clean water supply, electricity, heating), regularly denied citizenship papers and other related documents, and given minimal or no social services by the government.[7]

In the United States, for example, schools were separated by race until 1954, when the court case *Brown v Board of Education* found that "[s]egregation of children in public schools solely on the basis of race deprives children of the minority group of equal educational opportunities, even though the physical facilities and other "tangible" factors may be equal. The "separate but equal" doctrine . . . has no place in the field of public education."[8] The Civil Rights Act of 1964 extended additional rights in employment without regard to an individual's race, color, religion, or national origin.[9]

The principal international document that addresses racial discrimination, the Convention for the Elimination of All Forms of Racial Discrimination (CERD), defines *racial discrimination* broadly as "any distinction, exclusion, restriction or preference based on race, color, descent, or national or ethnic origin which has the purpose or effect of nullifying or impairing the recognition, enjoyment or exercise, on equal footing, of human rights and fundamental freedoms in the political, economic, social, cultural or any other field of public life" (Article 1). Significantly, ethnicity is explicitly included in this definition.

The following are important features of CERD:

- Racial discrimination applies to discrimination on grounds of national or ethnic origin, although it does not apply to discrimination on grounds of religion or nationality. Nationality is different from national origin in that it relates to place of birth rather than to current legal nationality.
- The definition of *discrimination* is broad, encompassing intentional discrimination as well as laws, norms, and practices that may appear to be neutral but in actuality have a discriminatory effect.
- CERD requires states to take action when either public or private persons engage in discrimination. In other words, states have a responsibility to prevent discrimination by police, state employees, and other state actors.

States are also obligated to take administrative and/or court actions against any private person who discriminates against others.

- Temporary affirmative measures aimed at securing the advancement of certain racial or ethnic groups or individuals, and necessary to ensure the equal enjoyment or exercise of human rights and fundamental freedoms, fall outside the definition of discrimination.
- Education is recognized as an essential component of combating discrimination. In Article 7, CERD provides that "States Parties undertake to adopt immediate and effective measures, particularly in the fields of teaching, education, culture and information, to combat racial prejudice and promote racial understanding, tolerance and friendship."

CERD also requires governments to ensure that effective protection and remedies are provided for treaty violations through competent national tribunals and other state institutions. The right to a remedy has proven highly controversial when entire groups of people seek reparations. At the 2001 UN World Conference Against Racism, for example, some countries pressed for financial and other forms of reparations for past violations such as slavery. In contrast, some Western governments, many of them former colonial powers, strongly denied the existence of any obligation to remedy past abuses.

✠ Learning Activity 4: Defining and Analyzing Racism ✠

Objective   To encourage reflection about assumptions regarding the meaning of race

Time   30 minutes

Materials   Chart paper and markers or blackboard and chalk

1. Define

Ask participants, working in pairs, to write a definition of *race* that they can both agree on and to give some specific examples of a race. When they have finished, each pair should join with another pair to compare their definitions and examples.

2. Discuss

Consider the following questions:

- How did you experience the process of defining *race*?
- What disagreements arose about the definition and examples?
- Why is *racism* difficult to define?
- Why are specific examples difficult to agree upon?

3. Explain

Explain that the Convention Against All Forms of Racial Discrimination explicitly includes ethnicity in its definition of *racial discrimination:* "any distinction, exclusion, restriction or preference based on race, color, descent or national or ethnic origin." Ask for examples of what is included under each of these terms: *color, descent, national origin, ethnic origin.*

Note to Facilitator: Emphasize that *national origin* refers to place, not nationality.

Discrimination Against Indigenous People[10]

Indigenous people comprise an estimated 370 million humans living in more than seventy countries and maintaining social, cultural, economic, and political characteristics distinct from those of the larger societies in which they reside. Although they are among the most resilient people worldwide, systematic marginalization throughout history has made them one of the poorest and most vulnerable groups as well.

Indigenous women are often targets of gender-specific and racially motivated violence and discrimination. They face interrelated forms of discrimination due to their status both as indigenous people and as women (and sometimes as disabled people, too). For example, many indigenous women have been imprisoned or abused because of their own—or a family member's—involvement in activism or politics. And because of their resistance to political, social, or cultural oppression, many have been raped.

The escalating militarization and conflict in many indigenous territories have severely affected the members of indigenous communities, women in particular, who then face significant internal displacement and devastation of natural resources and ancestral homelands. In Colombia, for example, indigenous women are the primary victims of forced displacement by paramilitaries and are often also subject to widespread sexual abuse.[11]

Canada: Stolen Sisters—A Human Rights Response to Discrimination and Violence Against Indigenous Women in Canada[12]

Helen Betty Osborne was a 19-year-old Cree student from northern Manitoba who dreamed of becoming a teacher. On November 12, 1971, she was abducted by four white men in the town of The Pas, sexually assaulted, and brutally murdered. A provincial inquiry subsequently concluded that Canadian authorities had failed Helen Betty Osborne. The inquiry criticized the sloppy and racially biased police investigation that took more than fifteen years to bring only one of the four men to justice. Most disturbingly, the inquiry concluded that police had long been aware of white men sexually preying on indigenous women and girls in The Pas but "did not feel that the practice necessitated any particular vigilance."

Violence against women, and certainly violence against indigenous women, is rarely understood as a human rights issue. To the extent that governments, media, and the general public consider concerns about violence against women, they more frequently describe it as being a criminal concern or a social issue. . . .

Amnesty International's research demonstrates that violence experienced by indigenous women gives rise to human rights concerns in two central ways. First, one must consider the violence itself and the official response to that violence. When private individuals target indigenous women for racist, sexist attacks, and the women fail to receive the necessary levels of official protection in response to that violence, their fundamental human rights are at stake. These rights include the right to life, the right to be protected against torture and ill treatment, the right to security of the person, and the right to both sexual and racial equality.

Second, the range of concerns, both historical and contemporary, that Amnesty International's research shows are factors placing indigenous women at heightened risk of experiencing violence also directly entail a number of fundamental human rights provisions. For instance, the United Nations Human Rights Committee (UNHRC) has found that past policies

continues

Canada: Stolen Sisters Continued

revoking the legal indigenous status of indigenous women who married nonindigenous men violate minority cultural rights under Article 27 of the International Covenant on Civil and Political Rights. The UNHRC reported that indigenous women and children are "particularly vulnerable" to the denial of "due process and are frequently victims of violence and physical abuse.[13]

Currently, increasing numbers of indigenous individuals are accusing the Canadian government of abuse and ill treatment in the form of its now-defunct residential schools program. Beginning in 1874, the Canadian government established residential schools, including a variety of institutions such as industrial schools, boarding schools, student residences, hostels, billets, and residential schools for indigenous children. Under the weight of heavy domestic criticism,these schools, never numbering more than one hundred, were gradually shut down in the 1970s, 1980s, and 1990s. Approximately 100,000 children attended these schools over the last century.[14] Only recently are former students reporting the physical, psychological, and sexual abuse and ill treatment they experienced during their time in these programs. This development obviously raises a range of concerns regarding human rights as well as economic, social, and cultural rights, including the right to access to education for indigenous children.

During the past two decades, indigenous women have mobilized to address the needs of their communities and to ensure that indigenous issues, and indigenous women's involvement in addressing key challenges, are visible on the international agenda. Indigenous women have formed confederations, legal and cultural centers, and political parties and platforms, all galvanized by their indigenous identity.[15]

Discrimination Based on Culture

Culture is not an unchanging norm but a feature of societies that is constantly renegotiated by all of the people that make up a social unit. Women play an integral role in the definition, creation, and maintenance of culture. Indeed, they are often perceived as the guardians and transmitters of culture. Yet, because women usually lack power in society, they are oppressed by certain aspects of culture. Many calls for human rights norms to be sensitive to culture mask the interests of those who benefit from women's oppression, especially state and religious forces. For women, the challenge is to maintain the integrity and beauty of their own culture while simultaneously changing those aspects of culture that treat women or any oppressed communities as inferior human beings.

In many parts of the world, women from marginalized communities often use culture as a way of resisting dominant groups—specifically, by insisting on the recognition of diversity. Yet while the use of culture has been an important means of empowering such minority groups, many of the women in these constituencies have found themselves in a double bind. The assertion of culture or religion has often been made in such a way as to consolidate the patterns of oppression within that particular community. For example, minority women who raise their voices against domestic violence and rape within their communities are often silenced because their struggle is perceived as threatening to the men of the community or to the entire community itself.

The issue of culture is further complicated in the context of women organizing on behalf of women's rights. The failure of many women from dominant Western cultures to recognize the patterns of oppression fostered by their own culture sometimes creates barriers to solidarity with women from minority cultures. For example, women from dominant cultures may be quick to point out the forms of violence experienced by women in minority communities, yet fail to recognize the systematic and structural forms of violence directed against women in their own communities. This difficulty is exacerbated when female members of dominant groups perceive the oppression of women in minority communities as an inevitable aspect of that culture.

In short, human rights advocates must respect cultural diversity and integrity while ensuring that the assertion of cultural rights does not become an excuse for denying the fundamental human rights of women.[16]

To build a global human rights movement, women from different parts of the world need to understand that cultural practices that deny women's human rights exist in every part of the world and that all cultures have liberating and oppressive practices. In targeting any cultural practice, whether domestic violence, dowry deaths, rape in war-torn areas, plastic surgery, arranged marriage, or female genital cutting (FGC),[17] the leadership should come from women in the regions affected and assumptions about the superiority or inferiority of any culture must be avoided. (For a more detailed discussion of culturally determined gender roles, see Chapter 1, "Introduction to Women's Human Rights."

Proposed Strategies for Analyzing Culture[18]

In examining a cultural practice that appears to disadvantage only women, or to have a disproportionately burdensome impact on women, the cost of violating the human rights norm must be weighed against the benefit of the cultural practice. We should begin such an analysis by asking the following questions:

- What is the origin of the cultural practice? What is its value?
- What is its level of significance to the culture? Within the community?
- How does the practice intrude on a protected individual right?
- How significant is the violated individual right to the international community?

By addressing the following questions, we can place this inquiry in context:

- What is the nature of the practice being challenged?
- Who is challenging the practice (e.g., an insider versus an outsider)?
- What are the motives for opposing the practice? What are the claimed harmful outcomes of the practice?

The key rights relating to culture are summarized below:[19]

- *The right to cultural identity* may be defined as the right for individuals, either alone or in community with others, to freely choose their own cultural identity (or identities) in all its manifestations such as language, traditions, religion, and heritage. No one may be forced to assimilate into another culture. This right is supported in a number of international documents, including Article 27 of the International Covenant on Economic, Social, and Cultural Rights (ICESCR), which affirms that members of ethnic minorities have the right to enjoy their own culture; Article 29 of the Convention on the Rights of the Child, which stipulates that education of the child shall be directed to developing respect for his or her cultural identity; and the Recommendation on Cultural Identity adopted by the World Conference on Cultural Polices, which calls on Member States to respect and work to preserve the cultural identity of countries, regions, and peoples and to promote the development of cultural identity through all appropriate means.

- *The right to participate in cultural life* is provided for, in one form or another, in a number of international and regional human rights documents. It implies both the right to actively express oneself in creative processes and the passive enjoyment of culture. Access to and participation in the cultural life of one's community and freedom from discrimination in that regard are core components of the right to participate in cultural life.

- *The right to education* is closely associated with cultural rights, inasmuch as states must respect the right of minorities to be taught in the language of their choice in institutions outside the official system of public education. In addition, states are obliged to incorporate cultural studies into their educational programs by teaching about civilizations and cultural heritage and foreign languages. Cultural education is seen as a tool for enhancing peace and stability and combating ethnic and racial disputes.

- *The right to cultural heritage* covers the enjoyment and protection against destruction or illegal appropriation of cultural heritage. A number of UNESCO documents address the protection of cultural property in times of war and peace, including the Convention Concerning the Protection of World Cultural and Natural Heritage, adopted in 1972 under the auspices of the United Nations Educational, Scientific and Cultural Organization (UNESCO). This Convention established a system of international protection for designated world cultural and natural heritage.

- *The right to international cultural cooperation*, as expressed in the UNESCO Declaration on the Principles of International Cultural Cooperation (1966), provides that cultural cooperation is a right and a duty for all peoples and all nations and that states should facilitate the sharing of cultural knowledge and skills. A number of general international human rights documents address international cooperation in broad terms and should, therefore, encompass cultural cooperation. Other documents relating specifically to minorities express rights to international as well as internal cultural cooperation.

- *The right to be protected from harmful cultural practices* is one to which international human rights treaties are increasingly making reference. In 2002, for example, the Ugandan police force officially identified female genital cutting as a cultural practice that greatly harms and oppresses women.[20] For further discussion of this practice, see Chapter 5, "Women's Human Right to Health."

Discrimination Based on Religion

Closely related to discrimination based on culture is discrimination based on religion. Article 18 of the Universal Declaration of Human Rights states:

> Everyone has the right to a standard of living adequate for the health and well-being of himself and of his family, including food, clothing, housing, and medical care and necessary social services, and the *right to security in the event of* unemployment, sickness, disability, widowhood, *old age* or other lack of livelihood in circumstances beyond his control." (italics added)

According to this article, "freedom of religion" is related to "freedom of belief," while "freedom of worship" includes the following indivisible, interdependent, and interrelated human rights:

- the human right to freedom of thought, conscience, and religion
- the human right to manifest one's religion or belief in worship, observance, practice, and teaching
- the human right to freedom from discrimination based on religious beliefs or activities, or because of refusal to conform to a certain religion
- the human right to freedom of expression and of association
- the human right to conscientious objection on grounds of religious belief.

International human rights instruments mentioning religious freedom tend to be nonspecific about women. In particular, they tend to emphasize protection of religious minorities and do not consider that women may be victims of discrimination based on religion. Nonetheless, the issue of discrimination against women under the guise of religion has received attention at the United Nations at international meetings and has increasingly found its way into UN reports. Significantly, in his 1999 report to the UN Commission on Human Rights, Abdellefatah Amor, Special Rapporteur on Freedom of Religion or Belief, stated unequivocally:

> Discrimination and intolerance against women, supposedly prescribed by religion or tradition, must be resolutely condemned. To that end, the Special Rapporteur reiterates his recommendation that a seminar should be held on the status of women from the standpoint of religion, traditions and human rights, so as not only to identify manifestations of discrimination and intolerance, but also to formulate practical recommendations and a plan of action for eradicating such practices.[21]

Three years later, in 2002, the Special Rapporteur published a comprehensive report on women's rights and freedom of religion or belief: the Study on Freedom of Religion or Belief and the Status of Women from the Viewpoint of Religion and Traditions.[22] The study urged that states take action to address intolerance and discrimination against women based on religion. A significant international nongovernmental project—The Women's United Nations Report Network and Program (WUNRN)—established a coalition in 2003 to build on the Special Rapporteur's study through exchange of information and other activities.[23]

Some argue that changes supported by the international community can be contrary to a people's religion and culture. Such was the case involving the family code in Morocco, the Moudawana, which, under pressure from human rights advocates, was revised in January 2004. The Moudawana gave women rights they did not previously enjoy, including the right to get married without consent of a male relative. The newly revised code raised the minimum marriage age from 15 to 18, gave women the right to initiate divorce and obtain property from the divorce, and required a wife's consent for her husband to take a second wife. While some Moroccans charged that the revisions were forced upon them, others believed that Islam provided women with rights that merited support under Moroccan law.[24]

✠ Learning Activity 5: Analyzing Culture and Religion ✠

Objective To examine the negative and positive aspects of culture and religion

Time 30 minutes

Materials Chart paper and markers or blackboard and chalk

1. List/Discuss

Ask the group to list some cultural practices in their community that are different for women and men (e.g., both men and women must wear distinctive clothing, men must undergo initiation rituals, women cannot divorce, only women are allowed to perform certain rituals, women must be married when they are very young, it is acceptable for men to beat their wives).

Pick a few examples and ask the following questions:

- Who is imposing the practice (e.g., family, father, mother, government, religious authority, dominant ethnic, or religious group)?
- Why is the practice being imposed (e.g., to protect women, to protect the economic interests of some individual or group, to prevent a group from competing for jobs, housing)?
- Who benefits from the practice (e.g., the community through cultural continuity, those whose power is maintained)?
- Who suffers from the practice (e.g., women specifically or entire communities, as in India where the institution of caste is detrimental to both men and women of lower castes)?
- If someone is harmed by the practice, what are the reasons that she or he continues the practice (e.g., ostracism, lack of alternatives, fear of violence, retaliation, or loss of job)?
- If a practice is detrimental, can it be modified? Is it being modified?
- What human rights are being violated by the practice? (For example, female genital cutting can violate rights to bodily integrity, health, and sexuality; inability to work can violate rights to livelihood; inability to go to school can violate rights to education, work, livelihood, and freedom of expression; domestic violence can violate rights to life, health, and security.)

continues

✠ Learning Activity 5 Continued ✠

2. List

Ask the participants to identify and list positive aspects of their culture with respect to women. Examine the list and discuss how these aspects support or promote women's human rights.

- Identify interpretations of culture that are not oppressive to any group of people. How would women go about promoting those interpretations? List some strategies. These could include reinterpreting religious texts, increasing political participation, taking direct action, and creating alternative rituals.
- Identify how perceiving human rights as women's rights might conflict with community cultural practices. What should happen when a clash occurs?

3. Discuss

Based on the lists made in Steps 1 and 2, discuss who should intervene when women's human rights are violated by cultural practices.

- The community? If so, which institutions or individuals?
- The government? If so, which institutions or individuals?
- The United Nations or international organizations?

Discrimination Based on Disability

According to the United Nations Program on Disabilities, there is no universally agreed definition of disability. The World Program of Action for Disabled Persons and the Standard Rules on the Equalization of Opportunities for Persons with Disabilities define *disability* not as a physical or mental attribute of an individual but, rather, as a socially created problem that exists as a result of a combination of social, personal, physical, and environmental factors. Following are some additional definitions related to disability:

- *Disability:* Any restriction or lack—resulting from an impairment—of ability to perform an activity in the manner or within the range considered normal for a human being
- *Impairment:* Any loss or abnormality of psychological, physiological, or anatomical structure or function
- *Handicap:* A disadvantage for a given individual, resulting from an impairment or disability, that limits or prevents the fulfillment of a role that is normal, depending on age, sex, social, and cultural factors, for that individual[25]

Women with disabilities make up a disproportionate percentage of disabled persons. Approximately 300 million women around the world, or one woman in ten, have mental and physical disabilities. In countries with poor and below-average economies, women constitute 75 percent of disabled people.[26] Traditional models of disability have reinforced the disempowerment of and discrimination against women and girls with disabilities. The "charity model" of disability is rooted in a sense of tragedy, pity, or paternalistic responsibility. There is a human impulse to take care of those who are considered weak and pitiful, poor and helpless. Unfortunately, however, society often wrongly assumes that people with disabilities automatically fall into this category and lack the potential to be self-sufficient. The effect of the charity perspective is that many people with disabilities are not given an opportunity to live independently or to earn a living, despite the fact that many would be capable of doing so if given the chance.

Equally disempowering to women with disabilities is the "medical model," which assumes that disability is primarily a health problem and the responsibility of the medical community. Society ignores its own responsibility to integrate people with disabilities by assuming, instead, that it is the duty of the health profession to help such people through treatment and rehabilitation. Physicians and other health professionals have an important role to play in helping all people maximize physical and mental strength and health—including people with disabilities. The medical model approach to disability, however, fails to consider society's critical role in integrating people with disabilities into the community.

Over the last two decades, the global disability community has worked to combat perceptions of people with disabilities as objects of charity or as sick people in need of a cure. Instead, it has sought to redefine people with disabilities as members of society with important contributions to make to both their families and their communities. This revisionist approach, often called the "social model" of disability, emphasizes that people with disabilities face barriers to inclusion not because of their disabilities but, rather, because of unhealthy and disempowering attitudes and actions. This social perspective is concerned with identifying, exposing, and examining the limitations imposed on people with disabilities by the physical and social environments in which they live, including:

- legal barriers that result in fewer rights for people with disabilities
- physical barriers that prevent access to voting places, shops, restaurants, schools, work, transportation, and other places
- communication barriers that inhibit access.

Eliminating the limitations created by these external environments requires complementing the social model with a human rights–based approach that:

- recognizes people with disabilities as rights holders who can and should determine the course of their lives to the same extent as any member of society
- defines limitations imposed by the social and physical environment as infringements on the rights of people with disabilities.

The oppression and dehumanization of women with disabilities that accompany stigma and discrimination have marked human rights consequences in a variety of contexts. For example, in the United States, men with disabilities earned 55 percent more than women with disabilities in 1994–1995. Workplace harassment of women with disabilities is commonplace, including particularly severe biases with regard to those with "hidden disabilities" such as mental disabilities. And pervasive ignorance frequently leads potential employers to reject disabled women, because they mistakenly assume that the women will not be able to fulfill job requirements or that reasonable accommodations will be extensive and costly.[27]

Women with mental and physical disabilities must fight to participate in decisions about their health care, and all too frequently the decisions are simply made for them, without their consultation or consent, leading to a variety of human rights abuses including forced abortion and sterilization[28] and psychiatric drugging.[29] In 1997, the government of Japan acknowledged that some 16,500 women with disabilities were sterilized, without their consent, between 1949 and 1992 in order to protect "against birth of defective descendants."[30] The government rejected calls by the disability community for compensation on the grounds that the procedures were legal according to the domestic Eugenic Law.

Because women with disabilities are falsely assumed to lead asexual lives, they are far less likely to receive reproductive health care services. They may also be regarded as unfit for parenting and, in some cases, may be falsely told that having a child would be unsafe or unwise because of their disability.[31] Human Rights Watch reports that, when seeking reproductive health care, women with disabilities frequently face abusive treatment at the hands of physicians who do not understand their particular circumstances.[32] One U.S. study in particular showed that women with disabilities were significantly less likely to receive pelvic exams than nondisabled women.[33]

Violence against women with mental disabilities who are confined to institutions and insulated from public scrutiny often goes virtually unaddressed. As reported in a number of countries by Mental Disability Rights International, the gross mistreatment of women in institutions is widespread and includes the practice of forced sterilization and abortion, rampant sexual abuse by staff and patients, arbitrary denial of parental rights, and an array of coercive treatments.[34] In some parts of Africa, having sex with a virgin is rumored to cure HIV/AIDS; thus women and girls with disabilities are sometimes targeted for rape because they are presumed to be virgins.[35]

Studies show that people with disabilities are less likely than others to receive education and often leave school with fewer skills and qualifications than their nondisabled counterparts. UNESCO estimates that the overall literacy rate for persons with disabilities worldwide is 3 percent, and 1 percent for disabled women and girls.[36] In addition, despite the fact that 51 percent of disabled people are women, "international development programs rarely address the needs of disabled women or include them in community development ventures."[37]

A report on gender and disability by Mobility International USA found this situation compounded by the problem that "most [development] organizations do not collect data showing the extent to which people with disabilities, in particular women and girls with disabilities, participate in the development assistance process."[38]

In addressing the challenges faced by women with disabilities, we must acknowledge the role played by poverty and poor environmental conditions. In the developing world, infectious disease, environmental hazards such as landmines, and a host of other conditions increase the likelihood of disability and therefore present serious obstacles to development efforts.

Women and girls with disabilities around the world are disempowered; pushed to the margins of their communities, they are forced to confront massive obstacles to their full participation in society as a result of deeply entrenched stigma and discrimination. Beyond the social and cultural resistance to the inclusion of people with disabilities in society, disabled people throughout the world continue to receive disparate treatment under the law. Of the 189 UN Member States, only about 40 have any form of antidiscrimination law specifically for persons with disabilities, and in those that do, much is lacking in the realms of implementation and enforcement of the provisions on the books.[39] In the United States, the chances of succeeding in a discrimination claim under Title I of the Americans with Disabilities Act is remote: A mere 6.1 percent of cases tried between 1992 and 1999 succeeded.[40] International human rights law applies to all people, including disabled women and girls.

✠ Learning Activity 6: Myths and Stereotypes About Disability ✠

Objective	To address the differences in point of view with regard to disability
Time	45 minutes
Materials	Copies of the list of "Myths and Stereotypes About People with Disabilities" seen below

1. Read

Explain that discrimination is often based on mistaken ideas and stereotypes that one group holds about another group. Read the following list and explain that it was created by an international group of people with disabilities.

Myths and Stereotypes About People with Disabilities

It is often assumed that people with disabilities:

- cannot be self-sufficient/are excessively dependent
- are to be pitied
- are helpless
- are cursed, and disability is a punishment for evil
- are bitter because of their fate
- resent the nondisabled world
- have lives that are not worth living
- are better off at home
- cannot work
- cannot have a family and cannot be good parents
- are asexual
- need to be cured and helped by medical professionals
- need special, separate educational programs
- cannot be involved in cultural/recreational activities.

continues

✠ Learning Activity 6 Continued ✠

These assumptions tend to be made as well:

- Children with disabilities are unable to learn.
- People with intellectual disabilities are naïve, like children, and cannot make any decisions for themselves.
- People with mental disabilities are violent and dangerous.
- People with alternative ways of communicating are stupid.

2. Analyze
Divide participants into small discussion groups and give each group a copy of "Myths and Stereotypes About People with Disabilities." Then ask each group to discuss these questions:

What are some underlying reasons for these views (e.g., fears, cultural and religious attitudes, ignorance)?

How do these views affect the way people with disabilities are regarded and treated by their families? By their communities? In public policy and law?

3. Report/Discuss
Ask a spokesperson from each group to summarize their conclusions and discuss their findings.

- What seem to be the principal underlying reasons for these views?
- What seem to be the most serious effects of these views?

Discuss these or similar questions:

- Which of these views are most prevalent in your community?
- How do these views result in discrimination and prevent people with disabilities from enjoying their human rights?
- How can these views be confronted?

Human Rights at Stake

- The right to nondiscrimination and freedom from violence and harassment
- The right to life
- The right to freedom from torture and cruel, inhuman, or degrading treatment
- The right to freedom from arbitrary arrest
- The right to freedom of movement
- The right to a fair trial
- The right to privacy
- The rights to free expression and free association
- The right to work
- The rights to social security, assistance and benefits, and a decent standard of living
- The right to physical and mental health
- The right to form a family[41]

Discrimination Faced by Women in Nontraditional Relationships

Some women face discrimination, violence, and other violations of their human rights when they live in situations that are not accepted by their communities or culture. Others are subject to discrimination because they live apart from men, facing harassment in the street, at home, or in the workplace. These women often have a hard time finding housing and employment. Single mothers, in particular, are sometimes ostracized by their communities and denied opportunities to participate in public life. Women-headed households are common in rural areas when the men migrate in search of wage labor, leaving women to care for the farm or business and their children. And women who are abandoned by their husbands, divorced, or widowed may be subject to laws, traditions, and practices that disallow their rights to inheritance[42] and custody of their children.[43]

In some areas of Nigeria, women who lose their husbands may be subject to violent discrimination: Upon the death of the husband, a woman can be evicted from her home, lose her property, and be handed over as property to another man in the husband's family. (Physical abuse often accompanies this type of discrimination; however, laws are being enacted in Nigeria to protect women from such abuse.)[44] Similarly, widows whose husbands die of AIDS may face a ritual "cleansing," often involving unprotected sex, which can further spread HIV.[45]

In other parts of the world, single women are considered property of their fathers or sons and are unable to own property themselves. In Kenya, inheritance norms prohibit wives or daughters from owning or inheriting land; women may own property jointly with their husbands, but this is rare. Kenyan men who favor a woman's right to property inheritance often fail to act because of fear of community retribution.[46]

Hostility sometimes confronts women in intimate relationships not accepted by their community, such as a single mother, a woman refusing arranged marriages, a woman living unmarried with a man, a woman in a relationship with another woman, or a woman in a relationship with a partner of a different ethnicity, class, or religion.

Following are some of the consequences of these relationships:

- She can be thrown out of her job.
- She can lose her family and children.
- She can lose her house.
- She can become isolated from her friends and her community.
- She can be put in jail.
- She can be assaulted by family members, the community, or the state.
- She can be forcibly separated from her partner.
- She can be forced into marriage.
- She can be physically harmed or killed.

For more information on women's intimate relationships, see the section in Chapter 3 headed "Women Living Apart from Men."

✠ Learning Activity 7: Examining Women's Intimate Relationships ✠

Objective To explore the repercussions of prohibited relationships in society
Time 20 minutes
Materials Chart paper and markers or blackboard and chalk

1. Act

Ask the participants if they would like to share a story about themselves or others who are currently living in situations that are not accepted by society, and about the obstacles they face.

2. Discuss

- What are the consequences for a woman in your community who is in a relationship not accepted by your family, community, religion, or culture?
- Make a list of all the human rights violations a woman may experience as a result.
- Why do the prohibited relationships in your community cause extreme repercussions?
- Why are such relationships so threatening to society? Whom do they threaten?

Discrimination Based on Class

Discrimination based on class or economic status is a pervasive problem for people all over the world. Poor women often bear the most severe consequences of population control programs, welfare cuts, government austerity programs, and cuts in government subsidies. Poverty can make women more vulnerable to economic and sexual exploitation, trafficking, and other forms of human rights violations.

Women often find it difficult to address class differences among themselves. After all, a professional woman who works as a lawyer will probably have concerns different from those of the woman she hires as a domestic worker. As part of the landowning or professional class, some women benefit from human rights abuses of poor women. The growing disparity between rich and poor all over the world adds to the power differences that exist between women. Such economic inequalities impair the ability of advocates to create a holistic human rights movement. For further discussion of these issues, see Chapter 9, "Women's Human Rights and Globalization," and Chapter 10, "Women's Human Rights and Work."

✠ Learning Activity 8: Acknowledging Class ✠

Objective To address the differences in point of view between privileged and underprivileged people

Time 45 minutes

Materials Chart paper and markers or blackboard and chalk

Note to Facilitator: The following exercise, especially Step 1, may be inappropriate in some settings. Consider the more impersonal alternative method. With both methods, take great care to ensure that no social group is derided.

1. Describe

Put four chairs in the center of the room. Ask four participants who identify themselves as coming from privileged backgrounds to sit in these chairs. Ask them to describe what it has meant for them to have class privilege. Examples might include "I had a nanny," "I knew when I was a child that I would go to college," "I never have to worry about paying the rent," or "I always had nice clothes to wear."

After this group has finished, ask four participants who identify themselves as coming from underprivileged backgrounds to sit in the chairs. Have them list what it has meant for them not to have class privilege. Examples might include "I never knew if I would be able to keep going to school because my parents weren't sure they could pay the fees," "I had to use an outside toilet," or "My mother migrated in search of work."

Alternative: On chart paper draw the outlines of three to five female figures, which will represent women from different classes within this society. Assign a small group to each figure and ask them to write and draw some of the distinguishing features of a person from this class (e.g., dress, speech, mannerisms).

Ask each small group to present its work, eliciting additional characteristics from the whole group.

Discuss these illustrations of class distinctions:

- How accurate are these illustrations? To what extent are they based on myths and stereotypes?
- How do such myths and stereotypes prevent solidarity and reinforce social and cultural discrimination against all women?
- Beyond these visible class differences, what are some of the invisible differences among women of different classes?

2. Discuss/List

Discuss the feelings and issues raised in the listings by the two groups, and compare. Note whether those who have class benefits have a harder time describing their experience than those who come from poor or working-class families.

continues

✠ Learning Activity 8 Continued ✠

List the ways institutions and resources in society benefit from or discriminate against different classes of people. How is this discrimination perpetuated?

3. Discuss

- How are different classes of people separated in schools, hospitals, and other public places? In what situations do people of different classes meet? Interact? Discuss or solve problems together?
- Is there a pattern of groups of certain ethnic or racial groups belonging to one class or another?
- Are there similarities or differences in the ways in which men and women have access to class benefits?
- How does class intersect with race, ethnicity, or sex to define how power is exercised in your society?
- How do class and privilege inhibit women's ability to support and promote the rights of all women?

Discrimination Based on Age

According to the UN Department of Economic and Social Affairs, because of the trend toward lower birth and death rates, one out of every ten people on the planet is now 60 years of age or older—and this number is expected to nearly triple by 2050.[47] At the same time, the older-person support ratio (the number of persons 15 to 64 years old relative to those 65 years or older) is falling in both more- and less-developed regions. This situation could further decrease the ability of societies and governments to care for aging populations. While the number of older persons who have living children is increasing worldwide, the number of older persons living with a child has declined.[48]

Unfortunately, the cost of supporting a person over the age of 65 is two and half times that of supporting a person under the age of 20.[49]

By 2050, the United Nations predicts, the median age of almost every country's population will be at "historically unprecedented high levels," whereas the potential older-person support ratio will often be halved, from four or five persons of working age (15 to 64) per older person to only two.[50] Older women, in particular, may face such problems as:

- the inability to obtain full- or part-time work
- an inadequate pension or pension scheme that does not give older women credit for their years as caregivers to family members
- difficulty finding affordable housing in a safe environment
- problems with using public transportation
- no influence in decision-making bodies that arrange for older people's housing, health, and other care

- lack of representation in government and nongovernmental organizations
- inadequate health care
- violence on the street and at home.

Since the level of institutionalization of older women is much higher than that of men in most countries,[51] women are more likely to face abuse in institutional settings.[52]

The rights of older people can be divided into three main categories: protection, participation, and image. *Protection* refers to securing the physical, psychological, and emotional safety of elderly people with regard to their unique vulnerability to abuse and ill treatment. *Participation* refers to the need to establish a greater and more active role for older people in society. And *image* refers to the need to define a more positive—as well as less degrading and less discriminatory—impression of who elderly persons are and what they are capable of doing.

Recent detailed recommendations and agreements about the rights of the elderly are based on the fundamental premises established in documents like the charter of the United Nations and the Universal Declaration of Human Rights. Specifically, Article 25, paragraph 1, of the UDHR establishes that

> [e]veryone has the right to a standard of living adequate for the health and well-being of himself and of his family, including food, clothing, housing, and medical care and necessary social services, and the right to security in the event of unemployment, sickness, disability, widowhood, old age or other lack of livelihood in circumstances beyond his control.

An older person's right to security is particularly vulnerable to violation. For example, one component of the right to security is the right to health care. If a person, due to old age, is unable to afford or pursue health care on his or her own, that security is compromised. Although many countries currently have universal health care systems, these systems are beginning to feel the strain of an increasingly older population and there is uncertainty about how these systems will remain viable in the future. In other countries where federally and state-subsidized health care programs exist only for those who are indigent, disabled, or elderly, as in the United States, rising health care costs threaten the survival of these systems. These rights to security are related to the right to an adequate standard of living, which, in the case of the elderly, is often affected by lack of an adequate support system for them.

Elderly individuals also have the right to nondiscrimination. Many are considered "useless" to society simply because they need more care than the average younger person. Stereotypes of older people can lead to degrading treatment, inequality, and even abuse.

Similarly, elderly persons' right to participation is sometimes threatened because of prevailing negative images of the elderly. The aged are often denied opportunities to be productive members of society. What's needed, therefore, is government assistance in creating a more positive image of the abilities and strengths of older populations as well as in providing actual opportunities for elderly people to participate in their societies.

✠ Learning Activity 9: Responding to Concerns of Older Women ✠

Objective To explore the discrimination and other problems experienced by older women

Time 45 minutes

Materials Chart paper and markers or blackboard and chalk

1. List/Discuss

Ask the participants to list words and phrases commonly used in your community to refer to older women.

- What qualities do these phrases stress? Which are positive qualities? Which are negative?
- Which of these terms would you not want to be called if you were an older woman?
- What prejudices against older women do these words reveal?
- How would you want to be treated as an older woman?

2. Discuss

- What are the main concerns of older women in your community?
- What is being done in your community to address the problems of older women?
- Are older women included in the decision-making processes that address these concerns?
- If you do not know the answers to these questions, how could you gain additional information?

Remembering Core Concepts

As noted earlier, The protection of human rights is based on the following four principles: universality, equality, nondiscrimination, and indivisibility and interdependence. While these principles apply in all cases, differences among and between women influence the manner in which they experience human rights abuses and affect their capacity to address the resulting inequalities. This chapter has only begun to explore the multiple ways in which women experience human rights abuses. Subsequent chapters continue this analysis in greater detail.

✠ Learning Activity 10: Speaking Out Against Discrimination ✠

Objectives To examine discrimination in the community and consider how to take action against it

Time 60+ minutes

continues

✠ Learning Activity 10 Continued ✠

Materials   Chart paper and markers, chart developed in "Learning Activity 3: Examples of Discrimination"

1. Review

List and remind participants of the four human rights principles discussed at the beginning of this chapter:

- Universality
- Equality
- Nondiscrimination
- Indivisibility and interdependence.

List and remind participants of the kinds of discrimination addressed in this chapter:

- Discrimination based on race and ethnicity
- Discrimination against indigenous people
- Discrimination based on culture
- Discrimination based on religion
- Discrimination based on disability
- Discrimination faced by women involved in nontraditional relationships
- Discrimination based on class
- Discrimination based on age.

Remind them of how different kinds of discrimination intersect and interact, producing multiple layers of inequalities.

Reintroduce the chart developed in "Learning Activity 3: Examples of Discrimination," and remind participants of their discussion of the most common kinds of discrimination identified in their community.

2. List

On the basis of this review, ask participants to list what they consider to be the principal problems of discrimination in their community. Then, after dividing them into small groups, ask them to choose an issue on which they wish to concentrate. Encourage the selection of different kinds of discrimination.

3. Discuss/Plan

Ask each group to prepare a five-minute presentation to a "panel of community leaders" on their issue. Each presentation should:

- describe the discrimination in terms of how it intersects with other kinds of discrimination, the group(s) of women it affects, and, if possible, the cause(s) of the problem

continues

Learning Activity 10 Continued

- relate the discrimination to women's human rights
- clarify how the discrimination affects women's lives
- show how addressing the problem can improves women's lives
- propose specific actions that should be taken to address the problem
- show how members of the community can become involved in addressing the problem.

Now ask each group to choose a spokesperson who will make the presentation and a "community leader" to serve on the panel. While the groups plan their presentations, the panel of leaders meets to decide their roles. These roles should represent a variety of differing, but typical, attitudes within the community leadership.

4. Present/Role-Play
The spokesperson from each group makes a presentation and members of the panel listen and respond, asking questions and offering comments, objections, or suggestions in keeping with their chosen roles.

5. Discuss
After each presentation and role-play, discuss the following questions:

- How did the spokespersons feel when presenting the problem?
- How did the "community leaders" respond to the presentation? What attitudes in the community were they representing?
- How did the audience, which is composed of the rest of the group, respond to the presentations?
- Did any spokesperson discuss discrimination as a human rights violation? Did putting the problem in a human rights context strengthen his or her argument? Why or why not?
- Are these ideas for addressing discrimination feasible in your community? Why or why not?

6. Conclude
Challenge the participants by asking them to evaluate their knowledge of the problem and the inclusiveness of their perspective:

- How did you obtain your information about discrimination faced by women in your community? Was it accurate and complete? If not, what additional information do you need and how can you obtain it?
- Did you personally consult women about the problem and how it affects them? About actions that could improve the problem?
- Why is it important in real-life human rights advocacy to include the active participation of those directly involved and affected?
- How can you apply the example of this learning activity to planning and implementing advocacy for women in your community?

Notes

1. United Nations Office on Drugs and Crime, "The Protocol to Prevent, Suppress, and Punish Trafficking in Persons, Part I—Purpose, Scope and Criminal Sanctions," Articles 1–3 (United Nations, 2000).

2. U.S. Department of State, "Testimony Before the Senate Foreign Relations Committee by Secretary Colin L. Powell," September 9, 2004.

3. Human Rights Watch: Africa, "Crisis in Darfur," June 2007, available online at http://www.hrw.org/doc?t=africa&c=darfur.

4. UN Division for the Advancement of Women, "Meeting of States Parties to the Convention on the Elimination of All Forms of Discrimination Against Women" (fourteenth meeting), New York, June 23, 2006.

5. Office of the High Commissioner for Human Rights (OHCHR).

6. United Nations Sixty-First Session of the General Assembly, United Nations "Convention on the Rights of Persons with Disabilities," December 6, 2006.

7. Human Rights House Network, "Roma Still Suffer Discrimination," available online at http://www.humanrightshouse.org/.

8. U.S. Supreme Court, *Brown v Board of Education*, 347 U.S. 483 (1954) 347 U.S. 483, Appeal from the United States District Court for the District of Kansas, May 17, 1954.

9. U.S. Justice Department, Civil Rights Act of 1964, 88th Congress, H.R. 7152.

10. UNIFEM, *Securing Indigenous Rights and Participation*, available online at http://www.unifem.org/filesconfirmed/2/355_at_a_glance_indigenous_women.pdf#search='Key%20issues%20raised%20by%20indigenous%20women%20at%20various%20regional%20and%20international%20forums%20have%20included%20the%20need%20for%20protection%20of%20their.

11. Amnesty International, "Stop Violence Against Women: Colombia—Women's Bodies a Battleground," October 12, 2004, AI Index: AMR 23/046/2004, available in Library Online Documentation Archive at http://web.amnesty.org/library/Index/ENGAMR230462004?open&of=ENG-COL.

12. Amnesty International Canada, "Canada: Stolen Sisters–A Human Rights Response to Discrimination and Violence Against Indigenous Women in Canada," October 4, 2004, available online at http://www.amnesty.ca/resource_centre/reports/view.php?load=arcview&article=1895&c=Resource+Centre+Reports.

13. Rodolfo Stavenhagen, "Information Note on the Mandate of the Special Rapporteur on the Situation of Human Rights and Fundamental Freedoms of Indigenous Peoples," June 2004, available online at http://www.unhchr.ch/indigenous/rapporteur.htm.

14. Indian and Northern Affairs of Canada, "Backgrounder: The Residential School System," available online at http://www.ainc-inac.gc.ca.

15. Deborah J. Yashar, "Indigenous Politics and Democracy: Contesting Citizenship in Latin America," *Working Paper #238*, July 1997.

16. For a more detailed discussion of culturally determined gender roles, see Chapter 1, "Introduction to Women's Human Rights."

17. For more on FGC, see the box titled "The Case of Female Genital Cutting" in Chapter 5.

18. Hernandez-Truyol, Berta Esperanza, "Women's Rights as Human Rights—Rules, Realities and the Role of Culture: A Formula for Reform," *Brooklyn Journal of International Law*, vol. 21, p. 605 (1996).

19. Again, see the box cited in Note 17.

20. Helen Alyek, "Harmful Cultural Practices Against Women and Children [Girl Children] in Uganda and Africa," conference paper for the Australian Government Institute of Criminology, October 2002, available online at http://www.aic.gov.au.

21. Abdellefatah Amor, "Special Rapporteur on Religious Freedom or Belief, Report on Religious Freedom or Belief (to UN Commission on Human Rights)," E/CN.4/1999/58.

22. United Nations, *The Study on Freedom of Religion or Belief and the Status of Women from the Viewpoint of Religion and Traditions,* Unofficial Summary in English, E/CN.4/2002/73/add.2, available online at http://www.wunrn.com/un_study/english.pdf.

23. Leony Grich, "Women's UN Report Network (WUNRN) and the UN Study, Human Rights Education Associates," available online at http://www.wunrn.com/anthology/anthology.htm.

24. Brian Katulis, *Freedom House: Women's Freedom in Focus—Morocco, Findings from Focus Groups with Moroccan Citizens on Women's Rights,* March 5, 2004.

25. Adapted from United Nations Program on Disabilities, available online at http://www.un.org/esa/socdev/enable/faqs.htm#definition.

26. Human Rights Watch, "Women and Girls with Disabilities," 2004, available online at http://www.hrw.org/women/disabled.html.

27. Human Rights Watch, "Background on Abuses of Disabled Women's and Girls' Rights," 2004, available online at http://hrw.org/women/disabled.html#background.

28. U.S. State Department Human Rights Report, February 2000, available online at http://www.state.gov.

29. "Nearly two-thirds of the states have passed involuntary outpatient commitment [IOC] laws that involve court-ordered treatment [almost always medication] for people who are not physically dangerous to themselves or others. As a result, more people who find these medications debilitating are being forced to take them under court order." See National Council on Disability, *From Privileges to Rights: People Labeled with Psychiatric Disabilities Speak for Themselves* (January 20, 2000), p. 12.

30. Japan National Assembly of Disabled Peoples International, *Counter Report of the Report of the Japanese Government Made at the 26th Session of the Extraordinary Session of the Committee on Economic, Social and Cultural Rights,* Geneva, August 13–31, 2001.

31. Human Rights Watch, Women's Division, *Background Paper on Abuses of Disabled Women's and Girls' Rights,* available online at http://www.hrw.org/women/disabled.html.

32. Ibid.

33. Human Rights Watch, "Women's Rights: Women and Girls with Disabilities—Background on Abuses of Disabled Women's and Girl's Rights," available online at http://hrw.org/women/disabled.html.

34. Mental Disability Rights International, *Not on the Agenda: Human Rights of People with Mental Disabilities in Kosovo* (2002).

35. Human Rights Watch, "Background on Abuses of Disabled Women's and Girls' Rights," 2004. available online at http://hrw.org/women/disabled.html#background.

36. Harilyn Rousso, "Education for All: A Gender and Disability Perspective," October 2003, World Bank, Washington, D.C.

37. "Disability Awareness in Action," *Disabled Women,* vol. 5 (1997).

38. Tina Singleton et al., *Gender and Disability: A Survey of InterAction Member Agencies* (Mobility International USA, 2001).

39. Robert L. Metts, "Disability Issues, Trends and Recommendations for the World Bank," *Discussion Paper No. 0007,* February 29, 2000.

40. John W. Parry, *1999 Employment Decisions Under the ADA Title I—Survey Update, Vol. 24: Mental and Physical Disability Law Reporter* (May–June 2000), pp. 348, 349.

41. Adapted from Human Rights Education Associates, available online at http://www.hrea.org/learn/guides/lgbt.html.

42. Human Rights Watch, "Q&A: Women's Property Rights in Sub-Saharan Africa," available online at http://www.hrw.org/campaigns/women/property/qna.htm.

43. Human Right Watch News, "Statement in Support of U.S. Senate Ratification of the Convention on the Elimination of All Forms of Discrimination Against Women (CEDAW) to the Senate Foreign Relations Committee," June 13, 2002, available online at http://hrw.org/backgrounder/wrd/cedaw-statement.htm.

44. The Global Fund for Women, available online at http://www.globalfundforwomen .org/newsletter/2004-03/nigeria.html.

45. Human Rights Watch, "Double Standards: Women's Property Rights Violations in Kenya," 2003, available online at http://www.hrw.org/reports/2003/kenya0303/kenya 0303.pdf.

46. Ibid.

47. United Nations Department of Economic and Social Affairs, Population Division, "Living Arrangements of Older Persons Around the World," available online at http:// www.un.org/esa/population/publications/livingarrangement/report.htm.

48. Ibid.

49. United Nations Population Division, 2000 Report on Replacement Migration, available online at http://www.un.org/esa/population/publications/migration/chap5 .pdf.

50. United Nations Population Division Press Release, DEV/2234, POP/735, "New Report on Replacement Migration," March 17, 2000, available online at http://www.un .org/News/Press/docs/2000/20000317.dev2234.doc.html.

51. United Nations Population Division, 2000 Report on Replacement Migration, available online at http://www.un.org/esa/population/publications/migration/chap5 .pdf.

52. Ibid.

3

Women's Human Rights in the Family

States parties shall take all appropriate measures to eliminate discrimination against women in all matters relating to marriage and family relations.
—Convention on the Elimination of All Forms of Discrimination Against Women (CEDAW), Article 16

Objectives

The learning activities and background information in this chapter will enable participants to work toward the following objectives:

- Recognize the importance of decision-making about family matters and the diversity of choices women can make.
- Recognize situations in their communities where women's human rights in the family are being violated.
- Discuss the role that governments, community leaders, and women themselves could play in protecting and promoting women's human rights in the family.
- Define the *public-private split* and examine women's concerns in the context of this debate.
- Develop ways to promote women's human rights in the family and in the community.
- Remember core concepts.

Getting Started: Thinking About Power and Decision Making in the Family

Article 16.3 of the Universal Declaration of Human Rights (UDHR) emphasizes the importance of the family, proclaiming that "[t]he family is the natural and fundamental group unit of society and is entitled to protection by society and the State."

Yet it is within the bounds of this essential social unit that many women experience the greatest limitation of their human rights. While the family unit is entitled to protection, the rights of individuals within that family are often violated. The customary family norms of many cultures are highly hierarchal, giving most power and decision making to male family members. Such traditional structures are highly resistant to change, even when laws may exist regarding the equality of men and women.

Although human rights law does not define the family, many people assume that a family consists of a man and his wife or wives and their children, with the man holding the position of head of the household. Although there are many social variations, the extended or multigenerational family unit is often assumed to include the sons of the primary couple, and the wives and children of their sons, with power devolving to the sons, often on the basis of their birth order. The United Nations, too, has shown latitude in endorsing many definitions of the term *family*. The UN Human Rights Committee has noted that "the concept of the family may differ in some respects from state to state, and even from region to region within a state; it is therefore not possible to give the concept a standard definition."[1]

Even institutions such as development agencies, religious organizations, and governments perpetuate this model of male authority in the family, assuming that a man is always the head of the household, the primary wage earner, and the chief decision maker. The reality of family life for many women does not match this stereotype, however. Despite strong pressures to maintain traditional family structures, changing social situations, economic necessities, personal choices, and crises such as war or epidemics, including HIV/AIDS, have resulted in the development of diverse families, many headed by women or girl children.

By adhering to the presumption that men are the heads of households, social surveys and governments tend to overlook and undervalue women's roles in families. Immigration and nationality laws often discriminate against women by failing to address their independent concerns and claims contrary to, or against the will of, the male in their household. Governments may even base social security, legal inheritance, credit, development projects, and other laws or policies upon the presumption of a male head of household. For example, governments or social institutions may assume that male members of a household need more social assistance than female members because the male is the primary breadwinner. Women, therefore, may face greater difficulties when they attempt to obtain social services.

Throughout the world, many women are heads of households. (See Table 3.1 for the percentages of women-headed households in Africa as of 2003.) Some of the circumstances accounting for such households are as follows:

- Being single, with or without children
- Living with another woman, or with other family or community members
- Being divorced
- Being widowed
- Being abandoned permanently or for long or indefinite periods
- Long-term migration and/or economic or military crisis drawing the male household member away
- Refugee or migrant status due to war or economic downturn.

Table 3.1   Percentages of Women-Headed Households in Africa, 2003

Country	% Women-Headed Households
Benin	21
Burkina Faso	9
Cameroon	22
Chad	22
Comoros	32
Egypt	12
Eritrea	47
Ethiopia	24
Gabon	26
Ghana	34
Guinea	13
Kenya	32
Madagascar	22
Malawi	27
Mali	11
Mauritania	29
Mauritius	17
Morocco	15
Mozambique	27
Namibia	42
Niger	13
Nigeria	17
Rwanda	36
Senegal	18
South Africa	42
Togo	24
Uganda	28
Tanzania	23
Zambia	23
Zimbabwe	34

Source: The World's Women 2005: Progress in Statistics, Annex 1 (New York: United Nations, 2006), p. 130.

Little information is provided about the percentage of female households that come about as a result of circumstances that are seen as controversial, such as divorce. Only a few countries reported statistics for at least five years between 1995–2003 concerning the number of divorced women within their boundaries: Egypt, Mauritius, the Bahamas, Canada, El Salvador, Mexico, Panama, St. Lucia, Brazil, Armenia, Bulgaria, Croatia, Bahrain, Cyprus, Japan, and Jordan, among others. In fact, none of the fifty least-developed countries have reported statistics on marriage or divorce beyond numbers representing totals.[2]

Many female-headed households are poor because the women themselves lack access to employment, credit, and productive resources; such households also usually lack access to social services such as health and child care. Disabled women and women of minority races and ethnicities face even greater discrimination in these areas.

✠ Learning Activity 1: Decision-Making Power in the Family ✠

Objective To identify decision-making power in the family
Time 90 minutes
Materials Copies of Article 16(1)(d) of the Convention on the Elimination of All Forms of Discrimination Against Women (CEDAW), chart paper and markers

The text of Article 16(1)(d) of CEDAW reads as follows:

1. States Parties shall take all appropriate measures to eliminate discrimination against women in all matters relating to marriage and family relations and in particular shall ensure, on a basis of equality of men and women:

(a) The same right to enter into marriage;
(b) The same right freely to choose a spouse and to enter into marriage only with their free and full consent;
(c) The same rights and responsibilities during marriage and at its dissolution;
(d) The same rights and responsibilities as parents, irrespective of their marital status, in matters relating to their children; in all cases the interests of the children shall be paramount;
(e) The same rights to decide freely and responsibly on the number and spacing of their children and to have access to the information, education and means to enable them to exercise these rights;
(f) The same rights and responsibilities with regard to guardianship, wardship, trusteeship and adoption of children, or similar institutions where these concepts exist in national legislation; in all cases the interests of the children shall be paramount;
(g) The same personal rights as husband and wife, including the right to choose a family name, a profession and an occupation;
(h) The same rights for both spouses in respect of the ownership, acquisition, management, administration, enjoyment and disposition of property, whether free of charge or for a valuable consideration.

2. The betrothal and the marriage of a child shall have no legal effect, and all necessary action, including legislation, shall be taken to specify a minimum age for marriage and to make the registration of marriages in an official registry compulsory.

1. Brainstorm

Ask participants to call out answers to the following question: What decisions are made in a typical family? Participants are to offer their ideas without comment from facilitators. Record their responses.

Now ask: Which decisions are usually made by women? By men? By both? On the chart paper mark each category—"Men" and "Women"—with a check, using different-colored markers.

2. Discuss

Ask participants to comment on differences in the decisions that men and women make. Add any of the following that are not included in the list:

continues

Learning Activity 1 Continued

- Whom to live with and according to what arrangement
- Whether to marry
- Whom to marry
- When to marry
- Whether to retain one's own nationality and citizenship upon marriage
- Whether to bear children
- When to begin bearing children and how many children to bear
- Whether to adopt children and how many children to adopt
- Whether to raise another person's child outside of adoption
- Whether and when to divorce, and on what conditions
- Whether to own and control family property, alone or with other family members, and on what conditions
- Whether to own and control personal property, to borrow money, or to open a business
- Whether to apply for paid employment and what type of employment to enter.

Distribute Article 16(1)(d) of CEDAW and point out that it provides for women and men to have equal rights and responsibilities in the family. Have participants gather into small groups or pairs; then ask them to discuss the following questions and to report back to the full group:

- What does the text of Article 16(1)(d) mean?
- Should there be recognition of the possibility that women have needs different from men?
- To what extent is the article followed or not followed in your community? In your family?
- What strategies could be adopted by your community to begin the process of ensuring that men and women have equal rights as parents within the family?

Human Rights in the Family

International human rights law protects the right of all people to marry and have a family. In particular, it supports marriage that is equal and consensual. It does not dictate what form a family or marriage should take, as types of family and marriage differ within and between societies, as well as among individuals.

In supporting the family unit, human rights law obliges states to assist families facing social, economic, and political challenges. For example, it recognizes the right of families to be reunified if they have become separated as refugees. Human rights law also upholds maternity rights that facilitate the bonding of mothers with their children. And for children who cannot receive parental care, human rights law requires that states provide appropriate alternative care, such as through adoption or foster care.

Family-related human rights that are protected include the following:

- *The right to marry and establish a family.* The family is recognized as the most natural and fundamental unit of society; therefore, the right to marry and create a family is protected in human rights law. Human rights law does not, however, dictate the types of family units that are deemed acceptable.
- *Equal rights for men and women in the family.* Human rights law asserts the equal rights and responsibilities of both men and women at the beginning of a marriage, during the marriage, and at its dissolution. Article 5(b) of CEDAW specifically recognizes the "common responsibility of men and women in the upbringing and development of their children."
- *The right to give full and free consent to marriage.* Human rights treaties specify that no marriage should be entered into unless consent is freely given by the intending spouses. (Yet forced marriages for economic or cultural reasons continue to be practiced in many countries in the world today. Forced marriage of girls under 18 is an area of particular concern.)
- *The right to family planning.* The right of individuals to freely determine the number and spacing of their children has been recognized by major UN conferences, including conferences on population and development in Tehran in 1968 and in Cairo in 1994.
- *The rights of children to parental care.* The rights of children to parental care are specifically protected in children's rights treaties, such as the Convention on the Rights of the Child (CRC). A number of treaties emphasize the need of states to provide extra support.
- for pregnant women—specifically, by allowing them maternity leave before and after childbirth that is either paid leave or leave with adequate social security benefits.
- *The rights of children without parents.* Human rights law lays down a number of standards governing the treatment of children who do not have parents, covering such issues as fostering, adoption, and intercountry adoption. At the heart of these standards is the need to ensure that the best interests of the child are met and to guard against the exploitation and abuse of this especially vulnerable category of children.
- *The right to family reunification.* Where parents and children are residing in different countries, states are obliged to facilitate contacts and deal with requests to enter or leave a state party for the purpose of reunification in a humane and expeditious manner. Such rights are to be restricted only for reasons of national security and public order.

Human rights related to family and marriage are addressed in many international documents including:

- the Universal Declaration of Human Rights (1948) (Article 16), which establishes the right of men and women to marry and found a family, their equal rights as to the marriage, and the principle that consent to marriage should be freely given.
- the International Covenant on Economic, Social and Cultural Rights (1966) (Article 10), which reiterates some basic rights concerning family

life and establishes further rights of pregnant mothers to maternity leave and social security.

- the International Covenant on Civil and Political Rights (1966) (Article 23), which provides that (1) the family is the natural and fundamental group unit of society and is entitled to protection by society and the state; (2) the right of men and women of marriageable age to marry and to found a family shall be recognized; (3) no marriage shall be entered into without the free and full consent of the intending spouses; and (4) States Parties shall take appropriate steps to ensure equality of rights and responsibilities of spouses as to marriage, both during marriage and at its dissolution. In the case of dissolution, provision shall be made for the necessary protection of any children.
- the Declaration on Social and Legal Principles Relating to the Protection and Welfare of Children, with Special Reference to Foster Placement and Adoption Nationally and Internationally (1986), which provides guidelines for fostering and adoption, including intercountry adoptions of children who lack appropriate parental care.
- the Convention on Consent to Marriage, Minimum Age for Marriage and Registration of Marriages (1962), which reiterates the right to full consent and requires states to establish a minimum age for marriage.
- documents agreed to at world conferences, including the 1994 Conference on Population and Development Program of Action, the 1968 Tehran Declaration, and the 1985 Fourth World Conference in Beijing, all of which contain provisions regarding the rights of individuals to family planning.

UN treaties relating to specific categories of persons can also be used to protect the human rights related to the formation and conduct of families. The Convention Relating to the Status of Refugees includes guidelines and principles established under the auspices of the UN High Commissioner for Refugees strengthens provisions regarding refugee rights to family. CEDAW includes provisions on marriage and nationality. And the Convention on the Rights of the Child addresses such issues as children's separation from parents, family reunification, and measures for children lacking parental care.

Paradoxically, some regulations intended to protect women end up confining them to roles in the family while excluding them from the workplace and public life. One such obstacle to women's work outside the home concerns protectionism. For example, legislation preventing women from working at night for their protection excludes them from income that may be essential to their families' survival.

The application of human rights to women in the family has proven to be "a double-edged sword." For example, Article 25(2) of the Universal Declaration of Human Rights (UDHR) states: "Motherhood [is] entitled to special care and assistance."

According to legal expert Ratna Kapur, author of in *Gender, Justice, Citizenship, and Development*:

> The protectionist approach accepts the traditional and patriarchal discourses that construct women as weak, biologically inferior, modest and incapable of decision-making. Such so-called feminine characteristics are perceived as natural, immutable and, thus, as the appropriate starting place for legal regulation. Writers within this approach often extol the role of women within the family—roles which are assumed to be natural, selfless and sacred. . . . Women's roles as mothers are similarly cele-

brated, and naturalized as an inevitable consequence of the biological differences between women and men.

For example, Article 28(1) of the Bangladesh Constitution declares equal rights for men and women in all spheres of public life, and Article 28(4) provides that the state should not create special provisions in favor of women. In Bangladesh law, however, women are perceived as needing protection, perhaps from the state or a male guardian. Laws in Bangladesh that limit women's choice of employment include the Factories Act of 1934, The Tea Plantation Labor ordinance of 1962, and The Shops and Establishments Act of 1965. These laws prohibit employment of women and children between 8 P.M. and 6 A.M., to protect them from danger during evening hours.[3] By preventing women from taking jobs that may have higher wages, protectionism can be an additional factor in women's levels of poverty, thus impacting their families as well.

✠ Learning Activity 2 ✠
Indivisibility and Interdependence of Rights

Objective   To explore the interdependence of women's human rights in the family

Time   60+ minutes

Materials   Chart paper and markers, copies of the above section headed "Human Rights in the Family" (including the list of protected rights)

1. Introduce/Discuss

Explain that a basic human rights principle holds that all human rights are indivisible as well as interconnected and interdependent. Explain these definitions:

- *Indivisible:* Refers to the notion that there is no hierarchy of rights; civil and political rights are as important as social, economic, and cultural rights. Authorities cannot pick and choose which rights they wish people to have: All people are entitled to human rights.
- *Interconnected and interdependent:* Refers to the notion that each human right reinforces and relates to all other rights, and that denial of one human right has an impact on a person's ability to exercise other human rights. For example, to exercise the right to participate in political life, a person needs to enjoy the right to education, access to information, and the ability to express freedom of expression and thought as well as conscience and religion, among many other rights.

Note to Facilitator: See Chapter 2, "Women's Human Rights to Equality and Nondiscrimination," for a full discussion of these principles.

Discuss why these principles are essential for the full enjoyment of human rights. Ask for hypothetical examples of how the denial of one right affects the realization of others.

continues

✠ **Learning Activity 2 Continued** ✠

2. Plan

Divide participants into small groups and give each group a copy of "Human Rights in the Family." Ask each group to develop a hypothetical case typical of their community to illustrate why women need all of their human rights in the family. They may present their case to the whole group in a variety of ways, including a role-play, a mock trial, or a panel discussion. In addition, encourage groups to include the rights of children.

3. Present

Ask each group to make its presentation. At the end of each, ask the whole group to identify explicitly the rights in question and the consequences that follow when any one of them is denied.

4. Discuss

Discuss with the whole group the obstacles to women's rights in the family, asking questions like the following:

- Do women in your community enjoy all of these rights? If not, which ones are most frequently denied? Why?
- Does a particular group of women have more of these rights? Fewer? What factors determine which women have the greatest rights in the family?
- What social or cultural forces lead to this denial of rights?
- How does this denial of rights affect women's other human rights in the family?

Discrimination Within the Family

The family is often regarded as the most important unit in society, and women are often regarded as the heart of the family. As we have noted, however, it is within this structure that women experience some of the worst human rights violations. Domestic violence, sexual assault, psychological abuse, and other forms of violence are often overlooked within the family, if not outright condoned. Many women face physical violence or even death if they exercise their rights to marry or not to marry. One women's rights organization in the United Kingdom noted that among the Indian women who came to them after refusing to accept a forced marriage, 95 percent received death threats from family members.[4] Women can face similar consequences based on their choices about where to live or work. Women's rights to land, property, and inheritance are often limited within the family. The family can also limit women's freedom of movement and ability to participate in public or political life, as well as their right to education.

Patriarchy, which is widely practiced in some areas of the world, particularly in the Middle East and North Africa, limits women's autonomy on the basis of what male family members believe is best for women, and the entire family. As such, it is a function of "kin-based societies," which impact development of gender policies of the state as well as women's rights.

In Northern African countries such as Tunisia, Algeria, and Morocco, for example, women's privileges based on family norms differ widely. In post-colonial Morocco, laws severely limited women's rights, while Tunisia offered more rights to women. In the late twentieth and early twenty-first centuries, however, women's organizations and advocates played an important role in increasing women's rights in Morocco, including the reform of the Moudawana, or family code. Family reforms in the Northern Africa/Middle East region include raising women's legal age for marriage, offering women the option of initiating divorce, and obtaining rights to family inheritances.[5]

Women's work within the home and their work in family businesses, farms, and informal enterprises may be viewed as of less value than that of the men in the household. This issue is explored in greater detail in subsequent chapters.

Attempts to uphold women's human rights within various family structures have met with strong resistance from some religious and cultural forces and other powerful social institutions. And efforts by women themselves to change divorce, custody, or property laws have been opposed by religious leaders who condemn such efforts as counter to religious law and custom. In many parts of the world, women who do not act within the boundaries dictated by religious authorities, such as obeying and being faithful to their husbands or caring for their home and family, may even face physical violence perpetrated by individuals acting in the name of religion.[6] While the Islamic religion in particular is often cited as a reason that women's rights are curtailed, the interpretation of Islam varies across countries and communities; hence no single interpretation is an accurate or complete representation of Islamic law.

CEDAW specifically directs states to examine and address cultural practices that discriminate against women. For more on discrimination based on culture, see Chapter 2, "Women's Human Rights to Equality and Nondiscrimination."

✠ Learning Activity 3: Religion, Culture, and the Family ✠

Objective   To examine how aspects of religion and culture affect women's human rights within the family

Time   60 minutes

Materials   Chart paper and markers, copies of the above section headed "Human Rights in the Family" (including the list of protected rights)

1. List

List the major religious groups in your community, including both majority and minority religious groups.

continues

✠ Learning Activity 3 Continued ✠

2. Discuss

Divide participants into seven small groups, give each group a copy of "Human Rights in the Family" (the same sheet as that used in "Learning Activity 2: Indivisibility and Interdependence of Rights"), and assign each group one of the human rights relevant to the family. Then ask each small group to discuss the likely attitude of major religious groups in the community toward this right. Encourage participants to indicate clearly those instances in which they have no information and to consider how to obtain it.

Table 3.2   Religion, Culture, and the Family

	Religious Group 1	Religious Group 2	Religious Group 3	Religious Group 4
Right to marry and found a family				
Equal rights of men and women in the family				
Right to give full and free consent to marriage				
Right to family planning				
Right of children to parental care				
Rights of children without parents				
Right to family reunification				

3. Report

Ask each small group to present its conclusions. Record these on a chart like the one shown in Table 3.2, keeping in mind the following questions:

- What religious beliefs do the participants believe underlie the attitudes of these religious groups?
- What information did the groups lack about the likely attitude of these religious groups? How could this information be obtained?
- What patterns emerged from these discussions? (For example, did some rights meet with greater approval or rejection?)
- Do any of the groups' conclusions about a particular religion conflict with one another? Why could this be?

✠ Learning Activity 3 Continued ✠

4. Discuss

- What is the relationship of culture and religion to women's human rights in the family?
- Do you think customs and attitudes regarding the family tend to be resistant to change? Why?
- Given that customary law and religious law are often applied to women even when alternative state laws exist, what are some strategies to enforce women's human rights in the family?

The "Public-Private Split" and Human Rights in the Family

Human rights practices have primarily focused on what governments can or cannot do, but individuals, too, can be challenged to meet human rights standards. Sometimes governments try to make a distinction between public and private spheres, reasoning that everything within the public sphere, including government and state-operated workplaces, falls under human rights protections, while everything within the private sphere, including family and home, is excluded from public scrutiny.

Activists and scholars have challenged this distinction between public and private domains, arguing that there is an interrelationship between the two. For example, women's low status in that family has the effect of institutionalizing women's subservient position in other aspects of life, while at the same time the state influences the private domain through laws and regulations that impact family life, depending on the perceived needs or preferences of the state. What many women want is assistance from authorities in combating violence and discrimination within the family. According to Hou Zhiming, the director of a Beijing women's counseling center, "It is imperative that an anti-domestic violence network be set up, led by governments with the participation of . . . law enforcement organs and communities."[7]

Gradually, through local and national activism as well as a series of international documents, conferences, and agreements, the public-private split in human rights discourse began to be questioned. The 171 government representatives at the 1993 United Nations World Conference on Human Rights in Vienna specifically recognized that violence against women raised human rights questions—regardless of where such acts occurred. In the same year, the UN General Assembly adopted a Declaration on the Elimination of Violence Against Women that similarly recognizes both public and private violence. In addition, the Convention on the Rights of the Child (CRC) has been applied to protect children from violence in the home. Although parents may exert some control over their children, they cannot violate their human rights. And an abusive parent—like an abusive husband—cannot hide under the cloak of privacy. (See also Chapter 7, "Women's Human Right to Freedom from Violence.")

The 1995 Beijing Platform for Action, which resulted from the Fourth World Conference on Women in Beijing, reaffirms this principle by strongly condemning the range of physical, sexual, and psychological violence that women face in the private or family sphere, including "battering, sexual abuse of female children in the household, dowry-related violence, marital rape, female genital mutilation and other traditional practices harmful to women" (paragraph 113a).[8]

Despite the growing recognition that human rights apply to both public and private acts, in practice women often have great difficulty enforcing their human rights within the family. Since many women fear retribution and/or social ostracism, they may be reluctant to complain about family matters that are regarded as a part of their culture, or as a private family matter. As women and girls begin to learn about their rights, however, they are increasingly empowered to challenge human rights abuses in the family.

✠ Learning Activity 4: When Private Is Public ✠

Objective To understand that human rights violations need to be addressed within both the private and the public spheres
Time 60 minutes
Materials None

1. Discuss
Divide participants into two equal groups and arrange them in two concentric circles. Those in the inner circle face outward toward those in the outer circle. Explain the procedure:

- You will read aloud a statement about human rights in the public and private spheres.
- Participants will discuss this statement facing the other person for about five minutes.
- When you announce "SHIFT," everyone in the outer circle will move one place to the right to face a new person and discuss a new statement.
- Continue in this manner through several statements. Then ask if participants would like to offer a statement of their own, and continue the process.

Some sample statements follow:

- A husband should decide whether his wife should be allowed to work for wages or outside the home.
- Parents should decide if education is allowed or provided for their children.
- It is the right of parents to discipline their children.
- It is the right of husbands to discipline their wives.
- Police officers shouldn't interfere with private family disputes.
- Families have their own rules.

☒ Learning Activity 4 Continued ☒

- Family rules are above the rule of any government.
- Cultures and communities have a responsibility to uphold traditional ways of life.
- Like father, like son.
- Schools can play a role in teaching children about human rights in the family.
- Governments may sometimes have to intervene in family matters.

2. Discuss

Divide participants into small groups to discuss these questions:

- Are there circumstances under which the government should be required to involve itself in what appear to be private decisions made between individuals in a family?
- Why is it important to address the public-private split?
- Can you give examples of the public-private split in your community?
- What persons or institutions benefit from this split?

Ask participants to report on their discussions. Point out similarities and differences in their conclusions.

Human Rights and Marriage

Age at Marriage

Societies that force, permit, or even encourage early engagements or early marriages of girls may violate girls' human rights. Early marriage can pose significant health risks for girls and young women. The Population Council, an international nongovernmental organization (NGO), found that teenage mothers have higher rates of complications during childbirth and disease, including the risk of obstetric fistula—a loss of tissue between the vagina and bladder and/or rectum caused by obstructed labor. The maternal mortality rate for girls between the ages of 11 and 13 is three times greater than that for women between 20 and 24.[9]

In recognition of the widespread practice of child marriages and marriages without the woman's consent, the United Nations opened the Convention on Consent to Marriage, Minimum Age for Marriage and the Registration of Marriages for ratification in 1962. It was enacted into force in 1964. The convention reads in part:

> All States . . . should take all appropriate measures with a view toward abolishing such customs, ancient laws and practices by ensuring . . . complete freedom in the choice of a spouse, eliminating completely child marriages and the betrothal of young girls before the age of puberty, establishing appropriate penalties where necessary and establishing civil or other register in which all marriages will be recorded.

Although the convention does not specify a minimum age for marriage, it provides that the countries signing it agree to make and enforce a minimum age.[10] The internationally accepted minimum age of marriage can be found in a nonbinding but influential recommendation that calls on all states to specify a minimum age not less than 15 years.[11] Many countries also allow a much lower minimum marriage age for girls than for boys, particularly in cases where parents consent to the lower age. In Togo, for example, the legal age for marriage as of 2003 was 17 for women and 20 for men. In Kuwait, the legal age for women is 15, with the consent of the woman's guardian and the woman herself or the person acting on behalf of either, and 17 for men, without restrictions.

See Table 3.3 for a list of countries with low average marriage ages for women compared to the average ages for men.[12]

Table 3.3   Countries with Low Average Marriage Ages for Women

Country	Mean Age at Marriage (1995–2002)	
	Women	Men
Chad	18	24
Dominican Republic	21	26
Guinea	19	28
Mali	18	26
Nepal	19	23
Niger	18	24

✠ Learning Activity 5: Marriage Customs ✠

Objective   To identify the relation of religion and culture to the violation of human rights in the family

Time   60 minutes

Materials   Copy of "Case Study: Marriage in Mattlandia"

Case Study: Marriage in Mattlandia

Although the laws of Mattlandia set 16 as the minimum age for marriage, some small villages still practice arranged marriages, as they have for hundreds of years. The actual tradition varies from village to village, but in most, a girl's father, oldest adult brother, or uncle chooses her husband for her by the time she is 10 years old. The marriage will take place after puberty, when the girl moves into her husband's family and is legally no longer a member of her birth family or community. The male relatives discuss and come to agreement about the size of her dowry, which can include jewelry, household items, and other valuables that will accompany her on her wedding night.

1. Read

Read the case study to the whole group.

⚔ Learning Activity 5 Continued ⚔

2. Analyze

Ask participants in small groups to respond to the following questions in light of the case study and to report their findings to the full group:

- Do any of the practices in this scenario violate the girl's rights? If so, list them.
- Can these practices be justified in the name of tradition? In the name of religion?
- Are these customs detrimental to the girl's future?
- What difference would it make to the men in Mattlandia if they did not marry until the girls had reached the minimum age for marriage in this village? To the individual girls? To their families? To the community?

3. Discuss

Conclude by discussing local customs relating to marriage, the family, and property:

- Which customs relating to marriage, the family, and property in your community discriminate against women?
- Which customs relating to marriage are supportive of women? That inhibit women's human rights?
- Does government seek to modify or abolish these customs? How are women responding to the customs?

The Role of Authorities in Restricting Rights in Marriage

Many national, regional, and international laws protect the rights of women in the family. In practice, however, many social institutions, including the family, the media, and religious and cultural groups, as well as governments, place direct and indirect restrictions on women's choices. In different contexts and to varying degrees, many states have used the institution of marriage and family to mold the role of women to suit state needs.[13]

Some governments encourage women to have more children by increasing benefits to large families; for example, in Australia, parents with four or more children can receive a Family Tax Benefit.[14] Other governments encourage women to have smaller families by limiting such benefits. Governments may exert control over family size by promoting or inhibiting the provision of birth control, abortion, and sex education. Beginning in the 1970s, the Chinese government imposed strict limitations on family size, provided free birth control and abortions, and promoted party members and government workers who limited their family size.[15]

Governments may also restrict women's rights in marriage and the family through the use of nationality laws. In many countries, residents with official status as "nationals" are entitled to extra benefits, such as free education, health care, and other social services. Some states have laws that make a woman's status contingent upon her father's or husband's status. Other states, such as Saudi Arabia, prohibit a woman from transmitting her citizenship to her child, allowing only a man to do so.[16] These laws are contrary to international conventions, including Article 9 of CEDAW, that declare that women and men should be treated equally with respect to nationality, regardless of marital status. These provisions often become important when women refugees or migrant women seek to obtain legal recognition based on their national status.

Direct and Indirect Restrictions on Marriage

Direct restrictions can include:

- laws or customs that prohibit women from marrying someone of a different race, ethnicity, or social group or someone of the same sex
- restrictions on family size or requirements that women be sterilized after they bear a certain number of children
- marriage and divorce practices that restrict women's ability to own, control, and inherit land
- prohibitions against women buying or selling property, obtaining credit, opening a bank account, or applying for employment without a male guardian to sign for them
- laws that strip women of their nationality when they marry a foreign national
- laws that specify that a father's nationality (and not a mother's) determines the citizenship of children, and regulations or customs prohibiting certain groups of women, such as lesbians, single women, or women not attached to men, from adopting and/or raising children.

Indirect restrictions can include:

- incentives that benefit women who make choices that the government deems most desirable, such as tax benefits for families of a certain size
- day care, welfare, maternity leave, pension benefits, and other supports that are conditioned on marrying or not marrying and on bearing or not bearing children
- in some places, married women pay lower taxes and/or have better access to government-sponsored housing than single women (and in other places, the opposite incentives apply)
- condoning violence against people in nontraditional families by failing to prosecute perpetrators and stop the violence.

✠ Learning Activity 6: Nationality Laws ✠

Objective   To identify the impact of nationality laws on women
Time   75 minutes
Materials   Copy of "Case Study: Stateless in the Land of Their Birth"

✠ Learning Activity 6 Continued ✠

Case Study: Stateless in the Land of Their Birth

Manju, a young woman living in Hoda, married a foreigner, Joseph, from Tarikstan. They settled permanently in Hoda and had three children. However, the laws of Hoda provide that a child's nationality is determined by that of the father. The family plans to live in Hoda forever and wants the children to have the benefits of Hoda citizenship, which include free or low-cost education and health care and the ability to participate in national politics. The laws of Tarikstan, on the other hand, state that children born overseas cannot gain citizenship unless they have lived in the country for five consecutive years. Manju and Joseph do not wish to send their children to live in Tarikstan for an extended period of time. Hence, the children are without any nationality.

1. Read

Read the case study to the whole group.

2. Role-Play

Divide the participants into small groups. Each group chooses someone to play the role of Manju's lawyer. Groups may wish to assign other participants with the role of an official, a child, a parent, or a lawyer. In preparation for the role-play, the small groups address the following questions:

- Can it be argued that this law violates Manju's human right to equality in the family?
- Does Hoda place direct or indirect restrictions on Manju's human rights?
- Ask each group to present its role-play.

3. Discuss

Discuss the following questions with the whole group:

- Which role-plays made the strongest arguments?
- Why should this case study be of concern to all women in Hoda? In Tarikstan?
- Why is nationality such an important issue?
- What other rights are related to nationality?
- How could women in Manju's community support Manju?

Source: Adapted from *Dow v Attorney General for Botswana* (1991) L.R.C. (const.) 623; Court of Appeal of Botswana, on appeal from (1991) L.R.C. (const.) 574; reproduced in *Human Rights Quarterly*, vol. 13 (1991), p. 614.

The Role of Authorities in Promoting Rights in Marriage

Some argue that women have achieved equality in marriage and in the family when they have the same legal rights as men. In other words, authorities can place restrictions on marriage and the family as long as these restrictions apply in the same way to both men and women (e.g., if the minimum age for marriage is the same for both males and females).

However, a broader interpretation of equality is that "sameness" is not enough: Women can have equality in marriage and the family only when institutions, laws, and practices that disempower women in the family are changed. According to this viewpoint, it is not sufficient to establish laws that treat men and women the same. Rather, it is necessary to consider the broader context of structures, rules, and customs that perpetuate power imbalances in the family. To address these inequities, the government can adopt policies that apply only to women if they serve to improve women's low status in the family. Termed *affirmative action* or *reverse discrimination*, such policies could include state compensation for household work, reimbursement of child care costs for women workers and students, or continuing educational opportunities designed for married women, especially young mothers.

Article 7 of CEDAW includes a broad version of equality for women:

> The term "discrimination against women" shall mean any distinction, exclusion, or restriction made on the basis of sex which has the effect or purpose of impairing or nullifying the recognition, enjoyment or exercise by women, irrespective of their marital status, on a basis of equality of men and women, of human rights and fundamental freedoms in the political, economic, social, cultural, civil or any other field.

Some key attributes of this definition follow:

- It applies to both intentional and unintentional discrimination.
- It seeks more than the same treatment for women and men in that it forbids anything that has the purpose or effect of interfering with women's human rights.
- It applies to all spheres of life and draws no distinction between the private and public spheres.
- It emphasizes that all women should have rights irrespective of marital status.
- It applies to all human rights and fundamental freedoms, not just to civil and political ones.

Women Living Apart from Men

In communities where women are expected to live with men (whether their fathers, brothers, or husbands), women living apart from men may face discrimination and even open harassment. They may be widows, divorced women, women separated from their husbands for any reason, or women who have never married. They may live alone or with their children, other family members, or unrelated women, and they often serve as the head of household in terms of both child care and income generation. Whatever their circumstances, such women may have difficulty obtaining education or employment and be unable to access social services, including housing and health care. (See also Chapter 2, "Women's Human Rights to Equality and Nondiscrimination.)

While international conventions do not explicitly mention the rights of women living apart from men, the broad language of the Universal Declaration of Human Rights and other human rights treaties can be read to include them in the provisions granted to "all people." Further, the Beijing Platform for Action has advanced the concept of sexual rights, affirming that "the human rights of women include the right to have control over and decide freely and responsibly on matters related to their sexuality, including sexual and reproductive health free of coercion, discrimination and violence" (paragraph 97). Another group of women living apart from men, lesbians, are often subjected to grave discrimination. They often must suffer in silence as there is a fear that those who advocate for their rights will themselves be excluded and suffer discrimination as a result.

🞖 Learning Activity 7 🞖
Responding to Women Who Live Apart from Men

Objective To explore the discrimination and other problems experienced by women living apart from men

Time 45 minutes

Materials Chart paper and markers or blackboard and chalk

1. Brainstorm/Discuss

Ask participants to think of as many situations as they can in which women live apart from men, whether by choice or not.

2. List/Discuss

Using a chart like the one shown in Table 3.4, write down some possible reasons or motivations next to each of the groups listed in Step 1.

Table 3.4   Responding to Women Who Live Apart from Men

Women Living Apart from Men	Reasons/ Motivations	Words and Phrases for These Women

Ask the participants to list words and phrases commonly used in your community to refer to women who, for varying reasons, live apart from men.

- What qualities do these phrases stress? Which are positive qualities? Which are negative?
- Which of these terms would you not want to be called?
- What prejudices against women living apart from men or not in legal marriage do these words reveal?

continues

✠ Learning Activity 7 Continued ✠

3. Discuss

What conclusions can you draw about attitudes toward women in your community who live apart from men?

- What are the underlying reasons for these attitudes?
- Do the women face additional problems because of this status?
- How do these problems relate to women's human rights?

Widowhood

Widows comprise a significant proportion of all women worldwide, ranging from 7 percent to 16 percent of all adult women.[17] However, in some countries and regions, the proportion is far higher. In nearly all countries, older women are far more likely than older men to experience widowhood.[18] (See Table 3.5.) In developed countries, widowhood is experienced primarily by elderly women, while in developing countries it also affects younger women, many of whom are still rearing children. In some regions, girls become widows before reaching adulthood.

Widows are painfully absent from the statistics of many developing countries, and they are rarely mentioned in the multitude of reports on women's poverty, development, health, or human rights. Growing evidence of their vulnerability, both socioeconomic and psychological, has challenged many conventional views and assumptions about this "invisible" group of women. Widows are profoundly affected in terms of loss of status, domestic violence, lack of access to education and training, and lack of access to the economy. (See also Chapter 2, "Women's Human Right to Equality and Nondiscrimination.")

Widows receive varying treatment within different regions and countries. Today, millions of the world's widows of all ages endure extreme poverty, ostracism, violence, homelessness, ill health, and discrimination in both law and custom. Widow abuse, the practice of degrading and life-threatening mourning and burial rites, and a lack of inheritance and land rights are prime examples of human rights violations that are rationalized on the basis of "reliance on culture" and "tradition."[19] The Association for Women's Rights in Development has noted that, due to "traditional, colonial, and postcolonial economic, social and political structures . . . and customary laws, African widows have no choices other than those perpetuating the domination of widows by male relatives."[20]

Property Ownership

Property laws often work in conjunction with family laws to place both direct and indirect obstacles in the path of women. Most women suffer dual discrimination when it comes to owning property: first as women, and second as married women. In some countries, women lose their rights to inherit, own, and control property to their husbands once they marry. Even in cases where they

Table 3.5 Widowhood Around the World

Percentage of Those Aged 60+ Who Are Widowed 1985–1997		
	Women	Men
Africa		
Northern Africa	59	8
Sub-Saharan Africa	44	7
Latin America and the Caribbean		
Caribbean	34	12
Central America	36	12
South America	37	13
Asia		
Eastern Asia	49	14
Southeast Asia	49	14
Southern Asia	51	11
Central Asia	58	13
Western Asia	48	8
Oceania	44	15
Developed regions		
Eastern Europe	48	14
Western Europe	40	12
Other developed regions	39	11

Percentage of Those Aged Between 45–59 Who Are Widowed 1985–1997		
	Women	Men
Africa		
Northern Africa	19	1
Sub-Saharan Africa	16	2
Latin America and the Caribbean		
Caribbean	8	2
Central America	10	2
South America	10	3
Asia		
Eastern Asia	9	2
Southeast Asia	16	2
Southern Asia	17	5
Central Asia	16	3
Western Asia	13	1
Oceania	13	3
Developed regions		
Eastern Europe	12	3
Western Europe	7	1
Other developed regions	5	1

Source: The World's Women 2000, p. 14.

do not lose all property rights, in practice (and, in some cases, under law) the husband is presumed to be the owner of the home, land, credit, and other family property. The divorce laws in many countries provide greater advantages to men—again, under the presumption that they own all household property. Following a struggle at the 1995 Fourth World Conference for Women in Beijing between women's NGOs and certain governments, the Beijing Platform for Action was written to guarantee girl children and women the "equal right to inherit" (paragraph 274d).

Unmarried women, too, face disadvantages in property ownership. In some countries, fathers or brothers control the unmarried woman's property, due either to specific legal provisions or to traditional practice. In nearly all countries, banks and other lending institutions prefer dealing with men over married or unmarried women. As a result, women are far more likely than men to be denied credit, loans, approval on leases, contracts, and other commercial transactions. The International Center for Research on Women found that "lack of property ownership . . . has been found to contribute to women's low social status and their vulnerability to poverty. It also increasingly is linked to development-related problems, including HIV and AIDS, hunger, urbanization, migration and domestic violence."[21]

Remembering Core Concepts

✠ Learning Activity 8 ✠
Speaking Out for Women's Human Rights in the Family

Objective　To examine women's human rights in the family in your community and consider how to take action to make improvements

Time　60+ minutes

Materials　Chart paper and markers

1. Brainstorm

Ask participants to list problems women in their community face related to their human rights in the family. Next, divide them into small groups and have them choose a problem on which they wish to concentrate. Encourage selection of widely different kinds of problems.

2. Discuss/Plan

Ask each group to prepare a five-minute presentation to a "panel of community leaders" on their chosen problem. Each presentation should:

- describe the problem, identifying the group(s) of women it impacts and, if possible, the cause(s) of the problem
- relate the problem to women's human rights
- clarify how the problem affects women's lives
- show how addressing the problem can improve their lives
- propose specific actions that should be taken to address the problem
- show how members of the community can get involved in addressing the problem.

Ask each group to choose a spokesperson to make the presentation and a "community leader" to serve on the panel. While the groups plan their presentations, the panel of leaders meets to decide on their roles, representing a variety of differing but typical attitudes within the community leadership.

✠ Learning Activity 8 Continued ✠

3. Present/Role-Play
The spokesperson from each group makes a presentation and members of the panel listen and respond, asking questions and offering comments, objections, or suggestions in keeping with their chosen roles.

4. Discuss
After the presentations and role-play, discuss these questions:

- How did the spokespersons feel when presenting the problem?
- How did the "community leaders" respond to the presentation? What attitudes in the community were they representing?
- How did the audience, composed of the rest of the group, respond to the presentations?
- Did any spokesperson discuss the problem as a human rights violation? Did putting the problem in a human rights context strengthen the argument? Why or why not?
- Are these ideas for improving women's human rights in the family feasible in your community? Why or why not?

5. Conclude
Challenge the participants by asking them to evaluate their knowledge of the problem and the inclusiveness of their perspective:

- How did you obtain your information about the issues facing women in your community regarding their human rights in the family? Was it accurate and complete? If not, what additional information do you need and how can you obtain it?
- Did you personally consult women about the problem and how it affects them? About actions that could improve the problem?
- Why is it important in real-life human rights advocacy to include the active participation of those directly involved and affected?
- How can you apply the example of this learning activity to planning and implementing advocacy for women in your community?

Notes

1. General Comment 19: "Protection of the Family, the Right to Marriage and Equality of the Spouses," Human Rights Committee, UN Doc. HRI/GEN/1/Rev.2 (1990), at 2.

2. *The World's Women 2005: Progress in Statistics*, Annex 1 (New York: United Nations), p. 100.

3. Ratna Kapur, "Challenging the Liberal Subject: Law and Gender Justice in South Asia," in *Gender, Justice, Citizenship, and Development*, edited by Maitrayee Mukhopadhyay and Navsharan Singh (Ottawa, Canada: International Development Research Centre, 2007).

4. Rajeshree Sisodia, "'Honor' Most Foul," *Indianest*, November 28, 2004, available online at http://www.boloji.com/wfs3/wfs312.htm.

5. Charrad, Mounira Maya, "Unequal Citizenship: Issues of Gender Justice in the Middle East and North Africa," in *Gender Justice, Citizenship and Development,* edited by Maitrayee Mukhopadhyay and Navsharan Singh (Ottawa, Canada: International Development Research Centre, 2007).

6. Dr. Unaiza Niaz, "Overview of Women's Mental Health in Pakistan," *Pakistan Journal of Medical Sciences,* vol. 17, no. 4 (December 2001), pp. 203–209, available online at http://www.pjms.com.pk/issues/octdec01/article3.html.

7. Quoted in Chinacourt, "Anti-Domestic Violence Drive Needs Legal Support," *China Daily,* August 23, 2005, available online at http://en.chinacourt.org/public/detail.php?id=3934.

8. United Nations Division for the Advancement for Women, "The United Nation Fourth World Conference on Women. Platform for Action, 1995" (New York: United Nations).

9. Population Council, "The Risks of Early Marriage," Media Center, New York, June 17, 2004, available online at http://www.popcouncil.org/mediacenter/newsreleases/early_marriageJB.html.

10. United Nations Convention on Consent to Marriage, Minimum Age for Marriage and the Registration of Marriages, Article 2.

11. United Nations General Assembly Resolution 10/2018 of November 1, 1965 (New York: United Nations).

12. The World's Women 2005: Progress in Statistics, Annex 1, (New York: United Nations), pp. 130–135.

13. Julie Mertus, "State Discriminatory Family Law and Customary Abuses," in *Women's Rights, Human Rights: International Feminist Perspectives,* edited by Julie Peters and Andrea Wolper (New York: Routledge, 1995), pp. 135–143.

14. Australian Government Family Assistant Office, "Large Family Supplement," available online at http://www.familyassist.gov.au/Internet/FAO/FAO1.nsf/content/payments-large_family_supp.

15. Daisy Sindelar, "China: Population May Peak Under 'One-Child' Policy," *Radio Free Europe, Radio Liberty,* January 6, 2005, available online at http://www.rferl.org/featuresarticle/2005/01/5c329a6d-0678-4be8-b651-b198e1565b94.html.

16. Consulate General of the United States, Dhahran, Saudi Arabia, "Public Services, International Parental Child Abduction," U.S. Department of State, January 16, 2002, available online at http://dhahran.usconsulate.gov/dhahran/custody.html.

17. United Nations, "Widowhood: Invisible Women Secluded or Excluded," *The World's Women 2000* (New York: United Nations, 2001).

18. United Nations, *The World's Women 2000: Trends and Statistics,* Sales No. E. 00 XVII 14.

19. World Bank, "Case Study 9: Widows," *Voices of the Poor* (Washington, DC, 2000).

20. Vanessa Von Struensee, "Reports and Analyses: Widows, AIDS, Health and Human Rights in Africa," Association of Women's Rights in Development, February 10, 2005, available online at http://www.awid.org/members/reports.php?id=13.

21. International Center for Research on Women, "Property and Inheritance Rights for Women," 2005, available online at http://www.icrw.org/html/projects/projects_property%20rights.htm#context.

4

The Human Rights of Young Women and Girls

States must implement the rights of children "without discrimination of any kind, irrespective of his or her parent's or legal guardian's race, colour, sex, language, religion, political or other opinion, national, ethnic or social origin."

—UN Convention on the Rights of the Child

Objectives

The learning activities and background information contained in this chapter will enable participants to work toward the following objectives:

- Distinguish between biological and socially constructed differences between boys and girls.
- Recognize traditional practices that can have a harmful impact on young women and girls.
- Identify forms of violence against young women and girls, and appreciate the impact on victims.
- Gain information about adolescent sexuality and about ways to promote the human rights of young women and girls with respect to health care, privacy, and equality.
- Understand the ways in which girls' labor can be exploited, at home as well as in both the formal and informal work sectors.
- Debate the role of authorities in both perpetuating and combating human rights abuses against young women and girls.
- Strategize ways in which individuals, organizations, and authorities can improve the human rights of young women and girls.
- Remember core concepts.

Getting Started: Thinking About the Human Rights of Girls

The rights of girls are defined and protected by the Convention on the Rights of the Child (CRC), which, of all human rights treaties, has received the broadest global support. All but two UN Member States—Somalia and the United States—have ratified the CRC, agreeing to revise their national legal codes to conform to the provisions of the treaty and to submit periodic reports on their progress in implementing it.

The CRC defines as a *child* any human being before his or her 18th birthday, regardless of whether the child is a parent; in fact, this definition applies to all children regardless of the child's race, color, sex, language, and religion, and regardless of political or other opinions or those of his or her parents or legal guardian. The state assumes the responsibility to protect children from danger and exploitation and to make provisions for their welfare and development, including nutrition, health care, and education.

In a groundbreaking move, the CRC has also officially recognized a child's right to participate in society. Participation includes the right to an opinion in matters that concern her or him, the right to information, association, privacy, and expression, and the right to freedom of thought, conscience, and religion. However, the convention acknowledges the different stages of a child's development, specifying that a child's participation is based on her or his "evolving capacity." It also makes clear that the child's rights are not granted by parents or the community but, rather, are inherent to the child as a human being and a "rights-bearing entity."

In considering the human rights of girls, governments are obligated to listen to girls' concerns and to act in their best interest. The CRC must be read in conjunction with the Convention on the Elimination of All Forms of Discrimination Against Women (CEDAW) and other regional and international agreements protecting the rights of young women and girls.

UN world conferences have further advanced the recognition of the human rights of girls. The 1994 UN International Conference on Population and Development condemned harmful practices such as prenatal sex selection, female infanticide, female genital cutting or FGC (also known as female genital mutilation or FGM), trafficking of girl children, and the use of girls in prostitution and pornography. Girls figure prominently in the Beijing Platform for Action, which lists the recommendations agreed upon at the 1995 Fourth World Conference on Women; among these are special measures to ensure that young women have the life skills needed for "active and effective participation in all levels of social, cultural, political and economic leadership" (paragraph 42), based on the recognition that girls constitute half of the world's population under the age of 25. The Beijing Platform also calls for the equal sharing of domestic responsibilities by boys and girls.

The Socialization of Girls

In many cultures, girls are taught at an early age to be silent, passive, and accepting. The Harvard Project on Women's Psychology, which charted stages in girls' development, found that by the age of 10 girls had begun to shape themselves into the "Perfect Girl," a collective image of the attributes they see being rewarded by parents and teachers: ladylike, quiet, obedient, good in school, and always pleasant.[1]

Parents and teachers tend to reinforce this image of the "Perfect Girl," which varies from culture to culture but exists in some form nearly everywhere. This socialization process has a long-lasting impact on girls' ability to fulfil their potential and realize their human rights. As noted in the Beijing Platform for Action: "Girls are often treated as inferior and are socialized to put themselves last, thus undermining their self-esteem. Discrimination and neglect in childhood can initiate a lifelong downward spiral of deprivation and exclusion from the social mainstream."[2] (See also Chapter 11, "Women's Human Right to Education.")

The disparity in status between boys and girls in families and communities can largely be attributed to attitudinal differences rather than biological differences. This disparity is often exacerbated by both formal and informal education systems that favor boys over girls. Neera Kuckreja Sohoni, who has studied the burden of girlhood in many countries, observes that "[t]he real gender differential is attitudinal and, as with racism, its damage is immeasurable. Like colour, [sex] is an accident of birth, but entitlements are man-made. A different and discriminatory set of values and expectations are applied to the girl, and to her preservation and development. Boys, like men, command greater space and value: that differential is sustained through a process of covert or overt neglect of the girl."[3]

✠ Learning Activity 1: Childhood Myths ✠

Objective To understand the subtle ways in which society perpetuates gender roles

Time 60 minutes

Materials Chart paper and markers

1. Perform

After dividing participants into small groups, ask them to draw up a list of traditional and modern stories, songs, games, sayings, or rhymes from their childhood that reflect men's and women's roles and then to respond to the following questions:

- What message do these examples impart about male and female roles? Do any of them convey a preference for boys and/or a more restricted or lesser role in the family for girls?
- Which of these examples were the most important to you as a child? Were there any that you especially liked or disliked?

Ask each group to choose the most striking example to present to the full group.

2. Discuss

Ask the following questions (adapted, as necessary, for same-sex groups) and list the responses on the chart paper:

continues

✠ Learning Activity 1 Continued ✠

- How do these stories and songs reinforce myths about boys and girls, men and women?
- How do they reinforce the ways boys and girls are treated in a family?
- What are some of the repercussions against girls or boys who fail to adapt to these social norms? What are some of the names they are called?
- Were you praised for being a girl? Who said what? How did you feel?
- Were boys preferred in your family or community? If so, in what ways? How was their preference made known? How did you feel?
- Did you say or do anything at the time to protest a preference for boys? What do you wish you had said?
- Have conditions changed for girls since your childhood?
- If you have children, do you treat your girls and boys differently?

3. Conclude

To conclude, ask participants the following question: "What can women do to confront this discrimination in their own families and communities?"

Son Preference and the Right to Survival

One of the most basic human rights is the right to survival. Many girls face a fight for survival right from the moment they are born, and this struggle continues throughout their life cycle. Within the continent of Africa, there is approximately a 1:1 ratio of women to men; in Europe and North America, the ratio is 103:100 and 102:100, respectively. However, where there is a strong preference for male children, the male-to-female sex ratio is reversed. In Asia and the Middle East, for example, there are 96 females for every 100 males.[4] And in India, as many as 10 million female fetuses may have been aborted over the past two decades following prenatal exams.[5]

Misuse of Amniocentesis and Selective Abortions

Where are all these missing women and girls? In both developed and developing countries, parents practice sex selection through the use of amniocentesis and other techniques that allow doctors to analyze the fluid of the amniotic sac surrounding the fetus. Though developed to detect fetal abnormalities or other problems with pregnancy, these procedures can also detect the sex of the unborn child. Studies show that women rarely abort male fetuses, even when the amniocentesis discovers a fetal abnormality. A leading British medical journal reported that a half-million girls had gone missing in India due to selective abortion.[6] The 2001 census showed a relative drop over a decade's time in the number of girls aged 0–6 years: 927 girls for every 1,000 boys compared with 945 in 1991. In India's northwest area, the ratio of girls to boys has fallen below 900 to every 1,000 boys, and in the Punjab, the figure for girls was below 800.[7]

Son preference is even more evident when daughters are present: Couples that already have one daughter are less likely to accept another.[8] In most societies, there are between 102 and 106 male births for every 100 female births. In China, that number is estimated to be as high as 117.[9]

Female Infanticide

Some of the missing women and girls can be accounted for by infanticide, which is commonly practiced in developing countries. As Radhika Coomaraswamy, the former United Nations Special Rapporteur on Violence Against Women, observed: "Within cultures with a high level of son preference, female infanticide provides a disturbing alternative for women who do not have access to amniocentesis, sonograms and abortion."[10] One study in a remote area of southern India, for example, found that 58 percent of all deaths of female infants were due to infanticide, usually within seven days of their birth.[11] In China, female babies are drowned or abandoned at such a high rate that social scientists anticipate Chinese men may have trouble finding women to marry in twenty years.[12] In fact, the Chinese media are increasingly reporting cases of "bride stealing"—the kidnapping and trafficking of young single women for marriage.[13]

Mortality and Morbidity

Once born, female infants and girls die at a much higher rate than boys in many parts of the world. For example, in India, the risk of dying between the ages of 1 and 5 is 43 percent higher for girls than for boys.[14] These higher rates of mortality among girls can be explained by neglect of girl children. Boys are more likely than girls to receive immunizations, and they tend to get better nutrition and medical care, whereas parents frequently wait longer to bring girls to the doctor than boys. While malnutrition affects both boys and girls all over the world, girls suffer disproportionately from being severely underweight as a result of this male preference.[15] An estimated 450 million adult women in developing countries are stunted as a consequence of childhood malnutrition.[16] (See also Chapter 5, "Women's Human Right to Health.")

Examining Son Preference

Economic considerations partially explain the preference for sons. Although girls usually work longer and harder than boys, girls are more likely to work within the family for free, while boys work outside the family for a wage. Families may thus value boys' wage-earning contribution more than girls' non-waged contribution. This is particularly true in agricultural and trading economies, but less true in urbanized and industrialized societies where more women and girls work in the waged labor force. Nevertheless, in both rural and urban settings, families usually prefer boys. Other explanations include the importance of religious rites; inheritance law, which grants benefits to males; and the tradition whereby girls "marry out" of the family, leaving it forever and, in effect, becoming the property of the husband's family.

Son preference contributes to the violation of many of the human rights of women and girls. In the case of selective abortion and female infanticide, son preference can violate the right to life.[17] When girls are deprived of adequate nutrition and health care in favor of boys, not only is their survival threatened, but those who reach adulthood often are marked for life by stunted growth or weakened health. Furthermore, when girls are denied the educational and employment opportunities given to boys, their right to develop to their full potential is severely curtailed. As detailed in the Beijing Platform for Action, when "girls suffer discrimination in the allocation of economic and social resources . . . this directly violates their economic, social and cultural rights."[18] Indeed, preferential treatment of boys over girls can violate the provisions of the Convention on the Elimination of All Forms of Violence Against Women (CEDAW) and the Convention on the Rights of the Child.

The Convention on the Rights of the Child

In 1959 the United Nations issued the Declaration on the Rights of Children, proclaiming the entitlement of young people to adequate nutrition, free education, and medical care, as well as their right to avoid exploitation and discriminatory practices. Support for children's rights grew in the 1980s, culminating in the 1989 signing of a legally binding treaty, the Convention on the Rights of the Child (CRC).

The CRC establishes what is known as the "best interest of the child" standard:

> In all actions concerning children, whether undertaken by private social welfare institutions, courts of law, administrative authorities or legislative bodies, the best interest of the child shall be a primary consideration.[19]

In other words, when official decisions are made that affect children, their interests should be seen as paramount. But the preferences and views of children should be respected, too. When is a child capable of forming his or her own view? Most communities recognize the life-cycle division between childhood and adulthood. The age at which one ends and the other begins, however, differs from community to community.

The CRC, which is the most widely ratified of any UN human rights treaty, clearly establishes that *all* children have human rights. In considering the human rights of girls, then, governments are obligated to listen to their concerns and to act in their best interests.

Besides the recent CRC, other international agreements affirm children's rights:

- The Universal Declaration of Human Rights (UDHR) affirms the right of children to special care and assistance.
- Both the International Covenant on Civil and Political Rights (ICCPR) and the International Covenant on Economic, Social and Cultural Rights (ICESCR) provide special protection to children as part of family rights.

- The Declaration Concerning the Aims and Purposes of the International Labour Organisation instructs the ILO to develop international programs to make, among other goals, "provision for child welfare."
- Regional documents such as the African Charter on Human and Peoples' Rights, the American Convention on Human Rights, and the European Social Charter encourage the protection of minors in their working and living conditions.

The Status of Girls: Facing the Facts

- Estimates suggest that there are between 60 and 100 million fewer women alive today than there would be in a world without gender discrimination and social conditions that favor sons.[20]
- Water, sanitation, and hygiene are crucial to getting and keeping girls in school. While all schoolchildren suffer when schools have filthy or missing sanitation facilities, girls bear the brunt of unhygienic or nonexistent latrines. And the need for household water keeps many away from the classroom because the laborious task of fetching water is usually delegated to girls.[21]
- Eighty-two million girls in developing countries who are now between the ages of 10 and 17 will be married before their eighteenth birthday.[22]
- Two million children, mostly girls, are exploited in the sex industry.[23]
- In sub-Saharan Africa, of the 6.2 million children and adolescents infected with HIV, 75 percent are female.[24] Globally, this proportion is 64 percent.[25]

The Sexual and Reproductive Health of Girls

Although governments and parents alike are often reluctant to acknowledge that adolescents engage in sexual relationships and have reproductive and sexual health care needs, the rise of teen pregnancies and sexually transmitted diseases, including HIV/AIDS, have brought increased attention to the sexual and reproductive needs of girls.

Once they reach adolescence, girls in some societies are secluded within the home, denied their rights to education and participation, and married off early on the grounds of protecting them from sexual exploitation. In many countries young girls are principal targets for sexual violence and coerced sexual activity, especially from older men. Worldwide 40–47 percent of sexual assaults occur against people aged 15 and under.[26]

Given their subordinate position because of their age and gender, girls are often not in a position to refuse sexual advances; and in cases where they do freely consent to sexual experiences, many are exploited, unprotected from pregnancy and disease, and ignorant about birth control and sexually transmitted diseases.

A principal barrier to the promotion of good adolescent health is lack of effective sex education. Even when sex education does exist, it is too often limited to the physiology of reproduction, birth control is seldom mentioned, and boys may be excluded from responsibility for preventing pregnancy. Indeed, although HIV infection is rising in all parts of the world, including among young people, sex education courses tend to avoid the topic altogether. To be effective, sex education programs must address young people's real concerns and anxieties and promote a positive and healthy sexual life that emphasizes self-determination, equal communication and respect between partners, and shared responsibility for birth control.

Harmful Traditional Practices

Traditional practices may harm the health and violate the human rights of girls. One such practice, female genital cutting (FGC), can cause great physical and psychological injury. The United Nations estimates that at least 2 million girls undergo FGC each year. (A detailed discussion of this issue is provided in Chapter 5, "Women's Right to Health.")

Traditional practices often reflect a society's definition of what is gender-appropriate. Some traditions connected with engagement and marriage, present in most cultures in some form, are forced upon girls. Girls who rebel against such traditions or who refuse to pair off with a male partner may face extreme penalties if they don't adopt gender-appropriate roles or enter into marriage with a prescribed partner.

Early marriages compromise the health and autonomy of millions of young girls. Even where laws prohibit early marriage, traditions nonetheless persist as authorities turn a blind eye to the practice. Early marriage almost always ends girls' education and leads to early maternity. According to the United Nations Development Fund for Women (UNIFEM), 82 million girls in developing countries, aged 10 to 17, will be married before their 18th birthday.[27] And the World Health Organization notes that maternal mortality is five times higher among girls aged 10 to 14 than among women aged 20 to 24.[28]

Many women around the world are also subjected, or subject themselves, to unhealthy practices in order to meet their culture's beauty standards. For example, in industrialized countries, dangerous dieting and conditions such as anorexia and bulimia begin among young women who wish to attain a slim figure. Eating disorders are far more common in Western cultures than in others.[29] In the United States, the number of American women and girls affected by these illnesses has more than doubled in the past three decades.[30] In Guatemala, as many as 2 percent of women have had "intimate surgery" to restructure their hymen to "regain virginity" because unmarried women who are not virgins are unacceptable in their culture. The procedure is expensive and dangerous; the surgery can cause infections, hemorrhage, incontinence, fistulas, and extreme dyspareunia when performed in unsafe conditions.[31] Rhinoplasty is on the rise in Iran, which has the highest rate of cosmetic nose surgery in the world. Other forms of cosmetic enhancement are likewise more frequent in Iran, including chin operations, fingernail implants, fake diamonds embedded in the gums, and eyebrows tattooed on. One argument for the increase in these surgical procedures is Iran's strict Islamic dress code, which prohibits visibility of all body parts except the face.[32]

Women may also use dangerous cosmetic items to alter their skin color. In Asia, Latin America, and the Middle East, the concept that light-skinned women are more beautiful has convinced women to use unregulated creams that carry a danger of mercury poisoning, which can cause neurological, kidney, and psychiatric damage. Other whiteners contain hydroquinone, a chemical used in photo processing, which has been shown to cause cancer in lab animals. These products have been banned or regulated in industrial nations such as the United Kingdom and the United States, but these regulations often do not exist in developing countries.[33]

Learning Activity 2: Traditional Practices

Objective   To identify the human rights relevant to harmful traditional practices as well as the strategies a girl might use to resist such harmful practices

Time   60 minutes

Materials   Copies of the above section headed "Harmful Traditional Practices"

1. Role-Play

Divide participants into small groups. Ask each group to choose one of the potentially harmful traditional practices mentioned in the handout (e.g., early marriage and its consequences, beauty standards and anorexia, FGC, skin whitening), or use another example from their community to develop a role-play.

Assume that the girl in the role-play wants to go against tradition or societal norms. Ask each group to act out the scenario by assigning the roles of the girl and of important figures in her life, such as parents, family elder, sister, friend, schoolteacher, or religious leader. Have the girl approach each important figure to discuss her wish to break with tradition. Each role-player should reflect the position their role would be likely to express.

2. Discuss

After each group has presented its role-play, address the following questions:

- How did each of the role-players feel? Describe these feelings.
- What human rights are violated in this situation? Who is the violator in this case?
- What strategies can be used to resolve this situation? What can be done in the family? In the community? Nationally?
- Could protection of these rights be enforced?

Violence Against Girls

Some traditions and customs can actually be a form of violence against girls; examples include FGC, early marriage, and forced marriage. Furthermore, as pointed out in the Beijing Platform for Action, "[due] to such factors as their youth, social pressures, lack of protective laws, or failure to enforce laws, girls are more vulnerable to all kinds of violence, particularly sexual violence, including rape, sexual abuse, sexual exploitation, trafficking, possibly the sale of their organs and tissues, and forced labour."[34]

Sexual Violence

Girls around the world face sexual harassment and violence at home, in school, and on the street, and most justice systems lack the authority or political will to prevent such abuses. The harassment of girls by boys in school ranges from rude or insulting comments to pinches and grabs and, ultimately, to more physical assaults and rape. Following a 1993 survey with similar findings, a 2001 survey by the American Association of University Women (AAUW) found that 83 percent of girls report incidents of sexual harassment in schools in the United States, and that 30 percent experience it often.[35] Moreover, 44 percent of girls experience fear of being sexually harassed.[36]

Girls everywhere are also subjected to rape, especially in societies where penalties are weak or not enforced for this violence and where the burden of proof and public shame is placed on the victim. Especially vulnerable to sexual assault are girls who live or work outside the home, although rape does take place within the family. Rape of girls, in particular, has increased in areas where HIV infection is widespread, due to the belief among many adult men that sex with young women, especially virgins, reduces the risk of HIV exposure.[37] According to one report in 2000, the belief in the "virgin cure" was helping to fuel an increase in child prostitution in Cambodia; there are many Asian men who believe that having sex with a virgin will cleanse their AIDS.[38] The same is true in India, according to the *Harvard AIDS Review* (Fall 1995), and in Jamaica, according to the Jamaican Ministry of Health.[39] Due to this belief, the number of girls contracting HIV and transmitting the virus to their children is increasing rapidly. (See Table 4.1.)

Table 4.1 Young People 15–24 Living with HIV/AIDS, by Sex, December 2001

Region	Young Women (percent)	Young Men (percent)	Total
Sub-Saharan Africa	67	33	8,600,000
North Africa and the Middle East	41	59	160,000
East Asia and the Pacific	49	51	740,000
South Asia	62	38	1,100,000
Central Asia and Eastern Europe	35	65	430,000
Latin America and the Caribbean	31	69	560,000
Industrialized Countries	33	67	240,000
World	62	38	11,800,000

Source: "State of the World's Population," UNFPA, HIV/AIDS and Adolescents: Contributing Factors, 2003.

Child Prostitution

Children have long been sexually exploited, but in recent times this practice has become increasingly widespread and organized. Modern communication, trade, and travel have transformed child prostitution into a transnational business. Using strategies such as abduction, false documents, and sham marriages, children as well as sex clients are easily transported across frontiers, not only to neighboring countries but also across the globe. Increasingly organized criminal elements are profiting from child prostitution as procurers, pimps, and intermediaries.

Children from poor families and developing countries are especially vulnerable for recruitment into the sex trade. Such exploitation is often referred to as "sex trafficking"—the recruitment, harboring, transportation, provision, or obtaining of a person for the purpose of a commercial sex act. In the U.S. State Department's annual report on trafficking, gender and age disaggregated data show that of the approximately 800,000 people trafficked each year across international borders, 80 percent are women and girls and up to 50 percent are minors, the majority of whom are trafficked into commercial sexual exploitation.[40] Worldwide, it is estimated that more than 2 million children are exploited through prostitution and pornography, and 1.2 million children are trafficked every year both between countries and within their own countries.[41] Some girls are sold into prostitution by members of their own families; others are lured from home with promises of good-paying jobs in the cities. The problem is compounded by social upheaval and economic crises that cause parents to migrate from rural to urban areas or one country to another in search of a livelihood.

In some societies, traditional practices increase the possibility of trafficking women. The customs whereby women leave the home for marriage, inheritance laws that exclude girls, and a lack of education may lead girls to look for livelihoods abroad, leaving them susceptible to international trafficking.[42]

In 2000, an estimated 1 million children entered the sex trade—the vast majority of them girls.[43] In industrialized countries, children often enter the sex trade because they are fleeing abusive homes.[44] Child prostitution can also lead to other forms of exploitation and violation of human rights, such as torture and even death. While most countries have laws to protect children from sexual exploitation, problems with enforcement are common as well.

Countries with the highest levels of international trafficking include Algeria, Equatorial Guinea, North Korea, Sudan, Bahrain, Iran, Oman, Syria, Burma, Kuwait, Qatar, Uzbekistan, Cuba, Malaysia, Saudi Arabia, and Venezuela.[45]

Domestic Violence and Incest

Girls also face violence in their homes. Although general or specific criminal laws may be applied to domestic violence, they are rarely enforced. Incest—intrafamily sexual abuse of children—is one particularly vicious form of domestic violence against children. Incest victims suffer both severe psychological trauma and physical aliments, such as anal and vaginal lacerations, lack of bladder control, sexually transmitted diseases, and early childhood pregnancy. The psychological effects may manifest themselves in long-term behavior problems and acute depression. (See also Chapter 7, "Women's Human Right to Freedom from Violence.")

The Convention on the Rights of the Child requires governments that have ratified the convention to "take all appropriate legislative, administrative, social and educational measures to protect the child from all forms of physical or mental violence, injury or abuse, neglect or negligent treatment, maltreatment or exploitation including sexual abuse."[46] Nearly every country has laws criminalizing incest, yet few cases are ever prosecuted. Families in which incest occurs usually attempt to keep it secret. The adult abuser uses threats to keep the child quiet, and children who do tell are rarely believed. Often police and prosecutors are reluctant to press charges, claiming that they cannot interfere with the privacy of the family. And if charges are brought, children's rights are often not protected in the justice system. A child may be re-traumatized by being forced to testify at length during trial, without counseling or support before or after the testimony. Due to the shortcomings of the justice system and social services, incest remains one of the most invisible and difficult-to-document forms of domestic violence. One medical study in Africa found that 16 percent of patients in a Nigerian hospital with sexually transmitted infections were under the age of 5; another found that at a clinic in Zimbabwe more than 900 children under age 12 had been treated for an STD.[47]

Several types of domestic violence are described below.

Emotional Abuse. Emotional abuse by parents or caretakers, whether in the form of verbal abuse or psychological maltreatment, can cause serious behavioral, cognitive, emotional, or mental disorders in children.

Neglect. Neglect is the failure to provide for a child's basic needs. It can be physical, educational, or psychological in nature. Physical neglect includes failure to provide adequate food or clothing, appropriate medical care, supervision, or proper protection from the elements. It may include abandonment. Educational neglect includes failing to provide appropriate schooling or special educational needs and allowing excessive truancies. Psychological neglect entails a lack of love and emotional support and failure to protect the child from abuse, including allowing the child to participate in drug and alcohol use.

Physical Abuse. Physical abuse involves the inflicting of physical injury upon a child. This may include burning, hitting, punching, shaking, kicking, beating, or otherwise harming the child. Such injuries constitute abuse whether the adult intended to do harm or not. For example, an injury may result from overdiscipline or from physical punishment that is inappropriate to the child's age.

Sexual Abuse. Sexual abuse involves inappropriate sexual behavior with a child, including fondling a child's genitals, making the child fondle the adult's genitals, intercourse, incest, rape, sodomy, exhibitionism, and sexual exploitation. It also involves forcing, tricking, bribing, threatening, or pressuring a child into sexual awareness or activity. Sexual abuse occurs when an older or more knowledgeable child or an adult uses a child for sexual pleasure. It is thus an abuse of power over a child and a violation of a child's right to normal, healthy, trusting relationships.

Vulnerable Groups of Girls

Although girls in general are more vulnerable to human rights violations than boys, some girls are especially at risk. Among them are "the abandoned, homeless and displaced street children, children in areas of conflict and children who are discriminated against because they belong to an ethnic or racial minority group" (Beijing Platform for Action, paragraph 171).

Street Children. Homeless urban children, or "street children," conservatively estimated at 100 million globally,[48] face a high risk of drug abuse and sexual exploitation, especially girls. In the United States, the estimated number of homeless children is more than 1 million, and 50 percent of the women and children on the streets are fleeing violence in the home.[49] UNICEF reports that, of the 100 million street children in the world, half are found in Latin America.[50]

Street children work in the worst jobs: drug pushing, pornography, prostitution, begging, stealing, garbage picking, and petty trading. They are often blamed for the majority of street crime, despite statistical evidence to the contrary. As one researcher notes, "With very few exceptions, state provision for street children is undertaken less in their best interests and more in the interest of cleansing the streets of their presence."[51]

Child Soldiers. Armed conflict threatens all children, but recently the conscription or kidnapping of children to serve in militia groups has become a global problem. Human Rights Watch reports that "in over twenty countries around the world, children are direct participants in war. Denied a childhood and often subjected to horrific violence, an estimated 200,000 to 300,000 children are serving as soldiers for both rebel groups and government forces in current armed conflicts."[52]

Some girls become frontline combatants, but most are used as porters, cooks, and, especially, as sex partners, often being given as "wives" to soldiers as a reward for bravery. Both male and female children are often forced to witness or commit atrocities, such as killing others who try to escape. The fortunate few who do manage to escape face difficulties returning to their communities—especially the girls, almost all of whom are infected with sexually transmitted diseases and many of whom escape with their babies. They are often considered unmarriageable and rejected by their families, leaving the girls traumatized and without education or community support.[53]

Child Mothers. Another group likely to be denied their human rights are child mothers, who constitute a large percentage of the girls in societies that encourage early marriage or where teenage pregnancy is common. Although themselves still children and entitled to all the protections and provisions of the Convention on the Rights of the Child, they are widely assumed to have entered adulthood if they marry. They are thus caught in a kind of legal limbo, lacking the protections offered to children but too young to claim the legal rights of adults.

For many young women and girls, early pregnancy, whether within or outside marriage, brings their formal education to an end and limits their future economic and employment opportunities. In some communities, pregnant girls are expelled from school or their home.[54] In others, unmarried adolescent mothers suffer legal penalties and social ostracism, including possible death through "honor killings," a practice whereby girls are killed for dishonoring the family.[55] (For more on girls' education, see Chapter 11, "Women's Human Right to Education.")

Girls with Disabilities. Although children with disabilities are often the targets of abuse, including violence and sexual assault, child protection services rarely address their needs. Social services may in fact perpetuate the abuse of children with disabilities by stigmatizing them as "special" or "in need," a categorization that transmits negative messages to society, parents, the children themselves, and even their abusers. Rather than affirming that children with disabilities are capable and valuable, social attitudes tend to regard them as weak and incapable of independence. Indeed, many children with disabilities are taught to be "good victims"—especially girls, who are already valued less than boys. They are also less likely to be educated, to receive adequate health care and rehabilitation treatment, and to be permitted to participate in their communities.[56]

AIDS Orphans. Another side effect of the increasing incidence of HIV/AIDS is the loss of parents. According to the United Nations, more than 13 million children under age 15 have lost at least one parent to AIDS. By 2010, the number of orphans is projected to reach 25 million.[57] Worldwide, eight of every ten AIDS orphans lives in sub-Saharan Africa. The proportion of children orphaned by AIDS rose from 3.5 percent to 32 percent between 1994 and 2004.[58] A UNAIDS report puts this problem into perspective:

> Evidence shows that AIDS orphans living with extended families or in foster care are frequently subject to discrimination and are less likely to receive health, education and other needed services. The situation is yet more desperate for those living in child-headed households or on their own on the streets. The vulnerability of these children represents part of a vicious cycle: their circumstances put them at high risk for exploitation and abuse, and . . . exposure to HIV, and a lack of access to health care, education and social support perpetuates the conditions of poverty.[59]

✠ Learning Activity 3 ✠
Taking Action Against Sexual Harassment and Violence

Objective   To advocate against sexual harassment and/or violence
Time   60 minutes
Materials   Brochures, advertisements, posters, or public service announcements about sexual harassment and/or violence (if available), paper and drawing materials

1. Design
Divide the participants into small groups and ask them to design a radio or TV advertisement or a brochure advocating an end to harassment or violence against a particular age group of girls in the community.

✠ Learning Activity 3 Continued ✠

Present the following guidelines for the group work:

- Keep it short and simple.
- Identify the best target audience for this advertisement or brochure, and design it to reach that audience.
- Identify the main points to emphasize: Among the details to be conveyed by this ad or brochure, which ones are appropriate for the public? Which ones are inappropriate?
- How would the brochure be distributed? Is this realistic?

2. Critique

Ask each small group to present its ideas to the full group. Invite participants to question and comment on one another's products.

If actual samples of relevant brochures or advertisements are on hand, pass them around. Critique their content and effectiveness.

Alternative: Follow the same instructions to create a brochure for law enforcement officers, teachers, or social workers on the subject of violence against girls.

Adolescent Sexuality and Human Rights

In many parts of the world, adolescent girls are sexually active at younger and younger ages. Most girls have little information about how to protect themselves from unwanted pregnancy or sexually transmitted diseases. In addition, many girls are involved in sexual relationships with older boys and men, and the power differences between the partners can prevent the girls from making decisions "freely" with the information they do have.

Teen pregnancy has been explained on the basis of numerous factors, including early marriage and the lack of sex education and contraception services for young women. Economically disadvantaged girls and young women are hurt most by the limited availability of public information and free or low-cost gynecological health care.[60] In becoming involved with several sexual partners (and thereby increasing their risk of pregnancy), girls who are valued only as "objects" may be searching for acceptance, approval, and love that they do not find elsewhere in their lives. A society that values girls for their unique personality, intelligence, creativity, and skills—and promotes their human rights—encourages different behavior.

The Convention on the Rights of the Child specifically recognizes the right of children to have health care. Yet many young girls have no access to gynecological care, including prenatal care and contraception. Girls who choose to carry their pregnancies to term often suffer additional pregnancy-related complications, such as toxemia, anemia, premature delivery, and prolonged labor.[61] As a result, at least 1 million babies born to teenage mothers die every year at birth or because of related complications.[62]

Young Women and Girls at Risk

- Of the 10 million young people living with HIV/AIDS, 6.2 million are young women and 3.9 million are young men.[63]
- Nearly one-third of pregnant teenagers at an antenatal clinic in Cape Town, South Africa, said their first intercourse had been forced. More than three-quarters said they would be beaten if they refused sex.[64]
- Each year more than 4.4 million 15- to 19-year-old girls have abortions, 40 percent of which are conducted under unsafe conditions.[65]
- At the end of 2003, an estimated 2.5 million children worldwide under age 15 were living with HIV/AIDS. Approximately 500,000 children under 15 died from the virus or associated causes in that year alone.[66]
- Women and children comprise approximately 80 percent of the world's 35 million refugees and displaced people, and they are particularly vulnerable to sexual violence while in flight from their homes.[67]
- In Asia, there are 86.7 million children who have lost one or both parents to AIDS. In Africa, where the disease has ravaged an even higher percentage of the population, there are about 43.4 million AIDS orphans.[68]

Child Labor

Girls' labor is often exploited, both at home and in the workplace. UNICEF and UNIFEM have observed that "[c]hild labor is often veiled in industrialized countries where, as elsewhere, it is subsumed into basic culture. For example, girls are being enlisted as almost full-time caretakers for younger siblings while their mothers work outside the home to support the family or attend classes in an attempt to improve their learning power."[69] In developing-country populations, too, boys tend to have significantly more leisure time than do girls, as the latter spend more time in household labor than do their male counterparts.[70]

Some Facts About Child Labor

- The International Labour Organisation (ILO) estimates that 250 million children worldwide are currently working, 120 million full-time and 130 million part-time. Not only are these total numbers high, but the ILO reports that tens of millions of children are engaged in the worst forms of child labor—slavery and bonded labor, hazardous jobs, drug trafficking, and the sex industry.[71]
- Among children who attend school, 33 percent of boys and 42 percent of girls are involved part-time in economic activities.[72]
- On the average, girls work longer hours and are paid less than boys for the same work.[73]
- Girls are the first to drop out of school to go to work and support their families; when education becomes privatized and the choice is between educating a son or a daughter, the son usually remains in school.[74]
- Africa and Asia together account for more than 90 percent of total child employment,[75] and the highest rates for girls' participation in the labor force are in sub-Saharan Africa (37 percent), eastern Asia and Oceania (20 percent), and Latin America (11 percent).[76] However, female economic activity is more likely to be undercounted due to the nature

Some Facts About Child Labor Continued

of the work girls do: Providing child care, fetching fuel and water, and preparing food are considered not "work" but, rather, typical female tasks. Girls are concentrated in sectors such as agriculture, fishing and forestry, manufacturing (such as carpet-weaving), and social and personal services (such as domestic work).[77]

- Many young girls who are lured into prostitution began their working lives as bar girls or domestic help or in factories or sweatshops that serve as natural recruitment pools for pimps and procurers; these girls, often refugees or migrants, are among the most vulnerable victims of child labor. An estimated 4 million women and girls are bought and sold worldwide, into either forced prostitution, slavery, or forced marriage.[78]
- Each year 5.7 million girls are forced into debt bondage, a form of force or coercion in which a bond, or debt, is used to keep a person in subjugation—a form of slavery.[79]

Poverty and custom in some countries have created a class of child domestics—girls who are sent to urban households to work as servants. UNICEF estimates that 400,000 children, most of them girls, are part of the domestic workforce in New Delhi alone.[80]

Children are not, in fact, always dependent on adults. Sometimes, adults depend upon them. Many girl children, in particular, take care of disabled, ill, or elderly adult family members and/or make substantial contributions to family income.

Learning Activity 4: A Girl Laborer's Story

Objective To identify measures to be taken in educating about child labor

Time 60 minutes

Materials Copies of "Case Study: The Harassment of Cristina," questions written on chart paper or newsprint

Case Study: The Harassment of Cristina[81]

Cristina is an 18-year-old Costa Rican who lives in a suburban zone of San José. She is the youngest daughter of a family of twelve children: seven girls and five boys. The boys are mainly involved in agricultural labor; the girls do domestic chores and some also work in factories. Cristina was sexually abused at the ages of 5 and 7, first by an uncle and then by two older relatives. By 9 years of age, when she started school, she had already learned to do the housework and gather coffee beans. At 15 she finished primary school and started her secondary education, but soon she was "bored." Since then she has been working.

Her first job was in a clothes factory. "I was made an apprentice. I had never touched a sewing machine. . . . I couldn't meet the output expected of me." This work lasted fifteen days. Then she worked for a year in another factory until it went bankrupt. By then she already had a bit of experience and "knew the ropes." She went to work in a leather-producing factory but was fired within a month, "because I had to run an important personal errand . . . and as I hadn't completed my three-month probationary period, I couldn't miss one day."

continues

✠ Learning Activity 4 Continued ✠

Afterward she worked packing goods as an operator in a clothes factory. "I soon figured out what they were doing with us. . . . [W]e were all under age. They made us do a lot of sanding. You end up looking as though you've covered yourself in talcum powder. It's in your hair, on your face, up your nose . . . just talc in the mouth and all over your body. . . . I could see the dirty work the people were doing. We sanded without a mask, but once the Ministry [of Labor] inspectors came, we had to put masks on, and once the Ministry supervisors left, we had to return them." Cristina also added, "It was illogical to work like that. . . . I had problems with my boss. . . . [H]e sent me to do the dirtiest work because I wouldn't let him touch me. As the other girl let him, she got all the nicer jobs." Cristina finally left due to the harassment she was suffering.

Later she worked in a wine factory. The foreman tried to abuse her, but because she resisted, she was accused in front of the owner of having taken off her clothes. She was fired immediately. Cristina's average monthly salary has been around US$111. She is currently looking for a new job.

1. Read/Discuss

Divide the participants into small groups and distribute the case study. Ask participants to read it with the following questions in mind and then to discuss these in the full group:

- What are the human rights at issue in Cristina's situation? How can her rights be safeguarded?
- Discuss the ways in which the following concerns are reflected in Cristina's situation: (a) sexual harassment and abuse as systematic practices within the power structures of working relations, (b) deterioration in working conditions, and (c) roles attributed to women in the workplace.
- How can Cristina and her family be helped in both the short term and the long term?
- What can be done to educate parents, employers, and government agencies to prevent child labor and assist girls like Cristina?

2. Role-Play/Analyze

Assign each small group a part of Cristina's story to role-play. At the end of each presentation, ask the groups to consider what could have happened to protect Cristina's rights at this stage.

- What could the family have done? The community? Nongovernmental institutions? The government?

3. Discuss

- How can the human rights of children like Cristina be protected?
- What people or institutions are responsible for this protection?
- How can the Convention on the Rights of the Child be used to protect children like Cristina?

The Role of Authorities

Since all of the UN Member States except for Somalia and the United States have ratified the Convention on the Rights of the Child, the first obligation of governments should be to uphold their commitment to implementing its provisions. Government and community authorities as well as the media can play both indirect and direct roles in supporting or hindering the human rights of girls. Governments may be responsible in the latter instances due to either action or inaction.

Where private parties interfere with the human rights of girls, states must demonstrate "due diligence" in addressing the problem. In other words, they must take active steps under local laws to prosecute and punish private actors who commit abuses.

In order to support the rights of girls, governments must also take steps to eliminate female genital cutting, forced marriage, and other traditional practices that injure girls. At the same time, governments need to assess the content of their education systems and begin campaigns for nonsexist education, opening up opportunities for girls to play sports and to take technical classes of their choosing. In addition, they must take steps to ensure safety in the streets and eliminate the sexual harassment of girls in schools and other institutions. Community leaders and the media can play a leading role in encouraging such actions.

Positive Programs for Girls' Human Rights

- As of 2005, 192 countries had ratified the Convention on the Rights of the Child. Only two countries, Somalia and the United States, had not; however, they have shown their intention to ratify by formally signing the convention.[82]
- Genetic testing for sex selection has been banned officially in India since 1994, under the Regulation and Prevention of Misuse Bill, and in China since January 1995.[83]
- The seven-member South Asian Association for Regional Cooperation declared 1991–2000 the Decade of the Girl Child and created programs to raise the age of marriage and provide girls with health care and other services.[84]
- The Girls' Power initiative began in 1994 when fourteen daughters and friends of two Nigerian women began to promote human rights and gender equality. As of 2001, there were activity programs in twenty-eight schools and many more initiatives throughout Nigeria.[85]
- Since 1998, the Global Fund for Women has awarded over $1.8 million to seventy-two organizations in thirty-seven countries that have addressed some of the barriers preventing girls from gaining an education.[86]
- As of 2005, about twenty-five countries have banned female genital cutting.[87]

Remembering Core Concepts

✖ Learning Activity 5 ✖
Speaking Out for the Human Rights of Young Women and Girls

Objectives To examine the human rights situation of young women and girls in the community and consider how to take action to improve it

Time 60+ minutes

Materials Chart paper and markers

1. Brainstorm
Ask participants to list problems faced by young women and girls in the community. Then, after dividing them into small groups, ask them to choose a problem on which they wish to concentrate.

2. Discuss/Plan
Ask each group to prepare a five-minute presentation to a "panel of community leaders" on the problem they have selected. Each presentation should:

- describe the problem, identifying the group(s) of young women and girls it impacts and, if possible, the cause(s) of the problem
- relate the problem to women's human rights
- clarify how the problem affects the lives of these young women and girls
- show how addressing the problem can improve their lives
- propose specific actions that should be taken to address the problem
- show how members of the community can get involved in addressing the problem.

Ask each group to choose a spokesperson to make the presentation and a "community leader" to serve on the panel. While the groups plan their presentations, the panel of leaders meets to decide on their roles, representing a variety of differing but typical attitudes within the community leadership.

3. Present/Role-Play
The spokesperson from each group makes a presentation and members of the panel listen and respond, asking questions and offering comments, objections, or suggestions in keeping with their chosen roles.

4. Discuss
After the presentations and role play, discuss the following questions:

- How did the spokespersons feel when presenting the problem?
- How did the "community leaders" respond to the presentation? What attitudes in the community were they representing?

✠ Learning Activity 5 Continued ✠

- How did the audience, composed of the rest of the group, respond to the presentations?
- Did any spokesperson discuss the problem as a human rights violation? Did putting the problem in a human rights context strengthen the argument? Why or why not?
- Are these ideas for improving the human rights of young women and girls feasible in your community? Why or why not?

5. Conclude

Challenge the participants by asking them to evaluate their knowledge of the problem and the inclusiveness of their perspective:

- How did you obtain your information about issues faced by young women and girls in your community? Was it accurate and complete? If not, what additional information do you need and how can you obtain it?
- Did you personally consult young women and girls about the problem and how it affects them? About actions that could improve the problem?
- Why is it important in real-life human rights advocacy to include the active participation of those directly involved and affected?
- How can you apply the example of this learning activity to planning and implementing advocacy for young women and girls in your community?

Notes

1. Ms. Foundation report, citing Lyn Brown, "Narratives of Relationship: The Development of the Care Voice in Girls Age 7–16," Ph.D. dissertation, Harvard Project on Women's Psychology, 1989; Gilligan, C., A. Rogers, and D. Jolman, eds., *Women, Girls, and Psychotherapy: Reframing Resistance* (New York: Hayworth Press, 1991).

2. Beijing Declaration and Platform for Action, Fourth World Conference on Women, September 15, 1995, A/CONF. 177/20 (1995) and A/CONF. 177/20/Add. 1 (1995), paragraph 260.

3. Neera Kuckreja Sohoni, *The Burden of Childhood: A Global Inquiry into the Status of Girls* (Oakland, CA: Third Party Publishers, 1995).

4. United Nations Statistics Division, Department of Economic and Social Affairs, "Statistics and Indicators on Women and Men 2005" (New York: United Nations, 2005), available online at http://unstats.un.org/unsd/demographic/products/indwm/ww2005/tab1a.htm.

5. Associated Press, "10 Million Aborted Female fetuses in India," *International Herald Tribune Asia-Pacific*, January 9, 2006, available online at http://www.iht.com/articles/2006/01/09/news/web.0109india.php.

6. Ibid.

7. Peter Wonacott, "India's Skewed Sex Ratio Puts GE Sales in Spotlight," *Wall Street Journal*, April 18, 2007, p. A1.

8. United Nations, *The World's Women 1995: Trends and Statistics* (New York: United Nations, 1995).

9. Daisy Sindelar, "China: A Future with a Shortage of Brides, an Abundance of Elderly," *Radio Free Europe, Radio Liberty*, January 7, 2005.

10. Report for the United Nations Special Rapporteur on Violence Against Women, February 5, 1996, E/CN.4/1996/53, p. 26.

11. UNICEF/UNIFEM Press Kit on CEDAW, Fact Sheet on Girls' Rights, undated.

12. Amnesty International, *Women in China*, AI Index ASA 17/29/95, London, 1995, p. 2; UNICEF, *"Education of the Girl Child, Her Right, Society's Gain,"* Report of the Educational Working Group, NGO Committee on UNICEF, New York, April 21-22, 1992.

13. Sindelar, "China: A Future with a Shortage of Brides, an Abundance of Elderly."

14. "World Health Day 2005," *News India*, available online at http://www.health initiative.org/html/whd/2k5/.

15. UNICEF Statistics Bank, abstract, available online at http://www.childinfo.org/.

16. Stuart Gillespie, "Health and Nutrition," 2020 Focus No. 06—Brief 08, August 2001, International Food Policy Research Institute, Washington, DC, available online at http://www.ifpri.org/2020/focus/focus06/focus06_08.asp

17. International Covenant on Economic, Social, and Cultural Rights (ICESR) in *Human Rights: A Compilation of International Instruments* (ST/HR/1/Rev.5, Vol. 1., Pt. 1).

18. Beijing Declaration and Platform for Action, Fourth World Conference on Women, September 15, 1995, A/CONF.177/20 (1995) and A/CONF. 177/20/Add. 1 (1995), paragraph 220.

19. UN Convention on the Rights of the Child, Article 3(1).

20. UNICEF Fact Sheet, p. 1, available online at http://www.unicef.org/protection/files/discrimination.pdf.

21. UNICEF Annual Report, 2003, available online at http://www.unicef.org/publications/files/unicef_eng_final.pdf.

22. Population Council, "Married Adolescent Girls: Human Rights, Health, and Development Needs of a Neglected Majority," Working Group on Girls Steering Committee, September 6, 2001, New York, Population Council.

23. UNICEF, Status of the World's Children Report, 2005, available online at http://www.unicef.org/.

24. International Labour Organisation, available online at http://www.ilo.org/.

25. UNICEF Lifeskills, Abstract 2003, available online at http://www.unicef.org/lifeskills/.

26. Center for Reproductive Rights, "Ensuring the Reproductive Rights of Adolescents" (New York, February 1999), available online at http://www.crlp.org.

27. Cited in UNICEF, "Early Marriage: Child Spouses," *Innocenti Digest*, No. 7 (Florence, Italy: UNICEF Innocenti Research Centre, 2001), available online at www.unicef-icdc.org/publications/pdf/digest7e.pdf.

28. Ibid.

29. "Approaches to Abnormality: Eating Disorders," Michael Eyesneck, *Psychology: An International Perspective* (London: Psychology Press, 2004), 844–845, available online at http://www.psypress.co.uk/pip/resources/slp/topic.asp?chapter=ch22&topic=ch22-sc-07.

30. U.S. Department of Health and Human Services Office on Women's Health, "Eating Disorders Information Sheet," February 2000, Washington, DC, available online at http://www.4woman.gov/owh/pub/factsheets/eatingdis.htm.

31. H. Roberts, "Reconstructing Virginity in Guatemala" (Abstract), *Lancet*, vol. 367 (2006), pp. 1227–1228.

32. Robert Tait, "Vanity and Boredom Fuel Iran's Nose Job Boom," *Guardian*, May 7, 2005, available online at http://www.guardian.co.uk/iran/story/0,12858,1478562,00.html.

33. "The List, If Looks Could Kill," *Foreign Policy*, June 2007, available online at http://www.foreignpolicy.com/story/cms.php?story_id=3845

34. Beijing Declaration and Platform for Action, Fourth World Conference on Women, September 15, 1995, A/CONF. 177/20 (1995) and A/CONF, 177/20/Add. 1 (1995), paragraph 269.

35. American Association of University Women, "Hostile Hallways: Bullying, Teasing, and Sexual Harassment in School" (New York, 2001), p. 12, available online at http://www.aauw.org.

36. Ibid.

37. Mike Earl-Taylor, "HIV/AIDS, the Stats, the Virgin Cure and Infant Rape," *Science in Africa*, 2002, available online at http://www.scienceinafrica.co.za/2002/april/virgin.htm.

38. Rich Buhler, "Women and Children in Portions of Africa Are Being Sexually Violated by Men Who Believe That Sex with a Virgin Will Cure Their AIDS," *Truth or Fiction* (2000), available online at http://www.truthorfiction.com/rumors/a/aids-virgins.htm.

39. Cited in ibid.

40. U.S. Department of State, "Trafficking in Persons (TIP) Report," June 2007.

41. UNICEF," Child Prostitution," 2005, p. 81, available online at http://www.unicef.org.

42. Thanh-Dam Truong and Maria Belen Angeles, "Searching for Best Practices to Counter Human Trafficking in Africa: A Focus on Women and Children," report commissioned by United Nations Educational, Scientific and Cultural Organization, March 2005.

43. Cesar Chelala, "The Unrelenting Scourge of Child Prostitution," *San Francisco Chronicle*, November 28, 2000, available online at http://www.sfgate.com/cgi-bin/article.cgi?f=/c/a/2000/11/28/ED120190.DTL&hw=The+Unrelenting+Scourge+Of+Child+Prostitution&sn=001&sc=1000.

44. Ibid.

45. U.S. Department of State, "Trafficking in Persons (TIP) Report," June 2007.

46. UN Convention on the Rights of the Child, Article 2.

47. United Nations Population Fund, State of the World Population 2000, Chapter 3: Violence Against Women and Girls—A Human Rights and Health Priority, citing the Panos Institute, *The Intimate Enemy: Gender Violence and Reproductive Health*, Panos Briefing No. 27 (London: Panos Institute, 1998), p. 11; K. Meursing, T. Vos, and O. Coutinho, "Child Sexual Abuse in Matabeleland, Zimbabwe," *Social Science and Medicine*, vol. 41, no. 12, pp. 1693–1704.

48. Youth Advocate Program, "Street Children and Homelessness," March 17, 2004, Washington, DC, available online at http://www.yapi.org/street/

49. National Coalition for the Homeless, "Who Is Homeless?" *NCH Fact Sheet No. 3*, p. 3. available online at http://www.nationalhomeless.org/publications/facts/Whois.pdf.

50. Cited in World Bank Group, Regional Activities Latin America and the Caribbean, "Child Labor," Washington, DC, available online at http://www1.worldbank.org/sp/childlabor/lac.asp.

51. Judith Ennew, "Outside Childhood: Street Children's Rights," in *The Handbook of Children's Rights*, edited by Bob Franklin (London: Routledge, 1995), p. 206.

52. Human Rights Watch, "Children's Rights: Child Soldiers," (New York, 2007), available online at http://hrw.org/campaigns/crp/index.htm.

53. Lisa Kays, "Why We Cannot Find the Hidden Girl Soldier: A Study of Professional Attitudes Towards Gender Analysis in International Conflict and Development Work," *Peace, Conflict, and Development Journal*, January 2005, available online at http://www.peacestudiesjournal.org.uk/docs/Child%20soldiers%20final%20version%203.pdf.

54. UNICEF Evaluation Report (BZE 2001/oo3), "Examination of Discriminatory Behaviors and Practices Within the Education System," available online at http://www.unicef.org/evaldatabase/.

55. World Health Organization, "The Health of Youth, Facts for Action: Youth and Reproductive Health," A42/*Technical Discussions*/5, Geneva, 1989.

56. Margaret Kennedy, "Rights for Children Who Are Disabled," in *The Handbook of Children's Rights*, edited by Bob Franklin (London: Routledge, 1995), p. 149.

57. USAID, UNICEF, and UNAIDS, *Children on the Brink 2002: A Joint Report on Orphan Estimates and Programme Strategies* (Washington, DC: The Synergy Project, 2002).

58. United Nations Department of Public Information, 2004, available online at http://www.un.org/events/tenstories_2006/story.asp?storyID=400.

59. UNAIDS, the Joint United Nations Program on HIV/AIDS, available online at http://www.unaids.org/en/Issues/Affected_communities/orphans.asp.

60. UNFPA, "State of World Population 2005," *The Unmapped Journey: Adolescents, Poverty and Gender*, available online at http://www.unfpa.org/swp/2005/english/ch5/index.htm.

61. Population Reference Bureau and Centre for Population Options, "The World's Youth 1994: A Special Focus on Reproductive Health," Washington, DC, March 1994.

62. Andrea Evans, "Group Warns of Risks to Teenage Mothers and their Babies," *San Francisco Chronicle*, May 3, 2004.

63. UNICEF Statistics, available online at http://childinfo.org/areas/hivaids/.

64. S. Singh et al., "Gender Differences in the Timing of First Intercourse: Data from 14 Countries," *International Family Planning Perspectives*, vol. 26, no. 1 (2000), pp. 28, 43.

65. United Nations Population Fund (UNFPA), Population Issues Briefing Kit (New York: United Nations, 2001).

66. National Institute of Allergy and Infectious Diseases, National Institutes of Health, U.S. Department of Health and Human Services, "HIV Infection in Infants and Children," July 2004, available online at http://www.niaid.nih.gov/factsheets/hivchildren.htm

67. "The Health of Youth, Facts for Action: Youth and Reproductive Health," A42/*Technical Discussions*/5, World Health Organization, Geneva, 1989.

68. "Children Orphaned by AIDS," UNICEF Statistics, available online at http://childinfo.org/areas/hivaids/.

69. UNICEF/UNIFEM Information Kit on CEDAW, Fact Sheet on Girls' Rights, undated.

70. "Chapter 8: Rethinking Leisure Time: Expanding Opportunities for Young People and Communities," *World Youth Report 2003*, United Nations, available online at http://www.un.org/esa/socdev/unyin/documents/ch08.pdf#search=%22boys%20girls%20leisure%20time%22.

71. Progressive Policy Institute, "Worldwide Child Labor Rates Have Fallen by Half Since 1980," May 8, 2002, Washington, DC, available online at http://www.ppionline.org/ppi_ci.cfm?knlgAreaID=108&subsecID=900003&contentID=250458.

72. Ashagric Kebebew, "Statistics on Working Children and Hazardous Child Labour in Brief," International Labour Organisation, Geneva, 1998.

73. Canadian International Development Agency, "Child Labour," Quebec, January 23, 2004, available online at http://www.acdi-cida.gc.ca/index.htm.

74. Kebebew, "Statistics on Working Children and Hazardous Child Labour in Brief."

75. Faraaz Siddiqi and Harry Anthony Patrinos, "Child Labor: Issues, Causes and Interventions," *Human Capital Development and Operations Policy* (Washington, DC: World Bank, 2005), available online at http://www.worldbank.org/html/extdr/hnp/hddflash/workp/wp_00056.html.

76. International Labour Organisation, "Child Labour Risks Growing in Africa: Organization of African Unity and International Labour Organisation, Convene Tripartite Meeting," Geneva, 1998, available online at http://www.ilo.org/public/english/bureau/inf/pr/1998/4.htm.

77. United Nations, *The World's Women 1995: Trends and Statistics* (New York: United Nations, 1995), p. 117.

78. Action Canada for Population and Development, "Trafficking and Girls," Ontario, 2001, available online at http://www.crlp.org/pdf/pub_fac_adoles_trafficking.pdf.

79. Child Protection Abstract, UNICEF, 2005; U.S. United States Department of State, "Trafficking in Persons (TIP) Report," June, 2005.

80. Cited in "Chapter 8: Rethinking Leisure Time: Expanding Opportunities for Young People and Communities," *World Youth Report 2003*, United Nations, available online at http://www.un.org/esa/socdev/unyin/documents/ch08.pdf#search=%22 boys%20girls%20leisure%20time%22.

81. *Our Words, Our Voices: Young Women for Change!* A report from the project "A Young Woman's Portrait Beyond Beijing '95" (UNICEF, UNFPA, and WEDO, 1996), p. 24.

82. UNICEF, *Convention on the Rights of the Child*, available online at http://www .unicef.org/crc/crc.htm.

83. "The Girl Child," *Fact Sheet 8*, United Nations Press Kit for the Fourth World Conference on Women, Beijing, China, 1995.

84. Ibid.

85. International Women's Health Coalition, "Nigeria: Challenging a Culture of Silence: A Conversation with Dorothy Aken'Ova," available online at http://www.iwhc .org/programs/africa/nigeria/index.cfm.

86. Global Fund for Women, available online at http://www.globalfundforwomen.org/.

87. "The State of Human Rights: The Human Rights of Girls and Women," UNFPA State of the World Population 2005, available online at http://www.unfpa.org/swp/ 2005/english/ch3/chap3_page1.htm.

5

Women's Human Right to Health

States Parties shall take all appropriate measures to eliminate discrimination against women in the field of health care in order to ensure, on a basis of equality of men and women, access to health care services, including those related to family planning.
> —Convention on the Elimination of All Forms of
> Discrimination Against Women, Article 12

States Parties recognize the right of the child to the enjoyment of the highest attainable standard of health and to facilities for the treatment of illness and rehabilitation of health. States Parties shall strive to ensure that no child is deprived of his or her right of access to such health care services.
> —Article 24(1), Convention on the Rights of the Child

Objectives

The exercises and background information contained in this chapter will enable participants to work towards the following objectives:

- Define the right to health.
- Explain the importance of women's health for women's equality.
- Understand the interrelationship between the right to health and other human rights.
- Identify ways in which women's right to health has been promoted or denied.
- Explain women's double work burden arising from their multiple roles and its effect on their health.
- Identify ways to balance respect for culture and tradition with respect for women's health.
- Describe the provisions regarding health in the Convention on the Elimination of All Forms of Discrimination Against Women (CEDAW).
- Remember core concepts.

Getting Started: Thinking About Women's Health

Women's *de facto* second-class status in society gives rise to both direct and indirect threats to their health. Since women are far more likely than men to be poor,[1] they often receive less nourishment and are more vulnerable to disease. Many women who suffer from poor health lack information, skills, purchasing power, and access to health care services. Too often, women are not part of the formal decision-making processes concerning the formulation of health care laws and policies. Violence against women, substandard working conditions, and a poor living environment also undermine women's health. As noted by the International Labour Organisation (ILO):

> The health problems reported in the literature on the informal sector are generally the same as in the formal sector, with a common presence of poor housekeeping, poor lighting, long work hours, poor work place design, unawareness of chemicals risks and increased use of drugs as home medication. Job-related risk factors are compounded by overcrowding, poor nutrition and other public health problems, inadequate sanitation, lack of adequate storage and the more general effects of poverty.[2]

The World Bank estimates that health care costs plunge 100 million people into poverty every year, with 60 percent of care spent on medicine:

> Women bear the brunt of the high cost of health care. If someone falls ill in the family, women take on the added burden of becoming the carer, and women are often the last to seek health care for themselves if any cost is involved, because they prioritise the rest of their family over themselves.[3]

Women may experience some or all of these problems regarding their health-related rights:

- Exposure to HIV
- Pregnancy-associated health issues
- Lack of clean drinking water
- Insufficient vaccination programs for girls
- Failure to treat anemia in women and girls
- Lack of general gynecologic care
- Lack of birth control and sex education
- Unsafe abortions
- Unsanitary and otherwise inadequate birthing facilities
- Treatment with unsafe drugs
- Inadequate attention to diseases mainly affecting women, such as breast cancer
- Medical research predominantly based on male subjects, yielding inadequate evidence for making decisions about women's health
- Lack of mental health care and therapy
- Lack of therapy for women victims/survivors of rape, incest, and other forms of violence
- Insufficient number of women trained as counsellors, physicians, and health care professionals

- Cultural barriers to women's health, such as the prohibition against allowing women to be attended by male health care providers and researchers
- Lack of education for women about child care, hygiene, nutrition, and other family health matters
- Barriers to general health care services for people with disabilities, especially disabled women
- Lack of appropriate, responsive health care for women living in rural areas; migrant, refugee, and displaced women; older women; lesbians; women of ethnic and racial minorities; and women in prison.

In short, poor health can prevent a woman from realizing other human rights. Women and girls who are ill often cannot participate fully in society; for example, they may not be able to attend school, work outside the home, or organize and participate in groups.

✠ Learning Activity 1: Defining Women's Health ✠

Objective To write a broad definition of women's health
Time 60 minutes
Materials Chart paper and markers or blackboard and chalk

1. Brainstorm

Draw the outline of a woman on chart paper or a blackboard. As a group, brainstorm the qualities that characterize a healthy woman and list these inside the outline. Consider the emotional and psychological aspects of health in addition to the physical ones.

Brainstorm the factors that are necessary for women to achieve these qualities of good health and list them in the margins outside the outline. For example, if the group included *energetic* as a quality of a healthy woman, *adequate food* or *rest and leisure* might be listed as necessary factors.

2. Analyze

Circle the items on the list of factors necessary for health that most women in your community do not have. Discuss what happens when women lack these factors:

- What are the effects on the woman herself?
- What are the effects on her children? On other members of her family?
- What are the effects on the community, especially if many women lack good health?

3. Discuss

The image of the woman in Step 1 represents all women in the community. Make a list of three or four subgroups of women (e.g., disabled, refugee, older, widowed, or unmarried women) who might have special health care concerns different from most women.

✠ Learning Activity 1 Continued ✠

Divide into small groups and pick one of these subgroups to discuss. In the context of the factors necessary for health listed outside the outline during Step 1, address the following questions:

- Are there additional factors necessary for health among this subgroup?
- Are there additional factors necessary for health that this group generally lacks?
- What are the obstacles to this group's enjoyment of good health?

Compare the findings of the small groups and discuss:

- What are some of the main obstacles to these subgroups' enjoyment of good health?
- Do these obstacles prevent them from exercising their human rights?
- Is good health a human right?

Defining the Right to Health

Building on the broad definition of *health* adopted by the World Health Organization (WHO) in its Constitution and other principles, the Beijing Platform for Action reaffirms that *health* as it specifically relates to women is

> a state of complete physical, mental and social well-being and not merely the absence of disease or infirmity. Women's health involves their emotional, social and physical well-being and is determined by the social, political and economic context of their lives, as well as by biology. However, health and well-being elude the majority of women.[4]

International human rights law does not guarantee the right of people to be healthy. Rather, it recognizes the right of all to have access to health care to ensure that people may attain the highest standard of health of which they themselves are capable. States are required to guarantee the right to access health services, a right that is further elaborated in some international documents. Article 12 of the Convention on the Elimination of All Forms of Discrimination (CEDAW), for example, requires states to eliminate discrimination against women in their access to health care services, throughout the life cycle, particularly in the areas of family planning, pregnancy, confinement, and postnatal well-being.

As the above Platform for Action definition of *health* makes clear, access to health care is broadly defined. Indeed, states are required to take certain measures with the aim of safeguarding public health.[5] For women to be healthy, their basic needs must be fulfilled. These include assured income, safe working and living conditions, adequate and clean food and water, education, and available, affordable, and appropriate health care. In addition, women need equal status in society, equitable division of labor (including production, child care, and housework), and freedom from violence. Accordingly, rights relating to health care imply only access to hospitals, clinics, medicines, and health professionals. While this access is important, it is insufficient for comprehensive "health."

Often poor health can be traced to oppression and human rights violations. As noted in the Beijing Platform for Action:

> The prevalence among women of poverty and economic dependence, their experience of violence, negative attitudes towards women and girls, racial and other forms of discrimination, the limited power many women have over their sexual and reproductive lives, and lack of influence in decision-making are social realities which have an adverse impact on their health (paragraph 92).

One important aspect of health is *reproductive and sexual health*, which the Platform for Action defines as a "state of complete physical, mental and social well-being . . . in all matters relating to the reproductive system" (paragraph 94). This section focuses on the *totality* of women's health needs. (See also Chapter 4, "The Human Rights of Young Women and Girls.")

✠ Learning Activity 2: Health Needs at the Community Level ✠

Objective To identify the health needs of women at the community level
Time 60 minutes
Materials Small pieces of paper, pens, adhesive tape or tacks, chart paper or surface on which to attach pieces of paper

1. List/Prioritize/Compare
Divide participants into small groups and ask them to do the following:

- Write or draw the health needs of women and girls in your community. Use a separate piece of paper for each need.
- Arrange the needs in a triangle, according to their importance. Put the most pressing needs at the top.
- Circle those needs in the triangle that are poorly met or not at all. Star those needs that are particular to women and girls.
- Post your chart and compare with others.

2. Discuss
In the full group, discuss the following points:

- What were the principal differences among the triangles?
- In what respect(s) is each item in the triangle important to the health of women and girls?
- What happens if any of these health needs are denied? Give examples.
- Why are those needs that are circled not met?
- Is there any relationship between the needs you have starred and those you have circled? Discuss.
- What steps are being taken in your community to improve women's health? What further might be done?

Health for All

Many women live with long-term health problems. Countless women and girl children suffer from nutritional deficiencies and anemia that make them prone to illnesses such as tuberculosis, malaria, diarrhea, and pneumonia. Many are subjected to constant stress and injuries resulting from work responsibilities and social restrictions as well as abuse and violence. In industrialized countries, health-related problems are often worst among women of color and women from minority groups.

Within any country, great disparities exist in health needs among different regions and different socioeconomic, ethnic, and age groups. Although many countries have made significant advances in primary health care, the worldwide HIV/AIDS epidemic has eroded much of this progress, and women's general and maternal health care and treatment for complications from pregnancy and childbirth remain inadequate. Of the 515,000 women who die from childbirth-related illnesses each year, almost 99 percent come from developing countries.[6] Between 2005 and 2007, 1 million women died for lack of medical care during pregnancy or while giving birth—a figure equivalent to the total number of German and Canadian women who gave birth in 2006. During the same two-year period, 21 million children under the age of 5 died from inadequate care—the same number as the total of children under 5 born in Germany, France, Canada, Japan, Italy, and the United Kingdom combined.[7]

No matter what the country, not just poor women but women from rural areas, refugee, displaced, and migrant women, and women heads of households—who are also likely to be of lower economic status—usually face great obstacles in exercising their health rights. Women with disabilities, too, often have restricted access to general health care as a result of discriminatory attitudes, physically inaccessible health facilities, or ignorance about the health needs of disabled women.

Women's multiple work responsibilities often endanger their health. In many societies women bear a double burden, expected to work outside the home for pay as well as to be responsible for work inside the home and to take care of their husband and children's needs—and often those of other relatives as well. Even when women do not work outside the home, their work may be difficult and never ending. In many homes around the world, women are the first to rise in the morning and the last to go to bed at night. Some women may become conditioned to think of their own health needs last. In some societies, women can see a doctor only when escorted by a husband or father. As a result, women are likely to delay or do without treatment. In addition, in some families boys are more likely to receive proper medical care than girls.[8] When the family resources are limited, money for proper nutrition and medicines may go first to boys, leaving the girls with little or none.[9]

A sick woman faces particular problems, especially if her disease bears some social stigma, as with tuberculosis, HIV/AIDs, or other diseases commonly transmitted sexually. Women with such diseases may be ostracized by their family, get fired from their job, or suffer domestic violence. Fearing such repercussions, many women do not seek treatment and attempt to hide their illness. For example, women may avoid being screened for HIV/AIDS out of fear of the husband's or family's reaction and, as a result, fail to get medication or treatment.

Even women with a less stigmatizing illness such as heart disease, diabetes, or malaria often face greater obstacles to full recovery because of chronic overwork, poor care, and undiminished family responsibilities.[10]

Facts About Women's Health

- The World Bank has warned that violence against women is as serious a cause of death and incapacity among women of reproductive age as cancer, and a greater cause of ill health than traffic accidents and malaria combined.[11]
- The life expectancy of women has either remained the same or risen since 1995 in every region of the world except sub-Saharan Africa.[12]
- Pregnant women are more susceptible than the general population to malaria and its consequences. Malaria-related maternal mortality can be very high, particularly during epidemics and in areas of low transmission and therefore low immunity.[13]
- Women are more likely than men to become disabled during their lives, due in part to gender bias in the allocation of scarce resources and in access to services. When ill, girls and women are less likely to receive medical attention than boys and men, particularly in developing countries where medical care may be a considerable distance from home. They are also less likely to receive preventive care, such as immunizations. Due to social, cultural, and religious factors, disabled women are less likely than men to make use of existing social services, including residential services, and it is estimated that disabled women worldwide receive only 20 percent of rehabilitation care.[14]
- Globally, 45 percent of adults living with HIV/AIDS are women. By region, this percentage varies considerably, from 57 percent in sub-Saharan Africa to 28 percent in East Asia and the Pacific. In 2004, 17.6 million women were living with HIV/AIDS worldwide.[15]
- Women between the ages of 35 and 60 account for 60 percent of all cases of cervical cancer. There appears to be an increased risk of this cancer in women who are farm workers, cooks, cleaners, and maids as well as in those who work, or have partners who work, in environments that involve contact with certain chemical substances (i.e., those in the mining, textile, metal, or chemical industries).[16]
- Women living in poor social and environmental circumstances with associated low education, low income, and difficult family and marital relationships are much more likely than other women to suffer from mental disorders.[17]

Respecting Culture and Tradition

A number of international human rights instruments require that states take effective action to abolish traditional practices prejudicial to the health of women and girls. In 1990, for example, members of the Committee on the Elimination of All Forms of Discrimination Against Women, the body responsible for monitoring the implementation of CEDAW, expressed its concern at the continuation of traditional practices harmful to the health of women.[18] And in 1999 the fifty-fourth UN General Assembly adopted a resolution condemning traditional or customary practices that affect the health of women and girls. Yet despite these developments, many societies continue adhering to customs, often rationalized in the name of religion or culture, that endanger women's health. One such custom prevents a woman from travelling to see a doctor; another accepts violence against women by male family members.

In some societies, early marriage and pregnancy have a grave effect on the health of women and girls. A preference for sons often results in preferential treatment for male children that, in turn, results in neglect or discriminatory treatment of girls, compromising their health and well-being. According to UNICEF, more than 100 million women are "missing" from global population figures, a majority of them from South and East Asia, victims of infanticide, malnutrition, neglect, abandonment, and, more recently, sex-based abortion relating to the misuse of technologies for prenatal sex determination.[19] Another study estimates that 60–100 million fewer women are alive today than would exist in a world without gender discrimination and without social norms that favor sons.[20]

Because of their lower status, women and girls often eat only after all male family members have eaten and suffer higher rates of malnutrition as a result. In addition, although women are often expected to have numerous children, many are forbidden or unable to access professional medical help and die during childbirth. Traditional birth practices pose further health risks, including, for example, dietary restrictions for pregnant women, harmful practices during labor and childbirth, and inappropriate treatment of conditions such as obstructed labor. According to the United Nations, at least 1,600 women die from complications of pregnancy and childbirth every day. These complications are the leading cause of death and disability for women aged 15 to 49 in developing countries.[21] For more on the impact of culture and tradition on health and human rights, see Chapter 4, "The Human Rights of Young Women and Girls."

The Case of Female Genital Cutting[22]

The World Health Organization (WHO) estimates that, around the world, 100–132 million girls and women have been subjected to female genital cutting (FGC) or female genital mutilation (FGM). Each year, an estimated 2 million girls are believed to be at risk for the practice. The majority of survivors live in twenty-eight African countries; others live in the Middle East and in Asian countries and, to an increasing extent, among immigrant populations in Europe, Canada, Australia, New Zealand, and the United States of America.

Female genital cutting is a cultural practice harmful to women that violates women's human rights to life, bodily integrity, health, and sexuality. As noted by the WHO, "FGM is linked to gender inequalities entrenched in the political, social, cultural and economic structures of societies in which it is practiced. It is a reflection of the discrimination against women in both public and private life." The health consequences of the practice can be severe, leading to lifelong mental and physical disability and even death and implicating the right to life, the right to freedom from violence, the right to bodily integrity, and reproductive rights. Because it is practiced mostly on young girls, female genital cutting violates a range of human rights of the girl child, including informed consent.[23]

The WHO defines *female genital cutting* as "all procedures which involve partial or total removal of the external female genitalia or other injury to the female genital organs whether for cultural or any other non-therapeutic reasons."

The United Nations Population Fund has identified four types of female genital cutting practices:

continues

The Case of Female Genital Cutting Continued

Type 1: Excision of the prepuce, with or without excision of part or all of the clitoris.

Type 2: Excision of the clitoris with partial or total excision of the labia minora.[24]

Type 3: Excision of part or all of the external genitalia and stitching/narrowing of the vaginal opening (infibulation). Sometimes referred to as pharaonic circumcision.

Type 4: Others. For example, pricking, piercing or incising, stretching, burning of the clitoris, scraping of tissue surrounding the vaginal orifice, cutting of the vagina, introduction of corrosive substances or herbs into the vagina to cause bleeding or to tighten the opening.[25]

Abolition of these harmful cultural practices is a complex and challenging issue, as FGM has important cultural and symbolic significance for some women and communities. The practice, much like plastic surgery to increase breast size, is understood to enhance the femininity of women, and to make them more attractive to men. It is also seen as a ritual in the process toward womanhood. Although groups have been working against the practice of female genital cutting in African countries for many years, the increased visibility of this problem has resulted primarily from the growth of women's movements around the world as well as from attention from the international human rights community to issues related to gender.

✠ Learning Activity 3 ✠
Impact of a Woman's Health on Her Life Cycle

Objective To identify the impact of health on the life cycle of a woman
Time 45 minutes
Materials None

1. Create a Story

Divide participants into small groups. Explain that each group will construct a life story of a typical women from their community from the standpoint of health, covering her life cycle from birth to old age. Each group should decide in advance the social, ethnic, and economic setting for this woman and assign her a name, life, and health experience typical for that setting. Encourage a wide choice of such settings.

Begin the story with "A baby girl was born into the ___ community . . ." and let the story pass from one participant to another, with each telling about a different period in this woman's life. Include factors that affect women's health in this community, both positively and negatively, such as traditional health practices, access to health care, education, leisure, family planning, child bearing, and cultural influences reflected in the media.

Alternative: These stories might be illustrated by drawings, dancing, role-play, or other creative methods.

2. Present

Each small group summarizes its life story for the whole group.

Learning Activity 3 Continued

3. Discuss

Conclude with discussion of questions like these:

- What factors were common to all stories?
- Which illnesses and practices most affect women of low economic status? Women of high economic status?
- Aside from reproductive factors, how would the stories be different if the baby had been a boy?
- What factors contribute to a lifetime of good health? To bad health?
- How do poor childhood health care and nutrition affect a person's life cycle?
- Is it possible to justify any custom that has a negative effect on women's health?
- How can women's bodily integrity be protected at the same time that culture and religion are respected?

The Role of Authorities in Women's Health

Most public health systems aim to make health care available for the whole population. This goal is reinforced by evolving human rights documents that obligate the states that have ratified them not only to promote and guarantee health care but also to ensure that health care facilities are equally accessible to everyone.

The United Nations Charter (1947), the founding document of the United Nations, calls on the UN to promote solutions for international health problems (Article 55b), and the Universal Declaration of Human Rights (UDHR, 1948) states that everyone has the "right to a standard of living adequate for the health and well-being of his [*sic*] family, including food, clothing, housing and medical care and necessary social services" (Article 25). In short, all UN Member States have an obligation to create the conditions for the health and well-being of all people in those states. These general documents were followed in later decades by covenants and conventions that placed legally binding obligations on the governments that ratified them, referred to as "States Parties to the treaty."

Some of these legal responsibilities require a government to refrain from interfering with or harming people's health; others obligate a government to actively promote health. Whether acting directly through official government programs or indirectly through institutions such as hospitals and doctors, governments cannot discriminate between the health care available to women and girls and that available to men and boys.

States that are parties to the International Covenant on Economic, Social, and Cultural Rights (ICESCR, 1976) are obligated to take the steps necessary to "recognize the right of everyone to the enjoyment of the highest attainable standard of physical and mental health" (Article 12). The Convention on the Elimination of All Forms of Discrimination Against Women (CEDAW, 1979) guarantees women the right to equal access to health care (Article 12), as well as to information and advice on family planning (Article 10). And in addition to guaranteeing the right of the child to the "highest attainable standard of health" (Article 24), the Convention on the Rights of the Child (CRC, 1989) gives the child the right to sources of information including "those aimed at the promotion of his or her . . . physical and mental health," thus implicitly including information about sexuality and reproductive health.

In its 1999 General Recommendation on women's right to health, the Committee on the Elimination of All Forms of Discrimination Against Women recommended that states should "implement a comprehensive national strategy to promote women's health throughout their lifespan" and that "States Parties should allocate adequate budgetary, human and administrative resources to ensure that women's health receives a share of the overall health budget comparable with that for men's health, taking into account their different health needs." The Committee also issued the following more specific recommendations:

> 31. States parties should also, in particular:
> (a) Place a gender perspective at the centre of all policies and programs affecting women's s health and should involve women in the planning, implementation and monitoring of such policies and programs and in the provision of health services to women;
> (b) Ensure the removal of all barriers to women's access to health services, education and information, including in the area of sexual and reproductive health, and, in particular, allocate resources for programs directed at adolescents for the prevention and treatment of sexually transmitted diseases, including HIV/AIDS;
> (c) Prioritize the prevention of unwanted pregnancy through family planning and sex education and reduce maternal mortality rates through safe motherhood services and prenatal assistance. When possible, legislation criminalizing abortion could be amended to remove punitive provisions imposed on women who undergo abortion;
> (d) Monitor the provision of health services to women by public, non-governmental and private organizations, to ensure equal access and quality of care;
> (e) Require all health services to be consistent with the human rights of women, including the rights to autonomy, privacy, confidentiality, informed consent and choice;
> (f) Ensure that the training curricula of health workers include comprehensive, mandatory, gender-sensitive courses on women's health and human rights, in particular gender-based violence.[26]

Governments differ greatly in their ability to provide health care, but they are obliged, to the extent that they are able, to ensure that their citizens attain a standard of living adequate to their health and well-being. Too often, however, even the wealthiest nations fail to meet this standard in a fair and nondiscriminatory manner.

Health Care and Equality Between Men and Women

Governments have the obligation to avoid discriminating between men and women in the provision of health care. However, providing health care on the basis of equality between men and women means more than simply providing identical facilities. The Committee on the Elimination of All Forms of Discrimination Against Women, in its General Recommendation regarding women's human right to health (1999), emphasized that "States Parties should report on their understanding of how policies and measures on *health care* address the health rights of women from the perspective of women's needs and interests and how it addresses distinctive features and factors which differ for women in comparison to men."[27] This means recognizing and addressing the differing health needs of men and women. A prenatal health service does not discriminate against men because they do not need such a service. Similarly, screening for prostrate cancer does not discriminate against women as long as other programs exist that address women's cancer concerns such as breast cancer.

Adequate health services for women must address their particular health care needs. For example, women may suffer from forms of cancer and other illness that are rare or unknown in men. Women may also be particularly susceptible to the effects of chronic fatigue, malnutrition, and anemia as well as to the health consequences related to these conditions. Governments and communities have to take steps to make health care more accessible to women, such as ensuring that hospitals and clinics:

- maintain working hours that correspond to times during which women are available
- are conveniently located (as women are less likely than men to be able to travel distances)
- are affordable
- offer quality care and consistently available medications
- employ culturally appropriate staff (including, if possible, local health professionals who speak the same languages and female staff for gynecological exams)
- design services in consultation with women to fit their needs (including the particular needs of rural, refugee, migrant, displaced, older, single, widowed, and disabled women)
- offer a welcoming atmosphere, not one that is cold or frightening.

Remembering Core Concepts

✠ Learning Activity 4: Speaking Out for Women's Health ✠

Objectives   To examine women's right to health care in the community and consider how to take action to improve such care
Time   60+ minutes
Materials   Chart paper and markers

1. Brainstorm
Ask participants to list the health problems of women in their community and, after dividing into small groups, to choose a problem on which they wish to concentrate.

continues

✠ Learning Activity 4 Continued ✠

2. Discuss/Plan

Ask each small group to prepare a five-minute presentation to a "panel of community leaders" on their chosen problem. Each presentation should:

- describe the health problem as well as identify the group of women it impacts and, if possible, the cause(s) of the problem
- relate the problem to women's human rights
- clarify how the problem affects women's lives
- show how addressing the problem can improve their lives
- propose specific actions that should be taken to address the problem
- show how members of the community can get involved in addressing the problem.

For a group-oriented class: Ask each group to choose a spokesperson to make the presentation and a "community leader" to serve on the panel. While the groups plan their presentations, the panel of leaders meets to decide on their roles, representing a variety of differing but typical attitudes within the community leadership.

3. Present/Role-Play

The spokesperson from each group makes a presentation and members of the panel listen and respond, asking questions and offering comments, objections, or suggestions in keeping with their chosen roles.

4. Discuss

After the presentations and role-play, discuss the following questions:

- How did the spokespersons feel when presenting the problem?
- How did the "community leaders" respond to the presentation? What attitudes in the community were they representing?
- How did the audience, composed of the rest of the group, respond to the presentations?
- Did any spokesperson discuss the problem as a human rights violation? Did putting the problem in a human rights context strengthen the argument? Why or why not?
- Are these ideas for improving women's human right to health feasible in your community? Why or why not?

5. Conclude

Challenge the participants by asking them to evaluate their knowledge of the problem and the inclusiveness of their perspective:

- How did you obtain your information about the health issues facing women in your community? Was it accurate and complete? If not, what additional information do you need and how can you obtain it?

> ### **Learning Activity 4 Continued**
>
> - Did you personally consult women about the problem and how it affects them? About actions that could improve the problem?
> - Why is it important in real-life human rights advocacy to include the active participation of those directly involved and affected?
> - How can you apply the example of this exercise to planning and implementing advocacy for women in your community?

Notes

1. UN Platform for Action Committee Manitoba, Women and the Economy, "What Are the Causes of Women's Economic Inequality?" (2002), from the BRIDGE Briefing Paper on the feminization of poverty, available online at http://www.unpac.ca/economy/whatcauses.html.

2. International Labour Organisation, "Health Impact of Occupational Risks in the Informal Sector in Zimbabwe," Chapter 2, February 2000.

3. Oxfam International, "The World Is Still Waiting," *Oxfam Briefing Paper 103*, May 2007, available online at http://www.oxfam.org.uk/what_we_do/issues/debt_aid/bp103_g8.htm.

4. *The World's Women 1995: Trends and Statistics* (New York: United Nations, 1995).

5. Asbjørn Eide, "Economic and Social Rights," in *Human Rights: Concepts and Standards*, edited by Janusz Symonides (UNESCO, 2000).

6. UNICEF Maternal Health, December 4, 2005, available online at http://www.unicef.org/health/index_maternalhealth.html.

7. Oxfam International, "The World Is Still Waiting," *Oxfam Briefing Paper 103*, May 2007, available online at http://www.oxfam.org.uk/what_we_do/issues/debt_aid/bp103_g8.htm.

8. United Nations, Expert Group Meeting on the Elimination of All Forms of Discrimination and Violence against the Girl Child, *Violence and Discrimination—Voices of Young People: Girls About Girls*, Florence, September 25–28, 2006, available online at http://www.unicef.org/voy/media/UNICEFEGM_GirlaboutGirlsFINAL.doc.

9. Ibid.

10. *UNAIDS, "AIDS Epidemic Update, December 2004," from Why Is There Stigma Related to HIV and AIDS?* (Avert.org), available online at http://www.avert.org/aidsstigma.htm.

11. Cited in Shelley Anderson, "'More Training!' Towards Gender-Sensitive Nonviolence Training," International Fellowship for Reconciliation Women Peacemakers Program, The Netherlands, available online at http://www.ifor.org/WPP/TOT%20report%202002.pdf.

12. United Nations, *The World's Women 2000: Trends and Statistics* (New York: United Nations).

13. Philippe J. Guerin et al., "Malaria: Current Status of Control, Diagnosis, Treatment, and a Proposed Agenda for Research and Development," *The Lancet Infectious Diseases*, vol. 2 (September 2002), available online at http://www.accessmed-msf.org/upload/ReportsandPublications/25920021619148/malaria.pdf.

14. Human Rights Watch, "Women and Girls with Disabilities," available online at http://www.hrw.org/women/disabled.html.

15. USAID Health Overview, Washington, DC, available online at http://www.usaid.gov/our_work/global_health.

16. United Nations Sustainable Networking Development Program (SNDP), New York, United Nations, available online at http://www.sdnpbd.org.

17. World Health Organization, "Women and Mental Health," available online at http://www.who.int/mediacentre/factsheets/fs248/en/.

18. CEDAW, General Recommendation No. 24 (20th session, 1999), Article 12: Women and Health, available online at http://www.un.org/womenwatch/daw/cedaw/recommendations/recomm.htm#recom24.

19. UNICEF, "Equality, Development, and Peace," available online at http://womenshistory.about.com/library/etext/speech/bl_sp_beijing_un_1.htm.

20. UNICEF, "Early Childhood: Investment in Early Childhood Can Break the Cycle of Poverty," available online at http://www.unicef.org/earlychildhood/index_investment.html.

21. United Nations Chronicle, "Safe Motherhood: A Matter of Human Rights and Social Justice" (Rita Luthra, 2005), available online at http://www.un.org/Pubs/chronicle/2005/issue2/0205p14.html.

22. Unless otherwise noted, references in this section are to "Female Genital Mutilation Information Pack, FGM: Prevalence and Distribution" (1996), available online at http://www.who.int/docstore/frh-whd/FGM/infopack/English/fgm_infopack.htm#THE%20PRACTICE.

23. UNICEF, "Changing a Harmful Social Convention: Female Genital Mutilation/Cutting" (Alexia Lewnes, 2005), available online at http://www.unicef-icdc.org/publications/pdf/fgm-gb-2005.pdf.

24. Ibid. See also Fran Hosken, *The Hosken Report: Genital and Sexual Mutilation of Females*, 4th rev. ed. (Lexington, MA: Women's International Network News, 1993); National Demographic and Health Surveys, Macro International, Inc., 11785 Beltsville Drive, Calverton, Maryland; and Nahid Toubia, *Female Genital Mutilation: A Call for Global Action* (New York: Women, Ink., 1993).

25. UNFPA, "Harmful Practices: Frequently Asked Questions on Female Genital Mutilation/Cutting," available online at http://www.unfpa.org/gender/practices2.htm#2.

26. CEDAW, General Recommendation No. 24 (1999).

27. Ibid.; see also http://www.unicef-icdc.org/publications/pdf/fgm-gb-2005.pdf.

6

Women's Human Rights to Reproduction and Sexuality

[R]eproductive rights embrace certain human rights that are already recognized in national laws, international human rights documents and other consensus documents. These rights rest on the recognition of the basic right of all couples and individuals to decide freely and responsibly the number, spacing and timing of their children and to have the information and means to do so, and the right to attain the highest standard of sexual and reproductive health.
—Programme of Action, United Nations International Conference on Population and Development, Paragraph 7.3

We, the Governments participating in the Fourth World Conference on Women, are determined to . . . [e]nsure equal access to and equal treatment of women and men in education and health care and enhance women's sexual and reproductive health as well as education.
—Beijing Platform for Action, Paragraph 1.30

Objectives

The learning activities and background information contained in this chapter will enable participants to work toward the following objectives:

- Recognize the importance of reproductive and sexual rights for women and their interconnection with other human rights.
- Identify obstacles to women's reproductive and sexual rights.
- Define the role of government, community leaders, the media, and women themselves in protecting and advocating for women's reproductive and sexual rights.
- Critically analyze the relation between population policies and reproductive and sexual rights.
- Debate the issue of reproductive and sexual health education from the perspective of women's human rights.
- Remember core concepts.

Getting Started: Thinking About Reproductive and Sexual Rights

About half the world's female population is of reproductive age (15–49). Over the next twenty years, this group will increase by 30 percent. Half of the world's population is under the age of 25, and within fifteen years—less than one generation—all 3 billion will have reached reproductive age.[1] The lives and health of women of reproductive age are greatly influenced by their potential reproductive roles. Although rates of mortality and illness related to reproductive health have declined throughout the world, this progress is being eroded by the HIV/AIDS epidemic, especially in Africa and parts of Asia. As noted in the Beijing Platform for Action (paragraph 95):

> Reproductive health eludes many of the world's people because of such factors as: inadequate levels of knowledge about human sexuality and inappropriate or poor-quality reproductive health information and services; the prevalence of high-risk sexual behavior; discriminatory social practices; negative attitudes toward women and girls; and the limited power many women and girls have over their sexual and reproductive lives. Adolescents are particularly vulnerable because of their lack of information and access to relevant services in most countries. Older women and men have distinct reproductive and sexual health issues that are often inadequately addressed.

Facing the Facts on Women's Reproductive Health

- Pregnancy and childbirth and their consequences are still the leading causes of death, disease, and disability among women of reproductive age in developing countries.[2]
- Maternal mortality is highest by far in Africa, where the lifetime risk of maternal death is 1 in 16 women, compared with 1 in 2,800 in wealthy countries.[3]
- Worldwide, 61.1 percent of births are attended by a professional who, at least in principle, has the appropriate skills. In sub-Saharan Africa, however, only 40 percent of births are accompanied by a skilled attendant.[4]
- Over 300 million women in the developing world suffer from short-term or long-term illness brought about by pregnancy and childbirth; 529,000 die each year.[5]

Reproductive Decision Making

✠ Learning Activity 1: Discussion Circle on Reproductive Rights ✠

Objectives To get started discussing reproductive rights and to relate them to personal experience

Time 45 minutes

Materials None

1. Discuss

Arrange the group in two concentric circles, with each participant on the inside circle facing a participant on the outside circle. Explain that as you read out a question from the list below, each pair should speak to each other about the question for four minutes. For the next question, those on the outer circle rotate one place to the right to face a new partner. Repeat this process for every question.

Learning Activity 1 Continued

Note to Facilitator: Some of these questions would be inappropriate in certain cultural settings; develop a set of five or six questions appropriate to a particular group and its culture. Other questions may need to be rephrased from the personal to the general (e.g., not "How did your mother protect herself from unwanted pregnancy?" but "How did women of your mother's generation protect themselves?"). Still others may need to be omitted altogether; clarify that everyone is free to decline to discuss a question.

- What is the first thing that comes to mind when you think of reproductive and sexual rights? The next thing?
- What major decisions in your life have been related to reproduction and sexuality (e.g., choosing a partner, taking a job, finishing education or training)?
- Has anyone tried to make decisions about reproduction and sexuality for you?
- What are the main controversies in your community about reproduction and sexual rights?
- What are the main incentives in your community for large families? For small families? Which arguments are most influential to you?
- How many children did your mother have? How did she protect herself from unwanted pregnancy?
- What kinds of decisions have you made about having or not having children? Did you make these yourself? Did your partner pressure you in any way? Your partner's family? Your family? Your community?
- What is the main family planning method used in your community, if any? What method, if any, do you use? Did you or most women in your community always choose family planning methods freely, or did someone do it for you? How did you and/or women in your community learn about them?
- What is the general attitude in your community toward abortion?

2. Discuss

After participants have discussed a number of questions for about half an hour, ask them to form one large group and discuss what they experienced in discussing the questions with others.

- How did you feel about discussing these topics with others?
- What did you learn about others' attitudes and information? About your own?
- Did this exercise help you to focus on issues related to reproductive health in your community? What do you think are the main concerns of women in your community?

Women and girls face many decisions about their reproduction and sexuality, including the following:

- Whether to obtain information regarding sex
- Whether to engage in sexual activity and with whom

- Which contraceptive methods to use, if any
- Whether to require a male sexual partner, including a spouse, to use a condom
- Whether to have children
- Whether to seek medical attention during pregnancy
- With whom to have children
- When to have children
- How many children to have
- Spacing of children
- With whom to bring up children
- Whether to abort an unwanted pregnancy.

Women's choices are often imposed or limited by direct or indirect social, economic, and cultural factors. For example, in some countries where women are allowed little participation in reproductive decisions, or where governments impose strict population policies and there is a strong preference for sons, women may feel forced to decide between abortion of the female fetus, infanticide of the female newborn baby, or neglect of a female child until she dies. In many countries an unmarried pregnant girl is told to have the baby quietly and then to give the child away to a married couple. Her only other option may be to raise the child alone in poverty with few prospects for the future.

It is often assumed that women and girls with disabilities cannot or should not exercise reproductive choices, and as a result they are denied access to information and services needed to make such choices, pressured into making particular choices, or made subjects of substituted decision-making (whereby someone else, such as a doctor or relative, makes the decision for them).

✠ Learning Activity 2 ✠
Decisions About Reproduction and Sexuality

Objective   To identify decision makers over reproduction and sexuality
Time   60 minutes
Materials   Chart paper and markers or blackboard and chalk, slips of paper, string or tape, copies of the above section headed "Reproductive Decision Making"

1. List/Discuss
Hand out copies of "Reproductive Decision-Making" or post this list on a prepared chart or blackboard. Ask participants:

- Is the list comprehensive?
- If not, what would you add to the list?

2. Analyze
Ask participants which of these decisions women in their community make and mark them with a *W*. Mark with an *M* decisions made by men. Write both *M* and *W* only when the decision making is shared equally. Discuss these questions:

Learning Activity 2 Continued

- Do all members of the group agree?
- Did your mother make the decisions marked with *W*? Your grand-mother? You?
- If there has been a change over time, discuss what explains this change.

3. Create/Gallery Walk

Draw a long horizontal line on a blackboard or chart paper or hang a string across the room. Explain that this represents women's lifeline. Mark ten equal units along the line to represent each decade of life.

Divide participants into small groups and ask them to write or draw on slips of paper decisions about reproduction and sexuality that women are likely to make or have made for them at different periods of their lives. Then attach these slips to the line in the appropriate decade, forming a "reproductive lifeline." When all of the slips are attached, have everyone examine them.

4. Discuss

Ask these questions about the reproductive lifeline:

- At what stages in life do most decisions about reproduction and sexuality occur? Least?
- Are there any decisions on the reproductive lifeline that women in your community may not or cannot make? Remove those from the line. What percentage remains? What percentage was removed? What conclusions can you draw from these percentages?
- How would your own reproductive lifeline change if you had more or less access to economic resources? To education?
- How would your own reproductive lifeline change if you were from a different racial, ethnic, or social group in your community?
- What happens when women cannot make decisions about their reproduction and sexuality? How are women's human rights affected when they cannot make these decisions?
- What other factors would alter women's reproductive lifeline?

Defining Reproductive and Sexual Rights as Human Rights

Many reproductive rights advocates have long linked their cause to human rights, and support for reproductive rights as human rights can be found in many international instruments. Yet reproductive and sexual rights were not firmly at the forefront of human rights advocacy until the issue was raised at a series of international conferences in the 1990s.

A major advance in the international recognition of reproductive and sexual rights as human rights took place in Cairo, Egypt, in 1994 at the UN International Conference on Population and Development (ICPD). There, the 180 countries in attendance agreed that population growth can be stabilized and development efforts enhanced by the advancement of women. The documents that were agreed upon at the ICPD thus recognized reproductive rights as part of the international human rights agenda and as crucial measures for promoting development. Specifically, the ICPD Program of Action, the main document resulting from the 1994 conference, recognized the need for women and men to be informed about and have access to safe, effective, and affordable means of contraceptives and other health care services.

The 171 state representatives at the UN World Conference on Women in Beijing in 1995 reaffirmed that reproductive rights are human rights. The main action plan drafted at the meeting, the Beijing Platform for Action, provides the following definitions of reproductive rights:

- Reproductive health "is a state of complete physical, mental and social well-being and not merely the absence of disease or infirmity, in all matters relating to the reproductive system and to its functions and processes. Reproductive health therefore implies that people are able to have a satisfying and safe sex life and that they have the capability to reproduce and the freedom to decide if, when and how often to do so" (paragraph 94).
- Reproductive health care "is defined as the constellation of methods, techniques and services that contribute to reproductive health and well-being by preventing and solving reproductive health problems. It also includes sexual health, the purpose of which is the enhancement of life and personal relations, and not merely counseling and care related to reproduction and sexually transmitted diseases" (paragraph 94).
- Reproductive rights "embrace certain human rights that are already recognized in national laws, international human rights documents and other consensus documents. These rights rest on the recognition of the basic right of all couples and individuals to decide freely and responsibly the number, spacing and timing of their children and to have the information and means to do so, and the right to attain the highest standard of sexual and reproductive health" (paragraph 95).

With the momentum of the Cairo and Beijing meetings behind them, reproductive and sexual rights advocates increasingly framed their struggles in human rights terms. This strategy met the most success in Africa, where advocates succeeded in persuading the African Union—the regional body charged with promoting unity and solidarity among its fifty-three member nations—to include strong statements on reproductive and sexual rights in a new treaty on women's rights. The treaty, known as the "Protocol on the Rights of Women in Africa,"[6] which, in turn, supplemented the African Charter on Human and Peoples' Rights, went into effect in November 2005. Among many global "firsts," this was the first human rights treaty to include a specific provision on a woman's right to abortion when pregnancy resulted from sexual assault, rape, or incest; when continuation of the pregnancy endangered the life or health of the pregnant woman; and in cases of grave fetal defects incompatible with life. Among other measures, the treaty also called for the prohibition of harmful practices such as female genital cutting.[7] (For more information on women's health, see Chapter 5, "Women's Human Right to Health.")

Reproductive and sexual rights under international human rights law are considered to be a composite of several separate human rights, including:[8]

- the right to life, liberty, and security
- the right to health, reproductive health, and family planning
- the right to decide the number and spacing of children
- the right to consent to marriage and to equality in marriage
- the right to privacy
- the right to be free from discrimination
- the right to be free from practices that harm women and girls
- the right to not be subjected to torture or other cruel, inhuman, or degrading treatment or punishment.

Governments' obligations to respect these rights can be found in many international treaties, as well as in several consensus documents arising from international human rights conferences. As with other human rights, government has both an affirmative duty to promote reproductive and sexual rights and a negative duty not to interfere with these rights. For example, in order for women to have full reproductive rights, governments should provide a wide range of information and health services to all women to enable them to make informed decisions about their health.

One highly significant development has been the support for reproductive rights incorporated into the Human Rights Committee's "General Comment 28," on equality. This document represents the thinking of one of the most important international human rights bodies. Among other provisions related to reproductive health, "General Comment 28" notes that states may fail to respect women's privacy "where there is a requirement for the husband's authorization to make a decision in regard to sterilization . . . or where States impose a legal duty upon doctors and other health personnel to report cases of women who have undergone abortion. . . . Women's privacy may also be interfered with by private actors, such as employers who request a pregnancy test before hiring a woman."

Since the Cairo Conference on Population and Development, a number of countries have introduced laws to combat discrimination against pregnant women and also to ensure greater access to health care.[9] According to a survey of the UN Population Fund, nearly fifty countries have introduced such legislation since 1994.[10]

✠ Learning Activity 3: Taking Action for Reproductive Rights ✠

Objective   To define what women need for their reproductive health and strategies to achieve it

Time   60 minutes

Materials   Chart paper and markers or blackboard and chalk

1. Brainstorm
Ask participants to list all the factors a woman needs in order to achieve full reproductive health. List these and, when finished, read the full list

continues

✠ Learning Activity 3 Continued ✠

aloud. Ask participants which factors women in their community have access to and circle these.

Discuss the items not circled:

- What is the reason that each of these factors is not available?
- What happens to a woman when such needs are not met?

2. Prioritize

Consider the items not circled in Step 1 (i.e., the unmet needs). Read this list aloud and ask participants to rank each item on a scale of 1 to 5, giving the highest score to the most urgent needs.

3. Discuss

Compare your list with the list below.

For full reproductive health, all people need:

- information, education, and communication on reproductive health and reproductive freedom, sexually transmitted diseases (STDs), human sexuality, responsible parenthood, gender power relations, sexual abuse and incest, sexual differences, and the reproductive health effects of toxic substances
- safe, appropriate, available means of family planning, including a broad range of methods
- promotion of responsible sexual behavior, including increased condom use
- access to adequate medical care, including but not limited to gynecological care and maternal pre-, peri-, and post-natal care
- in countries where abortion is legal, access to safe and legal abortion and pre- and post-abortion care
- prevention and treatment of STDs, including but not limited to HIV/AIDS
- prevention of and appropriate treatment for infertility
- recognition and support of many kinds of family structures
- elimination of threats to women's reproduction, such as environmental and workplace hazards
- the inclusion of women's perspectives and women's organizations in the planning, implementation, research, and development of new reproductive methods and forms of family planning and prevention of sexually transmitted diseases, and in programs and policies for the provision of reproductive health care and sex education
- access to adequate employment, housing, health care, and education.

Keeping in mind the priorities from Step 2, ask these questions:

- What could women do to lobby the government for better information and services?

✠ Learning Activity 3 Continued ✠

- What could women's groups and other nongovernmental organizations (NGOs) do to meet these needs for full reproductive health?
- Can you begin a public education project or discuss family planning?
- Can you set up counseling, family planning, or other needed services?
- Could you conduct campaigns and demonstrations against unsafe contraceptive and coercive reproductive technology? Would this be safe in your country?
- Can you undertake research to document medical polices and practices that abuse the rights of women with respect to reproduction and sexuality?
- Which of these approaches are most likely to be feasible and successful in your community?

The World Health Organization Facts on Abortion

- Thirteen percent of maternal deaths worldwide are the result of unsafe abortions.[11]
- Thirty-eight percent of pregnancies each year are unplanned, and 22 percent result in abortions.[12]
- Of the 19 million unsafe abortions performed throughout the world each year, 18.5 million take place in developing countries.[13]
- Women aged 15–24 experience 59 percent of all unsafe abortions in Africa.[14]
- Complications from unsafe abortion procedures lead to the deaths of 68,000 women each year, primarily in developing countries.[15]
- The risk of death from unsafe abortion procedures in developing countries is estimated to be 1 in 270.[16]

Abortion

Many women's attempts to assert their claims to reproductive and sexual rights have centered on access to safe abortion. An unsafe abortion is "a procedure for terminating an unwanted pregnancy either by persons lacking the necessary skills or in an environment lacking the minimal medical standards, or both."[17] Where women are denied access to abortion, the death rate from illegal and self-induced abortions may increase. Lacking resources to pay for higher-quality care, women who are poor, those who live in isolated areas, and vulnerable women such as refugees and adolescents are most likely to rely on unsafe abortions without skilled providers. Unsafe abortions can cause complications including infections, infertility, and even death.[18]

According to a 2000 World Health Organization study, 19 million unsafe abortions take place each year. Almost all abortion-related deaths occur in developing countries, where unsafe abortions are most prevalent.[19] Health care providers have found several ways to reduce the number of deaths from abortion, including improving the quality of abortion services, where legal; better post-abortion care; legalization of the procedure; increased use and quality of contraception; and increased information and education about reproductive health.[20]

✠ Learning Activity 4 ✠
Conflicting Messages About Reproduction

Objective   To illustrate the pressure and conflicting messages women receive about reproduction
Time   30 minutes
Materials   None

1. Role-Play

Ask one volunteer to be the representative "woman." She can circulate and listen in on any of the groups while they plan their arguments. Divide the rest of the participants into six groups, which will prepare the arguments for each of the following roles:

- A government health official encouraging a large number of children
- A government health official advocating restricting the number of children
- A traditional authority opposing any form of family planning
- A feminist health worker encouraging family planning
- A government official offering food and medical support in return for sterilization
- A family elder encouraging the birth of many children as security for old age, a necessity for economic survival, and/or as a major component of a woman's social status.

Ask the representative "woman" to sit in the center while a spokesperson from each group tries to persuade her about how to use her fertility. She may ask questions at the end of each argument, but should not express any opinion.

2. Discuss

Discuss the role-play, considering some of these questions:

- How did it feel to be the "woman"? Do many women get such conflicting messages?
- What are some of the coercions or incitements offered the woman?
- What advice or support would the group like to give this woman?
- What might motivate the government actors?
- Imagine that these arguments were made to persuade a man to have a vasectomy; would they be persuasive? Why are so few population control programs directed toward men?
- Which argument is most likely to persuade a woman in your society? Why?
- Do women really get to make choices about their reproduction? Why or why not? What factors interfere with choice? Do women have the right to choose?

Reproduction, Sexuality, and Social Conventions

The 1995 World Conference on Women in Beijing recognized a woman's right to decision making in a broad range of areas, including choice of partner and the option of not marrying. In many societies, however, this right may be limited by a variety of factors, including prejudice against women who break traditional social codes. These conventions usually include certain ideals of what a woman is supposed to be (e.g., mother, caretaker of the house, dutiful wife).

This narrow vision of women is limiting for all women, inhibiting their ability to express and enjoy their sexuality, to choose their partners, to make decisions about whether and when to have children, to protect themselves from disease and violence, and to participate equally in all aspects of economic and social life. Because of such norms, women are often unaware that they can view experiences (especially those affecting their bodies)—and exercise choice in sexual and reproductive matters—in ways other than those into which they have been socialized.

Although limiting to all women, such conventional social expectations have a particularly harsh impact on women who are not married to men. These women face violence, harassment, and discrimination in all spheres of life, including family and work.

Reproductive Rights Versus Population Control

Global population growth is a cause for legitimate concern. Although fertility rates are falling in many regions, global population increased by 2 billion during the last quarter of the twentieth century, reaching 6 billion in 2000. Despite declining fertility rates, population is expected to increase by another 2 billion during the first quarter of the twenty-first century. Nearly all of this growth will occur in developing countries and will be concentrated among the poorest populations and in urban areas.[21] Fertility rates have a direct impact on the lives of women. Reductions in birth rates most often lead to the improvement of the overall status of women, and family planning can save the lives of mothers and their babies by reducing the burden of too many pregnancies. Moreover, high fertility rates in poorer countries are usually an indicator of high infant and child mortality; families feel they must have many children to guarantee at least one child's survival. High fertility rates also may be an indicator that families feel they must have many children to take care of the sick and elderly. Finally, high rates reflect poor education; for example, women lack access to information on how to safely regulate their own pregnancies and men do not learn about their reproductive roles and responsibilities.

Promoting reproductive and sexual rights implicitly includes promoting the means for regulation of fertility. However, this is not the same as advocating population control. The assumption behind promotion of reproductive and sexual rights is that individuals have the capacity to make decisions about their lives and that denying them this capacity can erode both their human dignity and their health, whereas advocates of population control assume that women cannot make such decisions and that government and/or international organizations must make them for women. When governments resort to coercive methods of population control, whether encouraging or discouraging reproduction, women need to respond by claiming their sexual and reproductive rights. They can demand programs that improve their well-being as well as enhance their ability to make decisions about choice in how to change fertility patterns, including guarantees of informed consent and proper counseling for all family planning methods, including their side effects.

Another difference between reproductive rights and population control concerns the focus of government programs. The population control policies of some governments have prejudicially targeted specific groups, especially minorities and the poor; they have also viewed women in the limited roles of procreators of children, devoted spouses, and mothers within the context of marriage, thus ignoring the sexual and reproductive health needs of other women such as childless, divorced, widowed, or abandoned women. Such policies thus violate the principle underlying reproductive and sexual rights, which are intended to apply to *all* women equally, regardless of their status or identity.

By contrast, policies based on reproductive and sexual rights prohibit coercive government laws, population politics, and adverse social customs. At the same time, reproductive and sexual rights policies promote affirmative efforts by governments and the international community to adopt social, economic, and cultural conditions that will protect women's self-determination, health, and livelihood.

Case Study: Reproductive Rights and Racism[22]

"Slovak healthcare providers throughout eastern Slovakia are complicit in the illegal and unethical practice of sterilizing Romani women. [There are] clear and consistent patterns of healthcare providers who disregarded the need for obtaining informed consent to sterilization and who failed to provide accurate and comprehensive reproductive health information to Romani patients, resulting in the violation of their human rights.

[In-depth interviews were conducted] with more than 140 women who were coercively or forcibly sterilized or have strong indications that they were forcibly sterilized. Approximately 110 of these women [were] sterilized or [have] strong indications that they were sterilized at the fall of communism. . . . In many of these cases, doctors and nurses furnished misleading or threatening information to Romani women in order to coerce them into providing last-minute authorizations for sterilizations that were performed when women were undergoing a cesarean delivery. . . . In other cases, Romani women were given no information about sterilization procedures nor were they informed that they would be sterilized *prior* to undergoing the procedure. . . . In a few cases, women under the age of 18 were forcibly sterilized without the authorization required by law from their legal guardians. Many other women were never even told that they had been sterilized. . . . It sometimes took these women years, if ever, to confirm that they had been sterilized."

The Politics of Population Control

Learning Activity 5: Blaming the Poor[23]

Objective To examine common attitudes toward the poor and overpopulation

Time 30 minutes

Materials None

1. Take a Position/Discuss

Draw or indicate a line at the front of the room. Explain that the left side represents strong disagreement, the center represents neutrality, and the right side represents strong agreement; when you read a statement, participants should take a position along the line according to whether they disagree or agree. After participants have taken their positions on a statement, ask those at opposite ends to discuss their differences. At the conclusion of the discussion, ask whether any participants wish to change their position and invite them to explain why.

Some sample statements follow:

- Overpopulation is the cause of poverty.
- Poor people have too many children. As a result, they need too much food and too many resources.
- The poor have too many children because they are illiterate.
- The world's problems arise because poor people are too many, and they multiply at an alarming and uncontrolled rate.
- Poor people stay poor because they mindlessly have children that they cannot afford.

2. Discuss

Ask these questions about attitudes toward the poor and overpopulation:

- What other factors contribute to overpopulation?
- Why would authorities want to blame the poor? Why would ordinary people?
- What kinds of policies are authorities who blame the poor likely to support?
- Who or what do you think is responsible for overpopulation?

The Needs of Young People

One of the main points of debate at the 1994 International Conference on Population and Development in Cairo concerned adolescents. Some governments simply refused to acknowledge that adolescents engage in sexual relationships and have their own reproductive and sexual health care needs. The conference recognized that male behavior and attitudes must change if the reproductive needs of all people are to be met.

Among the principal barriers to the promotion of good adolescent health is a lack of effective sex education, particularly a scarcity of information about family planning and sexually transmitted diseases for girls and boys. One consequence is that many young people are not treated for sexually transmitted diseases, some of which can lead to infertility or even death.

Another consequence is that HIV/AIDS has become a disease of young people, with young adults aged 15–24 accounting for half of the 5 million new cases of HIV infection worldwide each year. Yet young people often lack the information, skills, and services needed to protect themselves from HIV infection. Providing these is crucial to turning back the epidemic. An estimated 6,000 youth a day become infected with HIV/AIDS (1 every fourteen seconds), the majority of them young women. At the end of 2001, an estimated 11.8 million young people aged 15–24 were living with HIV/AIDS—one-third of the global total of people living with HIV/AIDS. Only a small percentage of these young people know they are HIV-positive.[24]

Adolescent girls have limited power to refuse sex or negotiate condom use, and in many countries married adolescent girls are at greater risk for HIV/AIDS than unmarried girls their age. Many girls do not understand the health dangers of early pregnancy, which can lead to permanent organ damage, infertility, and even maternal mortality, as well as low birthweight and survival rates for their babies. And, as noted, many girls are vulnerable because they are not in a position to refuse sexual advances, particularly those of older men.

Lack of information on sexual health can have a particularly devastating impact on gay, lesbian, bisexual, and transgendered adolescents. Suicide rates and severe depression are highest among this population, frequently because the boy or girl feels all alone with no way out.

Even when available, sex education is too often limited to information on the physiology of reproduction. Family planning is seldom mentioned, and little mention is made of boys' responsibility for preventing pregnancy. HIV is seldom addressed or is treated as a disease of some outside group of people, despite the fact that women's rates of HIV infection are rising in all parts of the world. The primary concern of most young people is not pregnancy but love, courting, and sexuality. Health care experts have found that to be effective, sex education programs need to address young peoples' real concerns and anxieties and promote a positive and healthy sexual life—one that emphasizes self-determination, equal communication between partners, and shared responsibility for birth control.

Designed principally for the adult population and usually ignoring adolescent sexual activity, health services often fail to meet the needs of young people. In particular, many young people avoid seeking sexual and reproductive health care because they fear exposure owing to lack of confidentiality on the part of health professionals. (See also Chapter 4, "The Human Rights of Young Women and Girls.")

Information on Adolescence and Reproductive Health[25]

- Adolescents are between the ages of 10 and 19 and make up 20 percent of the world's population.
- Adolescents bear about 10 percent of the children in the world. About 14 million adolescent girls give birth each year.
- In developing countries 1–4 million adolescent girls have illegal, and usually dangerous, abortions each year.
- In 1998, 30 million people were diagnosed with HIV/AIDS; at least one-third of these were between 10 and 24 years old. When this statistic was obtained, young people were contracting AIDS at a rate of 2.6 million per year, or 5 every minutes.

Learning Activity 6: Sex Education for Whom?

Objective To examine the need for information about sexuality and reproduction, and to evaluate the quality of information available to girls
Time 60 minutes
Materials Slips of paper, three baskets or bags

1. Remember
Give participants three slips of paper each. Ask them to write on the first a question or misunderstanding they had about sexuality or reproduction as a child; on the second, a similar question from adolescence; and on the third, a question from the present. Explain that all questions are anonymous. Gather the finished slips into the three different baskets or bags.

Invite a participant to draw a slip from the "childhood" basket and read it aloud. Based on this example, request input from other participants about how they learned such information as children. List these sources of information. Read at least three slips from each basket or bag.

Ask these questions regarding the sources of information about sex:

- What was the source?
- Was the information accurate and complete?
- What values, if any, did the information source emphasize?
- Was the information related to women's human rights? Could it be? Should it be?

2. Discuss
Ask these questions about sex education:

- How do young people in your community learn about reproduction and sexuality?
- Do they receive any information from schools, health care centers, and/or other social institutions?
- Is the information from these sources accurate and complete?

continues

✠ Learning Activity 6 Continued ✠

- What values do these sources of information emphasize?
- Does the information they receive mention women's human rights? Should it?
- How would you revise the information and materials about sexuality that are currently available?
- If no educational materials exist in your community on reproductive and sexual rights, would you want to create some?
- How would you evaluate the information on sexuality and reproduction available in your youth? Available today?
- Where improved information is needed, who is or could be acting for change? Who opposes change?
- If you had the resources to publish anything for girls on reproduction and sexuality, what would you do?
- Where would you distribute this publication? How?
- Would you also offer courses to teach information in your publication?
- Would parents be permitted to forbid their children from receiving materials?

Actions to Promote Reproductive and Sexual Rights

- *Ireland, Poland, and Portugal.* Women on Waves, a Dutch organization whose mission is to "prevent unwanted pregnancy and unsafe abortions throughout the world," provides safe reproductive health services to women on a ship that sails to countries where abortion is illegal. On ocean waters, such services as nonsurgical abortions, contraception, and counseling are fully legal. Thus far, the organization has operated off the coasts of Ireland and Poland. In 2004, it was blocked from entering Portuguese waters,[26] but on April 10, 2007, the Portuguese president ratified a law permitting abortion until the tenth week of pregnancy.[27]
- *Mexico.* In 2007, one year after Colombia legalized abortion, abortion was declared legal in Mexico City—the capital of the world's second-largest Roman Catholic country.[28]
- *Nepal.* Legal experts met for the first time in August 2004 "to look for remedies to human rights violations in women's reproductive health."[29] High-profile officials discussed such wide-ranging issues as gender inequality, child marriage, and sexual violence.[30]
- *Japan.* For more than thirty years, oral contraceptives were illegal in Japan. However, thanks in part to the persistent media advocacy of Midori Ashida and her organization, the Women's Center for Sexuality and Health in Tokyo, oral contraception was legalized in June 1999.[31]
- *United States.* When the Bush administration withheld money from the United Nations Population Fund (UNFPA) for the third year in a row, Jane Roberts and Lois Abraham decided to get involved. They founded an organization, 34 Million Friends for the UNFPA, which is dedicated to raising the amount of money for the UNFPA that the Bush administration blocked—$34 million—by asking 34 million Americans to donate $1.00 each.[32]

Actions to Promote Reproductive and Sexual Rights Continued

Women in the United States and worldwide have participated in similar fundraisers and other political actions to demonstrate against other U.S. policies such as the policy that "restricts foreign non-governmental organizations (NGOs) that receive U.S. family planning funds from using their own, non-U.S. funds to provide legal abortion services, lobby their own governments for abortion reform laws, or even provide accurate medical counseling or referrals regarding abortion."[33] This policy inspired the March for Women's Lives in Washington, DC, on April 25, 2004, which opposed the policy.[34] The march drew throngs of protesters numbering from 800,000[35] (according to police sources) to more than 1 million marchers from at least sixty different countries.[36]

Remembering Core Concepts

✠ Learning Activity 7 ✠
Speaking Out for Women's Reproductive and Sexual Rights

Objectives To examine women's right to reproduction and sexuality in the community and consider how to take action to improve it
Time 60+ minutes
Materials Chart paper and markers

1. Brainstorm
Ask participants to list reproduction- and sexuality-related problems faced by women in their community. Then, after dividing them into small groups, ask them to choose a problem on which they wish to concentrate.

2. Discuss/Plan
Ask each group to prepare a five-minute presentation to a "panel of community leaders" on their problem. Each presentation should:

- describe the problem, identifying the group(s) of women it impacts and, if possible, the cause(s) of the problem
- relate the problem to women's human rights
- clarify how the problem affects women's lives
- show how addressing the problem can improve their lives
- propose specific actions that should be taken to address the problem
- show how members of the community can get involved in addressing the problem.

Ask each group to choose a spokesperson to make the presentation and a "community leader" to serve on the panel. While the groups plan their presentations, the panel of leaders meets to decide on their roles, representing a variety of differing but typical attitudes within the community leadership.

continues

Learning Activity 7 Continued

3. Present/Role-Play

The spokesperson from each group makes a presentation, and members of the panel listen and respond, asking questions and offering comments, objections, or suggestions in keeping with their chosen roles.

4. Discuss

After the presentations and role-play, discuss these questions:

- How did the spokespersons feel when presenting the problem?
- How did the "community leaders" respond to the presentation? What attitudes in the community were they representing?
- How did the audience, composed of the rest of the group, respond to the presentations?
- Did any spokesperson discuss the problem as a human rights violation? Did putting the problem in a human rights context strengthen the argument? Why or why not?
- Are these ideas for improving women's human rights to healthy reproduction and sexuality feasible in your community? Why or why not?

5. Conclude

Challenge the participants by asking them to evaluate their knowledge of the problem and the inclusiveness of their perspective:

- How did you obtain your information about the reproduction- and sexuality-related issues facing women in your community? Was it accurate and complete? If not, what additional information do you need and how can you obtain it?
- Did you personally consult women about the problem and how it affects them? About actions that could improve the problem?
- Why is it important in real-life human rights advocacy to include the active participation of those directly involved and affected?
- How can you apply the example of this exercise to planning and implementing advocacy for women in your community?

Notes

1. Population Action International, "Young People's Reproductive Health Needs Neglected," April 26, 2002, Washington, DC, available online at http://www.population action.org/news/press/news_042302_Youth.htm.

2. World Health Organization, "Facts and Figures from the World Health Report 2005," in *The World Health Report World Health Day 2005: Make Every Mother and Child Count*, available online at http://www.who.int/whr/2005/media_centre/facts_en.pdf.

3. Ibid.

4. Ibid.

5. Protocol to the African Charter on Human and Peoples' Rights on the Rights of Women in Africa, 2nd Ordinary Session, Assembly of the Union, adopted July 11, 2003.

6. Ibid.

7. "Protocol on the Rights of Women in Africa," *Equality Now*, available online at http://www.equalitynow.org/english/campaigns/african-protocol/african-protocol_en.html.

8. Center for Reproductive Law and Policy, *Reproductive Rights are Human Rights* (June 2003), available online at http://www.crlp.org.

9. United Nations Population Fund, *State of World Population 2004: Reproductive Health and Family Planning* (2004), p. 38, available online at http://www.unfpa.org.

10. Center for Reproductive Rights, *Surviving Pregnancy and Childbirth: An International Human Right* (December 2003), p. 11, available online at http://www.reproductiverights.org/pdf/pub_bp_survivingpregnancy.pdf. See also "Key Actions for the Further Implementation of the Programme of Action of Special Session," New York, June 30–July 2, 1999, paragraph 62(b), UN Doc. A/S-21/5/Add.1 (1999), available online at http://www.unfpa.org/icpd.

11. Center for Reproductive Rights, *Surviving Pregnancy and Childbirth: An International Human Right* (December 2003), p. 10, available online at http://www.reproductiverights.org.

12. Alan Guttmacher Institute, *Sharing Responsibility: Women, Society, and Abortion Worldwide* (1999), p. 42, available online at http://agi-usa.org/pubs/sharing.pdf.

13. Elisabeth Ahman and Iqbal Shah, *Unsafe Abortion: Global and Regional Estimates of the Incidence of Unsafe Abortion and Associated Mortality in 2000*, 4th ed. (Abstract) (World Health Organization, 2001), p. 9, available online at http://www.who.int/reproductive-health/.

14. Ibid.

15. Ibid.

16. Ibid.

17. World Health Organization, "Safe Abortion: Technical and Policy Guidance for Health Systems" (2003), available online at http://www.who.int/reproductive-health/publications/safe_abortion/safe_abortion.pdf.

18. Ibid.

19. Elisabeth Ahman and Iqbal Shah, *Global and Regional Estimates of the Incidence of Unsafe Abortion and Associated Mortality in 2000*, 4th ed. (Geneva: World Health Organization, 2004).

20. World Health Organization, "Safe Abortion"; Ahman and Shah, *Unsafe Abortion.*

21. United Nations Population Fund, "Population and Demographic Dynamics: World Population Still Growing," available online at http://www.unfpa.org/pds/.

22. "Body and Soul: Forced Sterilization and Other Assaults on Roma Reproductive Freedom in Slovakia," Center for Reproductive Rights (2003), pp. 14–45, available online at http://www.reproductiverights.org.

23. Adapted from *Na Shariram Nadhi: My Body Is Mine*, edited by Dr. Mira Sadgopal (Bombay: Sabala and Kranti, 1995), p. 47.

24. United Nations Population Fund, "State of the World Population 2003," available online at http://www.unfpa.org/swp/2003/english/ch3/index.htm.

25. Center for Reproductive Rights, "Ensuring the Reproductive Rights of Adolescents," available online at http://www.reproductiverights.org/.

26. Feminist Majority Foundation, "Women on Waves Leaves for Portugal," August 23, 2004, available online at http://www.feminist.org/.

27. Women on Waves Press Release, "'Yes' to Abortion!" April 10, 2007, Amsterdam, available online at http://www.womenonwaves.org/article-1020.1745-en.html.

28. Ibid.

29. Center for Reproductive Rights, "Nepalese Legal Experts Seek to Remedy Reproductive Health Violation," August 3, 2004, available online at http://www.crlp.org.

30. Ibid.

31. Midori Ashida, founder, Women's Coalition for Sexuality and Health, Tokyo, at Annual Japan Studies Association of Canada Conference October 4–6, 2002, Calgary, Alberta. p. 1, Haskayne School of Business, University of Calgary Press Release, available online at http://www.haskayne.ucalgary.ca/news/media/2002/jsac2002pressrelease.pdf#search='women's%20activism%20Japan%20oral%20contraceptives.

32. "34 Million Friends of the UNFPA," available online at http://www.unfpa.org/support/friends/34million.htm. (See also "34 Million Friends of UNFPA homepage: www.34millionfriends.org.)

33. Center for Reproductive Rights, "The Bush Global Gag Rule: Endangering Women's Health, Free Speech, and Democracy" (July 2003), available online at http://www.reproductiverights.org/.

34. Planned Parenthood Federation of America, "More Than a Million March in Washington for Reproductive Rights," April 25, 2004, available online at http://www.plannedparenthood.org/.

35. Associated Press, "Abortion-Rights Supporters Rally in Washington: Marchers Take Aim at President Bush's policies," April, 25, 2004.

36. Ibid.

7

Women's Human Right to Freedom from Violence

Everyone has the right to life, liberty and security of person.
—Universal Declaration of Human Rights, Article 3

No one shall be subjected to torture or to cruel, inhuman or degrading treatment or punishment.
—Universal Declaration of Human Rights, Article 5

Objectives

The learning activities and background information contained in this chapter will enable participants to work toward the following objectives:

- Define and identify various forms of violence against women.
- Recognize that all forms of violence against women are human rights violations whether they occur in armed conflict, on the streets, in the home, in public, in the workplace, or in custody, prison, or other institutional settings.
- Identify the role of governments, United Nations human rights bodies, community leaders, the media, and individual women in addressing and eliminating violence against women.
- Explore the effect of armed conflict on women and identify ways to respond to violence against women in conflict situations.
- Develop ways to prevent violence against women in your community.
- Remember core concepts.

Getting Started: Recognizing Violence Against Women

Women's activism to gain legal recognition of rights and to have such laws enforced has been particularly effective in the area of violence against women. Increasing numbers of international courts, national legislation, and local ordinances are acknowledging violence against women as a crime, just as more community groups and institutions are working to change attitudes and behaviors, and more women are coming to recognize their own right to freedom from violence. Yet despite these considerable gains, violence against women and girls continues.

Much of this violence is committed in the private sphere of households. Many forms of violence are condoned by families and indirectly sanctioned by state failure to recognize such acts as criminal. And even when states do legislate against domestic violence, law enforcement may be selective or nonexistent.

One of the most extreme forms of violence against women—*gendercide* or *womancide*—involves violent behavior leading to the death of women and girls.[1] And the phenomenon of *female infanticide* has created lopsided demographics in some parts of the world, as shown in Table 7.1. Advocates point out that, around the world, a healthy female fetus is far more likely to be aborted than a male. In Maharashtra, India, for example, a study found that of 8,000 amniocentesis tests that resulted in abortion only 1 involved a male fetus.[2] As babies, girls may be killed or malnourished because the society in which they were born does not value girls as much as boys. In many communities, girls are forced into marriage and childbearing before their bodies are fully developed and, as a result, can suffer severe physical injury.[3] As women and girls, they may experience rape, domestic violence, and sexual harassment. Violence during pregnancy has been identified as a major reason for miscarriage and low-birthweight children.

Women's human rights to health are violated by practices such as female genital cutting (FGC), a traditional practice of some communities (see Table 7.2). Although there are laws and policies banning the practice helping to end FGC, more comprehensive efforts are also needed. These include:

- integrating eradication of FGC into a range of social and economic development initiatives that focus on women's empowerment
- developing alternative rituals to substitute for traditional cutting ceremonies
- empowering women through participatory decision making to collectively decide about FGC and to negotiate community support

Table 7.1 Number of Women to 100 Men in the Countries Where There Are 95 or Fewer Women per 100 Men, 2005

Country	Women per 100 Men
United Arab Emirates	47
Qatar	48
Kuwait	67
Oman	78
Bahrain	76
Saudi Arabia	85
Palau	89
Jordan	92
Brunei Darussalam	93
Pakistan	94
Afghanistan	94
India	95
China	95
Côte d'Ivoire	95

Source: United Nations, 2005 http://unstats.un.org/unsd/demographic/products/indwm/ww2005/tab1a.htm.

Table 7.2   UNICEF 2005: Occurrence of Female Genital Cutting

Country	Percentage
Benin (2001)	16.8
Burkina Faso (2003)	76.6
Cameroon (2004)	1.4
Central African Republic (2000)	35.9
Chad (2000)	44.9
Côte d'Ivoire (1998–1999)	44.5
Egypt (2003)	97.0
Eritrea (2001–2002)	88.7
Ethiopia (2000)	79.9
Ghana (2003)	5.4
Guinea (1999)	98.6
Kenya (2003)	32.2
Mali (2001)	91.6
Mauritania (2000–2001)	71.3
Niger (1998)	4.5
Nigeria (2003)	19.0
Senegal (2005)	28.2
Sudan (north) (2000)	90.0
United Republic of Tanzania (1996)	17.7
Yemen (1997)	22.6

Source: UNICEF, "Female Genital Mutilation/Cutting, A Statistical Exploration, 2005, http://www.unicef.org/publications/files/FGM-C_final_10_October.pdf.

- using an intensive social marketing approach to involve community stakeholders in evaluating the costs and benefits of continuing or abandoning FGC
- identifying as role models individuals who have challenged or "deviated" from conventional societal expectations and explored successful alternatives to cultural norms, beliefs, or perceptions about their communities[4]
- involving men in the effort to eradicate FGC.

The occurrence of FGC varies within countries. In different areas of Kenya, for example, FGC varies from 4 percent to 99 percent, depending on the ethnicity of the communities. Moreover, UNICEF has found an overall trend toward ending the practice of FGC by generation. In 2005, for example, 97 percent of women with daughters in Egypt reported that they themselves had undergone FGC, but only 47 percent reported that their daughters had experienced the procedure.[5] In 2007, the Egyptian health ministry banned the practice altogether.[6]

Support for FGC varies across regions; see Table 7.3 for statistics on women who believe FGC should continue. It also varies over time. For example, in Egypt, where more than 70 percent of women have undergone FGC, 81.6 percent of women believed in 1995 that FGC should continue. This number decreased steadily to 75.3 percent in 2000 and to 71.1 percent in 2003.[7]

Death by Marriage

Dowry-related abuse is also common in some countries, where a woman may be harmed or even killed when her family cannot meet her husband's demands for money and goods. In India, where this practice is commonly noted, an average

Table 7.3   Percentages of Women 15–49 Who Believe FGC Should Continue

Country	Percentage
Benin (2001)	4.8
Burkina Faso (2003)	17.1
Central Africa Republic (2000)	21.6
Côte d'Ivoire (1998)	30.0
Egypt (2003)	71.1
Eritrea (2001–2002)	48.8
Ethiopia (2000)	59.7
Guinea (1999)	68.3
Kenya (1998)	19.8
Mali (2001)	80.3
Mauritania (2000–2001)	59.4
Niger (1998)	9.0
Nigeria (2003)	11.1
Sudan (North) (1990)	78.5
Yemen (1997)	20.8

of five women per day are burned for dowry-related reasons. Many other incidents go unreported.[8]

Structural Violence

The poverty that so many women experience all over the world is a form of structural violence,[9] the physical and psychological harm that results from exploitive and unjust social, political, and economic systems.[10] In other words, the conditions of poverty—including lack of health care and inadequate food and nutrition—may perpetuate an oppressive system of patriarchy and discrimination. Since women and children are more likely to be poor—women constitute 70 percent of the poorest people in the world, living on less than one dollar per day[11]—they are more likely to be victims of such structural violence.

Women are also victims of violence in places where the government or party harasses, arrests, beats, or tortures members of opposition or minority groups. In prisons and other custodial or institutional settings such as hospitals, orphanages, and foster homes, women and girls confront particular forms of mistreatment based at least partly on their sex.

According to surveys throughout the world, at least one out of every three women has been abused in her lifetime, including being beaten or coerced into sex.[12] The recommendations agreed upon at the 1995 UN Fourth World Conference on Women acknowledge: "Violence against women both violates and impairs or nullifies the enjoyment by women of their human rights and fundamental freedoms."[13] The widespread violence against women serves as an impediment to employment, political engagement, and civil society activism. In developing countries alone, approximately 5 percent of working time lost by women was due to disability or sickness resulting from gender-based violence.[14] Moreover, violence is sometimes used to discourage the use of family planning and reproductive rights. It can also prevent women's access to education and to the full development of personal potential.

Examples of Different Types of Violence Against Women Around the World

- Worldwide, nearly one woman in four experiences sexual violence at the hands of a partner during her lifetime, and as many as one-third of all girls are forced into their first sexual experience.[15]
- In the United States, a woman is battered every fifteen seconds. Moreover, 700,000 women are raped every year.[16]
- Each year in Bangladesh, about 200 women are the victims of "acid-throwing," usually perpetrated by a husband, suitor, or other male relative. The acid causes permanent and painful injuries, including loss of eyesight or disfigurement such as joining chin to chest or lips to nose.[17]
- In the United Kingdom, over 2,000 cases of physical and/or sexual abuse against female domestic workers were reported between 1987 and 1998. Most were noncitizens who feared that employers would alert the authorities to their immigration status.[18]
- The Indian government issued a statement that 6,929 women died in 1998 in connection with dowry demands.[19]
- A Chinese crackdown on human trafficking in 2000 led to the rescue of more than 10,000 women and children in just one month. It was reported that these women were to be sold into prostitution and forced marriage.[20]
- Up to 70 percent of female murder victims are killed by their male partners.[21]

✠ Learning Activity 1: Defining Violence Against Women ✠

Objectives	To identify the elements that constitute violence against women and apply the UN definition of violence against women to women's real-life experiences
Time	60 minutes
Materials	Chart paper and markers, copies of or a prepared chart containing Article 1 (extract) and Article 2 (extract) of the United Nations Declaration on the Elimination of Violence Against Women (see the box at the end of this section for the text), stories from the media about violence against women (optional)

1. List

Divide participants into small groups and ask them to list on chart paper different types of violence against women. Star those examples that occur in their community.

2. Define

Ask the groups to use their list of examples as a basis for the following:

- Next to each example on the list write the principal human rights that are violated by this act of violence.
- At the bottom of the list write a definition of violence against women.

Ask each small group to present its chart and definition.

continues

Learning Activity 1 Continued

3. Compare

Post a chart or pass out copies containing the text of Article 1 and 2 of the United Nations Declaration on the Elimination of Violence Against Women. Ask participants to compare this definition with the types of violence against women listed in Step 1.

Do their examples include the following:

- physical harm or suffering?
- sexual harm or suffering?
- psychological harm or suffering?
- threats of physical, sexual, or psychological harm or suffering?
- coercion?
- arbitrary deprivation of liberty?
- acts in both public and private life?
- violence occurring within the family?
- violence occurring within the general community?
- violence perpetuated or condoned by the state?

4. Discuss

- What is the UN definition of violence against women? Do you agree with the UN definition?
- Are there parts of the participants' definition they would wish to see added to the UN definition?
- Based on the UN definition, are there further examples of violence to add to the original list?
- Are there types of violence against women that are not covered in the UN definition?
- How do you personally define freedom from violence?

Alternative: As part of a "gallery walk" exercise, provide newspapers and magazines to participants and ask them to find and cut out accounts of violence against women. Provide a bulletin board or paper on which to mount these stories, along with a list of the human rights involved and any personal comments the participants would like to make.

Ask the participants to walk around and read the stories, thinking about whether the UN definition applies and whether the women in the stories could or could not expect justice if that incident occurred in the participants' community. Discuss reactions to the stories.

> ## United Nations Declaration on the Elimination of Violence Against Women
>
> **Article 1**
>
> For the purposes of this Declaration, the term "violence against women" means any act of gender-based violence that results in, or is likely to result in, physical, sexual or psychological harm or suffering to women, including threats of such acts, coercion or arbitrary deprivation of liberty, whether occurring in public or in private life.
>
> **Article 2**
>
> Violence against women shall be understood to encompass, but not be limited to, the following:
>
> (a) Physical, sexual and psychological violence occurring in the family, including battering, sexual abuse of female children in the household, dowry-related violence, marital rape, female genital mutilation and other traditional practices harmful to women, nonspousal violence and violence related to exploitation;
>
> (b) Physical, sexual and psychological violence occurring within the general community, including rape, sexual abuse, sexual harassment, and intimidation at work, in educational institutions and elsewhere, trafficking in women and forced prostitution;
>
> (c) Physical, sexual and psychological violence perpetrated or condoned by the State, wherever it occurs.
>
> **Article 3**
>
> Women are entitled to the equal enjoyment and protection of all human rights and fundamental freedoms in the political, economic, social, cultural, civil or any other field. These rights include, inter alia:
>
> (a) The right to life;
> (b) The right to equality;
> (c) The right to liberty and security of person;
> (d) The right to equal protection under the law;
> (e) The right to be free from all forms of discrimination;
> (f) The right to the highest standard attainable of physical and mental health;
> (g) The right to just and favorable conditions of work;
> (h) The right not to be subjected to torture, or other cruel, inhuman or degrading treatment or punishment.

Women in Prison

International human rights law has long devoted attention to the treatment of prisoners. However, both human rights groups and prison authorities assume that the typical prisoner is male. Nearly everywhere men are incarcerated at a far higher rate than women. However, women prisoners do exist, often in substantial numbers, and in most parts of the world women are the fastest-growing category of the prison population. A narrow focus on the male prisoner ignores and neglects the specific concerns of women prisoners.

Most women in prison are poor or working class and/or members of a caste, ethnic, or racial group that has less power in society. Research has shown that a large percentage of women in prison have been victims of sexual abuse and/or other forms of violence in the family. In a 1999 report the U.S. Department of Justice noted that almost 60 percent of women in state prisons were subjected to physical or sexual abuse before incarceration (compared to 16 percent of men), two out of five women in federal facilities or on probation had had abusive experiences, and more than a quarter of women in state prisons had been molested before age 18.[22] And a 1998 study showed that 82 percent of women inmates in Scotland had been emotionally or physically abused during their lives, often on a daily basis, with 47 percent of the cases involving sexual abuse by a father, a male relative, or a guardian.[23]

Some women are in prison precisely because they attempted to stop their partner, boyfriend, or husband from continuing to harm them or their children.[24]

But no matter what brings them to prison, female prisoners, like male prisoners, have human rights that must be respected. International standards require states to treat prisoners humanely—that is, to ensure that they are free from torture or other cruel, inhumane, and degrading treatment or punishment; to provide them with adequate living conditions; and to avoid discriminating against prisoners on the basis of sex or any other grounds.

Standards set out in the UN Standard Minimum Rules for the Treatment of Prisoners require female prisoners to be attended and supervised only by female officers. However, this rule is often ignored. In the United States, for example, 41 percent of guards in women's correctional facilities are male.[25] Moreover, records show that U.S. correctional officials have subjected female inmates to humiliation and violence: rape, sexual extortion and assault, groping during body searches, observation while bathing or using the toilet, and retaliation, often brutal, against those who dare to report them.[26] Particularly targeted for violence and sexual abuse are women who are lesbians and other minorities who may not fit the norm.

International Standards on Prisons

International standards on the rights of prisoners can be found in these documents:

- The Universal Declaration of Human Rights (1949)
- The United Nations Standard of Minimum Rules for the Treatment of Prisoners (1955)
- The International Covenant on Civil and Political Rights (1966)
- The Convention Against Torture and Other Cruel, Inhumane or Degrading Treatment or Punishment (1984)
- The United Nations Standard Minimum Rules for the Administration of Juvenile Justice (also known as the "Beijing Rules") (1985)
- The United Nations Body of Principles for the Protection of All Persons Under Any Form of Detention or Imprisonment (1988)
- The UN Basic Principles for the Treatment of Prisoners (1990)

Regional conventions on human rights also provide for the rights of prisoners, and various international documents address specific issues facing prisoners, such as the spread of HIV/AIDS in prisons, the treatment of juvenile delinquents, and the protection of prisoners with mental illnesses or on hunger strikes. None of these international documents deals specifically, however, with the rights of imprisoned women.

> **International Standards on Prisons Continued**
>
> The rights of prisoners have not received adequate attention from the international women's community. The Convention on the Elimination of Violence Against Women (CEDAW) does not include women prisoners, and former prisoners or their advocates are rarely invited to speak at women's meetings or meetings dealing with women's issues. As a result, women prisoners remain nearly invisible and their voices remain largely unheard.

International Recognition

The United Nations first began addressing the problem of violence against women at its world conferences on women sponsored in Copenhagen, Nairobi, and Beijing in 1980, 1985, and 1995, respectively. Until that time, women's rights were not framed in terms of "human rights." All subsequent UN recognition of violence against women as a human rights concern has come as a consequence of significant pressure exerted by women's NGOs on governments as well as on international and regional human rights systems. The international recognition of violence against women as a human rights issue is a dynamic example of the importance both of people's advocacy to have their rights recognized and of the evolution of laws and attitudes over time.

Remarkably, CEDAW,[27] which most directly addresses women's rights issues, makes no mention whatsoever of violence against women. This omission reflects the prevailing invisibility of the issue at the time of CEDAW's drafting in 1979. However, recognition of violence against women as a human rights violation has steadily evolved since then, primarily due to continuous advocacy by women worldwide:

- In 1992, the Committee on the Elimination of All Forms of Discrimination Against Women, the body responsible for monitoring the implementation of CEDAW, reaffirmed that both public violence and private violence against women are human rights violations. The Committee's General Recommendation 19 establishes the links between violence against women and gender discrimination: "Violence against women is both a consequence of systematic discrimination against women in public and private life, and a means by which constraints on women's rights are reinforced. Women are vulnerable because of disabilities imposed on them in economic, social, cultural, civil and political life and violence impairs the extent to which they are able to exercise de jure rights."[28]
- The inclusion of public and private violence against women in the Vienna Declaration and Programme of Action of the 1993 World Conference on Human Rights was a result of a global campaign involving more than 800 women's groups worldwide.
- In 1993, the United Nations General Assembly adopted a Declaration on the Elimination of Violence Against Women. While this instrument is not legally binding on states, it does, however, indicate the recognition by the United Nations of violence against women as an important human rights issue and spells out areas of violence that governments should address.

- In 1994, a United Nations Special Rapporteur on Violence Against Women was appointed by the Commission on Human Rights with the authority to examine the underlying causes and consequences of abuse and to serve as a special investigator in individual cases. The first Special Rapporteur was Radhika Coomaraswamy of Sri Lanka, who was succeeded in 2003 by Yakin Ertürk of Turkey. The reports of this special investigator are presented each year to the Commission on Human Rights.

- The establishment of an International Criminal Tribunal for the Former Yugoslavia (ICTY) in 1994 was specifically empowered to investigate and prosecute rape as a crime against humanity. It broke new ground in recognizing war crimes against women. Trials were begun in 1995 and 1996 and included the charge of rape and other forms of sexual violence.

- In 1995, the Inter-American Convention on the Prevention, Punishment and Eradication of Violence Against Women went into effect, allowing women victims of violence in the Americas to have recourse to the existing regional mechanisms in the Americas' system: the Inter-American Court and the Inter-American Commission on Human Rights, as well as an Inter-American Commission for Women. An earlier declaration of the Council of Europe—the 1991 Solemn Declaration on the Elimination of Sexual Violence—similarly saw violence against women as a human rights violation.

- In 1995, the Beijing Platform for Action recognized violence against women as a key area of concern and called on governments to "cooperate with and assist the Special Rapporteur on Violence Against Women in the performance of her mandate and furnish all information requested."[29] Women can then encourage and assist their governments to give information about violence against women to the Special Rapporteur as well as request her to investigate violations in their countries.

- In 1998, the International Criminal Tribunal for Rwanda ruled that systematic rape, used as a tool of war in Rwanda, constituted both a crime against humanity and genocide. This ruling was critical in recognizing that rape is not simply a by-product of war but, indeed, is often used systematically as a weapon of war.[30]

- The Rome Statute of the International Criminal Court, which was adopted in 1998 and entered into force in 2002, specifically recognizes the status of violence against women as a war crime. In particular, the Statute defines the following as crimes against humanity: "Rape, sexual slavery, enforced prostitution, forced pregnancy, enforced sterilization, or any other form of sexual violence of comparable gravity . . . when committed as part of a widespread or systematic attack directed against any civilian population, with knowledge of the attack."[31]

- In 2005, the "Protocol to the African Charter on Human and Peoples' Rights on the Rights of Women in Africa"[32] entered into force, marking a major milestone in the protection of women's rights in Africa and internationally. The Protocol recognizes the reproductive right to abortion when pregnancy results from rape or incest or if the mother's health is endangered. It also calls for a ban on female genital cutting and recognizes rights of vulnerable groups of women, including widows, the elderly, the marginalized, and women in detention.[33]

These international advances have been accompanied by national legislative efforts. (Human rights advocates have had particular success in the area of FGC.) See Table 7.4 for a listing of such legislation.

Table 7.4   National Legislative Efforts to Eliminate Female Genital Cutting as of March 2007

African Nations
  Benin
  Burkina Faso
  Central African Republic
  Chad
  Côte d'Ivoire
  Djibouti
  Egypt
  Ethiopia
  Ghana
  Guinea
  Kenya
  Niger
  Nigeria
  Senegal
  South Africa
  Tanzania
  Togo
Industrialized Nations
  Australia
  Belgium
  Canada
  Cyprus
  Denmark
  Italy
  New Zealand
  Norway
  Spain
  Sweden
  United Kingdom
  United States

Source: Center for Reproductive Rights, Female Genital Mutilation (FGM): Legal Prohibitions Worldwide Factsheet, National Efforts to Eliminate FGM, March 2007.

✠ Learning Activity 2 ✠
The Cycle of Recognition and Enforcement of Rights

Objectives   To recognize the importance of advocacy to both the recognition and the enforcement of rights
Time   30 minutes
Materials   Chart paper and markers

1. Introduce
Review the evolution of violence against women from nonrecognition to an established human rights violation, as outlined in the above section headed "International Recognition." Point out how each successive step refined and expanded the definition of violence against women. Emphasize the role of women themselves in making this violation not only visible but also recognized by the international community.

continues

⌘ Learning Activity 2 Continued ⌘

2. Discuss

- What laws recognize violence against women as an offense in your region? Your country? In your home community?
- How do you evaluate these laws?
- How broadly do they define violence against women? How closely do they reflect the definition of violence against women developed in Learning Activity 1?
- Do they include violence on the part of both state and private individuals?
- Do they include violence in both public and private life?
- Do they include rape and other forms of sexual violence?
- Do they include threats of violence and psychological harm or suffering?
- Do they include taking away someone's liberty?
- If you are unsure about the existence of such laws, how can you find out? Why is it important to have this information?
- Is action needed in your community to improve the laws protecting women from violence? If so, what needs to be added or changed?

3. Evaluate

Divide participants into small groups to evaluate how well laws protecting women against violence are enforced. Address the following questions:

- Can you give some examples of enforcement of these laws? What might motivate officials to do so? What are some results when these laws are enforced?
- Can you give some examples of failure to enforce? Why do you think officials fail to enforce these laws? What are some results when these laws are not enforced?
- Is action needed in your community to ensure that women are protected from violence? If so, what kind of action would be most effective?

4. Conclude

Ask each group to report its suggestions regarding action for enforcement. List these on chart paper.

Ask participants to consider where their community is within the cycle of recognition and enforcement. What kind of advocacy would be most effective in the present situation—improved recognition of violence against women or improved enforcement of existing laws? Or both? List participants' suggestions.

Note to Facilitator: Keep these lists for reuse in "Learning Activity 6: Speaking Out on Violence Against Women."

Domestic Violence

Distinguishing the Myths from the Facts

Women suffer from many forms of violence outside the home including sexual harassment at their places of work; abuse by prison guards; attacks in public places and on streets and buses; derogatory remarks on the street, making it unpleasant or impossible for a woman to visit certain areas alone; attacks on women travelers; beatings, rapes, and murders of prostitutes; and attacks against disabled and older women, both at home and in public places. (See also Chapter 10, "Women's Human Rights and Work.") But the most frequent attacks against women occur in the home, by known perpetrators: partners, boyfriends, or husbands; former partners, boyfriends, or husbands; fathers, stepfathers, fathers-in-law, brothers, sons, or other relatives. According to a 2002 World Health Organization report, half of all women who die from homicides were killed by their current or former husbands or partners.[34] Table 7.5 provides statistics on the lifetime prevalence of partner violence in rural and urban areas of select areas of the world. (*Lifetime prevalence of partner violence* is defined as the proportion of women in relationships who report having experienced one or more acts of physical or sexual violence by a current or former partner at any point in their lives.)[35] As shown in the table, the city in Japan under study consistently reported the lowest prevalence of all forms of violence, whereas the provinces of Bangladesh, Ethiopia, Peru, and Tanzania reported the highest figures.[36]

In cases of domestic violence among members of a family or members of the same household, one person gains power through use of physical or emotional coercion. Any person in a household could be the target, but such violence is

Table 7.5   Prevalence of Lifetime Physical Violence and Sexual Violence by an Intimate Partner (%)

	Physical Violence	Sexual Violence
Bangladesh (C)	40	37
Bangladesh (P)	42	50
Brazil (C)	27	10
Brazil (P)	34	14
Ethiopia (P)	49	59
Japan (C)	13	6
Namibia (C)	31	16
Peru (C)	49	23
Peru (P)	61	47
Samoa	41	20
Serbia and Montenegro (C)	23	6
Thailand (C)	23	30
Thailand (P)	34	29
United Republic of Tanzania (C)	33	23
United Republic of Tanzania (P)	47	31

Note: C and *P* respectively designate either a city (typically an urban region) or a province (typically a rural area).

Source: World Health Organization, "Multi-Country Study on Women's Health and Domestic Violence Against Women," 2005, p. 29, available online at http://www.who.int/gender/violence/who_multicountry_study/Chapter3-Chapter4.pdf.

most frequently experienced by women and children. Although the criminal laws in some countries explicitly ban domestic violence, in many cases these laws are not enforced. In many other countries, it is not even acknowledged as a crime.

Domestic violence involves physical and sexual violence, marital rape, and the violation of reproductive rights. It also involves psychological abuse, such as forced isolation, humiliation, denial of support, and threats of violence or injury. Those who work with survivors of domestic abuse often report that women consider psychological abuse to be more devastating than physical assault. For example, when the researcher in a study of 127 battered women in Ireland asked "What was the worst aspect of the battering experience?" the top responses included mental torture, living in fear and terror, depression and loss of confidence, and negative effects on children.[37]

Surveys on violence against women, although important measures of reported abuse, tend to underestimate the number of incidents and to minimize the level of abuse. Nowhere is this more evident than in the arena of domestic violence. Indeed, "women are frequently reluctant to disclose abuse because of feelings of self-blame, shame, loyalty to the abuser or fear. Moreover, women in many cultures are socialized to accept physical and emotional chastisement as part of the husband's marital prerogative, making them less likely to self-identify as abused."[38]

✷ Learning Activity 3 ✷
Myths and Facts About Domestic Violence

Objective   To demonstrate misunderstandings about domestic violence
Time   45 minutes
Materials   Copies of the box below titled "Myths and Facts About Domestic Violence"

1. Discuss

Ask a volunteer to read a "myth" regarding domestic violence, which the full group will discuss for three minutes. Then ask another volunteer to read the accompanying "fact."

2. Anayze

When all the myths and facts have been read, address the following questions:

- Does this categorization of myths and facts hold true for your community?
- Are some of the myths ambiguous or misleading? Why or why not?
- Can you add to this list of myths and facts?
- How do these myths affect the attitudes and behaviors of men and women?
- How do these myths make the prevention of domestic violence difficult?

Myths and Facts About Domestic Violence

Myth 1: Domestic quarrels, beatings, and fights are characteristics of the lives of uneducated and poor people, members of lower social classes, people of minority races and ethnicities, and the inhabitants of slums. For people of higher economic, cultural, or educational classes, such occurrences are less frequent.

Fact 1: Violence against women has no economic, ethnic, or class distinctions. It happens everywhere in all social classes and groups.

Myth 2: Domestic violence is a new phenomenon caused by the economic and social changes of modern life, our speedy way of living, and new social stresses.

Fact 2: The custom of wife-beating is as old as marriage itself and in some cases has been openly encouraged and sanctioned by the law. Similarly, most forms of violence against women have had a long history.

Myth 3: Domestic violence is now rare. It is an occurrence of the past, when people were more violent and women were considered the property of men.

Fact 3: The incidence of domestic violence is very frequent in our time. Legal experts and women's human rights advocates in many countries consider it to be one of the most under-reported crimes.

Myth 4: Women provoke the beatings by their attitudes or actions. They deserve to be beaten because they have disobeyed their husbands or have done something "wrong."

Fact 4: This common belief illustrates that the problem of battered women is a social one that is deeply rooted in the way men and women are socialized. Also, this kind of thinking shows how society draws connections among marriage, property, ownership, sex, and violence. The reality is that no human being deserves to be beaten, and that batterers will find any excuse for their actions, no matter what their target does or does not do.

Myth 5: If women wanted to, they would leave. If they stay, they must find some masochistic pleasure in the beatings.

Fact 5: Women don't leave for many reasons, including the shame of admission, fear of future beatings or escalation of violence, economic dependence, lack of financial or emotional assistance, lack of a place to go—or, most likely, a combination of all of these factors.

Myth 6: The law provides adequate protection for women involved in domestic violence.

Fact 6: Depending on the country, the law may be weak in this area. Police in some countries hesitate to interfere in what they consider domestic disputes or private relationships. And the criminal codes in many countries don't include special protections for women against domestic violence. Some legal systems view the problem as a competition between two sides with equal power when, in fact, this is not the case: The male perpetrator may have more power in many respects—socially, economically, physically, and even legally.

Myth 7: Battered women are uneducated and have few job skills.

Fact 7: Battered women are successful executives, factory workers, full-time homemakers—the list goes on. Their profession does not determine their partners' violent behavior.

Myth 8: Violent men are mentally ill or are alcoholics.

Fact 8: Few violent men are mentally ill. They are just asserting what they see as their right to dominate women. Alcohol can exacerbate violence against women, but it does not cause it. Abusive men with alcohol problems abuse their partners both when they are drunk and when they are sober.[39]

Preventing Domestic Violence

Violence against women and girls "is a manifestation of the historically unequal power relations between men and women, which have led to the domination over and discrimination against women by men and to the prevention of women's full advancement."[40] Any strategy to address violence against women and promote women's human rights must thus confront the underlying power imbalances, cultural beliefs, and social structures that perpetuate such violence.

Many women do leave their abusers, but many more remain in violent situations for years. The reasons for this are complex. Many people react adversely to victims of violence of any kind. Victims may make us feel uncomfortable, guilty, afraid, confused, and unsure; they may force us to face our own weaknesses and fear. But when we cannot tolerate our own vulnerabilities, we may become angry with the victim herself. Furthermore, many women lack the means to support themselves and their children economically or socially. Where shelters exist, the space is usually full. Both families and authorities prefer to avoid such problems.

Factors That Perpetuate Gender-Based Violence[41]

Cultural: Gender-Specific Socialization

- Cultural definitions of appropriate sex roles
- Expectations of roles within relationships
- Belief in the inherent superiority of males
- Values that give men proprietary rights over women and girls
- Notion of the family as the private sphere and under male control
- Customs of marriage (bride price/dowry)
- Acceptability of violence as a means to resolve conflict

Economic: Women's Economic Dependence on Men

- Women's limited access to cash and credit
- Discriminatory laws regarding inheritance, property rights, use of communal lands, and maintenance after divorce or widowhood
- Women's limited access to employment in formal and informal sectors
- Women's limited access to education and training

Legal: Women's Lesser Legal Status Than That of Men, by Written Law and/or by Practice

- Laws regarding divorce, child custody, maintenance, and inheritance that favor men
- Legal definitions of rape and domestic abuse
- Low levels of legal literacy among women
- Insensitive treatment of women and girls by police and judiciary

Political: Underrepresentation of Women in Power, Politics, the Media, and the Legal and Medical Professions

- Lack of political will to address domestic violence
- Notion of the family as private and beyond control of the state
- Risk of challenging religious laws/the status quo
- Limited organization of women as a political force
- Limited participation of women in organized political systems

---

Learning Activity 4: Violence and Inability to Flee

Objective   To identify constraints that prevent women from leaving a situation of domestic violence and opportunities that might support their leaving

Time   75 minutes

Materials   Copies of the box titled "Factors That Perpetuate Gender-Based Violence," pieces of letter-sized paper, markers, tape

1. Present

Hand out the copies of "Factors That Perpetuate Gender-Based Violence." Go over the headings and choose some factors to highlight. Invite comments.

2. Role-Play

Describe the following scenario:

Your friend keeps leaving her husband because he beats her, but she also keeps returning.

Ask for a volunteer to sit in the center of the floor to represent "your friend." Ask participants to call out reasons the friend cannot leave the violent situation. Each reason the whole group agrees to is written on a piece of paper and taped to the volunteer's body (e.g., one paper could symbolize economic dependency; another, community attitudes; another, lack of independent housing opportunities; and so on).

When the list of reasons is complete, ask participants to name factors that would *enable* the woman to leave the situation (e.g., a shelter, child care, supportive friends, and family). Remove the relevant sheets of paper until they are all or almost gone, then ask the volunteer to stand up, symbolizing her ability to choose.

3. Discuss

- How can we avoid blaming the victim?
- How can we begin to blame the perpetrator?
- What can be done to remove the factors that keep women in violent situations?
- What can community organizations and social institutions do to help?
- What can you do to help?

Sexual Assault

Sexual assault includes rape and other forms of physical attack of a sexual nature. As with other forms of violence against women, the perpetrators of sexual assault are most likely to be known to the victim. For example, a multicountry study by the World Bank, drawing from justice system statistics and data from rape crisis centers, found that in 60–70 percent of rape cases, the victim knew the perpetrator.[42] In the United States, other studies have shown that 67 percent of rapes were committed by acquaintances of the victim, including 47 percent of perpetrators who were a friend or acquaintance, 17 percent who were an intimate partner, and 3 percent who were another relative.[43]

Nearly every country in the world has laws against sexual assault, but disputes often arise about the following issues:

- *The scope of the offense (i.e., the range of behaviors included).* Many laws include only a narrow definition of rape as forced penetration of the penis into the vagina. This narrow definition excludes other forms of sexual assault, such as insertion of objects, forced fellatio, and anal intercourse. Radhika Coomaraswamy, a Sri Lankan lawyer who served as the UN Special Rapporteur on Violence Against Women between 1994 and 2003, noted a general rule regarding the crime of rape: If no physical injury is evident, then the incident is not rape.[44]
- *Whether sexual assault in marriage is a crime.* Under many criminal codes, married women cannot charge their husbands with rape.
- *Whether the burden must be placed on the victim to prove she did not consent.* Rape is the only criminal offense in which the complicity of the victim may become a relevant consideration in the trial of the offender. Whether and how lack of consent becomes an issue in court is a matter of considerable debate.
- *Whether rape should be a crime of sex or violence, or both.* Some women advocates argue that the perception of rape as a sexual crime is responsible, to a great extent, for mitigating its seriousness and heinousness. Rape is a crime of violence that is one of the worst forms of physical and mental injury that can be inflicted upon a woman.[45]

Women human rights advocates have pressed for reform in criminal justice systems to ensure that women are dealt with fairly in court and that police, prosecutors, and courts treat rape complaints in a serious manner. However, rape and other forms of sexual assault remain among the least reported crimes throughout the world, largely because, given the precedents, many women believe that facing the police and the judicial process would be worse than not seeking justice at all.

✠ Learning Activity 5 ✠
Human Rights and Violence Against Women

Objective   To identify the relationship between human rights and violence against women

Time   60 minutes

Materials   Chart paper and markers or blackboard and chalk

1. Discuss

In small groups, discuss the way fear of violence (both public and domestic) has affected participants personally, both currently and in the past.

Also, discuss the rights lost when women are not free from violence.

2. Brainstorm/List

Post four sheets of chart paper labeled as follows:

✠ Learning Activity 5 Continued ✠

- Effect on Women's Lives
- Loss of Rights Due to Violence
- Gains When Free from Violence
- How to Become Free from Violence.

Ask a representative from each group to add to the list the effects discussed in that group. Subsequently, ask if anyone can add other effects. Do the same for the list of rights lost due to violence.

Ask participants to brainstorm these categories and then to list them on the chart paper:

- Rights women gain when they are free from violence
- Ways to help women become free from violence.

Lead a discussion about how the four lists are related:

- What important connections do you see among the lists?
- What conclusions can you draw about violence and women's human rights?

3. Discuss

Post a chart listing the following human rights. Ask how claiming these rights can help women and free them and others from violence:

- Right to life
- Right to equality
- Right to personal freedom and security
- Right to equal legal protection
- Right to protection against all forms of discrimination
- Right to health
- Right to equality in the workplace
- Right not to be tortured, or to be exposed to other inhumane, cruel, or degrading treatments or punishments.

Choose two of the rights from the above list and explain their relationship to violence against women.

Alternative: If some participants have knowledge of the law, ask them to circle on the list the rights that are legally guaranteed in their country.

- Is the right being enforced?
- Is the right enforceable? Why or why not?
- How does enforcement of the right affect women?

What can women do to obtain the right to be free from violence within the context of some of the rights listed above? What can men do?

The Role of Authorities

Government

There continues to be some resistance to viewing the question of violence against women as a human rights issue. Opponents argue that human rights concern relations between the state and the individual and therefore exclude what people do in their private lives. While protection against violence in armed conflict or in state custody may be considered a human right, opponents would argue that domestic violence is not and that a battered woman's claim is against her batterer rather than the state.

Those who see domestic violence as a human rights violation now point out that the government and other authorities do have a responsibility to intervene in private forms of violence. By fostering the conditions that allow male batterers to go unpunished, by failing to respond seriously to women's complaints of sexual assault, and by sponsoring institutions that do not take women's needs into account, the state becomes implicitly responsible for violence, in both its actions and its failures to act.

Some governments have assumed responsibility to stop gender-based violence and take steps to prevent future violence. Such actions entail changes in the training of police officers and prosecutors in order to improve their understanding of domestic violence and their willingness to take the issue of violence against women seriously. Prevention also entails education in schools to combat the belief that men have a "right" to abuse women. Preventive steps include state sponsorship of battered women's shelters and counselling services, as well as cooperation between law enforcement officers and groups that counsel survivors of violence.

A number of governments have recently passed legislation concerning different forms of violence against women. While legislation is an important step toward combating violence, most governments do not go further than viewing it as a purely legal issue. The law in most countries does not specifically mention domestic violence or other forms of violence against women, apart from perhaps sexual abuse. This means that women have to look to general provisions of law that were never meant to cover their situation. When the law does address the various manifestations of violence against women, it does so separately, with no suggestion that they have a structurally related cause. In other words, laws do not usually address the relationship between violence against women and discrimination and subordination of women generally, and, as a result, the law on violence against women has developed in a fragmented way.[46]

Where specific laws on domestic abuse exist, they ordinarily involve some kind of protective order. This involves a procedure in which a woman can go to court and argue that the court should order the abuser to stop his behavior and stay away from her. Police can then arrest the abuser should he violate the protection order. Even where such legal remedies are available, however, police, prosecutors, and judges may fail to take women's complaints seriously and block women from obtaining relief.

Media and Community Leaders

While efforts to criminalize domestic violence and reform the legal system are indeed important, they are not sufficient to bring about systemic change. Strategies for changing the underlying beliefs and attitudes that perpetuate male violence must also be devised. Relying on incarceration for abusers does not address situations where women do not want or cannot afford to have their husbands go to jail.

While religious and community leaders, teachers, and the media may play a role in perpetuating violence against women, they can also be a valuable resource for addressing and reducing the problem. After all, women tend to go first to family members, community leaders, health care professionals, and social workers in times of crisis. The legal system is often the last resort.

Women in many parts of the world have initiated education campaigns, workshops, petition drives, "speak outs," and other actions to help change the kind of social attitudes that lead to violence. In addition, women activists have been at the forefront of providing counseling, shelter, and other services to women survivors of violence.

Strategies to Combat Violence Against Women: Beyond the Legal System

- In Ghana in 2003, a program that fights domestic violence using community-based response systems was initiated in rural areas.[47]
- In the United States, a National Domestic Violence Hotline was established in 1994 in response to new legislation. Between 1994 and 2003, the hotline responded to more than 860,000 calls.[48]
- In Malaysia, the Women's Aid Organization received a grant from UNIFEM in order to assist and follow through the legal system those women who wanted to report domestic violence. As a result of their advocacy, Malaysian law has changed—in part, to make the system more accessible.[49]
- The Latin American and Caribbean Women's Health Network of Chile conducted a campaign to review the Inter-American Convention on the Prevention, Punishment, and Eradication of Violence Against Women. Their powerful campaign mobilized women's groups throughout the country.[50]
- In Pakistan, the Working Women Organization organized a Human Chain in front of a media club to advocate against abuse, discrimination, and exploitation on the basis of gender, ethnicity, and religion.[51]
- In India in 2003, an NGO called Swadhina organized a speech competition for women that focused on the topic of combating domestic violence.[52]
- In Ireland, Women's Aid held an event called the "Dining Out to Make a Difference Campaign." Local restaurants participated by donating a portion of their proceeds to fight against domestic violence.[53]

Remembering Core Concepts

✸ Learning Activity 6 ✸
Speaking Out on Violence Against Women

Objectives To examine women's human right to freedom from violence and consider how to take action to improve it, and to discover the importance of including the active participation of those directly involved in and affected by human rights violations

Time 60+ minutes

Materials Chart paper and markers

1. Brainstorm

Ask participants to list problems faced by women in their community related to gender-based violence. After dividing them into small groups, ask them to choose a problem on which they wish to concentrate.

2. Discuss/Plan

Ask each group to prepare a five-minute presentation to a "panel of community leaders" on their problem. Each presentation should:

- describe the problem, identifying the group(s) of women it impacts and, if possible, the cause(s) of the problem
- relate the problem to women's human rights
- clarify how the problem affects women's lives
- show how addressing the problem can improves their lives
- propose specific actions that should be taken to address the problem
- show how members of the community can get involved in addressing the problem.

Ask each group to choose a spokesperson to make the presentation and a "community leader" to serve on the panel. While the groups plan their presentations, the panel of leaders meets to decide on their roles, representing a variety of differing but typical attitudes within the community leadership.

3. Present/Role-Play

The spokesperson from each group makes a presentation and members of the panel listen and respond, asking questions and offering comments, objections, or suggestions in keeping with their chosen roles.

4. Discuss

After the presentations and role-play, discuss these questions:

- How did the spokespersons feel when presenting the problem?
- How did the "community leaders" respond to the presentation? What attitudes in the community were they representing?
- How did the audience, composed of the rest of the group, respond to the presentations?

✠ Learning Activity 6 Continued ✠

- Did any spokesperson discuss the problem as a human rights violation? Did putting the problem in a human rights context strengthen the argument? Why or why not?
- Are these ideas for improving women's human right to freedom from violence feasible in your community? Why or why not?

5. Conclude

Challenge the participants by asking them to evaluate their knowledge of the problem and the inclusiveness of their perspective:

- How did you obtain your information about how women in your community deal with gender-based violence? Was it accurate and complete? If not, what additional information do you need and how can you obtain it?
- Did you personally consult women about the problem and how it affects them? About actions that could improve the problem?
- Why is it important in real-life human rights advocacy to include the active participation of those directly involved and affected?
- How can you apply the example of this learning activity to planning and implementing advocacy for women in your community?

Notes

1. Maire Vlachova and Lea Bison, *Women in an Insecure World: Violence Against Women—Facts, Figures and Analysis* (Geneva: Centre for Democratic Control of Armed Forces 2005), p. 15.

2. UNICEF, "Equality, Development, and Peace," Beijing+5, 2000, available online at http://www.unicef.org/publications/.

3. David Graham Epstein and Mary Patricia Rimsza, "Medical Complications of Female Genital Mutilation," *Journal of American College Health*, vol. 49 (May 2001), pp. 6–9.

4. Population Reference Bureau, "Abandoning Female Genital Cutting: Prevalence, Attitudes, and Efforts to End the Practice," 2001.

5. Ibid.

6. "Egypt Outlaws All Female Circumcision," *Agence France Presse*, June 28, 2007.

7. UNICEF, "Female Genital Mutilation/Cutting, A Statistical Exploration," 2005, available online at http://www.unicef.org/publications/files/FGM-C_final_10_October.pdf.

8. World March of Women, "Sexism and Globalization," 2000, available online at http://www.ffq.qc.ca/marche2000/fr/index.html.

9. Josephine A. V. Allen, " Poverty as a Form of Violence: A Structural Perspective," *Journal of Human Behavior in the Social Environment*, vol. 4, no. 2/3 (June 1, 2001).

10. Robert Gilman, "Structural Violence: Can We Find Genuine Peace in a World with Inequitable Distribution of Wealth Among Nations?" *In Context: A Quarterly of Humane Sustainable Culture—The Foundations of Peace* (IC#4), last updated June 29, 2000.

11. UNHCR, "From the Foreign Land," no. 16 (March 2002), available online at http://www.unhcr.pl/english/newsletter/16/world_of_refugee_women.php.

12. Amnesty International, *It's in Our Hands: Stop Violence Against Women*, available online at http://web.amnesty.org/web/web.nsf/8bad1ff50703146980256e32003c42f0/316e14580e57b88680256ea90037305a/$FILE/SVAW%20report%20ENGLISH.pdf.

13. Beijing Declaration and Platform for Action, Fourth World Conference on Women, September 15, 1995, A/CONF. 177/20 (1995) and A/CONF. 177/20/Add. 1 (1995), paragraph 112.

14. Ibid.

15. World Health Organization, *World Report on Violence and Health*, 2002, available online at http://www.amnestyusa.org/women/index.do.

16. Amnesty International, *Broken Bodies, Shattered Minds: Torture and Ill Treatment of Women*, 2001, available online at http://web.amnesty.org/aidoc/ai.nsf/362d2dfa88d393cf80256cbf004dcabe/39cb2f2a6c51b8d8802569ed0062a274/$FILE/ATT855AM/ACT400012001.pdf.

17. Ibid.

18. Ibid.

19. Ibid.

20. Ibid.

21. Amnesty International, *It's in Our Hands*.

22. U.S. Department of Justice, "Prior Abuse Reported by Inmates and Probationers," 1999, Washington, DC.

23. Social Work Services and Prisons Inspectorates for Scotland, "Women Offenders—A Safer Way: A Review of Community Disposals and the Use of Custody for Women Offenders in Scotland" (United Kingdom: House of Commons, The Stationery Office, 1998), available online at http://www.archive.official-documents.co.uk/document/scotoff/women/women.htm.

24. Amnesty International, *It's in Our Hands*.

25. Amnesty International, "Amnesty International Calls for the Restriction of the Role of Male Guards in Female Facilities," Online Documentation Archive, August 9, 2000, available online at http://web.amnesty.org/library/Index/ENGAMR511242000?open&of=ENG-USA.

26. Ibid.

27. CEDAW was adopted in 1979 and entered into force in 1981.

28. Committee on the Elimination of all Forms of Violence Against Women, General Recommendation 19, 1992.

29. Beijing Declaration and Platform for Action, Fourth World Conference on Women, September 15, 1995, A/CONF. 177/20 (1995) and A/CONF. 177/20/Add. 1 (1995), paragraph 112.

30. The full text of this ruling can be found online at http://www.ictr.org/ENGLISH/cases/Akayesu/judgement/akay001.htm.

31. The full text of the Rome Statute can be found online at http://www.icc-cpi.int/.

32. "Protocol to the African Charter on Human and People's Rights on the Rights of Women in Africa," July 11, 2003, available online at http://www.pambazuka.org/en/petition/1/protocol.pdf. See also "Protocol on the Rights of Women in Africa: A Briefing Paper," February 2006, Center for Reproductive Rights, available online at http://www.reproductiverights.org/pdf/pub_bp_africa.pdf.

33. "Protocol on the Rights of Women in Africa," *Equality Now*, available online at http://www.equalitynow.org/english/campaigns/african-protocol/african-protocol_en.html.

34. Etienne G. Krug et al., *World Report on Violence and Health* (Geneva: WHO, 2002), p. 93. See also related information from UNIFEM, available online at ok http://www.unifem.org/gender_issues/violence_against_women/facts_figures.php?page=2.

35. Ibid.

36. Ibid.

37. M. Casey, "Domestic Violence Against Women: The Women's Perspective," in *Demanding Accountability: The Global Campaign and Vienna Tribunal for Women's Rights*, edited by C. Bunch and Niamh Reilly (New Brunswick, NJ: Center for Women's Global Leadership and UNIFEM, 1994).

38. L. Heise et al. *Violence Against Women: The Hidden Health Burden* (Washington, DC: World Bank, 1994), pp. 1165, 1168.

39. Adapted from Safe Harbor, Inc., "Myths About Domestic Violence," 2005, available online at http://www.safeharborsc.org/myths.htm.

40. Beijing Declaration and Platform for Action, Fourth World Conference on Women, September 15, 1995, A/CONF. 177/20 (1995) and A/CONF. 177/20/Add. 1 (1995), paragraph 118.

41. Amnesty International, *It's in Our Hands.*

42. Heise et al., *Violence Against Women*, p. 2.

43. *National Crime Victimization Survey, 2004*, available online at http://www.rainn.org/statistics/index.html.

44. Radhika Coomaraswamy, "Of Kali Born: Violence and the Law in Sri Lanka," in *Freedom from Violence: Women's Strategies from Around the World*, edited by Margaret Schuler (UNIFEM, 1992).

45. Hina Jilani, "Whose Laws? Human Rights and Violence," in *Freedom from Violence: Women's Strategies from Around the World*, edited by Margaret Schuler (UNIFEM, 1992), p. 71.

46. Jane Connors, "Government Measures to Confront Violence Against Women," in *Women and Violence*, edited by Miranda Davies (London: Zed Books, Ltd., 1994), pp. 182–183.

47. 16 Days Campaign Website, "Violence Against Women Violates Human Rights: Maintaining the Momentum Ten Years After Vienna (1993–2003)," available online at http://www.cwgl.rutgers.edu/16days/16days2003.html.

48. Ibid.

49. UNIFEM Trustfund, "In Support of Actions to Eliminate Violence Against Women," available online at http://www.unifem.org/index.php?f_page_pid=59.

50. 16 Days Campaign Website, "Violence Against Women Violates Human Rights: Maintaining the Momentum Ten Years After Vienna (1993–2003)," available online at http://www.cwgl.rutgers.edu/16days/16days2003.html.

51. Ibid.

52. Ibid.

53. Ibid.

8

Women's Human Right to an Adequate Standard of Living

The States Parties to the present Covenant recognize the right of everyone to an adequate standard of living for himself and his family, including adequate food, clothing and housing, and to the continuous improvement of living conditions. The States Parties will take appropriate steps to ensure the realization of this right, recognizing to this effect the essential importance of international co-operation based on free consent.

—International Covenant on Economic, Social, and Cultural Rights, Article 11(1)

States Parties shall take all appropriate measures to eliminate discrimination against women in rural areas in order to ensure, on a basis of equality of men and women, that they participate in and benefit from rural development and, in particular, shall ensure to such women the right . . . to enjoy adequate living conditions, particularly in relation to housing, sanitation, electricity and water supply, transport and communications.

—Convention on the Elimination of All Forms of Discrimination Against Women, Article 14(2)(h)

Objectives

The learning activities and background information contained in this chapter will enable participants to work toward the following objectives:

- Define the right to an adequate standard of living.
- Explain the importance of the rights to food, clean water, adequate housing, clothing, and basic needs for women and girls.
- Explore the specific gender dimensions of the rights to food, clean water, and adequate housing.
- Understand the interrelationship between the right to an adequate standard of living and other human rights.
- Identify the role of government, nongovernmental organizations, and women themselves in advancing the right of women to an adequate standard of living.
- Remember core concepts.

Getting Started: Thinking About Women and Adequate Living Standards

The right to an adequate standard of living addresses the most basic needs to which human beings are entitled: food, clean water, housing, clothing, and the continuous improvement of living conditions. Women should be able to obtain these through work with dignity, not exploitative or degrading forms of work. A standard of living that is "adequate" means having living conditions above the poverty line; this provision necessarily implies the need to eradicate poverty. Adequate care—immunization, prevention and control of disease, and measures to address malnutrition—is a human right of vulnerable groups such as girls, mothers and pregnant women, disabled women and girls, and women refugees. (See also Chapter 5, "Women's Human Right to Health.")

The rights to work, property, and social security are all sources of subsistence or income that should make it possible for women to enjoy a decent living standard. Women often confront discrimination in these sectors, however, and thus face obstacles in attaining an adequate standard of living. (See also Chapter 2, "Women's Human Right to Equality and Nondiscrimination.") Discrimination in the workforce means that women receive less income for the same work than men. The terms of employment for women are often exploitative, especially in low-skill, low-wage sectors. Moreover, much of women's work takes place in the informal sector, in the home, and in agriculture—work that is still not regarded as productive activity or taken into account in statistical economic measures. Such labor is rarely remunerated and reinforces dependency, often on a husband, leading to disempowerment and otherwise limiting options for women.[1]

Women also face difficulties in gaining secure access to and control over resources such as land, water, and credit, as they are often not recognized as producers or legal equals. Access to credit and secure land tenure is often denied to women because they are not officially recognized by government authorities as food producers or agricultural workers. Without access to productive resources, women's economic independence and ability to feed and clothe themselves—and their children—are limited. Customs and traditions in many parts of the world further limit women's equal access to productive resources. In some countries, this discrimination is expressly written into customary law. Understanding the human right to an adequate standard of living and the obstacles that women face in attaining this right is important for organizing around issues relating to access to food, clean water, clothing, housing, and the progressive enhancement of living conditions.

✄ Learning Activity 1: Identifying Basic Needs ✄

Objective To identify what is needed in order to have an adequate standard of living

Time 45 minutes

Materials Chart paper and markers or blackboard and chalk

continues

✠ Learning Activity 1 Continued ✠

1. Define/Discuss

In small groups, decide on a definition of "adequate standard of living" and provide examples of components that fit this definition. Include the components needed for someone in this community to have a decent standard of living.

Ask each group to write its definitions on chart paper and to post them around the room. Using these draft definitions, try to develop a common definition with the whole group.

Note to Facilitator: Encourage participants to illustrate their definitions with drawings, and don't spend too much time trying to reconcile conflicting definitions. Leave them as "alternate drafts."

Discuss the following questions:

- What happens when any one of the essential components of an adequate standard of living is missing?
- How does failure to achieve an adequate standard of living affect individual women? Their families? The community? Human rights?

2. List

Individually or in small groups, list the obstacles that women face in realizing their human right to an adequate standard of living, drawing from the components identified in the definitions provided by the group(s).

Alternative: Assign different components to different small groups.

3. Analyze/Discuss

Consider the conclusions that can be drawn from this discussion about women and attaining a decent standard of living.

- In what ways are women limited in their access to the things that are necessary in order to have a decent living standard?
- In what ways do women have control over such access? In what ways do they not exercise control over such access?
- Which of these factors are most important for governments and other institutions to address in order to raise women's standard of living?

Adequate Standard of Living as a Human Right

The Universal Declaration of Human Rights (UDHR) provides that "[e]veryone has the right to a standard of living adequate for the health and well-being of himself and of his family, including food, clothing, housing and medical care and necessary social services." The International Covenant on Economic, Social, and Cultural Rights (ICESCR) develops this right further in providing "[t]he States Parties to the present Covenant recognize the right of everyone to an adequate standard of living for himself and his family, including adequate food, clothing and housing, and to the continuous improvement of living conditions." Human rights law recognizes that not all countries will be able to meet economic and social rights in full. However, as stated by the Committee on Economic and Social Rights, even poor governments that are States Parties to the ICESCR are obligated to move as quickly and as effectively as possible toward the goal of full implementation. A State Party in which a significant number of individuals are deprived of essential foodstuffs, clean water, and basic shelter and housing is failing to meet its human rights obligations.[2]

Many other rights are closely related to—and in many cases cannot be separated from—the right to an adequate standard of living:

- The right to non-discrimination
- The right to enjoy the highest standard of physical and mental health
- The right not to be subjected to arbitrary or unlawful interference with one's privacy, family, home, or correspondence
- The right to freedom of residence
- The right to enjoy the benefits of scientific progress. There are many scientific developments regarding an adequate standard of living, such as those pertaining to access to nutritious food and clean water.
- The right to freedom from discrimination. This addresses a variety of concerns; for example, (i) circumstances in which food distribution is not equal between men and women violates the right to food and (ii) insecurity of land tenure for women severely restricts their right to adequate housing.

✄ Learning Activity 2: Impact of Poverty on Women ✄

Objective   To examine the impact of poverty on women and identify actions to address women's poverty
Time   60 minutes
Materials   Chart paper and markers or blackboard and chalk, small pieces of paper for drawings, copies of the *economic justice* definition in Step 1 below (optional)

1. Read
Write on chart paper/blackboard, hand out, or read aloud this definition:

economic justice: equitable distribution of income and wealth, economic security, and economic freedom. This includes the right of every woman to a safe, secure home, good health care, and secure child care; the right of every woman to earn a wage that will support her and her family, working either inside or outside the home; shared responsibility between men and women for care of the elderly, children, and the community; elimination of wage- and gender-based discrimination; the right of women to own property and other economic resources and to be sustainably self-employed.[3]

continues

Learning Activity 2 Continued

2. List
Divide participants into small groups and give each a copy of the chart below. Ask each group to respond to the following questions, recording their responses on a chart like the one shown in Table 8.1 or on individual charts for each topic.

Table 8.1 Impact of Poverty on Women

Who Are the Poor?	What Makes Them Poor?	Women in Poverty	Overcoming Poverty

List A: Under the heading "Who Are the Poor?" record responses to these questions:

- Which people in your community are poor?
- Do they belong to a specific racial, ethnic, religious, or other social group?

List B: Under the heading "What Makes Them Poor?" record responses to the following question:

- What makes these people poor?

List C: Under the heading "Women in Poverty," record responses to this question:

- How does poverty affect women who belong to this group?

List D: Under the heading "Overcoming Poverty" record responses to this question:

- What social changes and/or actions could help this group rise out of poverty?

3. Analyze
Review List D and do the following:

- Mark with a star (*) those actions that have already been taken or are currently being taken. Next to the action write who or what has taken it.

Learning Activity 2 Continued

- Mark with an exclamation point (!) those actions that could be taken in the future.
- Add any additional actions that could help people rise from poverty.
- Circle those actions that have been or could be undertaken by women.

4. Discuss

Ask the small groups to present their lists. Discuss, especially where differences of opinion occur, and ask these questions:

- What actions have proven to be effective?
- Have some of these actions failed? Why?
- What proposed new actions seem most likely to be effective? Why?

Facts Relating to the Human Right to an Adequate Standard of Living

- It is estimated that more than 1 billion people live in inadequate housing, and that more than 100 million people are homeless.[4]
- Approximately one-third of the world's women are homeless or living in inadequate housing and own less than 1 percent of the world's property.[5]
- According to the UN Food and Agriculture Organization (FAO), while the proportion of women heads of rural households continues to grow, reaching more than 30 percent in some developing countries, less than 2 percent of all land is owned by women.[6]
- Promises made at the World Food Summit to cut by half the number of undernourished people have had little effect, as few countries have been able to report progress in reducing the number of victims of hunger.[7]
- The number of undernourished people around the world increased in 2002 to 840 million: 799 million in developing countries, 30 million in countries in transition, and 11 million in industrialized countries.[8]
- One child dies every five seconds from hunger or related causes.[9]
- At present, 460 million people are suffering from water shortages. If the current rate of water consumption continues, 25 percent of the world's population will become water stressed by 2025.[10]
- Lack of clean water is implicated in 80 percent of all sickness and disease worldwide.[11]

Women's Right to Food and Clean Water

Food and water are essential elements that all human beings must have in order to live. A woman's human right to food and clean water implies access to "the minimum essential food which is sufficient, nutritionally adequate and safe" as well as "sufficient, safe, acceptable, physically accessible and affordable water."[12] Undertaking these obligations must be understood in a way that respects gender difference, understands existing obstacles confronting women, and seeks to improve the situation.

The minimum requirements for satisfying the right to food are as follows:[13]

- *Availability:* This refers to the very presence of food or means of production of food in a community or household and includes availability of a clean water source. Food must be available, either directly or through access to a well-functioning distribution, processing, and marketing system that responds to demand.
- *Dietary Needs:* Food must satisfy dietary needs. A diet consists of a mix of nutrients, calories, and proteins necessary for physical and mental health and growth.
- *No Adverse Substances:* Food must be free from adverse substances. This means that the government must establish and enforce health and safety standards for food quality.
- *Culturally Acceptable:* Food must be culturally acceptable, meaning that it is necessary to take into account non-nutrient-based values for judging the acceptability of food, including informing consumers of food contents.
- *Accessibility:* This refers to the ability of people to actually obtain the available food and resources; in many countries, lack of accessibility is more of a problem than lack of availability. Food must be accessible; in other words, it must be (i) economically affordable and (ii) physically available.

Women and Food Security

Advocates of the human right to food and clean water aim to ensure food security for all people. *Food security* refers to circumstances in which food and clean water are always available and accessible to the population, both at present and for future generations. Women, especially poor women, are particularly impacted by food insecurity for a variety of reasons.

Women living in poverty have limited access to food. They may not have access to land on which to produce their own food and may lack the financial means to purchase enough food. Within families living in poverty, women and children typically have less access to food than men.

Recognizing women's right to food and clean water means eliminating hunger, malnutrition, and starvation. *Hunger* refers to the condition of a person who does not have access to enough food. *Malnutrition* is caused by hunger, poor food quality, and disease. Although a person might be consuming the appropriate number of calories daily, she may still be missing vital nutrients in her diet. Malnutrition can lead to additional diseases, and numerous diseases are known to intensify malnutrition. Chronic malnutrition, especially during childhood, has profound long-term effects on survival.

The disruption of food production or distribution is another major cause of hunger and malnutrition. Natural disasters such as droughts, floods, or tornados may halt or disrupt food production, shipping, or marketing and result in food shortages. Disruption of oil distribution, too, may lead to problems in food production and distribution. Human disasters, including war, can likewise limit food accessibility by disrupting regular movement and distribution of food. During conflicts, food can be used as a weapon; intentionally withholding food from civilian populations causes *starvation*.

Some vulnerable groups, including women and girls who face additional obstacles, have been expressly addressed in international documents relating to the right to food and clean water:

- *Women* have the right to receive pre- and post-natal health care and the right to breast-feed their babies.[14] They also have the right of access to information and education regarding child health and nutrition, the advantages of breast-feeding, hygiene, and environmental sanitation.[15]
- *Infants* from birth to 4–6 months have the right to be breast-fed.[16]
- *Disabled women and girls* have the right to food and clean water without discrimination and, wherever they are unable to fulfill those rights directly by means at their disposal, states have the obligation to provide that right directly.[17]
- *Women prisoners* must be regularly provided with food of nutritional value as well as drinking water upon request.
- *Girls* have the right to nutritious food and clean drinking water, as well as the right to be free of suffering from disease and malnutrition caused by inaccessibility of food and clean water.
- *Refugees and displaced women* should be provided the same public relief as the nationals of the country where they take refuge.[18]

Gender Discrimination in Access to Food

In his first report, the Special Rapporteur on the Right to Food identified seven major economic obstacles that hinder or prevent the realization of the right to food, one of which is discrimination against women and its impact on the realization of the right to food.[19] Women continue to suffer de facto discrimination in access to and control over food. Discrimination often occurs within the home, where the distribution of food and income can severely affect women's right to food. In Bangladesh, the Special Rapporteur on the Right to Food found a marked gender disparity in malnutrition levels, with far more girl children underweight and stunted than boy children. There, as in many cultures, social and cultural customs demand that women eat last, after the male members of the family, which also means that women often eat least, contributing to high rates of female mortality.[20]

Continued discrimination in the workplace also means that women earn less than men, making them less able to feed themselves and their families, particularly in the case of female-headed households. Though women are increasingly being incorporated into the workforce, the terms of this incorporation are often exploitative, particularly in the low-skill, low-wage sectors. Many women do not work for wages and therefore face significant obstacles in accessing the resources necessary to obtain food and clean water for themselves and their households.

Women who are at particular risk of having their right to food and clean water violated as a result of discrimination include, for example, disabled women and refugee women. Disabled women and girls often face discrimination in their access to food or resources for food. States are obliged to ensure that food and water are indeed accessible to disabled women and girls. To provide

---

Coping with Food Insecurity[21]

A study conducted by the International Fund for Agricultural Development (IFAD) in 1998 reviewed the question of food security under three projects that the Fund had supported in India and Nepal. Among the key questions were how women coped with food shortages and the impact of the projects on the women themselves.

Poorer and single-livelihood households had a particularly difficult time finding ways of feeding their families, especially during the lean periods of the year. They tended to use a number of different coping strategies, such as selling smaller animals, borrowing money from moneylenders, performing wage work (for women and men), mortgaging land, underselling products to get quick cash, performing small income-generating activities such as collecting and selling fuel wood, and calling on children's labor.

Women were the most involved in finding ways to deal with food insecurity. Several of the women's coping approaches were disadvantageous to the women and had a negative impact on their health. These included:

- reducing food intake and the intake of their daughters
- sharing food surplus between households
- using food that expanded in the stomach (e.g., gruel), especially for themselves
- cooking food only once a day and using side dishes in order to reduce the fuel used and time spent (freeing up time for earning an income)
- consuming processed foods that could be kept without special storage (dried vegetables, flour of mango kernel)
- purchasing cheaper staples to replace costlier and more nutritious items
- working harder and longer on productive activities to earn cash for buying food.

---

just one example, the obligation extends to ensuring that wells are built in a manner that is accessible to a woman with a mobility impairment, who uses a wheelchair or is on crutches. The construction of wells on raised platforms would not meet the accessibility requirement. Girls continue the gender-based roles adapted at home, and the procurement of food and clean water usually becomes their duty in refugee camps. Aware of women's responsibilities and vulnerabilities, humanitarian agencies have established food security guidelines that take the gender dimension into account.

⊠ Learning Activity 3: Last in Line for Food ⊠

Objective   To examine obstacles to women's adequate nutrition
Time   45 minutes
Materials   Chart paper and markers or blackboard and chalk

1. Read
Read this story, titled "Women's Biscuits," to the whole group.

> Humanitarian aide workers at a refugee camp just across the border from a war-torn country were faced with a mysterious problem: Although there was a simple but adequate food supply for all of the refugees, two-thirds of whom were women

---

Learning Activity 3 Continued

and children, women in the camp showed growing signs of malnutrition, with resulting chronic disease, miscarriages, and other related health side effects. When questioned, women and girls claimed they were receiving enough to eat.

Finally aide workers consulted some local women familiar with the culture of the refugees and spoke their language. Under promises of anonymity, they explained the problem. Most of the men in the camp and many of the boys were warriors engaged in the civil war across the border, who came into camp periodically to rest and recover from their wounds before returning to the front. In this community, the men were the heroes who needed and deserved most of the available food as well as other services. For example, aide workers were shocked to discover that almost all the medications, antibiotics, anesthetics, immunizations, and health services were also going to men. Boys were also given priority, as they were viewed as new recruits for the cause. Accustomed to eating last and knowing that any claim on food or health care would be treated as disloyalty, women in the camp had simply accepted malnutrition for themselves, giving most of the remaining food to their children.

The local aide worker suggested a clever solution: they labeled boxes of high calorie and high-protein crackers "Women's Biscuits" and let it be known that they could cause growth of breasts in males. Overnight, the women had a reliable food source and their malnutrition rapidly disappeared.[22]

2. Discuss

What value systems are at work in this story?

- On the part of the refugees? What do you think motivated the men? The women?
- On the part of the aide workers?
- On your part? Do you approve of the aide workers' trick?
- How would you interpret this story from a human rights point of view?
- What does this story illustrate about obstacles to women's right to adequate nutrition? To health care? To an adequate standard of living?
- What can be done in situations like this, where women's needs are subordinated to those of men, to ensure women's human right to an adequate standard of living?

Adequate Housing

Despite the obvious importance of housing rights to attaining an adequate standard of living, women often face discrimination in many specific aspects of housing. This can occur in terms of policy development, control over household resources, rights of inheritance and ownership, community organizing, or even the construction of housing.

The right to adequate housing means more than having a roof over one's head. Decent housing requires a habitable space that fulfills the basic needs of human beings to personal space, hygiene, security, and protection from the weather. A woman's right to adequate housing means having equal access to a safe, habitable, and affordable home. It also means that she must be protected against forced eviction.

The Center for Economic and Social Rights has summarized the minimum requirements of the right to adequate housing as follows:

- *Legal security of tenure:* This protects people from eviction, harassment, and other threats. States must provide and enforce security of tenure in consultation with affected groups.
- *Availability of services, materials, facilities, and infrastructure:* This includes facilities essential for health, security, comfort, and nutrition. For example, there must be safe drinking water, energy for cooking, heating, lighting, sanitation facilities, refuse disposal, storage, and emergency services.
- *Affordability:* The cost of adequate housing should not compromise the satisfaction of other basic needs.
- *Habitability:* Housing must protect its inhabitants from cold, damp, heat, rain, or other health threats and structural hazards. It must also provide adequate space.
- *Accessibility:* All people are entitled to adequate housing, and disadvantaged groups in particular must be accorded full and sustainable access to housing, which may mean granting them priority status in housing allocation or land-use planning.
- *Location:* Housing should be located in areas with access to employment options, health care services, schools, child care, and other social facilities. This applies equally in urban and rural areas. Housing should not be built on or near polluted sites or sources of pollution.
- *Cultural adequacy:* Activities geared toward development or modernization of housing should ensure that the cultural dimensions of housing are not sacrificed, while simultaneously ensuring modern technical facilities.[23]

Insecurity of Tenure

Lack of secure tenure is a major factor impacting a woman's right to an adequate standard of living, and her right to housing in particular. Someone has secure tenure if she is protected from being removed arbitrarily and involuntarily from her home or land. Security of tenure is widely recognized in international human rights law as a central tenet of the right to adequate housing and increasingly seen as fundamental to the enjoyment of the right to life. International law provides that security of tenure should be extended to all, regardless of the type of tenure (e.g., squatter, rental, leasehold, freehold, communal). Tenure is considered secure only if it is protected by legislation rather than protected merely through custom and tradition, which are more easily altered and often subject to arbitrary change.

Security of tenure can be denied to women in a variety of ways, including gender-biased law, customary laws, tradition and dominant social attitudes, domestic violence, and financial barriers. Any one of these can threaten women's security of tenure by preventing them from owning, inheriting, leasing, renting, or remaining in housing and on land. The effect of insecurity of tenure is that at any time a woman can be forced to leave her home and be removed from her land. Security of tenure—or its absence—is particularly relevant to women, as household economic security often rests on women's shoulders.

Security of tenure can be threatened in many ways, all of which impact women's right to housing:[24]

- In many cultures a widow loses all claim to her home and land, which by tradition revert to her husband's family or clan, to which she no longer belongs.
- A squatter community targeted for forced eviction lacks security of tenure; those living in the community do not know how long they can remain in their homes.
- When a marriage dissolves, a woman will lack security of tenure if her name does not appear on the title of the house—even if she has lived in the house for many years. Without title, in many jurisdictions, her former husband can legally remove her from the home and do whatever he chooses with the house, land, or property.
- A low-income tenant paying market-level rent in a city where the rental market is not regulated and where rents are rising rapidly lacks security of tenure. Her landlord can raise the rent at any time, making it unaffordable and forcing the tenant out.

Forced Eviction

A major cause of tenure insecurity is forced eviction, the temporary or permanent removal against the will of individuals, families, or communities from the home lands they occupy. Forced evictions place women at major risk of having their right to an adequate standard of living violated. Vulnerable groups may be singled out for eviction, such as women who have lost their husbands or a male family member. When a husband dies or a couple divorces, a woman may be evicted if the land title was in her husband's name. Often girl children are not allowed to inherit property, and land is willed instead to a brother or other male family member. The argument is that the girl will be married, and that land is not useful to her. There is generally no recourse for women and girls in these circumstances, partially because they may hesitate to report the violation to authorities. Women also suffer disproportionably when they must rebuild a home or move elsewhere.[25]

Situations in which forced evictions are most likely to occur include:

- slum removals in urban areas
- development and infrastructure projects (e.g., construction of dams and other energy projects)
- prestigious international events (e.g., Olympics)
- urban redevelopment or city beautification projects
- conflict over land rights or lack of documentation for women (i.e., legal will or housing title)
- the removal or reduction of housing subsidies for low-income groups
- forced population transfers and forced relocations in the context of armed conflict
- separation of ethnic or racial groups
- loss of male family members, particularly loss of husband
- refugee movements
- reclamations of public land.[26]

Forced evictions have been widely recognized as a violation of the right to housing. In cases where eviction is unavoidable, states are required to ensure that it does not render people homeless or vulnerable to the violation of their human rights.[27]

Women may be subjected to violence during forced evictions or as a result of forced eviction. The threat and uncertainty of eviction places high levels of stress on women and can limit their mobility.

Women may be involved in acts of resistance to forced eviction, which is frequently met with violence by state officials, such as police officers and the military. Physical and sexual violence against women may be used as a tactic to intimidate the community and deter those who would resist forced eviction. Women may experience verbal abuse, beatings, rape, killings, burning and destruction of property, and destruction of homes during the eviction process.[28]

Women who become homeless as a result of forced evictions are at greater risk of experiencing physical, sexual, and psychological violence.[29] In addition, relocation and deprivation of traditional means of subsistence lead to greater poverty and unemployment as well as to breakdowns in family and community support networks.[30]

Evicted women also bear the burden of rebuilding housing, taking care of the family with limited resources, and rebuilding community support networks.[31]

Violence, Poverty, and Housing

For women who are victims of domestic violence, the challenge of accessing adequate housing may limit the option of escaping the violent environment and resettling elsewhere. Even temporary or emergency relief may be difficult to access since shelters for women fleeing abusive relationships are uncommon in many countries, especially in rural areas. In wealthy nations, budget cuts to social services have resulted in a decrease in the number of shelters and the number of spaces available in shelters, making them extremely difficult for women to access.

Women's poverty is another condition that can contribute to domestic violence. When housing is treated as a market commodity, the ability to pay rent or buy determines housing security. As governments reduce welfare entitlements and enforce policies based on economic restraint, already-vulnerable women, especially those who head households, face even higher levels of poverty. Housing activists fear that women who are unable to pay their rent may fall prey to the sexual advances of men in positions of power such as landlords and property managers. In each of these contexts women have nowhere to go to escape the violence, and thus they face an almost impossible dilemma: to endure physical or psychological abuse or to accept homelessness and its accompanying risks to themselves and their children, including more violence.

Gender-biased policies in financing for housing create additional barriers for women seeking adequate housing. Policies of financial institutions for mortgages and other forms of housing loans often put women at a significant disadvantage. In most countries the process of applying for a loan assumes literacy levels that many women lack. In addition, because housing loans are often large, they entail long-term repayment, often require possession of other property to serve as collateral, and cover only a percentage of the price.[32] In many instances the cost of a down payment or deposit far exceeds women's available resources. In some countries, women are classified as minors and can acquire credit only with a husband's or male relative's approval and guarantee. In Lesotho, for example, married women were considered legal minors who could not own property until 2006, when the Parliament of Lesotho enacted a law ending the minority status of married women and giving them rights to own property.[33]

Habitat II Agenda[34]

The Habitat Agenda was adopted at the UN Conference on Human Settlements (Habitat II) in 1996. Women's equal access to land, housing, and property is one of the overall guiding principles of the Habitat Agenda. Chapter II of the Habitat Agenda provides that equitable human settlements are those in which all people, without discrimination, have equal access to housing as well as an equal right to inheritance, ownership of land, and other property and credit. The Agenda also notes that women's empowerment is fundamental to sustainable human settlements and development (paragraph 27).

Commitment A (Adequate Shelter for All) commits states to "providing legal security of tenure and equal access to land to all people, including women and those living in poverty; and undertaking legislative and administrative reforms to give women full and equal access to economic resources, including the right to inheritance and to ownership of land and other property, credit, natural resources and appropriate technology" (paragraph 40[b]).

Commitment D (Gender Equality) commits states to ensure gender equality in all aspects of human settlements, such as integration of gender perspectives in settlements-related legislation, policies, programs, and projects; development of conceptual and practical methodologies for incorporating gender perspective into human settlements planning; development and evaluation; and formulation and strengthening of policies and practices to promote the full and equal participation of women in human settlements planning and decision making (paragraph 46).

These goals and commitments are complemented by strategies for implementation that recommend the eradication of legal and social barriers to women's equal and equitable access to land.

In paragraph 78 of the document, states are called upon to:

- promote awareness campaigns and education regarding women's legal rights with respect to tenure, land ownership, and inheritance
- review legal and regulatory frameworks to ensure that equal rights of women and men are clearly specified and enforced
- support community projects, policies, and programs that aim to remove all barriers to women's access to affordable housing and property ownership, economic resources, infrastructure, and social services while ensuring the full participation of women in all decision-making processes
- promote mechanisms for the protection of women who risk losing their homes and properties when their husbands die.

Obstacles to the Realization of Women's Right to Shelter

- In Mongolia, housing became privatized as the country transitioned to an open-market economy. Over a five-year period the cost of housing rose by more than 5,000 percent. By 1998, an estimated 70,000 families—most headed by single mothers—were living in poverty, an extremely difficult situation without adequate housing in the freezing winter season.[35]

continues

Obstacles to the Realization of Women's Right to Shelter Continued

- Between 1996 and 2006, 200,000 refugees in Shan State of Burma were forcibly evicted to Thailand as a result of the Salween Dam project and ongoing conflict. As of 2006, refugees continued to enter Thailand at a rate of around 300 per month. Women's groups have reported continuing sexual violence involving women refugees, including the use of "comfort women" by warring troops in the area.[36]
- Massive urban slum eviction occurred in Mumbai, India: "They came for three days crushing house after house. One woman died when her house was crushed. . . . They forced me to give [my own kerosene] to set my house on fire and burn it down, all I possessed, my life, destroyed in merely a few moments."[37]
- According to Fijian customs, a woman moves into her husband's house after marriage. Even if the couple build the house together, the woman can claim only the amount of money she contributed to building the house, but the husband retains ownership of the house. Thus in situations of domestic violence, women are expected to move out of the "husband's" home. Women's groups are raising awareness among women facing domestic violence about the possibilities of staying in the house and having the husband leave.[38]

✠ Learning Activity 4 ✠
Thinking About Adequate Housing as a Human Right

Objective　To describe the problem of inadequate housing, to uncover the interrelationship between the right to housing and other human rights, and to plan for change
Time　45 minutes
Materials　Chart paper and markers or blackboard and chalk

1. Describe

Divide participants into small groups. Ask them to discuss housing problems faced by women in your community.

- What are the housing problems in your community? How do they especially affect women?
- Are there homeless people in the community? How many?
- Are there characteristics that many homeless women have in common?
- Is there a typical age, racial or ethnic group, or social group (e.g., disability) for homeless women in the community?
- How do women become homeless in the community?
- What permanent housing is available to homeless people in the community? Is the housing adequate? Is it considered healthy (e.g. clean, access to clean water, secure, free of environmental pollution), and safe?

Ask a representative from each group to summarize their discussion. List their findings.

✠ Learning Activity 4 Continued ✠

2. Discuss

What are the connections between adequate housing and other human rights?

- Do you consider housing a human right to which everyone is entitled?
- What policies and practices contribute to the violation or denial of this human right?
- How is the right to adequate housing related to other human rights? To the right to food and water? To employment? To education? To health care? To freedom from violence?
- How do participants justify or explain that certain people enjoy the right to adequate housing while others do not? Are these explanations convincing? Why or why not?

3. Plan

- What can advocates do to help promote the right to adequate housing for women in the community?
- Identify existing policies, practices, and/or attitudes that need to be modified, strengthened, or eliminated.
- Identify prospective policies, practices, and/or attitudes that need to be introduced to address the problem of inadequate housing in the community.
- What conclusions can you draw from this discussion about women and the attainment of a decent standard of living?

Source: Adapted from *Human Rights Education, The Fourth R* (Chicago: Human Rights Educators Network, Amnesty International USA, Spring 1998).

Human Rights and Millennium Development Goals

In September 2000, representatives of 189 nations, including 147 heads of state, met at the United Nations to commit themselves to making the right to development a reality for everyone and to freeing the entire human race from want. This UN Millennium Declaration[39] acknowledged that progress is based on sustainable economic growth, which must focus on the poor, with human rights at the center.

The objective of the Declaration is to promote "a comprehensive approach and a coordinated strategy, tackling many problems simultaneously across a broad front." It calls for halving the number of people who live on less than one dollar a day by the year 2015. To achieve these "Millennium Development" goals, richer countries are to provide direct support to developing countries in the form of aid, trade, debt relief, and investment.[40] This effort involves goals such as finding solutions to hunger and promoting gender equality. (See the nearby box for a list of all eight Millennium Development goals.)

The Millennium Development Goals[41]

Goal 1: Eradicate extreme poverty and hunger.
Goal 2: Achieve universal primary education.
Goal 3: Promote gender equality and empower women.
Goal 4: Reduce child mortality.
Goal 5: Improve maternal health.
Goal 6: Combat HIV/AIDS, malaria, and other diseases.
Goal 7: Ensure environmental sustainability.
Goal 8: Develop a global partnership for development.

Remembering Core Concepts

✠ Learning Activity 5: Speaking Out for ✠ Women's Human Right to an Adequate Standard of Living

Objectives To examine women's right in the community to an adequate standard of living and consider how to take action to improve it

Time 60+ minutes

Materials Chart paper and markers

1. Brainstorm

Ask participants to list problems women in their community face related to an adequate standard of living. Encourage them to include clean water, clothing, health care and livelihood, as well as food and housing. Ask participants, working in small groups, to choose a problem on which they wish to concentrate.

2. Discuss/Plan

Ask each group to prepare a five-minute presentation to a "panel of community leaders" on their problem. Each presentation should:

- describe the problem, identifying the group(s) of women it impacts and, if possible, the cause(s) of the problem
- relate the problem to women's human rights
- clarify how the problem affects women's lives
- show how addressing the problem can improve their lives
- propose specific actions that should be taken to address the problem
- show how members of the community can get involved in addressing the problem.

Ask each group to choose a spokesperson to make the presentation and a "community leader" to serve on the panel. While the groups plan their presentations, the panel of leaders meets to decide on their roles, representing a variety of differing but typical attitudes within the community leadership.

❖ Learning Activity 5 Continued ❖

3. Present/Role-Play
The spokesperson from each group makes a presentation and members of the panel listen and respond, asking questions and offering comments, objections, or suggestions in keeping with their chosen roles.

4. Discuss
After the presentations and role-play, discuss these questions:

- How did the spokespersons feel when presenting the problem?
- How did the "community leaders" respond to the presentation? What attitudes in the community were they representing?
- How did the audience, composed of the rest of the group, respond to the presentations?
- Did any spokesperson discuss the problem as a human rights violation? Did putting the problem in a human rights context strengthen the argument? Why or why not?
- Are these ideas for improving women's human right to an adequate standard of living feasible in your community? Why or why not?

5. Conclude
Challenge the participants by asking them to evaluate their knowledge of the problem and the inclusiveness of their perspective:

- How did you obtain your information about standard-of-living issues faced by women in your community? Was it accurate and complete? If not, what additional information do you need and how can you obtain it?
- Did you personally consult women about the problem and how it affects them? About actions that could improve the problem?
- Why is it important in real-life human rights advocacy to include the active participation of those directly involved and affected?
- How can you apply the example of this learning activity to planning and implementing advocacy for the human right of women in your community to an adequate standard of living?

Notes

1. Martha Chen, Joann Vanek, Francie Lund, James Heintz, Renana Jhabvala, and Christine Bonner, *Progress of the World's Women, 2005: Women, Work, and Poverty* (New York: UNIFEM, 2005.)

2. Committee on Economic, Social and Cultural Rights, General Comment 3, 1990, HRI/GEN/1/Rev. 5, p. 20.

3. Mariama Williams, in *The Indivisibility of Women's Human Rights*, edited by Susana T. Fried (New Brunswick, NJ: Center for Women's Global Leadership, 1994), p. 68.

4. UN High Commissioner for Human Rights, Fact Sheet No. 21 (1996), *The Human Right to Adequate Housing*, available online at http://www.ohchr.org/english/about/publications/docs/fs21.htm.

5. Center on Housing Rights and Evictions, *Fact Sheet on Women's Right to Housing, Land and Property*, available online at http://www.cohre.org.

6. UN Food and Agriculture Organization, available online at http://www.fao.org.

7. UN Food and Agriculture Organization, Committee on World Food Security, Twenty-seventh Session (Rome, 28 May–1 June 2001), *Fostering the Political Will to Fight Hunger*, 2001.

8. UN Food and Agriculture Organization, *The State of Food Insecurity in the World*, 2002.

9. World Food Programme World Hunger Map (dynamic), available online at http://www.wfp.org/country_brief/hunger_map/map/hungermap_popup/map_popup.html.

10. World Bank, *World Resources 2000–2001*, pp. 25–26.

11. World Health Organization, *World Health Report 2002* (2007), available online at http://www.who.int/home.

12. Center for Economic and Social Rights, available online at http://www.cesr.org.

13. Ibid.

14. *Innocenti Declaration on the Protection, Promotion and Support of Breastfeeding* (1990).

15. Convention on the Rights of the Child, Article 24.

16. *Innocenti Declaration on the Protection, Promotion and Support of Breastfeeding* (1990).

17. Committee on International Covenant on Economic, Social and Cultural Rights, General Comment No. 12, paragraph 15.

18. *Protocol Additional to the Geneva Conventions of 12 August 1949, and relating to the Protection of Victims of Non-International Armed Conflicts (Protocol II)* Article 14 (1977).

19. Committee on Economic, Social and Cultural Rights, "General Comment 12," 1999, HRI/GEN/1/Rev.5, p. 57; see also "Report of the Special Rapporteur on the Right to Food," E/CN.4/2001/53 (2001).

20. "Report of the Special Rapporteur on the Right to Food," E/CN.4/2001/53 (2001).

21. IFAD, South Asia, "How Women and Their Households Cope with Food Insecurity," 1998, available online at http://www.ifad.org/gender/learning/; Azad, Nandini, *Engendered Mobilization—The Key to Livelihood Security: IFAD's Experience in South Asia* (Rome: IFAD, 1999); Siddiqur Rahman Osmani, *Food Security, Poverty and Women: Lessons from Rural Asia, Part I* (Rome: IFAD/TAD, 1998); Suman Subba and Aneela Z. Babar, *Strengthening Gender Initiatives in IFAD Projects: Case Study of Hills Leashold Forest and Forage Development Project in Nepal* (Draft) (Rome: IFAD, 2001).

22. Julie Mertus, *War's Offensive on Women* (West Hartford, CT: Kumarian Press, 2000).

23. Center for Economic and Social Rights, "The Right to Housing," available online at http://cesr.org/housing.

24. Habitat International Coalition Housing and Land Rights Network/Middle East and North Africa, "Women's Right to Housing—A Legal Overview," available online at http://www.hic-mena.org/.

25. Centre on Housing Rights and Evictions, "In Search of Equality: A Survey of Law and Practice Related to Women's Inheritance Rights in the Middle East and North Africa (MENA) Region," Geneva, Switzerland, October 2006.

26. Centre on Housing Rights and Evictions, "Forced Evictions: Violations of Human Rights—Global Survey 10, Geneva, Switzerland, December 2006.

27. CESCR General Comment 7, "The Right to Adequate Housing: Art. 11.1—Forced Evictions, available online at http://www.unhchr.ch/tbs/doc.nsf/(symbol)/CESCR+General+Comment+7.En?OpenDocument.

28. Centre on Housing Rights and Evictions, *Forced Evictions—A Manual for Action and Human Rights*, May 1999.

29. Centre on Housing Rights and Evictions, "Fact Sheet on Women's Right to Housing, Land and Property," undated.

30. Special Rapporteur on Violence Against Women, E/CN.4/2000/68/Add.5.

31. Centre on Housing Rights and Evictions, "In Search of Equality."

32. Centre on Housing Rights and Evictions, "Women and Housing Rights," Geneva, September 2000.

33. Kathryn McConnel, "Gender Equality Linked to Economic Growth, U.S. Official Says: New Policy Requires Data on Gender Inequality in Development Plans," U.S. Department of State, March 1, 2007.

34. "Report of the United Nations Conference on Human Settlements (Habitat II), Istanbul 3–14 June 1996," Habitat Agenda, U.N. Doc. A./CONF.165/14 (August 7, 1996).

35. World Vision International: Mongolia Country Profile, "Development Issues," July 2003, available online at http://www.wvi.org/wvi/country_profile/profiles/mongolia.htm.

36. Programme Report: July to December 2006, Including Revised Funding Appeal for 2007. Thailand Burma Border Consortium, 2006.

37. Birte Schulz, "Crushed Homes, Crushed Lives: Women and Forced Evictions," July 2003.

38. "The Interlinkages Between Violence Against Women and Women's Right to Adequate Housing," Discussion Paper, Asia Pacific Regional Consultations with the UN Special Rapporteur on the Right to Adequate Housing, Office of the United Nations High Commissioner for Human Rights, 2003, available online at http://www.ohchr.org/english/issues/housing/women.htm.

39. United Nations Millennium Declaration, available online at http://www.un-documents.net/a55r2.htm A/RES/55/2.

40. "The Millennium Development Goals Indicators," United Nations Statistics Division, July 2006.

41. "The Millennium Development Goals Report: 2006, Inter-Agency and Expert Group on MDG Indicators," Department of Economic and Social Affairs of the United Nations Secretariat, New York, 2006.

9

Women's Human Rights and Globalization

Although some new employment opportunities have been created for women as a result of the globalization of the economy, there are also trends that have exacerbated inequalities between women and men.
—Beijing Platform for Action, paragraph 157

Objectives

The learning activities and background information in this chapter will enable participants to work toward the following objectives:

- Analyze the impact of globalization on women's human rights.
- Think critically and constructively about the role of multinational corporations.
- Begin to explore the impact of development models on women.
- Identify the role of government, community leaders, the media, and women themselves in transforming the economy to better promote women's human rights.
- Remember core concepts.

Getting Started:
Thinking About Women and Globalization

Globalization is the process by which worldwide interconnectedness increases due to changes in technology, capital, transportation, and rapid communication and informational flow. Historically and politically complex, it is defined by Thomas Friedman as

the inexorable integration of markets, nation-states, and technologies to a degree never witnessed before—in a way that is enabling individuals, corporations and nation-states to reach around the world farther, faster, deeper and cheaper than ever before . . . the spread of free-market capitalism to virtually every country in the world.[1]

Globalization involves interdependent networks spanning continents and oceans. Throughout these networks flow capital and goods, information and ideas, and people. The networks are composed of multiple rather than single linkages, and relationships reach across continents, far beyond the once-regional networks.

The globalized economy of the twenty-first century offers many women access to new careers and flexible jobs in a seemingly ever-expanding labor market. Unprecedented choices for consumption present themselves, and new routes emerge to enhance personal development. Moreover, new channels of information and technologies of communication improve understanding of global issues, thus potentially helping social movements to organize and promote wider adherence to human rights standards.

Globalization, however, does not benefit all people equally. Nor do all people have an equal influence over the direction and impact of globalization. Women are among those most likely to be left out of the central decision-making process. Yet some men have also been affected negatively, though in a different manner: "[G]lobalization, economic change, poverty, and social change have eroded men's traditional roles as providers, causing men to seek affirmation of their masculinity in other ways—unsafe sexual practices, and domestic and social violence—which affects them, their families, and society."[2]

Globalization leaves in its wake increasing gaps between the rich and the poor.[3] Evidence of its impact also indicates that wealthier countries (and the wealthy people within those countries) are more likely to benefit from global market economies than poorer countries (and the poor people within them). Income per capita has grown from thirty times the difference between the richest country and the poorest country in 1960 to seventy times the difference at the turn of the century.[4] And as a European study has shown, job insecurity and unequal wages are on the increase, with incomes of the highest-paid workers in nineteen out of twenty-one European countries growing at a faster rate than incomes of the lowest-paid workers.[5]

This chapter analyzes both the positive and negative impacts of the global economy on the human rights of women. At the same time, it considers the ways in which women's human rights advocates have played a role in the reshaping of globalization, building up counterweights and countervailing forces.[6]

Globalization and development intersect with the women's rights topics covered in other chapters. In particular, see Chapter 8, "Women's Human Right to an Adequate Standard of Living"; Chapter 10, "Women's Human Rights and Work," which focuses specifically on the question of women's rights in the workplace; and Chapter 13, "Human Rights of Refugee, Displaced and War-Affected Women," which more closely examines the role of migration and the economy.

⊠ Learning Activity 1: The Global Marketplace ⊠

Objective To introduce and personalize the concept of the global market-place

Time 30 minutes

Materials Chart paper and markers or blackboard and chalk

1. Examine

Have eight to ten volunteers come to the front of the group. Ask them to work in pairs to check the labels on their clothes to find out where they were made. As participants call out the countries, list them, putting a check mark next to each multiple reference. Include shoes, eyeglasses, and headgear.

2. Analyze/Discuss

Once this list has been completed, ask the group to analyze the results. (In almost every case the labels will indicate that the garments were made in a developing country.) Address the following questions:

- Are most of the clothes made locally or imported?
- Are they mostly handmade or factory-made? Why?
- Would this list be different if it had been created five years ago? Ten years ago? Twenty years ago?
- Why do you think this small group of people is found to be wearing clothing from such diverse countries?
- Were the brand names from corporations headquartered in countries other than where they were manufactured? Why would clothing corporations manufacture their products in another country?
- Who do you think made the fabric in your clothes? Made the buttons and the sleeves? Was it likely a man or a woman?
- What do you think were the working conditions of the people who made these clothes? Were they children? Did they enjoy safe working conditions? Did they have the right to belong to a union?
- How does this learning activity illustrate the effects of globalization? If necessary, read aloud the definition of *globalization.*
- What is the responsibility of consumers to the human rights of workers who make the products they buy? Can consumers actually influence economic factors? If so, how?

What Is the Impact of Globalization on Women?

The Bejing+5 report of the 2000 United Nations General Assembly notes that globalization presents opportunities to some women but at the same time threatens to harm women economically, politically, and culturally.

As pointed out in a five-year review of the Beijing Platform for Action in 2000, the benefits of changing economies in a globalized society are unevenly distributed. While some women are achieving great economic security, for others globalization has led to increased economic disparities, increased gender inequality, deteriorating work conditions, and unsafe working environments.[7]

According to the UN's International Research and Training Institute for the Advancement of Women (INSTRAW):

> During the last decade there have been several changes in the way poverty is addressed, including changes to poverty eradication policies. These changes are reflected in the shift from a psychological model of deprivation, focused on the failure to meet basic material and physiological needs, to a social model of deprivation focused on such elements as lack of autonomy and dignity and powerlessness.[8]

In this view, poverty is caused by exclusion and lack of power to claim legitimate rights;[9] therefore, expanding the opportunities and choices of impoverished individuals and groups, including women, is a reasonable strategy for reducing poverty.

Diversification of Women's Employment Opportunities

As noted, the impact of globalization is not always negative for women: For some it has offered greater possibilities for job training and skill development. The majority of women workers, however, labor under inferior working conditions with serious implications for their social and physical health. Some women in the lower-end labor-intensive consumer electronics industries, for example, suffer from health problems ranging from extreme fatigue to general health problems due to chemical hazards and job stress.

The International Labour Organisation (ILO) has found that women migrant workers, in particular, experience low wages, long shifts, unhealthy and dangerous conditions, and psychological, physical, and sexual aggression from men.[10] In developing countries, where informal employment comprises 80 to 95 percent of all employment,[11] women who work in their own or others' homes may handle toxic substances in spaces not equipped for proper storage or ventilation. And those who work in public places, such as in the streets or in parks, are not only exposed to pollution and the weather but also must deal with possible harassment, confiscation of goods, and physical assault by authorities.[12]

Migration, Breakdown of the Extended Family, and Kinship Networks

As of 2005, there were 191 million migrants worldwide.[13] Globalization has led to greater movement of peoples across traditional borders. Increased numbers of male migrants have also led to increased numbers of female heads of households, many of whom live in poverty. These changes have led to societal changes in beliefs regarding traditional gender roles, and divorce is occurring in much higher numbers as a result.[14]

The UN's *2004 World Summary on the Role of Women in Development* noted that migration can be an empowering experience for women themselves, allowing them to "move away from situations where they live under traditional, patriarchal authority to situations where they are empowered to exercise greater autonomy over their own lives . . . [taking] on new roles and [assuming] new responsibility for decisions affecting the social and economic well-being of their households."[15] Migrating women thus have the opportunity to break the bonds of traditionally oppressive family structures; however, they may not have a well-defined family support network on which to rely.

✠ **Learning Activity 2: Weighing the Positive and** ✠
Negative Effects of Globalization on Women

Objective   To evaluate the positive and negative effects of globalization on
women
Time   45 minutes
Materials   Pens and paper

1. Discuss/Plan
Remind participants of the key issues discussed in the preceding section on globalization's impact on women: migration and employment trends. Divide the participants into two (or an even number of) groups. Ask half the participants to brainstorm all the positive impacts of globalization on women, especially on women in their own country and local community. Ask the other half to list negative impacts.

When this task is complete, each group should choose the five most significant impacts from their lists and assign each of these points to five different participants or pairs of participants, who will present the list to the whole group.

2. Debate
Call on each group to present one of its points, alternating between positive and negative impacts. After each presentation, ask for comments or rebuttals from the opposite group. Be careful to limit discussion time so that all points are discussed equally.

3. Discuss
Conclude the debate by asking what actions are needed to enhance the positive impacts of globalization and to decrease the negative ones.

- What actions can women take in their own communities?
- What actions are already being taken?

Human Trafficking: The Intersection of Poverty, Migration, and Commodification of Women

Globalization has been a major factor in the increase of human trafficking, often referred to as modern-day slavery. The United Nations Protocol to Prevent, Suppress, and Punish Trafficking in Persons defines *human trafficking* as "the illegal trade of human beings, through abduction, the use or threat of force, deception, fraud or 'sale' for the purposes of sexual exploitation or forced labor."[16] Globalization, along with liberalized borders, has increased migration of all people, and a greater market for women and children has made human trafficking a worldwide problem. Increased poverty creates economic necessity, which drives trafficking—particularly for women aged 18 to 25 and children aged 12 to 17—for illegal labor and sexual services. Trafficking victims are often poor, unemployed, uneducated, illiterate, or have a history of abuse.[17] Human rights activists estimate that 200–400 young Bangladeshi women and children are smuggled every month from Bangladesh into Pakistan. Most of them end up in prostitution.[18]

A worldwide market for sex tourism has created an increasing demand for trafficking victims. Traffickers have created complex networks to create thriving businesses that circumvent international legislation and immigration policies. New globalized tools such as international media and the Internet allow traffickers to target foreigners around the world to attract them to nightclubs, brothels, massage parlors, sex tourism destinations, and even arranged marriages to facilitate trafficking.[19]

International responses to the trafficking in women and girls fall into one of two categories: law enforcement or human rights advocacy.

- The law enforcement approach to combating human trafficking refers to all activities related to writing and implementing anti-trafficking measures; capturing and prosecuting traffickers; and training police and other defenders of the law such as lawyers and judges. Such strategies, designed to stop illegal or undesirable activities, are mainly enacted by law enforcement agencies and are intended to punish those who are found guilty of crimes related to trafficking.[20]
- The human rights approach refers to activities that emphasize prevention of trafficking; protection of trafficked persons after they have been removed or have escaped from the trafficking situation; and rehabilitative services. Strategies within a human rights framework are thought to empower the victims of trafficking. Empowering strategies are activities that enable people to protect themselves from trafficking by addressing the root causes of the crime. Such strategies might include measures to overcome poverty, procedures to address discrimination, and mass education and public-awareness programs to publicize the risks and dangers involved in trafficking.[21]

Today, many international law enforcement agencies are working with organizations to combine these two approaches to combating trafficking. The operationalization of anti-trafficking measures has taken much longer because it has entailed rewriting laws, providing legal and social protection of victims as witnesses in criminal investigations, training of police to be sensitive to victims of trafficking, creating a national referral mechanism, and training and providing technical assistance to officials in the judicial system. At the turn of the century, law enforcement and anti-trafficking organizations began to take steps to address human trafficking. Between 2000 and 2005, Bangladeshi authorities arrested 296 traffickers and convicted 56 of them. Of the persons who had been trafficked, 170 were repatriated. These successes were supported by Bangladeshi community trafficking awareness campaigns and public awareness—raising marches in the streets with 30,000 Bangladeshis, including government officials, turning out to celebrate.[22]

Efforts to Combat Trafficking: Japan's Action Plan[23]

Vital Voices Global Partnership, a U.S. NGO, began a program in 2004 to address the serious problem of women who were trafficked from the Philippines to Japan. Japan had an "entertainer" visa that was used to exploit Filipino women. These women came as singers or dancers on a six-month visa. However, the women were performing not as singers and dancers but, rather, in large numbers as "bar girls," working for low wages and obliged to do *Dohan*, a date with customers in the daytime. They were fined penalties for low sales and at times were working as prostitutes on overdue visas. The Philippine government, conversely, received enormous remittances from migrants overseas and did not wish to stem the emigration tide. NGOs in Japan and the Philippines were working for an immigration policy change.

Vital Voices began a dialogue with civil society and government officials to determine the best methods of combating human trafficking in Japan. The U.S. State Department's Office to Combat and Monitor Trafficking in Persons was also consulted. In order to manage relationships among the government of Japan, the U.S. government, and civil society in the Philippines and Japan, Vital Voices facilitated direct communication among the diverse stakeholders.

Through this process, in 2006, Japan created an Action Plan to Combat Trafficking. The entertainer visa was no longer given unless an individual could prove that she had two years of experience as a singer or dancer. The government surveyed victims of trafficking in Japan and created shelters for them. It also began a campaign aimed at drafting legislation for protection of and assistance to trafficking victims as well as prevention of trafficking and an awareness-raising campaign.

✠ Learning Activity 3: Trafficking and Gender Bias ✠

Objective To understand the relationship between trafficking and gender bias

Time 45 minutes

Materials Pens and paper

1. Read

Ask someone to read aloud this report, written by Filipino Judge Nimfa Cuesta Vilches, a tireless international advocate for the protection of young women and girls against trafficking:

> A girl child in the Philippines is discriminated upon early in life due to culture-based and family-reinforced gender biases. For instance, despite her special nutritional needs in preparation as future mother and nurturer, the girl child is allotted less food than her father and her brothers. When money for education is scarce, her brothers are given the preference.
>
> The Filipino girl child takes on the stereotyped role of her mother who is portrayed as an abused and submissive woman relegated to domestic work. Moreover, the public considers girls and women as sex objects and typifies them as club/bar entertainers, beauty pageant contestants, and racy or pornographic film stars.
>
> The pejorative expectations that Filipino society has for women and children are compounded by problems of extreme poverty; massive labor export; globalization; porous borders; aggressive tourism campaigns; negative portrayal of women by mass media; pornography on-line and Internet chat-rooms; the practice of mail-order brides; inter-country adoption; and joint military exercises in

✠ Learning Activity 3 Continued ✠

the country with visiting forces from abroad. These factors cause women to become easy victims of sex-trafficking and other forms of sexual exploitation either in the Philippines or in countries of destination.

Because of the dire employment situation in 2000, around 600,000 prostitutes worked in the Philippines' sex trade, 50,000 of them children. With the trafficking in human beings reaching global proportions, the Philippine legislature was prompted in 2003 to enact the Anti-Trafficking in Persons Act, which protected trafficked persons under the category of "overseas Filipino in distress." This law entitled them to legal assistance extended by the Migrant Workers and Overseas Filipinos Act, without penalty to the person, and any issue of consent deemed irrelevant.[24]

2. Discuss

- How do the forces of globalization and poverty described by Judge Vilches exacerbate the sexual trafficking of women and girls? How does this trafficking violate their rights? What other factors also diminish their human rights?
- How and why do Filipino girls and women come to be treated as commodities? What overall strategies would you suggest to lessen these trends among girls and women in the Philippines?

The Role of Multinational Corporations

Multinational corporations (MNCs) draw heavily on female workers, and women in export factories account for between 70 percent and 90 percent of the total workforce.[25]

> Typically female industries have been the processing of textiles, leather and foodstuffs, the production of toys, electronic goods, and pharmaceuticals, as well as occupations in chemicals, rubber and metal-working. . . . Export production and liberalized trade thus serve as the engine of female employment. . . . But women have paid a high price for this in the shape of appalling working conditions, few rights, meagre pay, and no social security or sustainable livelihood. They are subjected to exhausting and monotonous work routines that are often injurious to their health.[26]

MNCs exert great influence over local economies, and their actions are often unrestricted by international laws. They can voluntarily choose to uphold international labor standards and conduct business as "model world citizens." They can also choose to advocate corporate social responsibility initiatives, "achieving commercial success while valuing people, communities, and the natural environment."[27] Indeed, there is a growing trend toward certification of products and corporations as Fair Trade, which ensures that workers and producers are paid fairly and that biodiversity is protected.[28]

Conversely, MNCs may attempt to maximize their own profits without concern for how this affects local communities and the environment. When challenged for their questionable practices, they may leave for other locations, resulting in loss of jobs. Also, many multinational corporations use contracting and subcontracting as strategies to keep costs low; this practice may divorce MNCs from the circumstances under which their product is manufactured and may permit them to claim no knowledge of or accountability for poor working conditions, treatment of workers, or environmental damage. In 2003 the UN adopted the Convention Against Corruption,[29] which was ratified by ninety-three countries as of June 2007.[30]

UNIFEM has found that organizing "is both an end in itself—as women achieve a sense of empowerment and are able to support each other—and a means to leveraging wider impact on the local, national, and international stage."[31] When women workers organize, they are able to confront such challenges as lack of knowledge of the outside world, insufficient crisis support, and underrepresentation in policy-making forums. In addition, by working together in different countries, across borders, they are better able to prevent companies from simply crossing borders for cheaper wages.

Strategies used by women's organizations include collective bargaining, often in the form of negotiations and planned strikes, and collective action such as marches, demonstrations, rallies, passive resistance, and use of the media.[32] When their numbers are small, women workers may choose to organize in cooperatives based either on the issues affecting them or on their trade, as in traditional trade unions.

Debt and the Global Economy

Structural Adjustment Programs and Poverty Reduction Strategies

The International Monetary Fund (IMF) was established to "promote international monetary cooperation, exchange stability, and orderly exchange arrangements; to foster economic growth and high levels of employment; and to provide temporary financial assistance to countries to help ease balance of payments adjustment."[33] For years, the IMF used the term *structural adjustment programmes* to refer to loans given to a nation with certain conditions attached. Under these programs, the indebted government was encouraged to adopt stabilization or austerity measures that entailed cutting government spending on services viewed as "non-essential," often in the areas of health and education. According to the head of the Gender Unit of the Third World Network African Secretariat, "The distributional effects of SAPs have been criticized as undemocratic in that they support accumulation by the trading and propertied classes at the expense of poor peasants, workers and the urban poor, the majority of whom are women."[34]

One study of the Kenyan agricultural sector showed that during the SAP era, women's burdens seem to have increased as SAP-related reforms placed more demands on their time:[35] "The more the state pulls out of social services, the more community tasks are taken over by groups within civil society, especially women doing voluntary [unpaid] work."[36]

The agricultural, anti-land-reform, and food-trade policies associated with SAPs were major engines in the urbanization of the global South, the worldwide ballooning of megacities, the migration toward the global North, and the growth in urban poverty and slums. As the Third World Network points out:

> By promoting external liberalization, SAP[s have] encouraged the increase in the extraction and export of raw materials in many countries, thus contributing to resource depletion and degradation. The growth of poverty and inequities resulting from debt and SAP[s] has also pushed poor farmers and communities to opening up forests to eke a living from the land."[37]

Since the turn of the century, the term *structural adjustment* has been little used; emphasis is now directed to *poverty reduction*. Developing countries are currently being encouraged to draw up poverty reduction strategy papers (PRSPs). Officially governments prepare PRSPs through a participatory process involving civil society and development partners, including the World Bank and the International Monetary Fund.[38] One observer has suggested that, although there may be a negative effect in a SAP's first year, gains tend to occur in subsequent years; therefore, a country under adjustment programs will ultimately see positive results from such changes.[39]

Critics argue, however, that many of the policies deemed "poverty reducing" actually increase poverty rather than decreasing it. Policies with unintended negative impacts include those described in the following sections.

Privatization. The International Monetary Fund's SAPs and PRSPs may call for the sell-off of government-owned enterprises to private owners, often foreign investors. Privatization is typically associated with layoffs and paycuts for workers in the privatized enterprises. According to a 2000 study on SAPs' effects in Tanzania, the requirement of privatizing agricultural enterprises increased the prices of fertilizer and other agricultural items while reducing access to credit: "While large farmers and private traders have benefited from . . . privatization, small farmers, who constitute the majority of Tanzania's population, have not."[40] Additionally, the Structural Adjustment Participatory Review Initiative (SAPRI), a network of 250 NGOs collaborating with the World Bank to evaluate the impact of adjustment lending and policy advice in selected countries, found in 2004 that, globally, "privatization of the mining sector [has] further eroded the environment and the viability of the land of small farmers and indigenous people."[41]

UNIFEM states that the PSRPs' "record on recognizing the importance of women's labor—both paid and unpaid—is [rather] spotty," as these programs fail to recognize that "women frequently face a higher risk of poverty due to low quality and instability of . . . employment."[42] It is possible that in the long term, PRSPs will contribute to the generation of the economic growth necessary to reduce overall poverty. However, until economic policies acknowledge and act upon the different roles and positions accorded to men and women around the world, especially in poor countries, such policies are likely only to exacerbate the impoverishment and economic subjugation of women.

Cuts in Government Spending. Reductions in government spending frequently reduce the services available to the poor, including health and education services, resulting in significant effects on women and girls. John Bomba, the national coordinator of Students Against Privatization in Zimbabwe, made this point about SAPs' negative effects:

> With the SAPs, public services were hit hard. Expenditure on medical staff and drugs were cut significantly. Education budgets were slashed. Exorbitant fees were introduced for all secondary schools and colleges which were previously free. This whole new dispensation brought the greatest disadvantage to the most vulnerable. States' subsidies on food and price controls were removed and people started starving. The country sank deeper and deeper into debt as the structural adjustment program depended on huge borrowings. By [19]97, the country was now spending 7 times more on debt servicing than on education and health.[43]

Higher Interest Rates. Higher interest rates exert a recessionary effect on national economies, leading to higher rates of joblessness and to the closure of many small businesses. The Committee for Cancellation of Third World Debt has argued that policies with high interest rates can "only increase domestic recession—the peasant farmer or craftsman who has to borrow to buy articles required for his production hesitates to do so or reduces his production through lack of funds—while invested capital thrives."[44] These high interest rates are justified by the claim that they attract foreign investors, but "in reality, capital attracted by high interest rates is volatile and flies to new horizons at the slightest hint of trouble or when a more profitable opportunity arises."[45]

Exports and Trade Liberalization. Countries are pressured to undertake a variety of measures to promote exports, at the expense of production for domestic needs. In the rural sector, the export orientation is often associated with the displacement of poor people who grow food for their own consumption, as their land is taken over by large plantations growing crops for foreign markets. As researchers at the University of Ghana have noted, "There is consensus that low commodity prices have not brought the economic returns expected from the promotion of export agriculture . . . [and] the promotion of export crops has implications for women farmers, most of whom have to work harder on export crop farms they do not own."[46]

The elimination of tariff protections for industries in developing countries has often led to mass layoffs. According to a 2003 study commissioned by the Organization for Economic Co-operation and Development, trade liberalization in Latin America and Africa resulted in a shift in the distribution of earnings away from the poorest, most unskilled workers by expanding exports of certain sectors that combined natural resources and skilled labor.[47]

Imposition of User Fees. Many IMF and World Bank loans have called for imposition of "user fees"—namely, charges for the use of government-provided services such as schools, health clinics, and provision of clean drinking water. For very poor people, even modest charges may result in the denial of access to services. Ghana, Swaziland, and the former Zaire were among the first African countries in which user fees replaced free services, and in each of these states it has been shown that the introduction of fees led to decreased use of such services.[48] Furthermore, investigations in Côte d'Ivoire have revealed that people with incomes below the median tend to decrease their use of services that require fees.[49] In fact, across Africa, attendance at hospitals and clinics dropped significantly after the introduction of user fees. In 2001, Uganda boosted its health care budget by 19 percent and stopped charging user fees; in some cases, attendance increased 100 percent at clinics.[50]

Debt Cancellation

In response to global outcry, the World Bank and the International Monetary Fund agreed in 2005 to cancel an estimated $40 billion of debt carried by eighteen poor countries in Africa and Latin America. Under the plan, twenty more of the world's poorest countries would become eligible for debt relief. The eighteen nations to become debt-free were Benin, Bolivia, Burkina Faso, Ethiopia, Ghana, Guyana, Honduras, Madagascar, Mali, Mauritania, Mozambique, Nicaragua, Niger, Rwanda, Senegal, Tanzania, Uganda, and Zambia. These countries were spending $100 million a day making bank payments that could have been used to fight HIV/AIDS, build literacy skills, and fund social development needs.[51]

Since 2005, the majority of debt—an average of 65 percent for each of the eighteen African countries[52]—owed to the World Bank and the IMF has been cancelled for twenty-two countries that qualified for debt relief.[53] As of 2007, 20 million more students are in school and more than a million more HIV and AIDS patients have access to treatment. Ghana has free education, Malawi has trained 4,000 more teachers each year.[54]

In the same year, to complement the World Bank and the IMF's efforts, the Inter-American Development Bank (IADB) granted the poorest countries in the Western Hemisphere 100 percent debt relief. Bolivia, Guyana, Haiti, Honduras, and Nicaragua were forgiven approximately $4 billion for investment in education, health, and social services in an effort to reach the United Nations Millennium Development Goals, which, as noted in Chapter 8, aim at halving poverty by 2015. The IADB will provide Ecuador, El Salvador, Guatemala, Paraguay, and Suriname access to a $250 million-a-year lending program as well.[55]

Beyond the eligible countries named for debt cancellation and assistance, others such as Bangladesh and Kenya are crippled with debt.[56] Nigeria, Iraq, and Indonesia are burdened by past regimes that misused loans and held no accountability.[57]

In 2005, the Group of Eight (G-8) Summit of world leaders—from the United States, Japan, Germany, the United Kingdom, France, Italy, Canada, and Russia—pledged a sum of $850 billion in aid to the poorest nations through 2010; by 2007, however, they had fallen short of that by $30 billion. Oxfam calculated that if this $30 billion had been made available for medical assistance to mothers, children, and HIV and AIDS patients, 5 million lives could have been saved.[58] In 2007 the G-8 pledged $60 billion to Africa to fight AIDS, tuberculosis, and malaria.[59]

✠ Learning Activity 4: Women and Poverty Reduction ✠

Objectives To clarify the reasons for poverty reduction policies, recognize their possible negative effects on women, and understand how women may prosper

Time 60 minutes

Materials None

1. Introduce

Review these poverty-reducing policies in the context of their effects upon women:

- Privatization
- Cuts in government spending
- Imposition of user fees
- Promotion of exports
- Higher interest rates
- Trade liberalization
- Debt cancellation.

Divide participants into seven groups and assign each one of these policies to discuss.

2. Discuss

Ask participants to address these questions:

- Why would this policy be recommended to governments? How could it help to reduce poverty? What questions would you like to ask economic planners about this policy?
- Have you ever experienced this policy in your own community and/or heard about such a policy in other countries or communities?
- Why do you think this policy could have a negative effect on women? List some specific effects.

Note to Facilitator: Facilitators and participants with little background in economics may be unable to answer some of these questions. Explain that if they lack knowledge, they should express this in the form of questions they would like to have answered. Emphasize that knowing what information is needed is a critical step toward learning.

3. Plan

Based on this discussion, create skits that illustrate how each poverty-reducing policy is intended to work and how it might have a negative effect on women. For example, participants might play the roles of a woman complaining to a member of the legislature, a government minister, an employer, or a lending institution.

Learning Activity 4 Continued

4. Present/Discuss
Ask the participants in each group to explain the policy they have discussed, to present their skit, and to explain the points they are trying to illustrate. Invite other members of the group to comment on and contribute to this discussion.

- Do you know of any examples of action to overcome these negative effects?
- Who is taking this action?

Women, Gender, and Development

Opinions differ on how best to promote equality and development for women. Some people argue that women-only projects are most effective at promoting women's needs while others feel that integrating women into development projects should be the goal. Certain organizations promote a welfare approach to women in development through, for example, free food programs. Other organizations feel that such an approach increases dependency and encourages income-generation activities. Indeed, this "add woman and stir" approach has been criticized for simply adding women into an inequitable system that itself should be examined for perpetuating inequalities.

For many years women's contribution to the economy went unrecognized, owing to assumptions about gender roles and to male ownership of land. International development projects and programs targeted men as the primary beneficiaries of training in the use of new technology and agricultural methods, even though agriculture often was predominantly women's work. Similarly, because the preponderance of those given training, credit, and other assistance were men, their access to the means of production was greatly enhanced.

To an increasing extent, however, development agencies are recognizing that women have multiple responsibilities related to work and family; such agencies now consult with women at the community level in the design and implementation of projects and, in some cases, build in a component that helps women assert their own needs and fundamental rights. These initiatives have been accompanied by acceptance of the concept *gender and development*. This concept holds that the gender roles of men and women—those qualities determined by society rather than by biology—lead to differences in needs, skills, and access to resources, which development plans should take into account if they are to be effective and equitable. The urgency associated with this concept proceeds from the fact that, as recognized by the World Bank, there is no region in the world where women's social, economic, and legal rights equal those of men.[60] At the same time, women consistently have less access to and control over resources (whether education, land, or finances), a circumstance that greatly lessens their ability to influence familial, community, and national decisions.[61] Therefore, in order for women to be able to participate in development, gender equality must be a central and non-negotiable goal of any governmental or international policy.

Accordingly, development planners have adopted the gender perspective. In 2001, the World Bank Group commissioned a report on gender and development whose authors concluded that "ignoring gender disparities comes at great cost—to people's well-being and to countries' abilities to grow sustainably, to govern effectively, and thus to reduce poverty."[62] The gender perspective rejects the traditional lens for examining the world—the lens through which differences between men and women are accepted as "natural" and the deeply embedded impact of structural inequalities is overlooked. Instead, such a perspective exposes the ways in which roles, attitudes, and relationships between women and men are constructed by all societies throughout the world, often to the detriment of women.

The gender perspective can be used to challenge dominant assumptions about central areas of concern, thereby bringing the experiences and capacities of women more to the forefront of development analysis and project implementation.

On the other hand, gender advocates who include men in the gender equation argue that "women are not always the losers and men are not always the winners," and that making generalized statements risks overlooking gender-specific inequities and vulnerabilities. As gender constructs differ from culture to culture,[63] an understanding of these constructs can contribute to supporting greater equality between men and women.

The inclusion of gender in development planning, then, is not just a matter of fairness; it is also a matter of effectiveness: "Studies suggest that when women and men are relatively equal, economies tend to grow faster, the poor move more quickly out of poverty, and the well-being of men, women and children is enhanced."[64] Nonetheless, differences between men's and women's needs traditionally have received less than full recognition in poverty analysis and participatory planning, and are frequently not taken into consideration in the selection and design of poverty reduction strategies.[65]

Gender-Based Budgeting

Gender-based budgeting is a tool that is increasingly being used to assess the fairness and effectiveness of state budgeting processes. The Council of Europe Informal Group on Gender Budgeting has defined the concept as "an application of gender mainstreaming in the budgetary process. It means a gender-based assessment of budgets, incorporating a gender perspective at all levels of the budgetary process and restructuring revenues and expenditures in order to promote gender equality."[66]

In short, gender-based budgeting is a method of looking at a budget, usually at the national level, to determine how to financially address gender equality. Allocating a specific amount or percentage of a budget to gender goals strengthens the connection between policies (e.g., laws to strengthen gender equality) and financial commitment. Allocating funding in a budget increases the accountability of a government to deliver on its promises.[67] The budget of a nation can arguably demonstrate the priorities of that nation. When equality-promoting laws or treaties are denied financial support, however, these initiatives may never become reality.

Steps to Create a Gender-Sensitive Budget[68]

- Identify and prioritize the problems facing women in a particular country.
- Assess existing government policies and programs to determine their current response to these problems.
- Assess the extent to which the government budget is adequate to implement the policies and programs needed to address the problems of the nation's women.
- Monitor the extent to which resources are used for their intended purpose and reach intended beneficiaries.
- Evaluate the impact of the resources spent on the problems identified in the first step.
- Reform policies if needed and begin the cycle anew.

Empowering Women Through Development

There is broad agreement in the development literature that women's empowerment is multidimensional. It comprises cognitive, economic, political, psychological, and also physical components that interact with one another:

- The cognitive dimension requires that women have an understanding of the conditions and causes of their subordination at various levels and entails making choices that challenge cultural expectations.
- The economic dimension stresses the overall importance of women's access to, and control over, productive resources such as land and credit. While this dimension accounts for a degree of financial independence, it is important to note that changes in the economic balance of power do not automatically translate into changes in traditional gender roles and norms.
- The political dimension requires that women have the capacity to analyze, organize, and mobilize for social change.
- The psychological dimension refers to the belief that women can act at personal as well as social levels to improve their individual relations and the societies in which they live.
- The physical dimension emphasizes women's control over their own bodies and sexuality and the need to protect themselves against violence.[69]

✠ Learning Activity 5 ✠
Gender and Development—Taking a Stand

Objective To set gender and development priorities
Time 60 minutes
Materials Chart paper and glue or tape for each group, set of eleven statements for each group (listed below) written on strips of paper

1. Discuss
Divide participants into small groups, and give each group a set of statements on strips of paper, glue or tape, and a sheet of chart paper divided into five columns labeled "Strongly Agree," "Moderately Agree," "Slightly Agree," Mildly Disagree," and "Strongly Disagree."

continues

⚜ Learning Activity 5 Continued ⚜

Explain the procedure:

- Someone reads each statement without comment.
- The group decides where to place the statement and attaches it to the sheet. Take a vote if the group cannot reach consensus.

2. Analyze

Ask each group to post its completed chart and allow time for everyone to compare charts. Ask the groups to identify differences in priorities and explain their decisions, especially where there are disagreements.

Following are the statements to be placed on strips of paper:

- A development project that benefits the whole community will automatically include women.
- Local development must be understood within the context of global economic forces.
- All development efforts should focus on women because women are responsible for holding the family and community together.
- We aim to help the poorest of the poor. Therefore, all our efforts should be aimed at helping poor women.
- When the situation is serious, you can't waste time thinking about gender issues.
- Development and human rights cannot be separated.
- If a community is involved in a national liberation struggle, focusing on women's needs is divisive.
- The important thing is to help the people most in need, not just the women.
- If women are educated, then development will automatically follow.
- True development for women would enable them to have the power to make meaningful choices about their lives.
- We should not talk about power because it is too threatening to the men.

3. Create a Story

Imagine a community that could result from ten years of ideal development. One participant starts and the next adds to the description until a full vision of the new society is presented.

The following points should be included in the story:

- What fundamental human rights promote your vision of development?
- What specific steps can each woman take right away to move herself and her community toward her vision of an ideal community?

Alternative: Draw images of this ideally developed community and discuss.

Source: Adapted from Suzanne Williams with Janet Seed and Adelina Mwau, *The Oxfam Gender Training Manual* (Oxfam, U.K., 1994).

Advocacy Strategies

According to the Montreal Principles (2002), improving women's human rights in the economy

> requires an understanding that focuses upon the subordination, stereotyping and structural disadvantage that women experience. It requires more than just formal legal recognition of equality between the sexes. It requires commitment by all responsible parties to take all necessary steps to address the actual material and social disadvantages of women.

The Center for Economic and Social Rights has identified two main types of strategies. One is *adversarial,* which includes "naming and blaming": applying pressure through public opinion and public actions, such as boycotts, designed to raise awareness and attract media attention; initiating lawsuits; and pushing for changes through diplomatic and political means. The other method is *cooperative:* networking and building alliances with unions, community-based organizations, international NGOs, national advocacy organizations, and government officials to assess the economic situation, jointly develop a plan of action, share implementation, and monitor progress.

The following list includes both adversarial and cooperative strategies for promoting and protecting women's human rights in the economy:

- *Promote collective action.* In August 2002, local women protestors who demanded basic services in their communities shut down at least six Chevron-Texaco installations in the Niger Delta.[70] In another area, peaceful protests by women crippled the oil giant's Nigeria operations and won them an unprecedented corporate pledge to build modern towns out of poor villages.[71]
- *Strengthen national laws on employment and corporations.* The Corporate Responsibility Coalition, representing over 130 organizations, including several women's organizations, is currently lobbying the British government "to enact laws that will ensure making profits is done so within the context of businesses' responsibilities to their stakeholders and their obligation to ensure their businesses are sustainable long term," while minimizing environmental and social harm.[72]
- *Form national or international coalitions.* In 2005, NARAL—a U.S. pro-choice organization that advocates for women's reproductive health—took action "naming and shaming" private pharmacies, including Wal-Mart, Rite-Aid, CVS, Walgreen's, and Eckerd, in more than twenty states that refused to dispense birth control to women with valid prescriptions.[73]
- *Push for more women to occupy decision-making positions in national governments and international trade and economic bodies.* In 2005, women held the greatest percentage of parliamentary seats in Rwanda (45 percent), but in 139 other states fewer than 25 percent parliamentary seats were held by women.[74] In 2005, women accounted for 52 percent of all staff at the World Bank but held only a quarter of the management and senior technical positions.[75] In 2002, women held only 15 percent of upper-management positions at the International Monetary Fund and

only 25 percent of senior positions at the UNDP.[76] Although these statistics represent an improvement over the past quarter-century, the situation they reflect is still far from being equitable.

- *Promote leadership and access to credit among working-class women.* The Working Women's Forum in India is a microfinance program with a grassroots history, based on the promotion of leadership among working-class women through cost-effective, large-scale outreach. Its credit program reaches more than 4 million poor entrepreneurs, with a 98.66 percent loan recovery rate in the urban slums and rural areas of India. By addressing the two most critical needs of poor women in the region, credit and health, the Working Women's Forum "has enabled poor women to be trainers and leaders; to express themselves; to articulate their problems; to learn by listening to others; and to prove that the poor are not problems but can be solutions as well."[77]

Remembering Core Concepts

✜ Learning Activity 6 ✜
Making Women's Economic Rights a Reality

Objective   To assess local economic conditions and strategize for action
Time   60 minutes
Materials   Chart paper and markers or blackboard and chalk, copies of the above list of adversarial and cooperative strategies for promoting and protecting women's human rights in the economy

1. Read/Discuss

Read aloud, post a chart, or pass out copies of the list of strategies for promoting and protecting women's economic rights, focusing on the italicized sentences only. Divide participants into small groups, and ask them to discuss these questions:

- Which of these strategies are already working in your community?
- Which strategies do you think could work?
- What other actions can you suggest?

2. Analyze

Ask participants to fill in the conditions of their community or country on a chart like the one shown in Table 9.1. They should list ways in which their group, working with allies, could reach the goals or undertake the strategies described in Step 1 above. Make sure that they include the needs of diverse people in the community.

3. Discuss

Ask the small groups to present their findings and to address these questions:

✖ Learning Activity 6 Continued ✖

Table 9.1   Making Women's Economic Rights a Reality

Sectors	Present Conditions/System	Future Goal	What Needs to Change
Economic			
Political			
Social/Cultural			
Environmental			
Legal			

- What difficulties did you have in doing this exercise?
- Do you need more information or resources?
- What kinds of difficulties would you have in carrying out your plans?
- What are your fears? Your hopes?

Notes

1. Thomas L. Friedman, *The Lexus and the Olive Tree* (New York: HarperCollins, 2000), pp. 7–8.

2. Ian Bannon, and Maria C. Correia, eds., *The Other Half of Gender: Men's Issues in Development* (World Bank, 2006), p. xix.

3. Joseph S. Nye and John D. Donahue, *Governance in a Globalizing World* (Washington, DC: Brookings Institution Press, 2000).

4. Gao Shangquan, "Economic Globalization: Trends, Risks and Risk Prevention," United Nations Economic and Social Development, CDP2000/PLEN/32, 2000, available online athttp://www.un.org/esa/policy/devplan/cdp00p32.pdf.

5. Marcus Walker, "Free-Trade Alert: A Warning on Globalization Backlash," *Wall Street Journal Online*, June 20, 2007, p. A4, available online at http://online.wsj.com/article/SB118226440519540516-search.html?KEYWORDS=OECD&COLLECTION=wsjie/6month.

6. Christa Wichterich, *The Globalized Woman* (London: Zed Books, 2000).

7. United Nations Division for the Advancement of Women, "Report of the Ad Hoc Committee of the Whole of the Twenty-Third Special Session of the General Assembly" (2000), available online at http://www.un.org/womenwatch/daw/followup/as2310rev1.pdf.

8. INSTRAW, "Women and Poverty" (2004), available online at http://www.un-instraw.org/en/index.php?option=content&task=blogcategory&id=143&Itemid=171.

9. UNDP, *Human Development Report 2000: Human Rights and Human Development* (New York: Oxford University Press, 2000).

10. International Labour Organisation, "Gender and Migration: The Importance of Considering Gender Issues in Migration," June 14, 2002, available online at http://www.ilo.org/public/english/protection/migrant/projects/gender/.

11. UNIFEM, *Progress of the World's Women 2005, Women, Work, and Poverty* (New York: United Nations Development Fund for Women, 2006), p. 39.

12. Ibid, p. 60.

13. International Organisation of Migration, available online at http://www.iom.int/jahia/jsp/index.jsp.

14. Adapted from Cecilia Ng, "Globalization and Women," November 22, 2000, available online at http://www.hrsolidarity.net/mainfile.php/2001vol11no2/25/.

15. UN Department of Economic and Social Affairs, Division for the Advancement of Women, "2004 World Survey on the Role of Women in Development, Women and International Migration" (New York: United Nations Publishing Section, 2005), available online at http://www.un.org/womenwatch/daw/Review/documents/press-releases/WorldSurvey-Women&Migration.pdf.

16. "United Nations Protocol to Prevent, Suppress, and Punish Trafficking in Persons," available online at http://www.uncjin.org/Documents/Conventions/dcatoc/final_documents_2/convention_%20traff_eng.pdf.

17. International Organization on Migration, "Data and Research on Human Trafficking: A Global Survey," 2005, available online at http://www.nswp.org/pdf/IOM-GLOBALTRAFFICK.pdf.

18. *Trafficking of Women and Children in Bangladesh*, p. 3, available online at http://www.usaid.gov/bd/files/trafficking_overview.pdf.

19. International Organization on Migration, "Data and Research on Human Trafficking."

20. Barbara Limanowska, "Trafficking in Human Beings in South Eastern Europe: 2004—A Focus on Prevention" (New York: UNICEF, UNOHCHR, OSCE/ODIHR, 2005).

21. International Organization for Migration, 2001.

22. USAID Bangladesh Anti-trafficking Program Successes, available online at http://www.usaid.gov/bd/trafficking_successes.html.

23. Vital Voices Global Partnership, available online at www.vitalvoices.org.

24. Judge Nimfa Cuesta Vilches, "Trafficking in Women and Children, from the 4th World Congress on Family Law and Children's Rights," the Mackay Centre for Research on Community and Children's Services (CROCCS), March 20–23, 2005, available online at http://www.croccs.org.au/downloads/2005_conf_papers/JudgeNimfaCuestaVilches Paper.pdf.

25. Wichterich, *The Gobalized Woman*, p. 1.

26. Ibid, p. 2.

27. Susan Ariel Aaronson, "Can Corporations Safeguard Labor and Human Rights?" *Yale Global*, June 24, 2004, available online at http://yaleglobal.yale.edu/display.article?id=4131.

28. "Fair Trade Product Certifier TransFair USA Partners with Whole Foods Market® to Help Launch Whole Trade™," March 29, 2007, available online at http://www.transfairusa.org/.

29. Oxfam International, "The World Is Still Waiting," *Oxfam Briefing Paper 103*, May 2007, available online at http://www.oxfam.org.uk/what_we_do/issues/debt_aid/bp103_g8.htm.

30. United Nations Convention against Corruption (UNCAC), "Transparency International: The Global Coalition Against Corruption," available online at http://www.transparency.org/global_priorities/international_conventions/regional_coverage/list/uncac.

31. UNIFEM, *Progress of The World's Women 2005*, p. 75.

32. Ibid, p. 78.

33. International Monetary Fund, "About the IMF," 2007, available online at http://www.imf.org/external/about.htm.

34. Dzodzi Tsikata, "Effects of Structural Adjustment on Women and the Poor," *Third World Network*, 2005, available online at http://www.twnside.org.sg/title/adjus-cn.htm.

35. Africa Institute, "Women's Burden has Increased: Gender Implications of Structural Adjustment in the Kenyan Agricultural Sector, " June 11, 2004. Available http://www.nai.uu.se/forsk/previous/sap/summaries/109.html.

36. Wichterich, *The Globalized Woman*, p. 110.

37. Third World Network, "TNCs and Globalization: Prime Sources of Worsening Ecological Crisis," available online at http://www.twnside.org.sg/title/pri-cn.htm.

38. World Bank, "Poverty Reduction Strategies," available online at http://web.worldbank.org/WBSITE/EXTERNAL/TOPICS/EXTPOVERTY/EXTPRS/0,menuPK:384207~pagePK:149018~piPK:149093~theSitePK:384201,00.html.

39. Patrick Conway, "IMF Lending Programs: Participation and Impact," *Journal of Development Economics*, vol. 45 (1994), pp. 365–391.

40. Rob Weissman, "Structural Adjustment Program (SAP) Alert on IMF and World Bank Lending to Tanzania, Executive Summary," Globalization Challenge Initiative, A Project of the Tides Center, USA and the Integrated Social Development Programme (ISODEC), Ghana, November 2000, available online at http://www.hartford-hwp.com/archives/36/347.html.

41. SAPRI Report, "Investigation by Civil Society and World Bank Challenges Structural Adjustment Programs," April 2004, available online at http://www.hartford-hwp.com/archives/36/347.html.

42. UNIFEM, *Progress of The World's Women 2005*, p. 20.

43. Interview with John Bomba at Friends Center, Philadelphia, 2004, available online at http://www.afsc.org/africa/new-africa/activism/john-bomba.htm.

44. Eric Toussaint, "From North to South: The Debt Crisis and Structural Adjustment Policies," *Nadir* (August 2000), Hamburg, Germany, available online at http://www.nadir.org/nadir/initiativ/agp/free/imf/sap.htm.

45. Ibid.

46. Dzodzi Tsikata, "Finance and Trade: Effects of Structural Adjustment on Women and Poor," CSD NGO Women's Caucus, 2002, available online at http://www.earthsummit2002.org/wcaucus/Caucus%20Position%20Papers/finance%20&%20trade/sap.htm.

47. M. Bussolo and J. Lay, "Globalisation and Poverty Changes in Colombia," *OECD Development Centre Working Paper* (Paris: OECD, 2003).

48. Ann-Louise Colgan, "Hazardous to Health: The World Bank and IMF in Africa," *Africa Action* (April 2002), available online at http://www.africaaction.org/action/sap0204.htm#privat.

49. Ibid.

50. Oxfam International, "The World Is Still Waiting."

51. Radio Free Europe/Radio Liberty, "World: IMF and World Bank Cancel 18 Countries' Debt," September 26, 2006, Prague, available online at http://www.rferl.org/featuresarticle/2005/09/a517765f-d7ad-4560-a7d8-c21473346c0a.html.

52. Africa Action Talking Points on the G8 and Africa, "The 2005 Gleneagles G8: Pledges Made and Broken," *Africa Action*, June 5, 2007.

53. Ibid.

54. Oxfam International, "The World Is Still Waiting."

55. Santiago Real de Azua, "IDB Governors Approve $4.4 billion in Debt Relief for Bolivia, Guyana, Haiti, Honduras and Nicaragua," Inter-American Development Bank Press Release, March 16, 2007, available online at http://www.iadb.org/NEWS/articledetail.cfm?artid=3665&language=En#.

56. Oxfam International, *The World Is Still Waiting*, available online at http://www.oxfam.org/en/files/bp103_g8_world_is_still_waiting.pdf/download.

57. Ibid.

58. Ibid.

59. "G-8 Pledges $60 Billion to Fight AIDS in Africa," *Wall Street Journal Online*, June 8, 2007, Associated Press, available online at http://online.wsj.com/article_print/SB118129174575028966.html.

60. Elizabeth M. King and Andrew D. Mason, "Engendering Development Through Gender Equality in Rights, Resources, and Voice," *The World Bank Group*, January 31, 2001, p. 26, available online at http://www-wds.worldbank.org/servlet/WDSContentServer/WDSP/IB/2001/03/01/000094946_01020805393496/Rendered/PDF/multi_page.pdf.

61. Ibid., p. 27.

62. "Documents and Reports: Summary of Engendering Development Through Gender Equality in Rights, Resources, and Voice," *The World Bank Group* (2001), available online at http://www-wds.worldbank.org/servlet/WDS_IBank_Servlet?pcont=details&eid=000094946_01020805393496.

63. Bannon and Correia, eds., *The Other Half of Gender*, p. xix.

64. Human Rights Internet, "Gender Equality and Human Rights," available online at http://www.hri.ca/HRDevelopment/chapter4/index.html.

65. Ibid.

66. Network of East-West Women, "Opinion on Gender Budgeting," May 2003, available online at http://www.neww.org.pl/download/badania/13/opinion_on_gender_budgeting_en.pdf.

67. Ibid.

68. Elaine Zuckerman, "An Introduction to Gender Budget Initiatives," *Gender Action* (September 2005), available online at http://www.genderaction.org/images/Intro_to_Gender_Budget_InitativesFINAL.pdf.

69. Maire Vlachova and Lea Bison, *Women in an Insecure World: Violence Against Women—Facts, Figures and Analysis* (Geneva: Centre for Democratic Control of Armed Forces, 2005), pp. 43–44.

70. Sam Olukoya, "Women's Protests Against ChevronTexaco Spread Through the Niger Delta," *CorpWatch*, August 7, 2002, available online at http://corpwatch.org/article.php?id=3428.

71. D'Arcy Doran, "Nigeria: Women Claim Victory in CheronTexaco Oil Terminal Takeover," *CorpWatch*, July 19, 2002, available online at http://corpwatch.org/article.php?id=3128.

72. The Corporate Responsibility Coalition was founded in 2001; for details, go to http://www.corporate-responsibility.org/.

73. NARAL Pro-Choice America, "NARAL: Tell Pharmacy Chains to Stop Discriminating Against Women," *CorpWatch*, April 4, 2005, available online at http://corpwatch.org/article.php?id=12045.

74. UN Human Development Reports, "Gender Empowerment Measure" (2005), available online at http://hdr.undp.org/statistics/data/indicators.cfm?x=239&y=2&z=2.

75. World Bank, "Annual Report 2005, About the Staff at the World Bank," available online at http://web.worldbank.org/WBSITE/EXTERNAL/EXTABOUTUS/EXTANNREP/EXTANN.REP2K5/0,,contentMDK:20639999~menuPK:1605938~pagePK:64168445~piPK:64168309~theSitePK:1397343,00.html.

76. Leena Lahti, "2002 Annual Diversity Report," International Monetary Fund, p. 17, available online at http://www.imf.org/external/np/div/2002/ar02.pdf.

77. The website address for Working Women's Forum is http://www.workingwomensforum.org/index.htm.

10

Women's Human Rights and Work

Everyone has the right to work, to free choice of employment, to just and favorable conditions of work and to protection against unemployment.
—*Universal Declaration of Human Rights, Article 23*

Objectives

The learning activities and background information contained in this chapter will enable participants to work toward the following objectives:

- Understand the difference between women's work and the informal and formal sectors.
- Explain the distinction between *nondiscrimination* and *equality of opportunity*, and define what it means to have human rights in the workplace.
- Define *affirmative action* and conclude whether it is an appropriate strategy.
- Define *sexual harassment* and identify possible cases in the community.
- Think critically about measures for promoting women's human rights related to work.
- Remember core concepts.

Getting Started:
Thinking About Women and Work

Work has increasingly come to be defined as an exchange of labor for wages in the market. As a result, many kinds of activities that are essential to society's growth and development are not valued as work. Many kinds of work performed by women are either not assigned any economic value at all or are valued at a lesser level than work performed by men. Work considered to be generally and often solely women's work includes the bearing and rearing of children, taking care of sick and elderly family members, household maintenance, subsistence agriculture, volunteer work, and local political organizing.

The chief United Nations organ charged with development—the UN Development Program—has recognized that women's work is greatly undervalued in economic terms. Most economic measures, such as the gross national product (GNP), do not, in fact, consider the work performed by many women in making their calculations. Actually, globally, women work more hours than men, especially in rural and developing countries. Many activists throughout the world have organized around the need to value women's labor. Especially undervalued is women's labor in the informal economy, which includes small unregistered enterprises as well as self-employed persons who work in their own or family businesses as globalization replaces full-time wage-paying jobs with outsourcing. One UN report indicates that the informal economy makes up 60 percent of the GNP in some countries.[1]

Understanding how tasks are divided between women and men is important for organizing around women's human rights both in the economy and in work. Although not explicitly stated, many economic policies are based on the assumption that women will continue to work within the family. When governments are unable or unwilling to provide essential social services such as education, housing, health care, and welfare, women usually pick up the burden of fulfilling their families' needs.

✠ Learning Activity 1: The 24-Hour Day ✠

Objective   To understand the significance of unpaid household labor in the daily lives of women

Time   45 minutes

Materials   Chart paper and markers or blackboard and chalk

1. Define

In small groups, decide on a definition of *work* and give examples that fit this definition. If possible, write these definitions on chart paper and post them around the room. You may wish to agree upon a common definition in the whole group.

2. List

Individually or in small groups, go through one day, hour by hour, asking participants to call out what they typically do during this hour. List these activities (e.g., "7 A.M.: Bathe, prepare breakfast, feed children, ride the bus to work, water and weed the garden, perform religious rituals). Analyze each activity:

- Put a plus sign if it fits your group's definition(s) of work.
- Put a minus sign if it is not work.
- Put a question mark for those activities you are unsure about.
- Circle any activities on the list for which women receive money.

3. Analyze/Discuss

In a large group, compare your definitions of work with the lists of activities:

⏣ Learning Activity 1 Continued ⏣

- What percentage of the items listed can be defined as work?
- What percentage of the items listed as work are circled as paid work?
- How much do you calculate it would cost to hire someone to perform tasks that are listed as unpaid work?
- Did listing all your activities for a day cause you to alter your definition of work?
- Are all the tasks you classified as *work* unpleasant or difficult?
- Are all the activities you listed as *not work* pleasant or fun?
- What does it mean to say, "My wife (or my mother/sister/daughter) doesn't work"?
- What definition of *work* is implied by this statement? Is it the same as your definition?
- What conclusions can you draw about women and work from this discussion?

Women in the Informal Sector

A great deal of women's work can be found in the informal sector, which, unlike work in the home, involves the exchange of money. The informal sector includes a wide range of work such as street vending, domestic work, piece-rate work, home-based businesses, and agricultural work. Family members often work together in the informal sector. Though an integral part of the economy, the informal sector is not regulated. In other words, women working in this sector do not receive fixed wages and they work under conditions that are not monitored by authorities. Because of the unregulated nature of their work, women's human rights in the informal sector are difficult to protect.

In 2005, UNIFEM released a report linking women's low status and poor treatment in the informal labor sector to high rates of poverty among women worldwide. The report found that

> in developing countries, except in those with large low-wage export sectors, women typically account for a relatively small share of informal wage employment. However, informal employment generally represents a larger source of employment for women than formal employment and a greater share of women's employment than men's employment. In developing countries over 60 per cent of women workers are in informal employment outside of agriculture—far more if agriculture is included. The exception is North Africa, where 43 per cent of women workers, and a slightly higher per cent of men workers, are informally employed.[2]

WIEGO

In addition to work in agriculture, women are more likely than men to be domestic workers, unpaid contributing workers in family enterprises, and industrial outworkers (i.e., persons who are employed by a firm but work primarily at home). Women have made great strides in organizing for their rights in the informal sector. One good example of these efforts is Women in Informal Employment:

Globalizing and Organizing (WIEGO). Founded in 1997, this network seeks to "improve the status of the working poor, especially women, in the informal economy through better statistics, research, programs, and policies and through increased organization and representation of informal workers."

WIEGO explains that the importance of the informal economy has grown rapidly in all regions of the world.

> [The informal economy has emerged] in unexpected places and in new guises. In developing economies, the majority of the working poor, more so women, work in the informal economy. In transition economies, many retrenched workers and many so-called "unemployed" work in the informal economy. And, in developed countries, an increasing share of paid workers is hired under flexible employment arrangements and a not-insignificant share of the total workforce is self-employed. . . . It is the contention of the WIEGO network that the quantity and quality of work generated by different patterns of economic growth and trade liberalization are key determinants of whether or not poverty is reduced, and for whom; and that the relative neglect of work and labor issues (especially from the perspective of informal workers) represents a "missing link" in the globalization-growth-poverty debate.[3]

SEWA

Other illustrations of women's organizing in the informal sector include trade unions that specifically address informal-sector activities. One of the most successful and well-known examples is the Self-Employed Women's Association (SEWA), an organization of poor, self-employed women workers in India, where more than 94 percent of the workforce is in the unorganized sector.[4] SEWA's main goals are to organize women workers for full employment and self-reliance. SEWA defines *full employment* as "employment whereby workers obtain work security, income security, food security and social security (at least health care, child care and shelter)." And by *self-reliance*, SEWA "means that women should be autonomous and self-reliant, individually and collectively, both economically and in terms of their decision-making ability." Since its establishment in 1972, SEWA's membership and activities have grown steadily. This innovative trade union annually evaluates its work with the following eleven questions:

1, Have more members obtained more employment?
2, Has their income increased?
3. Have they obtained food and nutrition?
4. Has their health been safeguarded?
5. Have they obtained child care?
6. Have they obtained or improved their housing?
7. Have their assets increased (e.g., their own savings, land, house, workspace, tools or work, licenses, identity cards, cattle, and share in cooperatives; and all in their own name)?
8. Have the workers' organizational strength increased?
9. Has workers' leadership increased?
10. Have they become self-reliant both collectively and individually?
11. Has worker's education increased?

Questions 1 to 7 are linked to the goal of full employment while 8 to 11 are those concerned with SEWA's goal of self-reliance. However, as SEWA stresses, each of these are interconnected to each other.[5]

✳ Learning Activity 2: Informal Work ✳

Objective To understand women's work in the informal sector
Time 45 minutes
Materials Magazines and newspapers, paper, scissors, glue, and markers

1. Brainstorm/ Draw
Brainstorm a definition of *informal work* by asking these questions:

- What types of jobs fall within the informal sector in your country?
- Who works in these jobs and what conditions do they face?

Next, divide participants into small groups, and ask them to create depictions of women working in the informal sector. They might draw a picture or make a collage using pictures from magazines and newspapers. Ask them to write in the margins of each picture the kinds of human rights issues that women face in each type of work illustrated.

2. Gallery Walk
Post the finished illustrations and invite participants to compare ideas. Ask what human rights issues were most commonly mentioned and list them.

Women in the Formal Sector

The risk of poverty is lower in formal employment. Nonetheless, as in the informal sector, women face many obstacles in the formal sector. The 2005 UNIFEM report on the status of women focuses on the links among gender inequality, labor, and poverty, noting that gender inequality in employment has multiple dimensions:[6]

- First, women are concentrated in more precarious forms of employment in which earnings are low. In developed countries, women make up the majority of part-time and temporary workers.
- Second, within employment categories, women's hourly and monthly earnings are generally lower than men's. A gender gap in earnings extends across almost all employment categories. A few exceptions exist among public-sector employees in certain countries, such as El Salvador, and in cases like Egypt where most of women's employment involves unpaid work in family enterprises, and the few women who do participate in paid employment tend to be highly educated. In these exceptional cases, women's average hourly earnings can be higher than men's.

- Third, in the countries for which data are available, women work fewer hours in paid work, on average, than do men. In part, this is due to women's long hours in unpaid household labor. Responsibilities for unpaid household work also reinforce labor force segmentation: Women can be restricted to own-account or home-based employment, even if they have to work longer hours and earn less than they would in other types of employment.
- Finally, despite the low earnings and the precarious nature of much of women's paid work, in both developed and developing countries, women's labor force participation can help keep a family out of poverty, provided there are additional sources of family income.

When a woman looks for a paying job, she faces a far more limited range of opportunities than a man. In every country some jobs are specifically defined as "women's work"—usually jobs that men reject and that have lower pay, status, and job security. When women enter previously male occupations in large numbers, the status of these occupations tends to fall, especially when they are higher-paying or professional jobs.[7]

Women's activism in the formal labor sector has taken on global implications as trade agreements open employment opportunities in low-wage-earning corners of the world. Some activists work within larger labor organizations that include women's rights as a vital part of their work, such as the AFL-CIO. This organization's figures show that women make up 39 percent of the world's workforce, yet they account for 70 percent of the world's population living in poverty.[8] Similarly, 80 percent of the nearly 50 million workers in export processing zones are women between the ages of 16 and 25.[9] Foreign companies operate virtually unfettered, though legally, in these tax-free zones; labor laws often are suspended, leaving workers without legal recourse for better wages or better working conditions. For example, in Mexico, as of 2003, women factory workers in these export processing zones earned US$4.20 a day, or less than fifty cents an hour.[10] The maquila program in Mexico is highly attractive to foreign companies—first, because they enjoy unlimited foreign investment in the capital and, second, because they are afforded special customs treatment, such as duty-free temporary import of machinery, equipment, parts, and materials. The potential for worker exploitation is great, and labor activists provide organizing support for issues of concern to women workers.

✠ **Learning Activity 3: Women Wage Earners in Your Community** ✠

Objective   To assess the impact of wage-earning work on women
Time   75 minutes
Materials   Chart paper and markers or blackboard and chalk, paper and pens (optional)

1. Discuss
Divide the participants into small groups and ask them to discuss the following questions:

✠ Learning Activity 3 Continued ✠

- Did your mother or grandmother work outside the home?
- If so, what led them to do this work?
- Where did they work?
- How were they treated at their jobs?
- In what ways was their work important to them?
- How did she manage to take care of her household responsibilities?
- How did their working affect you and your family?
- How do the same questions apply to you?

2. Discuss

Moving from home to the public workplace is a critical step in the lives of many women. Ask participants to discuss these questions and record their responses:

- What factors motivate women in your community to work outside the home?
- Which factors are positive (e.g., improved training, new opportunities)? Which are negative (e.g., financial hardship, unemployed spouse, widowhood)?
- When a woman works outside the home for wages, what are some of the effects on her family? On her marriage? On the woman herself?

3. Role-Play

Divide participants into small groups and ask them to plan and perform a role-play that shows the reasons a woman might decide to work outside the home and some of the reactions she may encounter. Some roles might be the woman, her husband, her child, her mother-in-law or some other family elder, a neighbor, or a friend. The role-play might show "before" and "after" versions of her experience.

After the role-plays are performed, discuss the common issues and perspectives they raise. Which of these relate to women's human rights?

Discrimination Against Women in the Workplace

As noted in an analysis performed by the Council of Europe, women face several types of discrimination in the workplace:[11]

- They lack access to the labor market.
- Their rate of participation in the labor market is lower than that of men.
- The unemployment rate of women is higher than that of men—although there are strong regional variations.
- More women than men work in part-time jobs, often not of their choosing.
- Many women are overqualified for the work they do and become what the ILO calls "discouraged workers"; they are not included in unemployment statistics because they are not actively seeking work; although they want

to work, they feel no work is available, or they face discrimination or structural, social, or cultural barriers.

- A wage gap exists in that women are paid 15–30 percent less than men for the same work or work of equal value.
- High educational achievements are no safeguard; in many countries, the better the woman is educated, the greater the wage gap.
- Women earn less than men in their lifetimes; they also have less pension insurance and receive smaller retirement pensions, even though they live longer than men.
- Women face a "glass ceiling" whereby they are routinely passed over for promotions. The higher the post, the less likely a woman will be promoted—even one whose qualifications are equal to or greater than those of her male counterpart.
- Women who break through this "glass-ceiling" into decision making positions remain the exceptions to the rule; even in female-dominated sectors where there are more women managers, a disproportionate number of men rise to the more senior positions.
- Women pay a gender penalty as actual or potential mothers inasmuch as many employers wrongly fear the cost and hassle that motherhood may entail. ILO research has found that the additional cost of hiring a woman is less than 1 percent of the monthly gross earnings of women employees.
- Women are discriminated against mainly because of stereotyping and misguided preconceptions of women's roles, abilities, level of commitment, and leadership style.
- Owing to stereotypes, women are often offered employment that is precarious, badly paid, lacking any possibility of career advancement, and nongratifying in the sense of not allowing for the full development of their abilities.
- Women are often excluded from informal networks and channels of communication.
- Some of them suffer from moral and sexual harassment, bullying, and mobbing.
- Family responsibilities—housework, child care, caring for elderly relatives—are not equally shared between women and men, preventing women from entering and staying in the workforce, and from having a career.
- Lower participation in the labor force and higher unemployment contribute to economic loss and inequality, which translate into economic dependence and poverty—particularly among the elderly.
- Women who are disabled or who belong to an ethnic and/or religious minority suffer double discrimination.
- Women rarely receive recognition for unpaid work performed within the home.[12]
- Men are more likely to own or have access to land for agriculture, to farm machinery, and to tools.[13]
- Men have greater access to credit and other financial services. While there may be a larger number of loans given to women, the monetary amounts of the loans to men are higher.[14]

Unequal treatment in the workplace can create a mutually reinforcing cycle of discrimination and poverty. For example, a woman who has primary parenting responsibilities may need flexible hours and/or affordable day care, which few jobs offer; as a result, she may earn less and also be forced to leave her children under inadequate supervision. A woman who is able to take a break from her work to raise children is at a disadvantage when she returns to the workforce, having lost wages and promotions. And a woman who quits her job due to sexual harassment may be labeled a troublemaker and have a difficult time finding a new job.

Although large numbers of women work, they are not represented in economic decision making in large public or private corporate structures. Similarly, women are rarely involved in national economic policy formulation, including decision making about resource allocation. Even many unions, formed to improve conditions for workers, exclude women from leadership or from membership altogether. Discrimination against women in the workforce and the workplace contributes to lower economic growth, diminishing tax incomes, and higher outlays in unemployment and social security benefits. The elimination of this discrimination is thus a sound economic policy goal in itself—one that promises to improve social cohesion.[15]

✖ Learning Activity 4: Discrimination on the Job ✖

Objective   To understand ways in which women are discriminated against in the workplace
Time   90 minutes
Materials   Paper and markers

1. Role-Play/Discuss

Divide the participants into small groups to plan a role-play. Describe this scenario:

> One person represents a male employer who has never hired women (or never hired a woman for a management position); a second person represents a woman applying for a managerial job. The employer is meeting the woman for the first time; the woman needs to explain the reasons why she wants to work for the firm. Ask groups to perform their scenarios for everyone.

Discuss the attitudes brought out in the role-play:

- How would the role-play be different if the employer were a woman? If the employer were a woman and the applicant a man?
- Summarize the applicants' advantages and disadvantages in both scenarios.

2. Discuss/List

In small groups, list or draw pictures that illustrate the ways in which women are disadvantaged in employment. Consider the following points:

continues

⛑ **Learning Activity 4 Continued** ⛑

- Have you experienced any of these kinds of discrimination in the workplace?
- What, if anything, did you do about the situation?
- What could you do?
- Did anyone support you?
- Who might be your allies in challenging such discrimination?

The Role of Authorities

Many national laws prohibit discrimination in the workplace. Some obligate governments to take actions to promote equality in all sectors of work; others reach only the state sector. Women's rights in the workplace also can be found in several international human rights conventions, including the International Covenant on Economic, Social, and Cultural Rights, which provides for the following rights:

- The right to work
- The right to fair wages, equal pay, safe and healthy working conditions, and equal opportunity for promotion
- The right to rest and leisure
- The right to join trade unions
- The right to social security
- The right to maternity leave and benefits
- The right of children to protection from exploitation
- The right to an adequate standard of living, which includes adequate food, clothing, housing, and living conditions.

The International Labour Organisation (ILO) also recognizes numerous worker rights for women through its various conventions, including freedom from forced labor and the right to equal wages. Many early ILO principles prohibiting discrimination against women in work were reaffirmed by the Convention on the Elimination of All Forms of Discrimination Against Women (CEDAW).[16]

CEDAW specifically allows for "special measures" aimed at accelerating equality between men and women, which would include temporary affirmative action measures in employment. CEDAW also explicitly protects women from discrimination in employment on grounds of marriage or maternity. A separate section of the convention, Article 15, protects the human rights of rural women, including their right to have access to agricultural credit and loans, marketing facilities, appropriate technology, and equal treatment in land and agrarian reform.

CEDAW is silent, however, on women's unpaid work in the home and offers little guidance on what it takes for governments to fulfill their obligations to promote equal opportunities for women at work.

The Beijing Platform for Action, the document resulting from the 1995 World Conference on Women, is more explicit. It calls on governments to "promote women's economic rights and independence, including access to employment and appropriate working conditions and control over economic resources" (paragraph F.1). This commitment includes enacting and enforcing legislation that would end discrimination in employment, provide social security and tax benefits, and give full recognition of the value of women's unpaid work.

The Beijing Platform for Action also recommends specific ways to eliminate all occupational segregation and employment discrimination. In particular, it emphasizes the need to work toward elimination of child labor, including the excessive demands made on girls to perform unpaid work in the informal sector (paragraph F.5). In addition, the Platform for Action calls for affordable support services for working women such as child care (paragraph F.3) and encouragement for women to participate in nontraditional work (paragraph F.5).

One measure intended to remove the barriers that women face when participating in the workplace—a measure the Human Rights Committee of the United Nations has explicitly endorsed—is *affirmative action* or *positive discrimination*. In formal comments issued in 1989, the Human Rights Committee found that governments have an obligation to undertake "affirmative action designed to ensure the positive enjoyment of rights." CEDAW, too, allows for affirmative action (in Article 4), as long as the steps taken are temporary ones. This means that in order to correct historic discrimination, governments or employers should take positive steps to encourage the hiring of women and the incorporation of women into their workforce.

✠ Learning Activity 5 ✠
Affirmative Action—Should Mano Be Hired?

Objective	To define *affirmative action* and assess whether it is an appropriate strategy
Time	60 minutes
Materials	Copy of "Case Study: The Zadako Soap Factory"

Case Study: The Zadako Soap Factory

The Zadako Soap Factory has had a long history of discriminating against women. Its workforce is 90 percent male. To help correct this situation, the management has decided to hire two women for every man until the workforce is at least 40 percent women. Consequently, although Mano applied for a job and passed the qualifying test, he was turned down, and a woman was hired instead. He complains that Zadako's new policy discriminates against qualified men like himself.

1. Read

Read the case study to the whole group.

continues

✠ Learning Activity 5 Continued ✠

2. Role-Play

Divide participants into two groups to brainstorm for or against Mano's claim that the Zadako factory has discriminated against him. Have spokespersons from one group present the arguments of Mano and his lawyer. Have spokespersons from the second group present the arguments of the Zadako management and the woman who has been hired. Have the audience direct questions to the spokespersons at the end of the role-play.

3. Discuss

- Do you support *affirmative action* plans? Why or why not?
- Is your support conditional? If so, what factors influence your opinion?

Sexual Harassment

Women's right to access to employment and to the same working conditions as men includes the right to freedom from gender-based harassment, often known as sexual harassment. Unwelcome sexual advances, requests for sexual favors, and other verbal or physical conduct of a sexual nature constitute sexual harassment when submission to or rejection of this conduct explicitly or implicitly affects an individual's employment, unreasonably interferes with an individual's work performance, or creates an intimidating, hostile, or offensive work environment.

Several countries have laws prohibiting sexual harassment. Definitions of sexual harassment vary. These are at least two types:

1. *Quid pro quo sexual harassment*[17] ("this for that"), whereby an employer says that an employee must submit to gender-based harassment in order to receive a tangible job benefit, such as being employed, promoted, given access to training programs, and paid well. An essential aspect of quid pro quo harassment is the harasser's power to control the employee's employment benefits. This kind of harassment most often occurs between supervisor and subordinate.

2. *Hostile work environment sexual harassment,*[18] whereby the overall conditions of the workplace create an atmosphere and culture in which disrespect and unfair treatment of women are tolerated or condoned. Hostile work environment harassment is unwelcome conduct that is so severe or pervasive as to change the conditions of the claimant's employment and create an intimidating, hostile, or offensive work environment.

Hostile work environment sexual harassment is different than quid pro quo sexual harassment in that it:

- does not entail an impact on an economic benefit
- can involve co-workers or third parties, not just supervisors
- is not limited to sexual advances but, rather, can include hostile or offensive behavior based on the person's sex

- can occur even when the conduct is not directed specifically at the victim individually but still affects her or his ability to perform the job
- typically involves a series of incidents rather than one incident (although a single offensive incident may constitute this type of harassment).

It is important to remember that sexual harassment is about power, not sex or attraction between two adults. In the workplace, sexual harassment can interfere with women's ability to perform their jobs and can intimidate women such that they avoid asking for raises and decent working conditions. It is also a form of violence against women.

✠ Learning Activity 6: Is This Sexual Harassment? ✠

Objective To define *sexual harassment*
Time 60 minutes
Materials Chart paper and markers or blackboard and chalk

1. Decide
Ask participants to work in pairs to decide whether or not an example from the list below represents sexual harassment; a pair should stand and take a position only if they can reach consensus. Designate one side of the room as "Sexual Harassment" and the other side as "Not Sexual Harassment." Pairs who cannot agree remain seated while people standing briefly explain their position. Ask those who take the "Sexual Harassment" position whether it is "Quid Pro Quo" or "Hostile Environment." Keep discussion brief. Take a vote to determine the majority view among all participants, and record the vote before going to the next example.
Choose from these examples:

- A male boss tells his female subordinate that she will be promoted only if she sleeps with him.
- A male boss tells a job applicant that part of her duties as a new employee will be to wear short skirts each day to work.
- A male employee pressures a female employee at the same job level to sleep with him.
- A male employee pressures a female employee at the same job level to sleep with him; the female employee complains to her boss, but the boss only laughs or accuses her of flirtatious behavior.
- Fellow workers make loud comments about a particular woman's body and often try to touch her breasts or buttocks.
- Fellow workers whistle or make panting noises when a particular woman passes and sometimes grab their crotches.
- The lunchroom at the workplace is decorated with photos of half-dressed women, and male employees regularly tell sexually explicit jokes.

continues

✠ Learning Activity 6 Continued ✠

2. List

Ask participants to identify other situations in which sexual harassment could occur (e.g., between student and teacher, policeman or government official and petitioner, politician and constituent, doctor and patient, landlord and tenant). Record their suggestions.

3. Role-Play/Discuss

Ask participants in small groups to describe any forms of sexual harassment they themselves have experienced. What kind was it? How did they respond? Ask each small group to choose one incident to role-play for everyone.

After the role-plays, discuss these questions:

- How can women support one another in these circumstances?
- What kinds of support should management offer women in the workplace?
- What happens if management doesn't work to stop harassment?

Protective Labor Legislation

Where a country has no equal opportunity or equal access legislation to protect women in the workplace, women have traditionally been included in international employment laws under protective labor legislation. As the name suggests, many of these "protective" laws were designed on the basis of the assumption that women are more fragile than men and need protection from particular employers and tasks, and even from themselves. These laws involve a particular vision of woman as mother or potential mother. Laws forbidding women from working in mines, for example, have been justified as protecting women's fertility and motherhood capacities.

The first international norms regarding women and work were adopted in 1919, soon after the establishment of the ILO, the international labor group now connected with the United Nations. These norms protected women from such demands as nightwork and strenuous manual labor. In countries where such laws were adopted nationally, women were unable to choose to increase their earnings by working long hours at night or by taking jobs that were highly paid because of the work's difficult nature.

For several years afterward, international bodies such as the ILO maintained the view that women workers were primarily homemakers and men were primarily wage earners. With the 1981 Convention and Recommendation on Workers with Family Responsibilities, the ILO formally recognized that men as well as women had parental responsibilities. Nonetheless, employers still often restrict women's work opportunities under the assumption that doing so helps women fulfill parenting responsibilities.

✠ Learning Activity 7: Unsuitable Work for a Woman ✠

Objective   To examine attitudes that keep women from competing with men in the workplace and relegate women to "women's work"
Time   60 minutes
Materials   Copy of "Case Study: Adelina Joins the Workforce"

Case Study: Adelina Joins the Workforce

During World War II, when most men in Europe and North America were drafted into the army, heavy industry turned to women to fill empty positions. Adelina, who had previously stayed at home with her young children, was hired at the steel mill where her husband had worked. Because of her intelligence and ability to drive a car, she was trained to operate a heavy crane, a job never held previously by a woman. At first, Adelina worked in the railyard, loading finished steel onto boxcars; however, she proved so skillful that after a year she was promoted to the foundry floor, pouring huge vats of molten metal into molds. This work called not only for dexterity and judgment on her part but also for careful teamwork. Adelina continually demonstrated both high technical competence and natural leadership. She enjoyed the high salary her skilled work earned for her family as well as the respect and comradeship she experienced with her fellow-workers, who soon elected her as representative to the union.

When the war was over, however, Adelina and other female industrial workers were asked to give up their jobs to men returning to the workforce. When she protested that she didn't want to quit, she heard many different arguments defending the need for women to return to their homes or to take on more menial jobs that the men did not want.

Finding no support for continuing her work, Adelina gave up her job to a returning veteran and eventually found "more appropriate work" driving a school bus for a third of her previous salary.

1. Read

Read the case study to the whole group.

2. Discuss

In small groups, with each group taking a different role, list arguments that might be made—by Adelina's husband, female co-workers, male co-workers, the Steel Worker's union, and factory management—to convince her to justify giving up her job.

Here are some possible comments:

- Her husband: "I'm embarrassed to have a wife who works, especially one who earns more than I do. Besides, the children need you at home."
- Her female co-workers: "After all, we were just filling in while the men were away fighting for us. Men need these jobs for their self-respect. It's not right for a woman to keep a man out of a job. They have families to support."

continues

⊠ Learning Activity 7 Continued ⊠

- Her male co-workers: "Under normal conditions a man doesn't want to take orders from a woman. Steel-making requires teamwork."
- The steel workers' union: "Well, we waived a lot of rules during wartime, but our real membership is almost entirely male, and these guys need jobs."
- Management at the steel factory: "Crane operating is unsuitable work for a woman—operating heavy machinery and pouring molten metal is dangerous. Your children have a right to a mother. Besides, women distract men in the workplace."

3. Role-Play

Have one participant role-play Adelina, and have others represent the different voices she hears. After the role-play, consider these topics:

- How might Adelina respond to each of these arguments?
- What support from friends, family, co-workers, union, management, and other sources—including the law—would Adelina have needed to keep her job?

4. Discuss

Adelina's story took place more than a half-century ago; but have conditions for women in the workplace changed? Very much?

- If you were Adelina, how would you feel about giving up your job? What would you do?
- Are any of the arguments she heard still prevalent in your community? What principles or values underlie each position? Have women's attitudes changed? Have men's? Have union's or management's?
- If Adelina lived in your community today, where could she find allies whose support would help her to keep her job?
- What possible dangers for women are posed by protective labor legislation?
- Can women's choices and decision-making capacity be limited in the name of "protection"?

Globalization and Women in the Workplace

The globalization of the world economy has had impacts on the workplace in almost every part of the world. Some common trends are described below.

- *Corporate downsizing:* This includes many cost-cutting measures such as laying off staff, reducing salaries and benefits, firing older staff who are about to receive pensions, and making staff perform additional duties or the work of laid-off staff instead of replacing them.[19]

- *Export processing zones (EPZs):* These zones are designated areas within a country where regulations and labor protection laws are relaxed or unenforced in order to attract foreign investment. Workers in EPZs are perceived to be easier to control and less likely to unionize. Many young women and girls work in such zones.[20]
- *Shrinking power of unions:* With the growth of export processing zones, unions face the challenge of developing appropriate responses on workers' behalf in an environment dominated by human resource management.[21]
- *Increased competition:* Global competition obliges enterprises to look for ways to keep costs and practices competitive to remain attractive to foreign investors. As a result, lower wages, less job protection, and deregulated industries are common in both developed and developing countries.[22]
- *Declining wages for unskilled workers:* Over the past two decades, unskilled workers have borne the brunt of globalization with their share of income from the economic pie on the decline. Even so, skilled workers themselves earn a relatively small share of national income in developed countries, compared to business owners who enjoy the lion's share.[23] The IMF estimates that the gap between real earnings of skilled and those of unskilled workers in the United States has grown by 25 percent.[24]

For more on the impact of globalization on the human rights of women, see Chapter 9, "Women's Human Rights and Globalization."

The Way Forward?

UNIFEM's 2005 report, *The Progress of the World's Women 2005: Women, Work and Poverty*, made several specific suggestions to improve gender equity. Among other measures, it stressed the following four core priorities:

- Core Priority #1: To promote decent employment for both women and men as a key pathway to reducing poverty and gender inequality.
- Core Priority #2: To increase visibility of informal women workers in national labor force statistics and in national gender and poverty assessments.
- Core Priority #3: To promote a more favorable policy environment for the working poor, especially women, in the informal economy through improved analysis, broad awareness building, and participatory policy dialogues.
- Core Priority #4: To support and strengthen organizations representing women informal workers and help them gain an effective voice in relevant policy-making processes and institutions.

Many labor organizations, women's human rights groups, and activist networks have supported these goals and, in particular, have demanded better conditions in the informal sector. Sweatshop Watch, for example, was organized in 1995 with a commitment to eliminating exploitation of workers in the garment industry. Composed of more than thirty labor, community, civil rights, immigrant rights, women's, religious, and student organizations, Sweatshop Watch has educated consumers about substandard garment worker conditions and supported several winning campaigns for low-wage garment workers nationally and globally.[25] Similarly, the Workers Action Center of Toronto organizes to promote the rights of workers in low-wage and unstable employment.[26] Although these efforts are not directed solely at women workers, they do promote gender equity.

Remembering Core Concepts

✠ Learning Activity 8: Speaking Out for Women at Work ✠

Objectives To examine women's human right to work and consider how to take action to improve it
Time 60+ minutes
Materials Chart paper and markers

1. Brainstorm

Ask participants to list problems faced by women in their community related to work in both the formal sector and the informal sector. Ask participants, working in small groups, to choose a problem on which they wish to concentrate.

2. Discuss/Plan

Ask each group to prepare a five-minute presentation to a "panel of community leaders" on their problem. Each presentation should:

- describe the problem, identifying the group(s) of women it impacts and if possible the cause(s) of the problem
- relate the problem to women's human rights
- clarify how the problem affects women's lives
- show how addressing the problem can improve their lives
- propose specific actions that should be taken to address the problem
- show how members of the community can get involved in addressing the problem.

Ask each group to choose a spokesperson to make the presentation and a "community leader" to serve on the panel. While the groups plan their presentations, the panel of leaders meets to decide on their roles, representing a variety of differing but typical attitudes within the community leadership.

3. Present/Role-Play

The spokesperson from each group makes a presentation and members of the panel listen and respond, asking questions and offering comments, objections, or suggestions in keeping with their chosen roles.

4. Discuss

After the presentations and role-play, address these questions:

✠ Learning Activity 8 Continued ✠

- How did the spokespersons feel when presenting the problem?
- How did the "community leaders" respond to the presentation? What attitudes in the community were they representing?
- How did the audience, composed of the rest of the group, respond to the presentations?
- Did any spokesperson discuss the problem as a human rights violation? Did putting the problem in a human rights context strengthen the argument? Why or why not?
- Are these ideas for improving women's human right to work feasible in your community? Why or why not?

5. Conclude

Challenge the participants by asking them to evaluate their knowledge of the problem and the inclusiveness of their perspective:

- How did you obtain your information about the work-related issues facing women in your community? Was it accurate and complete? If not, what additional information do you need, and how can you obtain it?
- Did you personally consult women about the problem and how it affects them? About actions that could improve the problem?
- How can the affected woman emerge the victor and not the victim?
- Why is it important in real-life human rights advocacy to include the active participation of those directly involved and affected?
- How can you apply the example of this learning activity to planning and implementing advocacy for women in your community?

Notes

1. UN Department of Economic and Social Affairs Division for the Advancement of Women, "Enhancing Women's Participation in Development Through an Enabling Environment for Achieving Gender Equality and the Advancement of Women," Report of the Expert Group Meeting, Bangkok, Thailand, November 2005, available online at http://www.un.org/womenwatch/daw/egm/enabling-environment2005/EGM-WPD-EE-2005-REPORT%2013.2.pdf.

2. UNIFEM, *The Progress of the World's Women 2005: Women, Work and Poverty* (New York, 2005).

3. "Women in Informal Employment: Globalizing and Organizing," available online at http://www.wiego.org/about/.

4. Self-Employed Women's Association, "We the Self-Employed," January 2005, available online at http://www.sewa.org/newsletter/newsletter1.html.

5. Self-Employed Women's Association, available online at http://www.sewa.org/aboutus/goals.asp.

6. UNIFEM, *The Progress of the World's Women 2005: Women, Work and Poverty* (New York, 2005).

7. Robert M. Blackburn and Jennifer Jarman, "Gendered Occupations: Exploring the Relationship Between Gender Segregation and Inequality," *GeNet Working Paper No. 5,*

January 2005, ESRC Gender Equality Network, Centre for Research in the Arts, Social Sciences, and Humanities, University of Cambridge, United Kingdom, p. 14, available online at http://www.genet.ac.uk/workpapers/GeNet2005p5.pdf.

8. "Women in the Global Economy," available online at http://www.aflcio.org/issues/jobseconomy/globaleconomy/women/.

9. Ibid.

10. "Life on the Line: Violence Against Women Working in Factories in Mexico," available online at http://www.aflcio.org/issues/jobseconomy/globaleconomy/upload/Juarezflyer.pdf.

11. Adapted from Council of Europe Parliamentary Assembly Recommendation 1700, "Discrimination Against Women in the Workforce and the Workplace" (2005), available online at http://assembly.coe.int/Documents/AdoptedText/ta05/EREC1700.htm.

12. Jayati Gosh, "Integration of Gender Perspectives in Macroeconomics," United Nations Commission on the Status of Women, Forty-Ninth Session, February 28–March 11, 2005, Panel 1.

13. International Food Policy Research Institute, "Report Finds Severe Gender Inequities" (Washington, DC: World Bank, October 2005), available online at http://www.worldbank.org/html/cgiar/newsletter/Oct95/3ifprw.htm.

14. Angela E. V. King, "Statement to the Meeting of the Preparatory Committee for the International Conference on Financing for Development," UN Inter-Agency Network on Women and Gender Equality October 16, 2001 (New York: United Nations), available online at http://www.un.org/womenwatch/ianwge/activities/Oct16_01_aevk_st.html.

15. Council of Europe Parliamentary Assembly Recommendation 1700 (2005).

16. CEDAW, Article 11.

17. Minnesota Advocates for Human Rights, "Stop Violence Against Women," available online at http://www.stopvaw.org/Quid_Pro_Quo_Sexual_Harassment.html.

18. U.S. Equal Employment Opportunity Commission, Information on Sexual Harassment, Legal Definitions of Sexual Harassment, available online at http://www.de2.psu.edu/harassment/legal/eeoc.html.

19. Kevin Danaher, "Globalization and the Downsizing of the American Dream," *Global Exchange*, April 3, 2007, available online at http://www.globalexchange.org/campaigns/econ101/americanDream.html.

20. ILO International Institute for Labour Studies, "Global Production and Local Jobs: New Perspectives on Enterprise Networks, Employment and Local Development Policy (Export Processing Zones: The Cutting Edge of Globalization)," International Workshop, Geneva, March 9–10, 1998, available online at http://www.ilo.org/public/english/bureau/inst/papers/confrnce/gps/heerden.htm.

21. Ibid.

22. Ibid.

23. Owen F. Humpage and Michael Shenk, "Do Workers Benefit from Globalization?" May 3, 2007, *Cleveland Federal Reserve*, available online at http://www.clevelandfed.org/research/trends/2007/0507/01intmar_050107.cfm.

24. Ibid.

25. Sweatshop Watch, "Empowering Workers, Informing Consumers," available online at http://www.sweatshopwatch.org/.

26. *Workers Action Centre Annual Report 2006*, available online at http://www.workersactioncentre.org/documents/AnnualReport2006.pdf.

11

Women's Human Right to Education

Everyone has the right to education. [Elementary] education shall be free . . . and compulsory. Technical and professional education shall be made generally available and higher education shall be equally accessible to all on the basis of merit. . . . Education shall be directed to the full development of the human personality and to the strengthening of respect for human rights.
—*Universal Declaration of Human Rights, Article 26*[1]

Objectives

The learning activities and background information contained in this chapter will enable participants to work toward the following objectives:

- Understand that every woman and girl has the right to education and assess the importance of education in women's lives.
- Define illiteracy and functional illiteracy and analyze their impact on the lives of women and girls.
- Examine the role that governments, community leaders, the media, and women themselves can play in promoting women's and girls' full access to education.
- Define gender-role stereotyping in education and strategize ways to combat it.
- Identify the link between education and other human rights.
- Strategize ways to promote the right to education in their community.
- Remember core concepts.

Getting Started: Thinking About Women and Education

People can be motivated to seek education both for practical reasons and for the love of learning. Women and girls, in particular, may also see education as a way out of poverty, a chance for mobility, or an opportunity to break out of binding traditions to attain self-sufficiency and freedom. With the number of

235

female-headed households rising worldwide, women's self-sufficiency has become increasingly important. Women with children may seek an education in order to become better providers, teachers, and role models for their own daughters and sons. In addition, women may see education as a way to contribute to their communities and to participate in the public and political sphere. Despite widespread recognition of the importance of education, many women and girls do not have access to education.

Women and Education

- In 2000, there were 236 million more illiterate women than illiterate men; it is projected that by 2015 the difference will be 215 million. Women account for two out of three illiterate adults.[2]
- In 2004, girls worldwide were 60 percent more likely than boys to be deprived of school completely.[3]
- In 2005, 56 percent of the world's children lived in countries where there is a proven disparity between girls and boys in primary school enrollment levels; UNICEF estimates that 121 million primary-school-aged children worldwide, the majority of whom were girls, did not attend school and that 16 percent of girls worldwide missed out on school altogether.[4]

⊠ Learning Activity 1: Why We Learn ⊠

Objective To identify the benefits of education in the lives of women
Time 45 minutes
Materials Chart paper and markers or blackboard and chalk, copies of the section below headed "Social Benefits of Education," paper and colored pens

1. Brainstorm
Ask the full group to call out responses to this question: "What are some of the benefits of education to women and girls?" List their responses.

2. Discuss
Write out on chart paper or read aloud the benefits of education listed in "Social Benefits of Education." Add the phrases that are italicized to the brainstormed list, if not already mentioned.

Lead a discussion on each of these benefits. Ask for personal examples that support the benefits or show the consequences of a lack of such benefits. How can this list of benefits be used to contribute to better educational opportunities for women?

3. Create
Ask participants in small groups to create posters or television "advertisements" that make people aware of the benefits of women's education both to women themselves and to society in general. Have participants present these for everyone.

Learning Activity 1 Continued

4. Discuss

Discuss the following questions about the human right to education:

- Why is education a human right?
- What is the connection between women's education and their other human rights?

Social Benefits of Education

Although education across the globe favors boys, when women are educated the whole society benefits. Lawrence Summers, former chief economist at the World Bank, stated that girl's education may be the investment that yields the greatest returns in the developing world. Not only does the education of young girls yield a higher return than the education of men, but children benefit more from an increase in their mother's schooling than from an equal increase in their father's schooling.[5]

Of course, education is not a magic solution. Where poverty and disease are rampant, education alone cannot cure the ills of society. However, education can help women to improve their lives within the limitations set by other factors. Some benefits of education are listed below:

- *Better health:* Children with educated mothers are more likely to live healthfully because of better nutrition and immunization rates. Educated women marry later, have fewer children, and are less likely to die in childbirth than uneducated women.[6]
- *Better resistance against HIV/AIDS:* Girls' education is one of the most important weapons in the prevention of HIV/AIDS. It slows and reduces the spread of the virus by contributing to female economic independence, increased marriage age, and HIV/AIDS awareness.[7]
- *Better pay:* For every year of schooling, wages for women, like those of men, increase by about 10 percent. Moreover, educated women often send their children to school, increasing their chances of breaking out of poverty.[8]
- *Better protection against abuse:* Education keeps girls in school and makes them less vulnerable to exploitation and abuse.[9]
- *Better chances of becoming good citizens:* Education gives girls and women the knowledge to influence the nature and direction of society and to engage in political life.[10]
- *Better family planning:* When women have more education, they generally have fewer children and are thus better able to provide for the children that they do have. Indeed, national statistics suggest that lower fertility rates translate into more resources for the next generation.[11]
- *Better production:* For women involved in agricultural work, education helps to increase productivity, thereby increasing household incomes and decreasing rates of poverty.[12]

- *Better GDP:* Research shows that female education levels have a positive impact on a country's GDP levels, while male education has a much less significant impact.[13]

⚜ Learning Activity 2: Education Makes a Difference ⚜

Objective   To understand the impact of education on a woman's ability to make decisions, evaluate information, and obtain her human rights

Time   45 minutes

Materials   Chart paper and markers or blackboard and chalk

1. Role-Play

Ask three participants to sit in the center of the group. One plays a woman who has had twelve years of education; another, six years; and the third, none at all.

The remaining participants in the group play these or similar roles:

- A politician who wants to get women's votes or recruit women to run for office
- A public-health worker who introduces a new contraceptive or child nutrition program
- A personnel officer who wants to hire workers for a new factory
- An employment agent who wants women to sign contracts to work abroad
- A government official who issues permits to operate a small business
- A family elder or religious authority who claims that a certain behavior is forbidden or required by religious law or traditional practice.

Each of these "spokespersons" in turn interacts with the three women, who respond according to their level of education.

2. Discuss

Ask these questions about the role-play:

- What were the principal differences in the ways the "spokespersons" approached the three women? In the ways the women responded?
- How does education affect each woman's feelings about herself? Her willingness to make decisions? Her ability to evaluate or use information?
- What impact might their differences in education have on each woman's health and well-being? Her family? Her community? Her future development and opportunities?
- What impact do their differences in education have on their ability to enjoy their human rights? Which specific rights are limited or denied by lack of education? List these rights.

Female Illiteracy: Causes and Effects

Illiteracy rates for women are disproportionately high. Yet these figures do not include the percentage of women who are *functionally illiterate*—that is, who possess basic literacy skills that are not sufficient for full functioning in society. This type of illiteracy is widespread, even throughout the industrialized world. In Germany alone, the number of functionally illiterate adults is estimated at 4 million.[14]

Literacy is fundamental to the overall process of women's empowerment, raising their analytic skills and opening to them the storehouse of information and knowledge they have long been denied.

The reasons for female illiteracy include:

- lower social status of women and girls
- less access to education
- longer working hours for women and girls, both inside and outside the home
- lower income
- family and community emphasis on education of sons and discrimination against girls in the family
- cultural or traditional restraints that require young women to stay in the home
- curriculum and teaching methods with a gender bias that favors boys and/or is inappropriate for local culture
- considerable distances between home and school
- lack of child care
- inadequate classrooms and lack of teachers.

In most communities, rates of illiteracy and functional illiteracy are likely to be highest among ethnic and racial minorities and the disabled. Thus, failure to combat illiteracy among these groups perpetuates discrimination based on race, ethnicity, and disability.

The effects of illiteracy or functional illiteracy on women and girls include:

- unemployment
- poverty
- crime and imprisonment
- teenage pregnancy and young marriages
- prostitution
- poor health
- perpetuation of family and community discrimination against girls in education.

All of these effects contribute to continuing illiteracy, thus making illiteracy a self-perpetuating cycle. As increasing numbers of women end up supporting their families, their lack of education can lead to poverty and limited opportunities for children.

✠ Learning Activity 3: I Can't Read It![15] ✠

Objective   To understand the personal impact of illiteracy on negotiating life
Time   15 minutes
Materials   Copies of the nearby box headed "Asylum Application"

1. Imagine/Write
Ask participants to imagine the following:

> After a terrifying five-day journey through a war zone, you and your four children cross the border of a neighboring country, where officials are already overwhelmed by thousands of people like you. You need a place to live and some way to care for your family. Someone hands you a sheet of paper. This is, in fact, an application for asylum, without which you cannot stay or receive assistance. You have five minutes to complete it.

Asylum Application

1. APPELLIDO:________________ A#________________
2. PRIMER NOMBRE:________________________________
3. FECHA DE NACIMIENTO:___________________________
4. PAIS, CIUDAD DE RESIDENCIA:_____________________
5. OU GENYEN FANMI NE ETAZINI?____________________
6. KISA YO YE POU WOU:___________________________
7. KI PAPYE IMIGRASYON FANMI OU YO GENYEN ISIT:________
8. KI LAJ OU?________________ KI SEX OU? FI GASON
9. ESKE OU ANSENT? WI NON
10. ESKE OU GEN AVOKA? WI NON
11. NON-AVOKA-W?________________________________
12. HA RECIBIBO ALGUNOS PAPELES DE LA MIGRA? CUALES SON?________
13. OU JAM AL NAHOKEN JYMAN? WI NON
14. CANTIDAD DE FIANZA:___________________________

---

2. Discuss
Ask these questions about the exercise:

- How did you feel and what did you do when you saw the "Asylum Application"?
- This form is an application for refugee status written in Haitian Creole, a blend of French and Spanish. Over 80 percent of refugees are women and their children. What impact does the lack of education have on illiterate woman who become refugees? On their children? (For further discussion of the needs of refugee women, see Chapter 13, "Human Rights of Refugee, Displaced, and War-Affected Women.") In what other crisis situations does lack of education impact women's human rights?

Women's Literacy Programs

- A program of the United Nations, "Education for All," hopes to achieve equality in education by 2015.[16]
- With funding from UNESCO and the Norwegian government, the government of Laos has created a project to improve literacy among women and girls.[17]
- A Peruvian organization called Peru Mujer works to provide literacy and education services to poor women and girls throughout Peru. The organization offers bilingual, culturally inclusive curricula.[18]
- The Afghan Women's Education Center, established in Afghanistan in 1991, provides literacy training and other services to women.[19] According to a 2004 survey, 47 percent of Afghans said that women's greatest problem was illiteracy, and only 8 percent disagreed that women had a right to education. Sixty-five percent of the female respondents agreed that women should have the same opportunities for education as men.[20]
- In Santakulam, India, Aid India provides life-skills training to women, including literacy training.[21]
- The Feminist Dalit Organization of Nepal helps to empower the Dalit women in Nepal through advocacy around many issues affecting women, including illiteracy.[22]

Beyond Literacy: Educating for the Needs of Girls and Women

Around the globe, fewer girls enter primary school, and the number of girls in school continues to decrease each year. In each successive year of education, fewer and fewer girls remain. In most countries, only a fraction of the women reach higher education levels and receive a professional degree.[23]

Why do girls drop out? While it is important to know that these reasons vary according to region, a 1994 study in Africa[24] sheds some light on this question by suggesting the following reasons:

- Negative parental attitudes stemming from cultural practices and value systems, including emphasis on early marriage and childbearing rather than on formal education
- The high cost of education, such as school attendance fees and money for uniforms, school supplies, and books
- Poverty that makes a girl's formal employment essential to family survival
- Sexual harassment both within and outside the school environment, with resulting parental fears for their daughters' safety and the family's honor
- Girls of school age who become pregnant
- Unfriendly teachers and dilapidated physical facilities in schools
- Curricula that are rigid and irrelevant to girls' experience.

Most educational systems are designed for students who can attend school all day during the school year for at least ten consecutive years. In addition, families are often required to pay for school fees, books, and uniforms. Such systems exclude poor children, especially girls, who often must work alongside their parents for family survival. In cultures where early marriages are customary, girls are usually withdrawn from school before they can achieve literacy or fully develop other skills. The costs of girls dropping out are very high; they become trapped in poverty and powerlessness, with few skills and little hope for change.

What is needed worldwide are flexible structures to extend educational opportunities to out-of-school women and girls, especially young mothers, girls at home, the disabled, those living on the streets, and those displaced and affected by armed conflict—all of whom receive low priority in national programs.

Yet women face many obstacles to continuing education. Because of their long workdays, few women have the leisure to attend continuing-education programs. Such educational opportunities need to be close to home and to accommodate child care, or at least occur in conjunction with child care programs. Another obstacle is the opposition of husbands. During a training program on land reform and women's issues in South Africa, for example, rural women cited their husbands' antagonism. The men were antagonistic "because we [women] came here to learn about our rights," and many reported either being forbidden to attend or being beaten because they dared to do so.[25]

Community-based programs that offer health care and other social services can provide women of all ages training programs in literacy and nontraditional vocational skills, as well as gender awareness, legal information, and knowledge of their options in family life, employment, and social relations.

Poverty and Education: Catalina's Story[26]

Catalina is a Guatemalan Indian who is the youngest in a family of six children. Although none of her siblings finished grade school, her father urged her to continue her education, seeing it as something prestigious and a good business investment. He also did so "as an expression of love," says Catalina. After she completed high school, Catalina's family made an extra effort to get money to put her through a college-preparatory institute so that she could go to the university. Here, however, Catalina's dissatisfaction with her education began. Institute attendance meant leaving her village, family, and friends. Her fees, she knew, drained the resources of her family, and it hurt her knowing that her brothers and sisters worked hard everyday while she studied. And it was at the institute that she experienced racism for the first time: "The teachers and the non-Indian students thought of us as second-class. . . . My preparation was deficient since the teachers in our village school had been poorly prepared. It was hard for me to reach the level of the others."

After leaving the preparatory institute, Catalina found that her father couldn't continue to pay for her studies. On her own, she signed up to study medicine at San Carlos University, where she became aware of how few Indians there were at the university level and how few of those would ever attain a degree. It was as if, she said, "we Indians are trapped in a huge net and we cannot get out." In order to support her studies, Catalina had to work in a restaurant and open a small business to sell hand-woven blouses made by women in her village. Eventually this pace exhausted her. She finished the year, but switched from medical school to study secondary education, which required two years less.

After her studies, Catalina taught in village schools where her pupils were taught only in Spanish, as their indigenous languages were forbidden, and where, compared to schools in wealthy areas, supplies were almost nonexistent and teacher preparation poor. Catalina ends her tale reflecting that, while her father had wanted her to study so that she could help her village, "He didn't know what suffering a little knowledge brings with it. . . . When I am depressed, I think it would be better to be illiterate. . . . When I am optimistic, I dream that one day all of us will know more than just reading and writing."

✠ Learning Activity 4: Bringing Education to All Women ✠

Objective   To understand the educational needs of out-of-school women
and strategize how to meet them
Time   60 minutes
Materials   Chart paper and markers or blackboard and chalk

1. List

Ask participants to identify categories of out-of-school women and girls in their community who could benefit from education, whether formal or non-formal. Write their answers under "Who Needs Education?" on a chart like the one shown in Table 11.1.

Table 11.1   Bringing Education to All Women

Who Needs Education?	What Kind of Education?

Next, ask the participants to identify what kinds of learning these women and girls would wish for or benefit from, and write their answers under "What Kind of Education?" Referring to the nearby box headed "Poverty and Education: Catalina's Story," suggest that they consider how Catalina, in particular, might benefit from improved kinds of formal or nonformal education.

2. Plan

Divide participants into small groups. Ask each group to select a category of women from their list and design an education program to suit their needs.

Alternative: Ask the whole group to select one category to work on and then develop the separate parts of the program in small groups.

Suggest the following guidelines:

- What are the educational needs of the women in this category? Do not limit your thinking to "school" subjects or "schoolroom" settings and hours.
- Determine what subjects this model program will offer. How will you know if the women need these subjects? How can you justify these subjects to the women in the community? To their husbands? To the authorities? To possible funders?
- What methods will you use to make learning relevant and effective for these women?
- Consider the logistical problems women may have in attending, such as scheduling, transportation, and child care. How can your program accommodate their needs?

continues

✠ Learning Activity 4 Continued ✠

- Consider the personal problems women may have in attending, such as spousal or parental opposition, fear of embarrassment, self-doubts, and community criticism.
- Are there community organizations with which you might ally yourself to reach and teach these out-of-school women?
- Give your model program an attractive name and devise a thirty-second television or radio announcement to advertise it. What strategies are needed to attract women to your program?

3. Report/Analyze
Ask each group to present its radio/TV announcement as a way of describing the model program the group has developed. Compare these presentations:

- What were viewed as the most important subjects to teach?
- What methodologies seemed appropriate for this learning situation?
- What were the greatest logistic and personal problems?
- What community resources and strategies did the group identify?

4. Discuss

- What is the role of women in bringing these educational opportunities to other women?
- How will this educational program benefit the community?
- How will this program further women's human rights?

Gender-Role Stereotyping in Education

Access to education alone is not sufficient to fulfill girls' human right to education. Indeed, girls and women may face discrimination in the education system: schools, special programs, and training programs open only to boys and men; higher-paid, higher-status teaching positions open only to male educators; and testing methods biased in favor of boys (e.g., questions that reflect the interests and vocabulary of most boys). In most parts of the world, female teachers predominate at the primary level, yet women are generally underrepresented in higher-status, decision-making posts in education, especially at universities. Not only do female students need positive role models, but female teachers may be better able than male ones to address the needs of female students.

School programs can be one of the primary vehicles for reinforcing stereotyping of the expected roles of men and women that society imposes from infancy onward. Schoolbooks often portray boys as big, brave, active, adventurous, and clever people who take action as leaders, explorers, and inventors. Girls, on the other hand, are seen as small, modest, sensitive, cautious, and beautiful, playing traditional reproductive and care-giving roles. In some countries, gender-role stereotypes encourage boys to study the sciences but depict girls as fearful of subjects, such as math and science, that they perceive as being too difficult for them, thus reinforcing girls' sense of inadequacy.

However, properly designed school programs can reverse such stereotyping and combat discrimination against girls and women. The 1995 Beijing Platform for Action explicitly recognizes the importance of combating gender-role stereotyping:

> The creation of an educational and social environment . . . where educational resources promote non-stereotyped images of women and men would be effective in the elimination of the causes of discrimination against women and inequalities between women and men.[27]

Many teachers are not conscious of the discrimination faced by women as a group. And because they do not perceive it, they are unable to challenge damaging stereotypes in educational material, career options available to girls, and school environments that may discriminate. (See also the discussion of gender stereotypes in Chapter 1, "Introduction to Women's Human Rights," and Chapter 3, "Women's Human Rights in the Family.")

From early childhood, girls are socialized to accept the ideology of male supremacy that makes them prey to a range of discriminatory practices. Thus women and girls are not only ill-equipped to identify or confront the injustices to which they themselves are subjected, but, lacking any alternative models of behavior, they actually reinforce and pass on to their children cultural values that are harmful to women. For this reason, women need powerful social, cultural, and economic support to develop a sense of self-worth and encouragement and to transmit this sense of women's value to the succeeding generation. (See also Chapter 4, "The Human Rights of Young Women and Girls.")

✠ Learning Activity 5: Gender-Role Stereotyping in Education ✠

Objective To examine gender-role stereotyping in education and the community

Time 45 minutes

Materials Sample textbooks

1. Role-Play
Read aloud the following scenario:

> You have a small daughter who is just beginning to learn how to read in school. When you are helping her with her schoolwork, you notice that her book is about a boy and his sister. One story tells about the boy's hike in the mountains and his discovery of a secret treasure. The next tells about the girl's trip to her grandmother's house in the village where she learns how to cook.

Ask the participants to do the following:

continues

✠ Learning Activity 5 Continued ✠

- Discuss what this story tells us about male and female behavior.
- Role-play how they would discuss these stories with their own daughters.
- Role-play how they would discuss these stories with the teacher or school officials.

2. Discuss

Ask participants to remember some of their elementary school teachers, texts, and activities. What ideas about gender roles did they reflect?

3. Analyze

In advance, obtain or ask participants to bring in sample textbooks used in local schools. Ask the participants to review them and answer these questions:

- Identify the male and female roles depicted in the textbooks. Could they be changed to present more choices for male and female behavior? If so, how?
- Count the number of pictures of males and females in any section. Compare the ways in which male and females are depicted.
- If one of the books is an anthology of stories or poems, compare the number of male versus female authors and the number of male versus female protagonists.
- Pay special attention to the math and science texts. Are girls pictured at all in these texts? Are they actively engaged? Or are they watching boys perform experiments or manipulate equipment?
- Note the word problems: Does the subject matter include material familiar to girls as well as to boys?

4. Discuss

Ask these questions about gender-role stereotyping:

- How can education be used to combat gender-role stereotyping?
- What can women do to make these changes at both the local and national levels?

Sexual Harassment in Schools

Harassment on the basis of sex constitutes impermissible discrimination and interferes with a student's right to education. Unwelcome sexual advances, requests for sexual favors, and other verbal or physical conduct of a sexual nature constitute sexual harassment.

The laws on sexual harassment vary from country to country, but usually such conduct is illegal under the following conditions:

1. Submission to such conduct is made either explicitly or implicitly a term or condition of an individual's status in a class, school program, or activity.
2. Submission to such conduct is used as the basis for academic decisions affecting the individual, including, but not limited to, grade or academic progress.
3. The conduct has the purpose or effect of interfering with the individual's academic performance, or of creating an intimidating, hostile, or offensive educational environment.

Sexual harassment can be exhibited both verbally and/or physically. Examples of sexual harassment in schools include unwelcome sexual innuendos, suggestive or insulting sounds, humor and jokes about sex, implied or overt threats, and unwelcome patting, pinching, or touching.

The basic point to remember is that sexual harassment is unwanted, unsolicited, or undesired attention of a sexual nature. In most countries, sexual contact between an adult and a minor is illegal whether consensual or not. Sexual harassment is a breach of the trusting relationship that normally exists between a teacher and a student. One student can also harass another, and educators have an obligation to try to prevent this abuse.

Sexual Harassment in Schools: Nko's Story[28]

Nko has come to the university from a small village. In an attempt to fit in, she tries to become more modern. She arranges her hair in a new way and wears her headscarf much less frequently than usual.

One day the faculty dean, Professor Ikot, wants to see her. When she gets to his office, she finds four male students there. Staring at her, they comment on how different she looks. Professor Ikot then announces, to Nko's great surprise, that her work is to be supervised by him. The male students give Nko another curious, long look and leave. Later, Nko receives an anonymous letter that comments, "I wonder how beautiful female students always manage to come up with projects so interesting that they require the dean of faculty to supervise." This comment makes Nko feel cheap.

She realizes that word will get around campus that she is trying to get her degree without having to work for it, simply because the dean of her department is supervising her work. She begins to worry about losing her good name. Can she both keep her name and get a degree?

Nko relaxes when the professor tries to set her at ease. He assures her that people will get used to seeing her come into his office. Discussing her work and her future plans, she finds herself talking freely. She cannot believe anyone would think she was encouraging the professor by simply talking normally and smiling at him. When Professor Ikot invites Nko to join his family on Sunday for a car trip to the nearby falls, she accepts.

On Sunday, the professor picks Nko up and they head for his apartment to gather his family. Once there, his steward tells him that his wife has left to visit her mother. The professor already has the car started before announcing, "I'll show you the falls myself." On the way, Professor Ikot makes a number of sexual remarks to Nko. When they arrive at the falls, the professor says, "If you don't sleep with me, you don't get your degree."

❈ Learning Activity 6: Nko's Story ❈

Objective   To strategize ways to combat sexual harassment in education
Time   60 minutes
Materials   Copy of the nearby box headed "Nko's Story"

Read/Discuss
Read "Nko's Story" aloud, or ask participants to do so. Ask:

- Did Nko do anything wrong?
- Who is the violator in the story?
- What should Nko do now?
- What are the contributing causes?
- Do you think Nko's experience, or one like it, could happen in a school in your community?

What does a school, university, or workplace need to do to protect women and girls from the type of sexual harassment described in this story?

Note to Facilitator: Make clear that individual behavior and societal attitudes are at fault, not Nko herself.

Alternative: Ask the participants to draft the main points of a policy on sexual harassment for a school, university, or other institution in their community. Who should be responsible for setting such standards on sexual harassment? For enforcing them?

The Role of Authorities

Governments as well as social, cultural, and community institutions can greatly affect the education of women and girls. As with the other human rights discussed in this book, authorities can act both directly and indirectly, influencing the media and using culture as well as tradition to mold decisions and to sanction female students who do not comply. Governments have specific obligations: to open school doors to girls and women, to promote women's literacy, and to provide equal educational opportunities for both male and female students. However, beyond this initial step of access and equal opportunity, governments can also play a role in promoting education as a tool for advancing equality, for breaking down discriminatory practices, and for promoting positive images of women and girls.

Traditional and cultural practices need not be roadblocks to educational access for women and girls. Under national, regional, and/or local laws, states have the obligation to respect the human rights to education in all circumstances. Governments violate this principle when they turn a blind eye to traditional practices that interfere with the human right to education. Instead, they should work with communities in a positive way, promoting education for female students while still respecting local culture.

Strategies for Action on Women's Education[29]

- Set specific targets and time-frames to progressively reduce the gender gap.
- Increase access to schools by creating locations within walking distance of girls' homes, and increase the number of adolescent wives and mothers in schools by providing day care facilities.
- Recruit and train more teachers.
- Campaign to elicit parental support and participation in education.
- Adopt innovative programs to combine learning with income earning for out-of-school girls and women in poor communities, and prevent gender-role stereotyping in school curricula.

✠ Learning Activity 7 ✠
The Role of Government Versus the Role of Tradition

Objective To define the responsibility of government for the promotion of girls' education and to strategize action to further that role

Time 45 minutes

Materials Copy of "Case Study: The Girls of Tula"

Case Study: The Girls of Tula

In the village of Tula, girls older than the age of 13 rarely attend school. Some parents forbid them to attend; others simply do not encourage their girls. Fewer than 10 percent of the graduates from secondary school in Tula are girls. Only one girl has ever attended the university, and when she came back to the village, no man would consider marrying her as it was assumed that she had lost her virginity while in the city. Girls in Tula are expected to marry young, to stay at home, and to bear many children—particularly sons.

1. Read

Read the case study to the whole group.

2. Role-Play

Divide participants into small groups. Read the following scenario and ask them to use it to develop a role-play:

You are an educator speaking to Tula community members about the importance of education for girls. What could you say to various groups to encourage keeping girls in school? How might they respond? (Suggested roles among these community members: student, parent, head of family, teacher, local legislator, and local religious leaders.)

3. Imagine/Discuss

Ask the participants to imagine: You are a 15-year-old girl in Tula. You want to go to school, but your parents won't let you. What will you do? How could and should the government help you?

continues

✠ Learning Activity 7 Continued ✠

- Should the government force parents to send their older girls to school?
- Should the government fund "outreach" educators to explain the importance of education to members of the community?
- What other tactics could the government use in the community? In the school? In the university?

4. Discuss

Ask these questions about girls' education in the local community:

- Does your community equally value the education of boys and girls?
- Do more girls than boys drop out of school or attend irregularly? If so, at what age? For what reasons?
- Are government authorities doing anything to correct or challenge negative attitudes toward girls' education? Are people in the community doing anything?

The Human Rights at Issue in Education

Human rights to education include:[30]

- the right to free and compulsory elementary education and to easily available forms of secondary and higher education
- the right to freedom from discrimination based on sex in all levels of education, including equal access to scholarships and fellowships, career development, continuing education, and vocational training
- the right to information about health, nutrition, reproduction, and family planning.

These rights to education are linked to other important human rights, including:[31]

- the right to equality between men and women, including equality in the family and society (implementation of which requires the elimination of gender-based stereotypes in education that deny women opportunities for full and equal partnership)
- the right to work and receive wages that contribute to an adequate standard of living
- the right to freedom of thought, conscience, religion, and belief
- the right to an adequate standard of living
- the right to participate in shaping decisions and policies affecting one's community at the local, national, and international levels.

The right to education is recognized in many national, regional, and international laws. These are listed below.

- Signatories to the Convention on the Rights of the Child (CRC) must "recognize the right of the child to education," including "primary education compulsory and available free to all, secondary education available and accessible to every child," and "higher education accessible to all on the basis of capacity" (Article 28).[32]
- The International Covenant on Economic, Social, and Cultural Rights (ICESCR) similarly recognizes "the right of everyone to education," stating that "education shall be directed to the full development of the human personality and sense of its dignity" (Article 13).[33]
- The Convention on the Elimination of All Forms of Discrimination Against Women (CEDAW) prohibits discrimination in education: "States Parties shall take all appropriate measures to eliminate discrimination against women in order to ensure to them equal rights within the field of education" (Article 10).[34]

Education *for* Human Rights[35]

Some governmental human rights education initiatives have proved beneficial to women:

- In Ethiopia, the Ministry of Justice has promoted legal and human rights education through a media campaign, helping women to better understand the legal rights available to them. And the Ministry of Education has undertaken a revision of school curricula in order to include principles of human rights, including those related to gender justice.
- In Namibia, a Committee for Human Rights was established in 1995 within the Ministry of Justice. And in 1998, a series of human rights training workshops for key sectors (the private sector, parliamentarians, women's organizations, regional governors, and NGOs) were organized. The Committee has also been active in curriculum development within the school system and in a regional project involving Zimbabwe and Mozambique.
- In Jordan, human rights awareness-raising programs have been designed to promote the role of women leaders, the rights of the child, and conflict resolution methodologies. Accordingly, human rights and children's rights clubs have been set up in a number of schools.
- In Thailand, the Office of the National Commission on Women's Affairs (ONCWA), as the secretariat body of the national machinery for the advancement of women, has implemented legal literacy programs for women and published materials on the topic of women and the law.
- In Ecuador, a national action plan for human rights education was created in 2002. Human rights education components have been included at all levels of education. Poor women, children, and other vulnerable populations are targets for these educational programs.
- In Trinidad and Tobago, government ministries chair a National Plan of Action Committee, which strives for attainment of the goals of the 1990 World Summit for Children. Government divisions conduct seminars and workshops on children's rights, women's rights, and gender-based violence.

A lack of education prevents women from exercising other human rights. For instance, uneducated women may have difficulty understanding the political process and/or what electoral candidates stand for. Moreover, illiterate women are far less likely than literate women to be candidates for office or to be active in high-level politics, and they may have difficulty determining where and how to access health care. Employment options are also drastically reduced for illiterate women, who may not be able to read information about job positions or even fill out an application. And their property rights may be reduced, as illiterate women have trouble reading contracts or other papers needed to buy or sell property.

Education and the Beijing Platform for Action

The Beijing Platform for Action, a statement of intentions on the part of government representatives at the Fourth World Conference for Women in Beijing in 1995, recognizes education as a basic human right and an essential tool for achieving more equal relations between women and men. It recommends investing in formal and nonformal education and training for girls and women as one of the best means of achieving economic growth and development that are both sustained and sustainable.

In particular, the Beijing Platform for Action proposes these strategic objectives:

- Ensure equal access to education.
- Ensure the completion of primary education by at least 80 percent of children, with special emphasis on girls, by the year 2000.
- Close the gender gap in primary and secondary education by 2005 and achieve universal primary education in all countries before the year 2015.
- Reduce the female illiteracy rate, especially among rural, migrant, refugee, internally displaced, and disabled women, to at least half the 1990 level.
- Eradicate illiteracy among women worldwide.
- Improve women's access to vocational training, science and technology, and continuing education.
- Develop nondiscriminatory education and training by developing and using curricula, textbooks, and teaching aids free of sex-stereotyping for all levels of education.
- Allocate sufficient resources for and monitor the implementation of educational reforms.
- Maintain or increase funding levels for education in structural adjustment and economic recovery programs.
- Promote lifelong education and training for girls and women, and create flexible educational programs to meet their needs.

Remembering Core Concepts

✠ Learning Activity 8 ✠
Speaking Out for Women's Human Right to Education

Objectives   To examine women's and girls' right to education in the community and consider how to take action to ensure that it is upheld

Time   60+ minutes

Materials   Chart paper and markers

✖ Learning Activity 8 Continued ✖

1. Brainstorm

Ask participants to list the problems faced by women in their community who could benefit from improved access to education or improved quality of education, whether formal or informal. Then, after dividing them into small groups, ask them to choose a problem on which they wish to concentrate.

2. Discuss/Plan

Ask each group to prepare a five-minute presentation to a "panel of community leaders" on their selected problem. Each presentation should:

- describe the educational problem, identifying the group of women it impacts and, if possible, the cause(s) of the problem
- relate the problem to women's human rights
- clarify how the problem affects women's lives
- show how addressing the problem can improve their lives
- propose specific actions that should be taken to address the problem
- show how members of the community can get involved in addressing the problem.

Ask each group to choose a spokesperson to make the presentation and a "community leader" to serve on the panel. While the groups plan their presentations, the panel of leaders meets to decide on their roles, representing a variety of differing but typical attitudes within the community leadership.

3. Present/Role-Play

The spokesperson from each group makes a presentation and members of the panel listen and respond, asking questions and offering comments, objections, or suggestions in keeping with their chosen roles.

4. Discuss

After the presentations and role-play, discuss:

- How did the spokespersons feel when presenting the problem?
- How did the "community leaders" respond to the presentation? What attitudes in the community were they representing?
- How did the audience, composed of the rest of the group, respond to the presentations?
- Did any spokesperson discuss the problem as a violation of women's human rights? Did putting the problem in this context strengthen the argument?
- Are these ideas for preventing violations of women's human right to education feasible in your community? Why or why not?

continues

✠ Learning Activity 8 Continued ✠

5. Conclude

Challenge the participants by asking them to evaluate their knowledge of the problem and the inclusiveness of their perspective:

- How did you obtain your information about human rights educational problems facing women in your community? Was it accurate and complete? If not, what additional information do you need and how can you obtain it?
- Did you personally consult women about the problem and how it affects them? About actions that could improve the problem?
- Why is it important in real-life human rights advocacy to include the active participation of those directly involved and affected?
- How can you apply the example of this learning activity to planning and implementing advocacy for women in your community?

Notes

1. Universal Declaration of Human Rights, General Assembly Resolution 217A (III), 1948, Article 26, in *25+ Human Rights Documents* (Center for the Study of Human Rights, Columbia University, New York, 2001).

2. United Nations Literacy Decade, "Education for All (2003–2012)," 2005.

3. UNICEF State of the World's Children Report, 2004, available online at http://www.unicef.org.

4. Ibid.

5. Isobel Coleman, "The Payoff from Women's Rights," *Foreign Affairs*, May/June 2004.

6. UNICEF Fact Sheet, Facts on Children, "Girls' Education: Making the Case," available online at http://www.unicef.org.

7. Ibid.

8. Ibid.

9. Ibid.

10. UNESCO, "Gender and Education for All: The Leap to Equality," *Summary Report*, available online at http://www.unesco.org.

11. International Women's Health Coalition, Resource Library, available online at http://www.iwhc.org.

12. UNESCO, "Gender and Education for All."

13. World Bank, "Girls' Education: A World Bank Priority," 2005.

14. Literacy Exchange: World Resources on Literacy, *Overview: Literacy and Adult Education in Germany*, June 6, 2005.

15. David Donahue and Nancy Flowers, adapted from *Uprooted: Refugees and the United States* (Alameda, CA: Hunter House, 1995), p. 20.

16. See the Literacy Online website at http://www.literacyonline.org/explorer.model.html.

17. Ibid.

18. Ibid.

19. Jagriti International, "Currently Registered Women's Organizations," available online at http://www.jagritifoundation.org/organizations.asp?SelectAll=yes.

20. Asia Foundation, *Afghanistan in 2006: A Survey of the Afghanistan People*, pp. 61–64.

21. Jagriti International, "Currently Registered Women's Organizations," available online at http://www.jagritifoundation.org/organizations.asp?Country=India.

22. Jagriti International, "Currently Registered Women's Organizations," available online at http://www.jagritifoundation.org/organizations.asp?Country=Nepal.

23. Asian Human Rights Commission, "Women's Right to Education Teaching Modules," Lesson Series 12, Lesson I: Poverty and Education for Women, 2004.

24. Forum for African Women Educationalists, "Girls and African Education: Research and Action to Keep Girls in School," Nairobi, 1995.

25. Janine Hicks Hlomelikusasa et al., "Skills for the Future," in *Women's Rights as Human Rights: A Training Manual* (Community Law Centre, Durban, South Africa, 1995).

26. *Ch'Abuj Ri Ixoc* (The Voice of Women), news bulletin on Guatemala published in Washington, DC, No. 3, 1985.

27. Beijing Declaration and Platform for Action, Fourth World Conference on Women, September 15, 1995, A/CONF. 177/20 (1995) and A/CONF. 177/20/Add. 1 (1995), ch. 4, B.69.

28. Adapted from Buchi Emecheta, *Double Yoke* (George Braziller, 1982), pp. 132–142.

29. *Literacy: A Key to Women's Empowerment*, UN Public Information Department Press Kit for the Fourth World Conference on Women, Beijing, China, 1995.

30. *The Right to Education*, undated, adapted from the People's Decade for Human Rights Education Website, posted on The People's Movement for Human Rights Learning.org, available online at http://www.pdhre.org/rights/education.html.

31. Ibid.

32. Convention on the Rights of the Child, 1990, in *25+ Human Rights Documents* (Center for the Study of Human Rights, Columbia University, New York, 2001).

33. Ibid.

34. Ibid.

35. "Summary of Selected National Initiatives Undertaken Within the Decade for Human Rights Education, 1995–2004," available online at http://www.unhchr.ch/html/menu6/1/initiatives.htm.

12

Women's Human Rights in Politics, Public Life, and the Media

States Parties shall take all appropriate measures to eliminate discrimination against women in the political and public life of the country.
> —Convention on the Elimination of All Forms of
> Discrimination Against Women, Article 7

Objectives

The learning activities and background information contained in this chapter will enable participants to work toward the following objectives:

- Identify the advantages of participating in political and public life and the different forms that such participation takes.
- Understand the various human rights linked to political participation.
- Provide examples of the obstacles faced by women with respect to participating in politics and public life at the community level.
- Explore what governments, community leaders, the media, and women themselves can do to improve women's participation in public life.
- Understand the role of the media in reinforcing gender stereotypes.
- Explain the provisions of the Convention on the Elimination of Discrimination Against Women (CEDAW) regarding women's participation in politics and public life.
- Remember core concepts.

Getting Started: Thinking About Women's Participation in Politics, Public Life, and the Media

Women's participation in politics, public life, and the media is critical if women are to enjoy their human rights. Women's voices and perspectives are needed in the drafting of policies and legislation that protects and promotes women's human rights, and women's advocacy is needed to ensure that such laws are not only passed but also actively enforced. During the twentieth century women gained the right to vote and run for political office in almost every country with elected institutions. Yet women still have not won the vote in Saudi Arabia.[1]

In the twenty-first century, however, women are stepping to the forefront in waging peace as leaders in democratic governance. In Morocco, a law requiring a 10 percent quota of women representation increased the number of women parliamentarians in 2002 from 2 to an Arab-world record of 35.[2] In Liberia, Ellen Johnson-Sirleaf came to power in 2005 as the first woman to be elected president of an African country. To calm her troubled country, President Johnson-Sirleaf welcomed a United Nations peacekeeping force made up entirely of women from India who came in early 2007 to ease Liberia's transition from civil war to peace.[3] In Chile, Michelle Bachelet, a former woman minister of defense in the post-dictator era, was elected to the presidency in a runoff in 2006 and went on to appoint another woman as her defense minister. And in Guatemala, 1992 Nobel Peace Laureate Rigoberta Menchu Tum, a Quiche-Maya, announced her candidacy for the 2007 Guatemalan presidential race; she is the first indigenous woman ever in the Americas to run for presidential office. At the other extreme, however, 72 percent of Afghans did not consider women capable of serving in the National Parliament, citing insufficient knowledge of politics, less education than men, and the need to remain at home with their families.[4]

Despite remarkable progress, women remain underrepresented in positions of power both locally and nationally, whether in elected and other government positions or in other decision-making roles. An assessment made by the Inter-Parliamentary Union in October 2005 shows that women are far from equally represented in decision-making structures. Even the goal of 30 percent by 1995, set by the UN Economic and Social Council, is still a dream for most women.

In only a few countries—such as Wales and certain Scandinavian countries—is the proportion of women and men in decision-making structures more or less equal. Indeed, some countries, particularly those undergoing fundamental political, economic, and social change—Croatia, Bosnia and Herzegovina, Russia, Armenia, Kyrgyzstan—have experienced a significant decline in the number of women in legislative bodies.[5] Such an absence of representation means that women's skills, experience, and concerns are still largely missing when plans and decisions affecting the whole population are formulated. A 2002 study analyzed by World Bank experts and other prominent researchers showed that women worldwide are less tolerant of corruption in government, suggesting that an increased number of women in governing roles would improve governance, thereby attracting greater economic investment from abroad.[6]

Yet women face daunting opposition to their participation. In some cases, they are obstructed by the "glass ceiling," an invisible barrier within business and professional hierarchies that restricts them to minor positions in professions, business, and government; in others, cultural and religious practices exclude women from public life altogether. Some governments use threats or acts of violence to inhibit women who work to bring about social change. The media, whether state-owned or private, tend to reinforce traditional roles for women and often fail to represent their perspectives and concerns.

The lack of women's participation in political decision making has important consequences for society:

- It deprives women of important rights as well as responsibilities as citizens.
- It excludes their point of view from policies and legislation.
- It prevents their input into national budgets and resource allocation.
- It deprives society of women's skills, knowledge, and perspectives.

The Right to Participate

The International Covenant on Civil and Political Rights (ICCPR) spells out the political and civil rights of all people. This important document specifically states that men and women shall be provided political rights on an equal basis and that each citizen shall have the right and the opportunity—without unreasonable restrictions—

- to take part in the conduct of public affairs, directly or through freely chosen representatives
- to vote and to be elected at genuine periodic elections, which shall be by universal and equal suffrage.

The Convention on the Elimination of All Forms of Discrimination Against Women (CEDAW) also contains provisions concerning women's right to participation:

- Article 7 specifically mentions women's right to participate in nongovernmental organizations, thus recognizing this work as meaningful political participation. Still, the measures suggested in Article 7 are only suggestions: Governments may find that other measures are necessary to eliminate discrimination in political and public life.
- Article 13 further provides that "States Parties shall take all appropriate measures to eliminate discrimination against women in other areas of economic and social life in order to ensure, on a basis of equality of men and women, the same rights, in particular (a) the right to family benefits; (b) the right to bank loans, mortgages and other forms of credit."
- Article 14 of the convention specifically guarantees the human right of rural women to have access to agricultural credit and loans, marketing facilities, appropriate technology, and equal treatment in land and agrarian reform as well as in land resettlement schemes.

Note, however, that these provisions of international human rights law grant only formal equality to participation in politics and public life. For example, they guarantee women the right to vote, but they neither obligate governments to do anything to ensure that women do vote (e.g., voter education) nor require governments to take any actions to correct historical discrimination against women in the political sphere. In most cases, it is women themselves who have pressured governments to make their human rights real. Women around the world have also developed strategies to overcome challenges and gain access to power; such strategies include participation in grassroots movements and nongovernmental organizations as well as use of alternative and electronic media.

To participate in the public life of their societies, women need to enjoy the full spectrum of their civil and political rights. Not only civil freedoms such as expression, access to information, assembly, and association but also the fulfillment of basic survival and social needs such as education, health, and an adequate standard of living are essential if women are to participate in public life as equals. Just as important is freedom from family and community violence, especially in countries where freedom of association is limited and women's political activity is under close surveillance and sometimes threatened by their own governments.

If women's human right to political participation is to be on truly equal terms with that of men, the following must occur:

- Women must be *elected* to government structures.
- Government structures must demonstrate a general *understanding of women's equality* and gender roles.
- Women must be *employed* as civil servants in government.
- *Women in civil society must be empowered* to participate in formal structures of government not only as individuals but also as members of NGOs and other civic lobbying organizations.[7]

Women in Political Life

- Of some 180 countries, only 13 are headed by women. Among the other women leaders in government are 15 vice presidents and deputy heads of state and 2 governor-generals.
- Seventeen percent of members of national parliaments worldwide are women.
- Women hold only 8.8 percent of the seats in Arab states' parliaments, 17 percent of the seats in sub-Saharan African nations' parliaments, 19.2 percent of the seats in national parliaments in Europe, and 19.9 percent of the seats in the Americas.
- Rwanda has the highest proportion of women parliamentarians in the world, inasmuch as 48.8 percent of its National Assembly members are women. This outcome followed the passage of a constitutional referendum guaranteeing that a minimum of 30 percent of parliamentary seats and other leadership positions would be held by women.
- In 1995, Sweden became the first country to have an equal number of women and men in ministerial posts. At present, 52.4 percent of its cabinet members are women ministers.
- In the developing countries of Mozambique, Vietnam, and Namibia, 34.8 percent, 27.3 percent, and 26.9 percent, respectively, of seats in the Lower House of Parliament are held by women.
- By contrast, in the developed nations of the United States, France, and Japan, only 16.3 percent, 12.2 percent, and 9.4 percent, respectively, of the members of the House of Representatives or Lower House of Parliament are women.
- Austria was the only state to have elected a woman to the presidency of one of the Parliament's Chambers (the Bundesrat) before World War II.[8]

✠ Learning Activity 1: A Recipe for Political Success ✠

Objective To consider the qualities a woman needs to become an effective leader
Time 45 minutes
Materials Charts prepared with the two leaders' quotations featured below, chart paper and markers or blackboard and chalk

1. Read
Ask for volunteers to read out these quotations, which are also displayed on chart paper:

- "If you're not completely sure of yourself and you're not completely sure of the direction you are taking you give up very quickly. You have to be completely unconcerned with other people's opinion. . . . You don't get into being a leader in a country unless you go through the nasty role of politics. And it can be nasty. Oh, it's vicious." (Eugenia Charles, Prime Minister, Dominica, 1980–1995)[9]
- "We all know women have to do everything a little better than men. . . . We're all so tolerant when men make mistakes but I don't know of any society that is tolerant when women make mistakes. . . . [T]here is a tendency to say: Well, she's a woman. You'd never say: Well, he's a man; it's natural that he makes mistakes." (Vigdis Finnbogadottir, President, Iceland, 1980–1996).

2. List
Ask participants to list and discuss the following:

- The qualities a woman needs to succeed in politics
- The names of women who hold elected or appointed offices in your community, region, or country
- Aspects of background, experience, or character that are shared by these women office holders. (Add to your first list any additional qualities you observe.)

3. Discuss
Go down your list of qualities needed to succeed in politics and check every woman on your list of officials who has these qualities. Which qualities occur most often?

Using this information, develop the profile of a typical woman engaged in politics in your community. When complete, discuss this profile:

- Does the profile differ among women at the regional and national levels?
- Ideally, what other qualities would you like to see in a woman political leader? Describe the kind of leadership such a woman could provide.
- What are some of the advantages and disadvantages of participation in the political life of your community? For women in particular?

⌗ Learning Activity 1 Continued ⌗

- Is it ever possible for a woman lacking the qualities in your profile to become a political leader? What kind of leadership might such a woman provide? What can women do to bring more women from diverse backgrounds and experience into politics?
- How do you evaluate the women who hold office in your community, region, or country? Do your criteria for rating women leaders differ from those you use to rate men?

Barriers to Women's Political and Public Participation

Women face many barriers to political and public participation. These may include the following:

- Discriminatory attitudes and practices
- Unequal power relations between women and men in the family
- Household and child care responsibilities
- Exclusion of women's concerns from the political agenda
- Lack of education
- Lack of experience in public affairs
- Lack of role models of and support from women in power
- Fear of violence, harassment, and criticism and of being divorced by one's husband
- Poverty
- High cost of seeking and holding public office
- Discrimination against minority women
- Culture of political confrontation, which creates "winners" and "losers"
- Designation of male as "head of household" for all social, economic, and political purposes
- Low self-esteem.

Family, Culture, and Religion: Barriers to Women's Participation

Many of the barriers to women's participation in political and public life are related to women's role in the family. In many instances, male members of a family determine a woman's ability to leave the house, get an education, find a job, attend meetings, or even meet people. Women often have to vote for candidates supported by their husbands or fathers or are not allowed to vote at all. And women can be thrown out, abandoned, abused, or ridiculed for attempting to have a public role. For further information on these aspects of women's political participation, see Chapter 3, "Women's Human Rights in the Family"; Chapter 10, "Women's Human Rights and Work"; and Chapter 11, "Women's Human Right to Education."

Cultural and religious beliefs are closely connected to gender roles within the family and can act as barriers to women's public and political participation. While cultural and religious factors have long been implicated in the reinforcement of women's principal roles as that of wife and mother, in recent years the rise of religious extremism has further constrained women's public participation. In particular societies, religious extremism also constitutes a political movement that seeks to impose strict notions of identity, culture, and religion to enhance the political power of certain communities of men.

✠ Learning Activity 2: Obstacles to Public Participation ✠

Objectives Identifying the obstacles to women's participation in public life
Time   60 minutes
Materials Copies of the nearby box headed "Barriers to Women's Political and Public Participation," chart paper and markers or blackboard and chalk

1. Discuss
Divide the participants into small groups and ask them to consider the following:

- Do women participate in decision making in the public life of your community? If not, why not?
- What are the obstacles to participating equally with men in public life? You may wish to draw or dramatize the experiences of a woman who wants to effect change in your community, showing some of the obstacles she might encounter.

2. Analyze
Read or hand out the box headed "Barriers to Women's Political and Public Participation." Ask participants to add to this list any other barriers they feel are relevant and to circle those barriers that apply to their community. Have each small group consider the following questions:

- What can be done to overcome these obstacles?
- Are women in your community already working on these obstacles?
- What are some of the alternative paths women are taking to affect decision making?
- Are there grassroots movements that promote women's interests?
- What nongovernmental organizations support women's issues?

3. Evaluate
Ask each group to report three responses to the questions in Step 2. List ideas.

Conclude by summing up the positive actions the community can take to support women in leadership.

State Violence Against Women

The government itself often prevents or hinders women's political participation through the violent acts of agents or officials. Indeed, women may face state violence for exercising their human rights through such activities as organizing, teaching advocacy and education about human rights, protesting government policies, writing political articles, being a member of a political party, providing legal representation, organizing women or other communities of people, and participating in national movements for change. In some countries, women are subjected to torture, beatings, detention, or execution; in others, they are denied rights such as the ability to report harassment or threats and violence by the state. In addition, many governments fail to protect women against violence perpetrated by nonstate actors.[10] (See also Chapter 7, "Women's Human Right to Freedom from Violence.")

Abuses of women in custody or in prison are severe human rights problems around the world. Women can be put in prison for many reasons,[11] including discriminatory laws or the discriminatory application of laws—especially in cases of adultery or rape—and membership in particular ethnic or social groups that are targeted by the dominant group. Although both men and women prisoners experience violence in prison, the latter are often abused in ways connected to their sex; moreover, prison-guards' sexual misconduct often goes unnoticed. A woman can be publicly strip-searched, touched inappropriately, raped, gang-raped, or have foreign objects inserted into her vagina.[12] And as Amnesty International reports, pregnant women prisoners have been sexually abused, shackled in the third trimester and during labor and delivery, and given inadequate or no health care.[13]

Women, Violence, and Political Participation

The Pakistani government is trying to silence human rights defender Mukhtar Mai, whose courage and refusal to be silenced have increased international attention to abuses against women in Pakistan. In 2002, Mukhtar Mai was gang-raped on orders of a traditional village council as punishment for acts allegedly committed by her younger brother. She courageously testified in court against the men responsible for her rape and, using compensation money, built schools for girls and boys and started a shelter for abused women.[14]

In Nepal, 100 women, members of the All Nepalese Women's Association, were arrested during a demonstration on International Women's Day, March 8, 2005. They were held in custody with an estimated 1,800 other activists and denied visits and communication with their families and colleagues.[15]

Marlene Garcia Esperat, a Filipino journalist, was killed in her home after writing a story that exposed government officials' and military officers' involvement in graft and corruption. She is one of nearly 40 activists to be murdered or disappeared in the Philippines in 2005.[16]

In the village of Taishi, in China's southern Guangdong province, dozens of democracy activists have been arrested, including three elderly women who carried out a sit-in to protect the village's account books. Other activists and journalists in Taishi have been beaten or denied travel to or from the village.[17]

✠ Learning Activity 3: Political Persecution of Women ✠

Objective   To identify the women's human rights issues involved in political persecution

Time   75 minutes

Materials   Copies of "Case Study: The Story of Guidem Ange Tekam" and "Case Study: The Story of Eliane Potiquara Lima dos Santos"

The Story of Guidem Ange Tekam

Guidem Ange Tekam from Cameroon was editor of her university's student newspaper. The government had a history of banning issues or harassing newspaper staff whenever the paper printed anything critical of it. Ange was also a leader in student and national politics, for which she was frequently physically attacked, even in class. Finally, soldiers surrounded her one day on campus, stripped her naked, and beat her brutally, firing guns and tear gas at crowds of students who ran to her defense. The soldiers ultimately arrested and tortured over 1,300 students during the three days of rioting that followed.

After a night of torture in a shed, Ange was thrown into a windowless jail cell 2 by 3 meters with more than 15 males. There she was kept for two weeks without access to anyone. Fortunately Ange's cellmates gave her protection and clothes to cover herself. Ange was released two weeks later without comment or explanation, except from the gatekeeper who told her if she made trouble at the university again, "There will be nothing to save you." She was immediately expelled from the university. However, she remains active in public life, continuing to oppose government oppression.[18]

The Story of Eliane Potiquara Lima dos Santos

When Eliane Potiquara Lima dos Santos first visited her indigenous family's homeland in the state of Paraiba in northeast Brazil, she learned about how her grandparents' generation had been forced either to leave or to become forced labor in foreign-owned plantations and factories. She became active in the indigenous movement and in 1986 founded GRUMIN (Indigenous Women Education Group).

As she became more visible as an activist at both the national and international levels, a campaign of persecution and defamation began against her. Landowners and right-wing politicians who did not want Indian problems exposed, especially conflicts over control and management of land, attacked her in the press. Some claimed she was only passing as an Indian; others accused her of being a thief and prostitute. Police began to call her in for questioning. Anonymous callers frightened her and her children, and strangers followed them and disturbed their home.

For a long time, no one took her complaints seriously, but through the support of the Attorney General of Paraiba, international NGOs and indigenous women's groups, the persecution finally ended. Today Eliane is working on national legislation to enable indigenous women to demand that the government assume responsibility for their human rights under both national and international law.[19]

1. List

Distribute both cases to be read in small groups. Ask participants to list the ways in which these women's public participation was discouraged. Who or what tried to stop them? Why?

✵ Learning Activity 3 Continued ✵

2. Discuss

- What human rights were violated?
- What aspects of their persecution are especially related to gender?
- Who or what were their allies? What aspects of their support are especially related to their being women?
- Are there examples of similar attacks on women active in the public life of your community? Are any of the tactics and motives similar to those described in the case studies? Have these women also found allies?

Strategies to Increase Women's Political Participation

Women's participation and leadership in the political sphere can be increased in several ways. Through education and information campaigns, women can be encouraged to vote. Women's skills in the areas of politics, public speaking, and leadership can be developed through training programs. And funding and campaign assistance can be made available to women candidates who are running for political office.

Affirmative Action

A commonly used strategy to increase women's political participation is affirmative action. Sometimes called affirmative discrimination or special measures, affirmative action refers to the steps taken by governments, educational institutions, businesses, and other bodies to eliminate existing discrimination, provide an immediate remedy for past discrimination, and prevent discrimination from taking place in the future. The goal of affirmative action is to enable both women and men to have an equal opportunity to compete for political office or other decision-making positions.

In some instances, governments have imposed specific quotas for women in certain political categories. For example, India has constitutionally mandated reserving one-third of positions for women at the rural government level.

Opinions differ, however, as to the effectiveness of this strategy to increase women's power in politics. Some argue that despite having quotas before the recent transitions to capitalism and democracy, women in Eastern Europe had no more impact on policies than their counterparts in countries without quota systems. Others argue that a critical mass of at least 30 percent female representation would influence decision-making bodies to integrate the needs and views of women, thus actually expanding women's access to political power. Still others suggest that quotas can have the effect of segregating women as tokens in marginal positions.

Proportional gender representation in electoral systems seems to have been more effective in increasing women's presence in state legislatures. In this model, political parties are encouraged to have a certain percentage of female representatives in their executive bodies and lists of candidates. Sweden, Denmark,

France, Norway, and Bosnia all had such quotas for women in their elections, and Afghanistan and Iraq have incorporated these quotas into their respective constitutions.[20]

Affirmative Action at the National and Local Levels of Government Around the World[21]

Quota systems are being established in some countries to ensure greater participation of women in decision making.

Quotas Regarding Number of Women in National and Local Government Seats

- In Mauritania, 17.9 percent of National Assembly seats were reserved for women after the 2005 military coup.
- Since 2003 in Jordan, six seats (5.45 percent) have been reserved for women in the national parliament. Women's groups are calling for a 20 percent quota for women.
- In India, 33 percent of seats at the local government level are reserved for women.
- In Tanzania, 20 percent of national seats and 25 percent of local government seats are reserved for women.

Legally Mandated Quotas for Political Parties

- In France, a 1999 constitutional amendment requires political parties to include 50 percent of women candidates on party lists submitted for election.
- In South Africa, a municipal act states that political parties must ensure that women comprise 50 percent of lists submitted for local-level elections.

Voluntary Quota Adopted by Political Parties

- In Norway, the Labor Party in 1993 introduced a 40 percent quota for women.

Beyond Traditional Politics

Women's empowerment rests on women's ability to participate in decision making at all levels: formal decision-making arenas such as the United Nations and local governments, religious structures, community groups, nongovernmental organizations, the formal economy, and the informal workforce. In the words of the Beijing Platform for Action: "Women's empowerment and their full participation on the basis of equality in all spheres of society, including participation in the decision-making process and access to power, are fundamental for the achievement of equality, development and peace."[22]

Faced with systematic exclusion from traditional avenues of power, women continue to empower themselves and their communities through alternative structures. Particularly through nongovernmental organizations (NGOs) and grassroots organizations, women have been able to bring their issues and concerns to the public arena and influence policy-making bodies from which they are otherwise excluded. Women's groups—including literacy programs, battered women's hotlines, health care groups, child care advocates, law groups, agricultural collectives—all take an active role in the public sphere.

For example, every four years, countries that have ratified the Convention on the Elimination of All Forms of Discrimination Against Women are required to submit a report outlining the progress that they have made in implementing CEDAW in their country. NGOs play an active role in monitoring government implementation by producing "shadow reports" that critique or support the official state reports. This method is critical to ensuring government accountability. In Morocco, for example, the Association Démocratique des Femmes du Maroc (ADFM), an NGO protecting women's rights, coordinated a shadow report with twenty-two women's NGOs. ADFM prepared a report in 1996 examining the official government and conducted field research to document cases of human rights violations and discrimination against women. ADFM then drafted a report based on the findings and workshops with other NGOs, and held a press conference to highlight their response. ADFM continues to use this model and submitted another shadow report in 2003.[23] Multiple countries submit shadow reports each year. In 2007 alone, 22 countries submitted shadow reports: Austria, Azerbaijan, Colombia, Greece, India, Kazakhstan, Maldives, Mauritania, Mozambique, Namibia, the Netherlands, Niger, Pakistan, Peru, Poland, Serbia, Sierra Leone, Suriname, Syrian Arab Republic, Tajikistan, Vanuatu, and Vietnam.[24]

As of November 2, 2006, 185 countries—over 90 percent of UN members—have ratified CEDAW. The United States signed the convention, but the U.S. Senate has yet to ratify it.[25] International demand for CEDAW compliance has proved a rallying tool to overturn cultural, economic, religious, and other practices that treat women like second-class citizens.

Gender Mainstreaming and Gender Budgets

Gender mainstreaming seeks to integrate gender perspectives and the goal of gender equality in government policy-making, planning, implementation, and evaluation. In this way, governments can better serve all citizens by making sure that women's needs and priorities are considered in the formulation and implementation of all policies and programs, even those that seem gender-neutral. Furthermore, gender mainstreaming efforts have produced strategies and tools for analysis and evaluation, using gender data and sex-disaggregated statistics that bring other concerns such as race, class, and ethnicity into government policy and planning. This inclusion benefits not only women but also other marginalized sectors to which women may also belong.

Gender budgets are a method of determining the extent to which government spending has matched its goal of gender equality. A gender budget is not a separate budget for women but, rather, a tool that analyzes budgets, public spending, and taxation from a gender perspective. Gender budgets can be used to advocate for changing government budgets to better respond to women's priorities. As a result of gender budgeting, governments have increased their expenditures for social services that benefit women and children such as health and nutrition, education, and other family and community services. Overall, gender budgets make a significant contribution to gender mainstreaming.[26]

In short, gender mainstreaming and gender budgets are not ends in themselves but tools for achieving gender equality. Their strength is that they facilitate efforts directed at woman-centered activities, such as daycare for mothers working outside the home. Their principal weakness, however, is that they do not address the factors that create women's subordinate status in society and instead reinforce traditional women's roles, such as caring for children.[27]

Learning Activity 4
Becoming a Public Person, Taking a Public Stand

Objective To identify ways of taking a public stand to bring about change at the community level and acknowledging the importance of women's representation in public life

Time 60 minutes

Materials Copies of "Case Study: Anna, Part One" and "Case Study: Anna, Part Two"

Case Study: Anna, Part One

Anna lives in a small village with her three children. Since her husband died two years ago, she has been quarreling with relatives over control of her house and land. Her late husband's brothers argue that they are entitled to the property, but Anna contends that she should own the land. The written law supports Anna's claim, but custom and tradition support the brothers' arguments. Anna tries to find a lawyer to represent her case in court, but no one will take her seriously. Then Anna tries to get a bank loan to buy a tractor for her land. The bank refuses to give her any money without the co-signature of a male relative.

1. Read/Discuss

Distribute or read aloud "Case Study: Anna, Part One." Ask participants to discuss the following in small groups:

- Is Anna considered a public person in this story?
- What would it take for Anna to be recognized as a public person?
- Where could she look for support?
- What factors would increase her chances of success? Literacy? Experience in public life? Understanding of the law? Community allies?
- Why did the lawyers fail to take Anna's case seriously? Do lawyers, judges, and other court personnel take women seriously in your community? In cases in which women report rape or violence in the family?
- Why is property ownership important to Anna? To women in your community?

2. Read/Discuss

Distribute or read aloud "Case Study: Anna, Part Two."

Case Study: Anna, Part Two

When her brothers-in-law continue their attempts to take over her land, Anna first seeks the advice of her family elders: her grandmother, great aunts, mother, and aunts. They advise her to speak to her deceased husband's family elders as well, but when Anna speaks to the women of his family, she sees that they favor their sons and grandsons over her.

When the brothers grow impatient and make threats to Anna and her children, Anna goes to the chief of police, who assures Anna that her officers will provide her with extra surveillance.

Anna then decides to consult a lawyer, a woman well known in the community for her astuteness in property cases. With her help Anna files a case against

✠ Learning Activity 4 Continued ✠

her brothers-in-law, but she and her lawyer also decide to try to make the local laws clearer about inheritance rights.

Because they first must gain support from the village council, they call on many of the women on the council to discuss their concerns. Some actively support their efforts. One agrees to submit to the next council meeting the new regulations that Anna's lawyer has drafted, and the mayor indicates that she will approve the measure.

To Anna's surprise, when the new proposal comes before the village council, every woman votes for it, and the new law goes into effect. When Anna's case comes before the local court, the judge announces that, according to her interpretation of the new law, Anna's right to the property is beyond question.

Word about this new law soon spreads to neighboring villages, which also adopt legislation to secure women's inherited property. Through news stories about Anna and her lawyer, the governor of the state hears about the movement, and she sends her private secretary to meet with them. She asks them to serve on a committee to draft such a law for the whole state.

Through serving on this committee, Anna gets to know many of the state legislators. She is inspired by the role model these women provide and now dreams of taking a greater part in her community.

As a full group, consider these questions:

- At which points did you experience any kind of emotional response to this story? How did you feel?
- Of course, this is a fictional story, but could any parts of it be true in your community? Which could not? Is a society like the one in this story desirable for women? Why or why not? What circumstances in this fiction encouraged Anna's increased participation in community life?

For more on the women's right to inheritance, see Chapter 3, "Women's Human Rights in the Family."

Groups Advocating for Change

Inter-Parliamentary Union (IPU)
http://www.ipu.org

The IPU is the international organization of parliaments of sovereign states. Established in 1889, it is the focal point for worldwide parliamentary dialogue, working for peace and cooperation among peoples and for the firm establishment of representative democracy. The IPU carries on an active campaign to increase women's political participation, particularly the balanced representation of women and men in parliaments worldwide.

Women's Environmental and Development Organization (WEDO)
http://www.wedo.org

The WEDO is an international advocacy organization that seeks to increase the power of women as policy-makers throughout the world at all levels in governments, institutions, and forums to

continues

Groups Advocating for Change Continued

achieve economic and social justice, a healthy and peaceful planet, and human rights for all. It leads "50/50: Get the Balance Right!," a campaign that targets balanced representation of women and men in local and national politics worldwide.

International Women's Rights Action Watch (IWRAW) Asia Pacific
http://www.iwraw-ap.org

IWRAW Asia Pacific contributes to the progressive interpretation, universalization, implementation, and realization of women's human rights through the lens of the CEDAW and other international human rights treaties. In particular, it facilitates a process through which the CEDAW is used as a tool for applying international human rights standards at the national level and in a wide range of contexts, including political participation, armed conflict, rights in marriage, violence against women, trafficking, reproductive rights, and employment.

Center for Legislative Development (CLD)
http://www.cld.org

The CLD addresses the need both for building the capability of legislatures and for strengthening participation of civil society in legislative decision making to ensure the passage of responsive and gender-fair legislation. It provides training, research, and information development services to legislatures, government agencies, nongovernmental organizations, and other players in the policy-making process.

International Women's Democracy Center (IWDC)
http://www.iwdc.org/

The IWDC was established to strengthen women's global leadership through training, education, research, and networking in all facets of democracy, with a particular focus on increasing the participation of women in policy, politics, and decision making. It organizes events for national and local women leaders around the world on a regular basis.

Women Learning Partnership (WLP)
http://www.learningpartnership.org

The WLP is an international nongovernmental organization (NGO) that aims to empower women and girls in the Global South to reimagine and restructure their roles in their families, communities, and societies. Its website provides online resources regarding women, including facts and figures on political participation and economic decision making.

The White Ribbon Campaign
http://www.whiteribbon.ca/

Based on the White Ribbon, which symbolizes a man's pledge to never commit, condone, or remain silent about violence against women, the White Ribbon Campaign is the world's largest effort by men to end men's violence against women. Started by a handful of men in Canada in 1991 on the second anniversary of the Montreal Massacre, this campaign now takes place in more than fifty countries around the world. The White Ribbon Campaign began as an annual awareness week but has become a year-round effort focusing on education and awareness and challenging men regarding their role in ending violence against women.

The Role of the Media

The media, whether radio, television, the printed page, or electronic news, have immense political power in the twentieth century. Advances in information technology have facilitated a global communications network that transcends national boundaries and affects public policy and private attitudes, especially of children. However, "[p]rint and electronic media in most countries do not provide a balanced picture of women's diverse lives and contributions to society."[28] On the contrary, the media often trivialize women's experience, reinforce women's traditional roles, and create a "climate in which advertisements and commercial messages often portray women primarily as consumers."[29]

Seen through the lens of the media, social and occupational roles are almost completely divided along gender lines. When women appear at all—and numerous studies around the world document their dramatic underrepresentation in almost all kinds of media content—they tend to be depicted within the home and are rarely portrayed as rational, active, or decisive. As the Beijing Platform for Action recognizes, such stereotyping through the media only "reinforces the tendency for political decision making to remain the domain of men" (paragraph 183).[30]

Violence is often portrayed on television as a normal way of life, reinforcing misconceptions about violence against women. In TV soap operas, images may be found of husbands and boyfriends beating and raping their wives. Commercials for products from motorcycles to liquor often use women and women's bodies to sell products. Popular songs and music videos portray women as ever-willing sexual objects to be used and abused.

The kind of programming that demeans women seems motivated by the desire of sponsors to sell their products to men rather than to reflect women's interest in media. Women themselves are enthusiastic users of the media, but their preferences differ from those of men. A United Nations Educational, Scientific, and Cultural Organization (UNESCO) study of television viewing patterns in nine countries found that women spend on average 12 percent more time watching television than men. Whereas men like sports, news, and action-oriented programs, women tend to choose drama, music, dance, and other entertainment programs—a contrast that seems to mirror a preference for programming that gives visibility to their own gender, whether in terms of the situations, the characters, or the issues presented.

The Beijing Platform for Action and the Media

The Beijing Platform for Action addresses the negative impact of the media on women's lives, as well as its potential for empowerment. In particular, it calls for "increased participation and access of women to expression and decision making in and through the media and new communication technologies" (Strategic Objective J.1). In response, many governments have committed themselves to review media policies and increase the number of programs for and by women and to "promote balanced and diverse portrayals of women in the media."[31]

In addition, the Beijing Platform urges governments to create legislation against the projection of violence against women and children in the media and to encourage training for women in using the media. It also encourages the media themselves to establish professional guidelines and methods of self-regulation for the way women are presented, as well as to support and finance alternative media and all forms of communication that support the needs of women. Yet despite these efforts, women remain underrepresented professionally in the media, especially in higher-paid and decision-making positions.

✠ Learning Activity 5: Portrayal of Women in the Media ✠

Objective   To analyze the portrayal of women in the media
Time   75 minutes
Materials   A wide variety of old magazines, chart paper and markers

1. Analyze
Choose one of the following options, engaging the full group. Or assign a specific activity to each of several small groups.

Activity A: Magazines

- Look through several magazines for images of women in advertising.
- Analyze the advertisements:
  - Try to determine whether the advertisements are aimed at a male or a female audience. How do the images seem to differ according to the intended audience?
  - Make a list of the activities in which women are engaged. How does this factor contribute to the media image of women?
  - What conventions of female beauty do the advertisements embody?
  - How might these images be different if they came from a different culture?
  - Is there more than one woman in an ad? How do they seem to relate to one another?
  - Are there also men in the ads? How do the women seem to relate to them?

Activity B: Television

- List the most popular television shows of all kinds in the community.
- Analyze and list the roles given to women in these programs. What qualities do the media value in women?

Alternative: Show a recording of a TV show to the full group. Discuss the same questions in small groups.

Activity C: Television News Programs, Newspapers, and News Magazines

- Consider the following:
  - What kinds of women appear most often in television news programs, newspapers, and news magazines? What qualities make these women "newsworthy"?

Learning Activity 5 Continued

- ○ Are any of these women admired for qualities other than their beauty or their relationship to an important man? In what qualities other than physical appearance do the media seem interested?
- Look through copies of the week's daily newspapers and consider the following:
  - ○ How much attention is given to women in sports? Politics? Business? The arts?
  - ○ Do any women appear on the front page or in the opening segment? Are there any bylines or editorials by women?

Activity D: Public Art Works

- List all the statues or artistic representations of people that appear in public places in your town.
- Consider the following:
  - ○ How many of these representations portray men? Women?
  - ○ Of the male statues, how many represent real men? Idealized men who represent some value (e.g., courage, the unknown soldier)? How many male statues are wearing clothes?
  - ○ Ask the same questions about the statues of women. How do you explain the differences?

2. Discuss

In the context of the analysis in Step 1, discuss how these images affect the following aspects of women's lives:

- Their participation in public life
- Their ideas about how they should look
- Their desire for consumer products
- Their experience of violence
- Sexual expectations placed upon them.

Also address these questions: What can women do locally to counteract or stop the negative images of women in the media? Regionally? Nationally? How can decision makers be persuaded to present images of women that reflect respect for women's human rights, talents, skills, and multifaceted individualities?

Access to the Media

Access to the media involves issues of power, decision making over what information and images appear in the media, and the way these are presented. In a 1994 survey in Great Britain, most women respondents said they would like to see more women journalists and experts on television because they would "act as significant role models for other women, stimulate female interest in public issues and—perhaps—speak in the interests of and for women." Indeed, although data from the Media Report to Women show that increasing numbers of women have been educated as communication professionals in recent years, the gap between men and women employed in the media persists, with males holding more than 60 percent of television news jobs and two-thirds of journalism positions.[32] In the technical area, where many jobs are highly skilled and highly paid and often lead to careers in program production or senior management, women are even less represented, making up just 27 percent of television news directors and 14 percent of radio news directors.[33] In radio and television, women tend to be concentrated in occupations such as announcers, presenters, or production assistants that may not lead to further career development.

Alternative Media

Electronic media, especially e-mail and the Internet, have permitted women to transcend the usual barriers to access. As technology becomes increasingly affordable, e-mail and the Internet strengthen more women's abilities to access informational resources, distribute news about their organizations, and work to create a cross-cultural, virtual community among regions that are not only remote and technically underdeveloped but sometimes in conflict with one other.

Women have shown ingenuity in developing other forms of alternative media as well. In many places they have adapted "comic book"–style publications to educate women with low literacy about their rights. And in India specifically, dowry deaths or bride burnings have become a common theme for street theater, a grassroots political art form used to portray unjust practices of society, the government, or, originally, foreign intervention. Street actors stage their impromptu plays in public spaces as a way to raise awareness and pressure authorities into action.

Another form of popular media is radio. The Feminist International Radio Endeavor (FIRE) is an all-women radio magazine produced and broadcast daily in Spanish and English at Radio for Peace International (RPI), a short-wave noncommercial radio station in Costa Rica. Another radio station, the Women International News Gathering Service (WINGS), was started by two feminists in 1985 and continues to broadcast both shortwave and on the World Wide Web.[34]

✠ Learning Activity 6: Alternative Media for Women ✠

Objective   To develop strategies for organizing women through the use of alternative media

Time   60 minutes

Materials   Paper and colored pens (optional)

1. Discuss

Divide participants into small groups and ask them to brainstorm ways to organize women in their community using traditional means of expression such as songs, dance drama, puppet shows, comedy routines, or whatever is appropriate in their culture.

Decide on the messages that could be conveyed by using these techniques. Would the audience be receptive? Would the messages reach women?

✠ Learning Activity 6 Continued ✠

2. Create

Ask each small group to develop a short alternative presentation using forms of expression and issues appropriate to their community. Especially consider effective techniques for reaching those women who have been excluded from mainstream media such as illiterate, disabled, rural, or homeless women.

Ask each group to deliver its presentation. Then pose the following questions for further discussion.

How could you use these techniques:

- to reach women in your community?
- to teach women about their rights?
- to mobilize women to act on an issue?

Media for Women's Human Rights Education

- In Tanzania, women activists are taking up cartooning to advance the messages of women's rights. One cartoon shows a doctor telling a woman patient that he'll treat her if she'll have intercourse with him. The cartoonist in Tanzania said she was trying to capture how doctors, like government officials, try to "use their position to fulfill their desires." (At the end of the strip, the doctor is led away under arrest for corruption.) Cartoons are popular because of their humor, and their messages reach people of all ages and all levels of education—even those who cannot read.[35]
- In the Indonesian organization known as "Woman Transforming Conflict," women have played the delicate role of peace mediators between communities torn apart by conflict. Women on both sides have enabled their communities to survive and carry on. Their story, *Perempuan untuk Perdamaian* ("The First Step"), is captured on CD-ROM.[36]
- The Maisha Yetu Media Campaign (*Maisha Yetu* is a Swahili phrase meaning "Our Lives") worked with six media outlets' coverage of HIV/AIDS, TB, and malaria in Botswana, Kenya, and Senegal, resulting in dramatic changes in coverage of these diseases and their impact on women. Between March 2005 and March 2006, the campaign trained some 1,000 journalists, half of them women, to link HIV/AIDS, TB, and malaria to social and development issues and to capture women's stories about the HIV/AIDS crisis. (Just under 64 percent of all people—and more than 76 percent of all women—living with HIV are in sub-Saharan Africa.)[37] The campaign was launched by International Women's Media Foundation to strengthen the role of African women in the news media and increase leadership by women journalists.[38]
- Between 2007 and 2011, the Africa Media Project will incorporate women's roles in the coverage of agriculture and rural economics and create more gender equality in African newsrooms. The project aims to "amplify the voices" on poverty, food insecurity, and malnutrition—all major challenges in sub-Saharan Africa.[39]
- West African film directors and actors are raising HIV/AIDS awareness among African youth with two- to eight-minute vignettes depicting young people in sensitive situations. These lively, nondidactic vignettes are based on ideas generated by thousands of young people about safe sex.[40]

Remembering Core Concepts

�֎ Learning Activity 7: Speaking Out for Women's �֎ Human Rights in Politics, Public Life, and the Media

Objectives To examine women's participation in public life in the community and consider how to take action to improve it
Time 60+ minutes
Materials Chart paper and markers

1. Brainstorm

Ask participants to name as many women as possible who are prominent in politics, media, and other forms of public life in their national, regional, and, especially, local communities. Enter these names on a chart like the one shown in Table 12.1.

Table 12.1   Speaking Out for Women's Human Rights in Politics, Public Life, and the Media

Politics		Media		Other Forms of Public Life	
Name	Factors	Name	Factors	Name	Factors

Next, ask people to comment on some of the factors that have contributed to the participation of these women. List them on the chart.

- What patterns appear from such data?
- What areas of public life seem to attract women? Are there other areas where women are not well represented?
- What factors do many of these active women share? Which are personality traits (e.g., energy, intelligence, inspiration) and which are socially determined (e.g., wealth, education, status)?

2. List

Ask why more women in your community don't participate in public life. List these obstacles.

Explain that, to encourage more participation in public life by women, these obstacles need to be addressed. Ask participants, working in small groups, to choose one obstacle on which they wish to concentrate. Encourage selection from a variety of obstacles.

✠ Learning Activity 7 Continued ✠

3. Discuss/Plan

Ask each group to prepare a five-minute presentation to a "panel of community leaders" on their obstacle. Each presentation should:

- describe the obstacle, identifying the group(s) of women it impacts and, if possible, its cause(s)
- relate the obstacle and its removal to women's human rights
- clarify how the obstacle affects women's lives
- show how removing the obstacle can improve their lives
- propose specific actions that should be taken to remove the obstacle
- show how members of the community can get involved in addressing the obstacle.

Ask each group to choose a spokesperson to make the presentation and a "community leader" to serve on the panel. While the groups plan their presentations, the panel of leaders meets to decide on their roles, representing a variety of differing but typical attitudes within the community leadership.

4. Present/Role-Play

The spokesperson from each group makes a presentation, and members of the panel listen and respond, asking questions and offering comments, objections, or suggestions in keeping with their chosen roles.

5. Discuss

After the presentations and role-play, discuss:

- How did the spokespersons feel when presenting the obstacle?
- How did the "community leaders" respond to the presentation? What attitudes in the community were they representing?
- How did the audience, composed of the rest of the group, respond to the presentations?
- Did any spokesperson discuss the obstacle as a human rights violation? Did putting the problem in a human rights context strengthen the argument? Why or why not?
- Are these ideas for improving women's participation in public life feasible in your community? Why or why not?

6. Conclude

Challenge the participants by asking them to evaluate their knowledge of the obstacle and the inclusiveness of their perspective:

- How did you obtain your information about obstacles to public participation facing women in your community? Was it accurate and complete? If not, what additional information do you need and how can you obtain it?

continues

✠ Learning Activity 7 Continued ✠

- Did you personally consult women about this obstacle and how it affects them? About actions that could remove the obstacle?
- Why is it important in real-life human rights advocacy to include the active participation of those directly involved and affected?
- How can you apply the example of this exercise to planning and implementing advocacy for women's participation in the public life of your community?

Notes

1. CIA, *The World Factbook: Saudi Arabia,* available online at https://www.cia.gov/library/publications/the-world-factbook/geos/sa.html#Govt.

2. *Online Women in Politics Statistics,* May 2007, available online at http://www.onlinewomeninpolitics.org/statistics.htm.

3. "All-Female Peacekeeper Squad to Deploy," *USAToday,* January 19, 2007, available online at http://www.usatoday.com/news/world/2007-01-19-liberia-women_x.htm

4. Asia Foundation, *Afghanistan in 2006: A Survey of the Afghan People,* p. 70.

5. United Nations Economic Commission for Europe, "Preparatory Meeting Reviews Subjects of Violence Against Women, Women in Power and Decision-Making," UN/ECE News Press Release ECE/GEN/00/8Geneva, January 20, 2000, available online at http://www.unece.org/press/pr2000/00gen8e.htm.

6. Anand Swamy et al., *Gender and Corruption,* joint publication of Williams College, the World Bank, the Korean Development Institute, and the IRIS Center-University of Maryland, independently analyzing a World Values Survey (August 2000).

7. "Women in Local Government: Breaking Barriers," *Proceedings of the Women in Local Government: Breaking Barriers Conference,* IDASA/LOGIC, Johannesburg, South Africa, June 17–18, 1996.

8. "Leadership Facts and Figures," Women's Learning Partnership, March 2007, available online at http://www.learningpartnership.org/resources/facts/leadership.

9. Ibid.

10. Victoria Collis, "Proceedings of the International Consultation on Women Human Rights Defenders," Women Human Rights Defenders' International Coordinating Committee, River Path Associates, December 22, 2005.

11. Human Rights Watch, "Libya: Women, Girls Locked Up Indefinitely Without Charge: 'Protective' Facilities Serve as Places of Arbitrary Punishment," available online at http://hrw.org/english/docs/2006/02/27/libya12725.htm.

12. Human Rights Watch, "Women in State Custody," available online at http://hrw.org/women/custody.html.

13. Amnesty International USA: Women's Human Rights, "Abuse of Women in Custody: Sexual Misconduct and the Shackling of Pregnant Women," available online at http://www.amnestyusa.org/Womens_Human_Rights/Abuse_of_Women_in_Custody/page.do?id=1108288&n1=3&n2=39&n3=720.

14. Jan McGirk, "Women's Rights in Pakistan: The Woman Who Dared to Cry Rape," *The Independent* (UK), June 15, 2005, available online at http://www.truthout.org/cgi-bin/artman/exec/view.cgi/35/11898.

15. Ibid.

16. Ibid.

17. Tim Luard, "China Village Democracy Skin Deep," *BBC News,* October 10, 2005.

18. N. Reilly, ed., *Without Reservation: The Beijing Tribunal on Accountability for Women's Human Rights* (New Brunswick: Rutgers, 1996), p. 16.

19. Ibid., p. 116.

20. International Institute for Democracy and Electoral Assistance, "Global Database of Quotas for Women" (Stockholm), available online at http://www.quotaproject.org/case_studies.cfm.

21. Women's Learning Partnership, March 2007, available online at http://www.learningpartnership.org/wlp.php//.

22. Beijing Platform for Action, September 1995, available online at http://www.un.org/womenwatch/daw/beijing/platform/.

23. "Shadow Reports: Holding Governments Accountable for Women's Human Rights," Women's Learning Partnership, July 2003, available online at http://www.learningpartnership.org/news/enews/2003/iss4/shadow.

24. International Women's Rights Action Watch (IWRAW), Asia Pacific CEDAW Shadow Reports, May 16, 2007.

25. WomenWatch, "CEDAW States Parties," available online at http://www.un.org/womenwatch/daw/cedaw/states.htm.

26. Collen Lowe Morna, *Gender Budgeting: Myths and Realities*, paper presented at the 25 years International Women's Politics Workshop, Bonn, October 13–14, 2000, available online at http://www.genderlinks.org.za/docs/governance/genderbudgeting.pdf.

27. Women Human Rights Net, "Women and Political Participation," available online at http://www.whrnet.org/docs/issue-women-politics-html.

28. Beijing Platform for Action, September 1995, available online at http://www.un.org/womenwatch/daw/beijing/platform/.

29. Ibid.

30. Ibid.

31. Ibid.

32. Radio and Television News Directors Association, 2003; Poynter Institute's American Journalist Survey, 2003; Media Report to Women, available online at http://www.mediareporttowomen.com/.

33. Ibid.

34. Women's International News Gathering Service, available online at http://www.wings.org.

35. Daniel Dickinson, "Drawing Attention to Tanzanian Women's Rights, *BBC Dar es Salaam*, June 5, 2003.

36. Search for Common Ground—Indonesia, *Women Transforming Conflict*, December 2006, available online at http://www.sfcg.org/programmes/indonesia/indonesia_transforming.html.

37. International Women's Media Foundation, *Maisha Yetu: Media Campaign for Our Lives* (Washington, DC), available online at http://www.iwmf.org/files/9464_WFOLforweb2.pdf.

38. Ibid.

39. International Women's Media Foundation Press Release, "IWMF Receives Grant from Buffett Foundation for African Media Project," June 6, 2007, available online at http://iwmf.org/print.

40. Scenarios from Africa, Gateshead, United Kingdom, available online at http://www.globaldialogues.org/homeEng.htm.

13

Human Rights of Refugee, Displaced, and War-Affected Women

Women suffer human rights violations in situations of armed conflict, including terrorism, torture, disappearance, rape, ethnic cleansing, family separation, and displacement, as well as lifelong social and psychological traumatic consequences. . . . If women are to play an equal part in securing and maintaining peace, they must be empowered politically and economically and represented adequately at all levels of decision making.

—Beijing Platform for Action
(paraphrase of paragraphs 132–151)

Objectives

The learning activities and background information contained in this chapter will enable participants to work toward the following objectives:

- Explore how each aspect of conflict—from attempts at conflict prevention, to the outbreak of conflict, to conflict resolution and post-conflict transition—is gendered: that is, influenced by the real and perceived needs and responsibilities, constraints, and opportunities of men and women.
- Discuss gendered forms of resistance to, and cooperation with, agents of war and peace.
- Understand the various legal classifications for war-affected women (i.e., *refugee* versus *displaced person*) and explore their impact.
- Identify the rights of refugee, displaced, and war-affected women and understand the importance of international protection of these rights as well as the obligations of receiving countries and countries of origin.
- Recognize the importance of involving women in the design and implementation of conflict prevention, conflict resolution, and post-conflict transformation and humanitarian assistance programs.
- Remember core concepts.

Getting Started:
Thinking About the Impact of War on Women

Since 1945, more than 23 million people have died from war-related causes. Civilians account for 90 percent of the casualties in modern warfare, and three out of four of these casualties are women or children.[1] Although men are more likely to be fighting the wars, women and children are more likely to be displaced or killed. Currently, more than 50 million people are being forced to flee their homes due to violent conflict; 75–80 percent of those people are women and children.[2] As the Beijing Platform for Action recognizes, gross violations of human rights and obstacles in war include "torture and cruel, inhumane and degrading treatment or punishment, summary or arbitrary executions, disappearances, arbitrary detentions, all forms of racism and racial discrimination, foreign occupation and alien domination, xenophobia, poverty, hunger and other denials of economic, social and cultural rights, religious intolerance, terrorism, discrimination against women and lack of the rule of law."[3]

Government, paramilitary, and other opponents target women on the basis of their ethnic, national, religious, racial, and/or political affiliations, but there is a gender component as well. Women in conflict often suffer abuses and consequences different from those visited upon their male counterparts. For example, throughout history soldiers have raped women as part of war. Mass rapes of women, often promoted as government policy, have been documented in recent years in a wide range of conflicts around the world including Bosnia, Cambodia, Haiti, Peru, Somalia, Uganda, and Sudan.[4] While men may also experience rape and sexual violence in conflict situations, women are particularly at risk for such abuse, often intended as a way to humiliate and defeat the men in the community. In addition to acts committed by individual soldiers that may not necessarily be planned (though they are often condoned), rape and sexual violence may form part of a planned strategy to terrorize a population. When women are tortured during interrogation or imprisonment, both in times of war and peace, the torture may be of a sexual nature.

In addition to experiencing direct violence, women must cope with the violence committed against their loved ones, husbands, parents, and children. When men are attacked or imprisoned, women are frequently left alone to take care of their families and to work for the release of male family members. Fear of violence also has a direct and particular impact upon women. Fear of rape and fear of being caught in the crossfire, for example, may cause women to stay at home or to go into hiding. Fear of violence limits women's ability to go to their workplaces, to work in the fields, to shop in the market, or to stand in line for humanitarian aid. For women with children, fear of violence entails the constant stress of monitoring the movements of their children, at times confining their children to the home, or even taking them into hiding.

Conflict situations may also increase the levels of domestic violence against women. Regimes that exercise power by undermining people's self-esteem and self-expression usually encourage domination based on gender as well as on class and ethnic differences.[5] Domestic violence is always difficult for women to report, but in conflict situations women may be particularly hesitant to report abuse due to additional social taboos, including bringing dishonor and shame to their families and communities.[6] In Colombia, for example, alleged perpetrators use stigmatization and harassment to keep their victims silent. In conflict areas, they often accuse "women or teenage girls of belonging to or collaborating with the guerrillas. The army's counter-insurgency strategy views civilian victims of the armed conflict, including those who inadvertently come into contact with guerrilla groups, not as innocent victims but as part of the enemy."[7] Societies in conflict may be more willing to overlook domestic violence when the male perpetrator is himself a victim of conflict.

Some Facts About Wartime Violence Against Women

- In the Sudanese province of Darfur, women were raped and gang-raped by Sudanese security forces and armed groups, according to the UN high commissioner for human rights. Victims were denied access to medical treatment to obtain evidence of a crime or were treated insensitively or sexually inappropriately to establish accountability for sexual violence.[8] An estimated 500 rape victims were treated by Medecins Sans Frontières between October 2004 and February 2006, although doctors acknowledged that the rapes continued.[9]

- Human rights reporting indicates that ongoing civil war in the Democratic Republic of the Congo has resulted in mass rapes of hundreds of thousands of women. In 2003, reports suggested that armed groups were practicing sexual mutilation and cannibalism, targeting Pygmy women in particular, as a part of a genocidal plan.[10]

- In Rwanda, at least 250,000—perhaps as many as 500,000—women were raped during the 1994 genocide. In a survey of 2000 widows whose husbands had been massacred during this genocide, 80 percent were found to be HIV-positive, and many had not been sexually active before the genocide.[11]

- In Bosnia, Muslim women were targeted for rape as part of the ethnic cleansing campaign to form an ethnically pure Greater Serbia. More than 20,000 women were reported to have been raped during the war as a part of an intimidation and humiliation strategy against Bosnian Muslims that included rape with the purpose of impregnating Bosnian Muslim women and diluting the Bosniak identity.[12]

- Violence in the form of sexual slavery and trafficking tends to increase during wartime. According to the United Nations Office on Drugs and Crime, "trafficking patterns are greatly influenced by conflict situations as combatants (or even peacekeepers) create a market for the services of victims and the effects of conflict erode the capacity of law enforcement and other authorities to combat the problem."[13]

- Sexual violence, or the threat of sexual violence, is used during periods of conflict and unrest to silence women and curtail their activism. In Burma, according to a 2002 report titled "License to Rape," the Shan Women's Action Network (SWAN) and the Shan Human Rights Foundation (SHRF) jointly found that many incidents of rape since 1996 were part of the military's strategic reaction to dissident voices.[14]

- Studies demonstrate that domestic violence increases during wartime and post-conflict transition due to ex-combatant trauma and the influence of militarism on domestic relations. Official statistics from East Timor during December 2002 indicate that nearly 40 percent of all reported crimes were cases of domestic violence or violence against women, such as rape and sexual assault.[15]

- Children born of rape and sexual exploitation from combatants or peacekeepers often symbolize war trauma and, therefore, may be ostracized from their communities.[16]

- According to a report from the International Conference on War-Affected Children, "as a result of their unique status, due to the gender relations and cultural traditions surrounding

---

Some Facts About Wartime Violence Against Women Continued

their origins, these children [born of rape] are likely to suffer infanticide, stigma, neglect and discrimination in addition to the difficulties facing all war-affected children."[17]

- Reports from Mental Disability Rights International indicate that in post-conflict Kosovo, women who were traumatized by war and experienced rape and other abuse have frequently been unable to receive trauma assistance and protection in their communities and have sought help in UN-administered psychiatric institutions, only to be retraumatized due to deplorable conditions.[18]

The rights of women in conflict, including the right to be free from sexual violence, can be enforced through national, regional, and international laws and policies such as the following:

- The Geneva Conventions of 1949—in particular, the Geneva Convention on the Protection of Civilian Persons in Time of War and its additional protocols
- The UN Declaration on the Protection of Women and Children in Armed Conflict, UN GA Res. 2200A (XXI), December 16, 1966
- The International Convention on the Elimination of Torture and Other Cruel, Inhuman and Degrading Treatment or Punishment (entered into force, 1987)
- Guidelines issued by the United Nations High Commissioner for Refugees (UNHCR): Refugee Women and International Protection, General Conclusion 64, 1990; and Refugee Protection and Sexual Violence, General Conclusion 73, 1993.

"Comfort Women"

During World War II, 100,000 to 200,000 women were systematically kidnapped, brutalized, and forced to provide sexual services to the Japanese soldiers as "comfort women."[19] While 80 percent of "comfort women" were from Korea, a Japanese colony at that time, they also included Japanese, Filipino, Chinese, Indonesian, and European women.[20] Each woman was expected to serve approximately twenty soldiers per day, for which she was paid little or nothing.[21]

The powerful testimonies and organizing strength of former "comfort women" and their supporters provided a catalyst for communities of women along with the governments of Korea, the Philippines, China, and Indonesia to demand that the former "comfort women" receive an apology and compensation from Japan.

In 1993, after more than fifty years of denial, the Japanese government issued an official apology. Compensation in the form of research and exchanges was also provided to countries of the former "comfort women," along with funds for medical and social assistance. And the government of Japan has been cooperating with the Asian Women's Fund in implementing these activities. The atonement projects were completed in the Philippines, in the Republic of Korea, and in Taiwan by the end of September 2002.[22] Though international demand for *individual* compensation continues, the Japanese response is a tribute to the strength and tenacity of "comfort women" survivors and the power of international collaboration among women and human rights groups.[23]

✠ Learning Activity 1 ✠
The Impact of Armed Conflict on Women's Lives

Objective To identify the impact of armed conflict on women's lives and the violation of women's human rights inherent in this impact

Time 45 minutes

Materials Copies of nearby box headed "Comfort Women," copies of "Case Study: Women and War in Country X"

Case Study: Women and War in Country X

Country X has just emerged from a series of civil wars and totalitarian regimes spanning a twenty-year period. Before the period of conflict began, gender relations in X were characterized by a clear division between men's and women's labor and resources such as livestock, grain, farm equipment, and money. In general, men had control of most resources.

A large percentage of the male population and a smaller but significant percentage of the female population died during the wars, and many of the surviving males are now migrant workers in neighboring countries. The surviving women have a greater share of the work in their communities, yet still-limited control over resources.

Some of the surviving women were raped by soldiers during the wars. Many of these women have suffered long-term health effects from self-induced and unsterile abortions. Those who have given birth to children born from rape are scorned by their communities.

Violence has increased in X since the end of the conflict. Thieves prey on women walking alone; male family members abuse the females in their household at an alarmingly high rate; guns from the wars can be bought and sold on the streets; and mothers now worry about their children becoming involved in increasingly popular youth gangs. In some areas, women have become "camp followers"—women who have no means of support apart from attaching themselves to the remaining military camps where they provide sexual favors.

Still, peacetime has brought some positive changes for women. Women have become increasingly involved in community affairs. Stepping in to fill roles previously occupied by men, women are now more influential in local government and women's groups play increasingly important community roles.

Source: Adapted from Activity 60, *Oxfam Gender Training Manual* (Oxford, UK: Oxfam, 1994).

1. Read/Discuss

Distribute the case study or read it aloud. Lead a discussion based on the following questions:

- Can you identify the human rights abuses in this story?
- Can you identify the abuses against women during and after the conflict?
- Which of these abuses are directly related to war? Incidentally related? Might have happened regardless of war?
- What effect will these abuses have on the future of this society?

✠ Learning Activity 1 Continued ✠

- What could women in your community do to help women victims and survivors of conflict?
- What motivates women to provide such help? What blocks such efforts?

Read the box headed "Comfort Women" and discuss it in the context of the case study.

Defining Refugee and Displaced Women

Refugees are people who are forced to leave their home country because of fear of persecution. They are treated differently from other people in need of humanitarian aid because they cannot look to their own government and state institutions to protect their rights and physical security. The state either is weak and unable to provide protection or is itself the perpetrator of human rights abuses. The need for international protection for refugees is great. *Non-refoulement*, the most fundamental principle of refugee protection, provides that refugees cannot be forced back to a place where they may be persecuted.

Reports indicate that as many as 80 percent of displaced people worldwide are women and children.[24] Refugee-receiving countries have been slow to recognize gender-based persecution, including the practices of female genital cutting, mass rapes, and systematic domestic violence, as legitimate grounds for asylum. Officials in receiving countries often lack the training and sensitivity to deal effectively with female victims of violence.[25]

Although some women actively choose to leave their home communities, flight is often precipitated by sexual harassment, gender-based violence, or sex discrimination. Many displaced women face discrimination throughout their flight, settlement, and return. Women and girls are among the most vulnerable groups due to both physical realities and traditional cultural roles and perceptions of women.[26] Therefore, as their homes, communities, and support systems disintegrate, they are at even greater risk for human rights abuses.

At least two-thirds of the world's more than 40 million refugees and internally displaced persons (IDPs) have fled their homes in countries in which there is a severe or significant threat of death or injury from antipersonnel mines.[27] In agrarian and subsistence-farming societies, landmines are often deliberately placed in agricultural fields and along routes to water sources and markets, areas regularly used by women and children. Therefore, the presence of antipersonnel mines overwhelmingly affects women in their roles as primary caregivers and sustenance providers in many affected countries. In Asia and Africa, for example, where women constitute a larger percentage of farmers than men, producing up to 80 percent of the food, landmine casualties are noticeably gendered.[28]

Yet the displacement experiences of women and girls often go unnoticed by the international community. For example, whereas the "Lost Boys of Sudan" received a great deal of attention and assistance, their female counterparts went unnoticed. In fact, of the 3,800 "lost boys" who were resettled in the United States in the 1980s, fewer than 100 were girls. This was due in part to the fact that when villages were attacked, women and girls were often taken captive, never having the chance to flee.[29] The boys roamed the desert for years or found themselves in Kenyan refugee camps, but the Sudanese refugee girls often ended up in foster homes with families who eventually would enjoy a "bride prize" when a girl was married off.[30] Once they were placed in those homes, their welfare and their very existence were not tracked by camp officials. As a result, the girls' experiences were invisible to policy-makers and their well-being was not a great concern of the international community.[31]

The United Nations High Commissioner for Refugees (UNHCR) is the international body entrusted with ensuring that the basic needs of refugees are met and that they receive adequate protection from the governments of the countries where they have sought asylum. UNHCR is mandated to lead and coordinate international action to protect refugees and resolve refugee problems worldwide. Its primary purpose is to safeguard the rights and well-being of refugees. Although the UNHCR's original mandate is limited to serving refugees who fall within the definition provided in the 1951 Convention Relating to the Status of Refugees (also known as the Refugee Convention), in practice UNHCR does attempt to provide assistance to all people who are war affected, regardless of whether they qualify as refugees.

In contrast to refugees, internally displaced persons (IDPs) are people who leave their homes to flee persecution but stay within their home country. Thus, they remain subject to the laws of their home state—a state that, in many cases, has caused or contributed to their displacement. The UNHCR estimates the total number of IDPs at 25 million. Although it does not have a specific mandate to protect IDPs, the UNHCR assists several million of them per year in operations initiated at the request of the UN Secretary General or Security Council, and with the consent of the country concerned. Although NGOs have urged the United Nations and its Member States to institute gender-sensitive policies for the protection of women IDPs, gender sensitivity training of refugee workers is more often the exception than the rule.[32] In addition, only recently have women's and children's specific health and well-being needs been considered in planning IDP operations and construction of facilities for IDPs. Yet this is a critical factor, as the gender-based discrimination that affects women and girls in most societies before and during conflict is usually replicated or even exacerbated during their forced migration.[33]

✠ Learning Activity 2: Political Flight ✠

Objectives To think about the conditions of flight and to understand the criteria for granting political asylum

Time 30 minutes

Materials Chart paper and markers or blackboard and chalk (optional)

1. Read

Read the following passage to the group:

✠ Learning Activity 2 Continued ✠

You are a teacher in the country of L. Your partner has "disappeared," probably because of his attempts to form a trade union. During the next few months you receive several threatening phone calls, and your name appears in a newspaper article listing suspected subversives. When you arrive home from school tonight, you find an anonymous letter threatening your life. You decide you must flee at once and seek political asylum elsewhere.

2. List

Ask participants to "pack their bags" by listing what they would take with them when they flee. They may take only what is in their house at the moment and what they can carry, and only eight categories of things (i.e., clothes, food, family documents, etc.).

3. Discuss

Ask individual participants to read their lists aloud and discuss their choices. Then read or write out on chart paper this definition of *refugee* from the 1951 Refugee Convention:

> [A person who,] owing to well-founded fear of being persecuted for reasons of race, religion, nationality, membership in a particular social group or political opinion, is outside the country of his nationality and is unable or, owing to such fear, is unwilling to avail himself of the protection of that country; or who, not having a nationality and being outside the country of his former habitual residence as a result of such events, is unable or, owing to such fear, is unwilling to return.

Explain that according to this definition, only those who, when fleeing, included among their belongings either the newspaper clipping or the letter would likely be able to prove the "well-founded fear of persecution" required to obtain refugee status.

The Human Rights Concerns of Refugee and Displaced Women

The human rights concerns of refugee and displaced women are varied and include the following:

- *Physical safety.* Long-term inhabitants of refugee camps are often lured into prostitution rings or made to perform sexual acts in return for food or favors such as an asylum hearing. Human rights groups have documented cases of women refugees or migrants being raped or sexually assaulted by border guards or security forces.
- *Inability to find meaningful work.* Some countries do not allow refugees to work legally, and women often do not have legal papers. Other countries discourage employment or provide opportunities that do not fully utilize women's skills. As a result, refugee and displaced women often work in low-paid, exploitative jobs where employers take advantage of their illegal status.
- *Changes in family relationships due to the uprooting.* Most women refugees are without male family support except from their young male children. If

the family is intact and a man is present, women must often deal with changes in male and female roles. Often the man, who used to work outside the home, is left without work or meaning for life. Yet the woman continues to be productive: cooking, cleaning, taking care of children, shopping, and, at times, providing for all the basic needs of the family. This imbalance increases the risk of alcoholism and domestic violence among the male family members. Many times the burden for women increases as their elderly relatives become more dependent on them. Parent-child relationships may also change. Because children often possess better language skills in the new country, they may take on adult roles, such as negotiating with government agencies, humanitarian aid groups, and asylum officials. Parents may feel a loss of control and a sense of inadequacy when this happens.

- *Lack of access to basic items needed for daily life.* Women usually have the burden of feeding and clothing themselves and their families. Humanitarian aid packages often do not provide for women's needs, such as feminine hygiene products.

- *Lack of access to health care and other services.* Access to reproductive and gynecological health care and contraception is crucial to a woman's well-being. However, such services are scarce or nonexistent in most refugee camps.

- *Inability to prove refugee status and insensitive asylum hearings.* Women who are persecuted because of their sex may have difficulty proving refugee status. In addition, women who are victims of military attack may have a hard time proving they are victims of persecution rather than of random violence. Since some asylum officers still see rape and sexual violence as random offenses, a soldier's rape of a woman, for example, may be discounted even though rape in war *is* defined as a violation of established international humanitarian law. Asylum officers often discount women's experiences of conflict as being "not severe enough" to constitute persecution. For example, some states give priority to survivors of concentration camps and to victims of state torture, categories that include more males. For this reason, although the majority of refugees are women, the vast majority of people who receive asylum are men. According to the European Council on Refugees and Exiles, "current procedures are based on the widespread assumption that asylum seekers are politically active men who have been persecuted by the State authorities as a result of those activities."[34] Another problem facing women who are seeking asylum is the "the failure of decision-makers to incorporate the gender-related claims of women into their interpretation of the existing grounds enumerated in the 1951 Convention . . . [as these decision-makers] have largely failed to recognize the political nature of seemingly 'private' acts of harm to women."[35]

- *Lack of recognition as independent beings with full legal capacity.* Sometimes a male head of household may migrate or receive asylum first. Women who join their husbands then become dependent on them for their immigration or refugee status. Should the family break up, the woman could face deportation. This policy places battered women in an especially difficult situation. They may refrain from seeking help from law enforcement officials for fear of being deported or because of language or other cultural barriers.

✠ Learning Activity 3: Possible Intervention for Women Refugees ✠

Objective To develop interventions and actions that could be taken to support women refugees

Time 60 minutes

Materials Chart paper and markers; copies of nearby box headed "Scenarios of Hope"

1. Imagine/Draw

Ask participants to make up a story of a refugee woman starting from her crossing the border of her home country. This might be one group story or several stories prepared by small groups. For example:

> A young woman refugee arrives at a camp without her family. In order to get enough food, she accepts an offer made by a guard to get her a "good job." Instead of a good job, she finds herself working in a brothel where she isn't allowed to keep her wages. She can't complain to the police because they are part of the racket. Most customers refuse to wear condoms. Ultimately, she contracts a sexually transmitted disease.

Once the story outline has been agreed upon, members of the group draw the different scenes of the story on the chart paper. Ask each group to present its story.

2. Discuss/Evaluate

Ask the groups to list an action or service that could have helped the woman in the stories escape the spiral of degradation at different points in the story. For example: "When the woman arrived in the refugee camp, she could either join a micro-enterprise to earn money for food or work with other refugee women to create one." Or "In the brothel, an NGO conducting public health training workshops could educate her on how to protect herself or help her escape prostitution."

Conclude by summarizing each group's story and suggested interventions. Evaluate: What can women do to help themselves and each other?

Note to Facilitator: You might want to supplement the discussion with some of the suggested interventions in the box below.

Scenarios of Hope[36]

Governments can advance the human rights of refugee women by doing the following:

- Involve refugee women in the design and implementation of all programs dealing with refugees.
- Employ female protection officers and female community social workers to work with all women, provide safe places for women to talk to one another, and provide remedies for women who are victims of violence.

continues

Scenarios of Hope Continued

- Offer gender-sensitive and culturally appropriate counseling to women victims. This counseling should be conducted by trained, experienced counselors, preferably from the refugees' culture and/or community.
- Support the operation of SOS hotlines and "safehouses" for women refugees, staffed by women refugees and/or women counselors from the refugees' same culture and/or community whenever possible.
- Provide emergency resettlement to refugee women who may be particularly exposed to abuse.
- Establish effective mechanisms for law enforcement to ensure that abusers are identified and prosecuted.
- Ensure that refugee women are not forced to stay for long periods in closed camps or detention centers where they are more likely to be victims of violence.
- Include information about refugee women, preferably written by and with refugee women, in all educational activities carried out in refugee programs; include information about uprooted women in public media campaigns to combat abuse of and discrimination against refugee women.
- Provide gender-sensitive training for border guards, police, military units, asylum officers, aid personnel, and others who come in contact with refugees and displaced persons.
- Improve the design of refugee camps to promote greater security according to the needs voiced by refugee women. Such measures could include better lighting, security patrols, and special accommodations for single women, women heads of household, and unaccompanied minors.
- Place international staff that has received gender-sensitive training in border areas where refugee women cross in order to enter countries of asylum. Also, place them in reception centers at refugee camps and settlements.
- Develop strategies to raise community awareness of the value of women's resources and labor, as well as women's rights.
- Build the capacity of local women's organizations and networks to function locally to advance the rights of women and girls.

The Refugee Convention and Asylum

A government's obligations to refugees are found in the 1951 Convention Relating to the Status of Refugees and its 1967 Protocol. As noted earlier, the 1951 Convention defines a refugee as a person who, "owing to well-founded fear of being persecuted for reasons of race, religion, nationality, membership in a particular social group or political opinion, is outside the country of his nationality and is unable or, owing to such fear, is unwilling to avail himself of the protection of that country; or who, not having a nationality and being outside the country of his former habitual residence as a result of such events, is unable or, owing to such fear, is unwilling to return." The Convention does not, however, apply to persons who have committed crimes against peace, war crimes, crimes against humanity, or a serious nonpolitical crime outside the country of refuge or who acts contrary to the purposes and principles of the United Nations.

The Refugee Definition, Step by Step

Step One: Outside Country of Origin. This is the easiest step. The person applying for refugee status must show that he or she has fled across national borders. If she left her home but remained in her country, she is not considered a refugee, but a "displaced person." Because no international conventions exist to protect the rights of internally displaced persons, those who cross national borders are in a much better position under international law.

Step Two: Well-Founded Fear of Persecution. This next step has two parts. According to *Part A: Showing "Persecution,"* there is no universal definition of what constitutes *persecution.* The individual applying for refugee status must argue that she herself faces persecution or that she has a legitimate fear of persecution because of the experiences of other people in similar situations. The refugee officer or adjudicator must decide when bad treatment is sufficient to be deemed *persecution.*

Defining *persecution* is not simple, but torture is definitely considered a form of it. The Convention Against Torture and Other Cruel, Inhumane, or Degrading Treatment prohibits torture committed by state actors or their agents. Rape in conflict situations may be defined as torture and therefore as a form of persecution. Similarly, forced pregnancy can be considered persecution or even a form of slavery. Severe sex discrimination may also be considered persecution. According to the United Nations High Commissioner for Refugees (UNHCR) handbook on refugees, discrimination may constitute persecution if it leads to "consequences of a substantially prejudicial nature for the person concerned." This definition opens the door for arguing that systematic sex discrimination can constitute persecution.

According to *Part B: Showing Relation to the State,* persecution must be an act committed by the state or by someone acting as an agent of the state. If a private person commits the harmful act, this will constitute *persecution* under the refugee definition only if one can show a strong connection between the private person and the state. For example, when a mob of private civilians stones a woman for refusing to wear a veil, this violence would constitute *persecution* under the refugee definition only if the mob was carrying out government orders or if the government knew of the plan and did nothing to prevent it. According to the UNHCR, state action may exist where one section of the population inflicts serious harm on another part of the population and the authorities are unwilling or unable to prevent it.

Step Three: Persecution Grounds. It is not enough to show a fear of persecution; the fear must be based on specified *persecution grounds.* This means that the persecution must be connected to reasons of race, religion, nationality, membership in a particular social group, or political opinion. No other reasons are included under the statute.

Note that gender is excluded. Some activists are seeking to add gender explicitly as a grounds for persecution. Others oppose this amendment as unnecessary because women usually can claim refugee status based on other grounds that are already listed (e.g., persecution based on race, religion, nationality, membership in a particular group, or political opinion). Another argument is that gender can be read into the existing refugee definition—for example, by including women in the category *social group.*

Learning Activity 4
The Right to Asylum—Refugees at the Border

Objective To heighten awareness of the experience of seeking asylum
Time 30–45 minutes
Materials Copy of "Immigration Officers' Arguments," copy of "Refugees' Arguments," copy of the above section titled "The Refugee Definition, Step by Step"

1. Read
Read this scenario to the whole group:

> It is a dark, cold, and wet night on the border between X and Y. A column of refugees, mostly women and children, has arrived, fleeing from the war in X. They want to cross into Y. They are hungry, tired, and cold. They have no money and no documents except passports. The immigration officials from Country Y have differing points of view: Some want to allow the refugees to cross into Y, but others don't. The refugees are desperate and use several arguments to try to persuade the immigration officials.

2. Plan
Assign roles to participants, and give them a few minutes to plan their parts and tactics:

- One group consists of "immigration officers" from Country Y. Give this group a copy of "Immigration Officers' Arguments."
- A second group consists of "refugees." Give this group a copy of "Refugees' Arguments."
- A third group is to act as observers, with one half listening in on the "refugees" and the other half listening in on the "immigration officers."

Explain to the participants that they may add additional relevant arguments of their own. Tell them that they have less than ten minutes to reach some kind of conclusion.

3. Role-Play
Draw a line on the floor to represent the border and start the role-play, stopping it when you feel the relevant points have been made.

Alternative: If time permits, repeat the role-play with the roles of "immigration officers" and "refugees" reversed.

4. Discuss
Discuss the role-play, stressing the relevant points that participants learned, both factually and emotionally.

- How did the situation work out according to the observers? What happened?
- Could the observers offer additional arguments for either side?
- Did the immigration officers do anything wrong?
- How did it feel to be a refugee? To be an immigration officer?

✠ Learning Activity 4 Continued ✠

- Were the "refugees" given their right to protection under the 1951 Refugee Convention? Why or why not?
- Should a country have the right to turn away refugees?
- What would you have done if you were a border guard?

Immigration Officers' Arguments

You can use these arguments and any others you can think of:

- They are desperate; we can't send them back.
- If we send them back we will be responsible if they are arrested, tortured, or killed.
- We have legal obligations to accept refugees.
- They have no money and will need state support. Our country cannot afford that.
- Can they prove that they are genuine refugees? Maybe they are here just to look for a better standard of living?
- Our country is a military and business partner of country X. We can't be seen to be protecting them.
- Maybe they have skills that we need?
- There are enough refugees in our country. We need to take care of our own people. They should go to the richer countries.
- If we let them in, others will also demand entry.
- They don't speak our language, they have a different religion, and they eat different food. They won't integrate.
- They will bring political trouble.

Refugees' Arguments[37]

You can use these arguments and any others you can think of:

- It is our right to receive asylum.
- Our children are hungry; you have a moral responsibility to help us.
- We will be killed if we go back.
- We have no money.
- We can't go anywhere else.
- I was a doctor in my hometown.
- We only want shelter until it is safe to return.
- Other refugees have been allowed into your country.

Before the role-play, think about the following options:

- Will you separate from your children if the immigration officers ask you to?
- Will you go home if they try to send you back?

✝ Learning Activity 5 ✝
The Right to Asylum—Refugees Before a Tribunal

Objectives   To add greater clarity to the asylum definition and to encourage thinking about the complexity of gender-based claims
Time   30–45 minutes
Materials   Copies of "Six Hypothetical Cases" and "Answer Key"

1. Read/Discuss

Divide the participants into small groups and assign each group one of the individuals in "Six Hypothetical Cases" below. Pretending to be UNHCR Protection Officers, the participants must decide whether the individuals in these cases are eligible for refugee status. Participants should base their decision on international law, specifically the 1951 Convention Relating to the Status of Refugees and its 1967 Protocol. Emphasize that their decisions will determine whether these people are granted asylum or sent back to their country of origin.

2. Report

Ask someone from each group to read the group's case aloud and someone else to explain the group's decisions in terms of the 1951 Refugee Convention. After each case, read the paragraph interpreting the case in the Answer Key.

3. Discuss

When all six cases have been reviewed, compare them with the role-play in "Learning Activity 4: The Right to Asylum—Refugees at the Border."

- Who should decide whether someone is granted asylum?
- How helpful is the 1951 Refugee Convention in deciding cases?
- What gives one asylum seeker advantages over another? Are these advantages that most women have?
- Are you aware of the policies of your country regarding the granting of asylum? If so, what are they?
- How are refugees treated in your country if they are granted asylum? What are some problems of refugee women?

Six Hypothetical Cases[38]

Case 1: Ms. K

Women in Ms. K's tribe are not subject to female genital cutting. However, when her parents died, the 16-year-old Ms. K came under the protection of her paternal uncle. He removed her from secondary school and arranged a marriage with a middle-aged friend from another tribe. The proposed bridegroom demanded that Ms. K undergo female genital cutting according to the customs of his tribe. Not only did Ms. K not want to marry this man, but she was horrified at the prospect of the procedure. With the help of an older sister, she managed to flee her country and wishes to obtain refugee status in Country A.

Case 2: Dr. Q

For the past two years, Zania has been ruled by a military regime. The country's parliament has been dismissed, and all laws are made by decree. As part of an ambitious plan to employ all able-bodied working men, the government orders all women to leave their jobs and remain in their homes. Women who disobey this decree are severely punished. Dr. Q, a physician, had to abandon her profession. But thanks to an influential patient, she obtained a false passport and escaped the country. She is now requesting asylum in Country A.

Case 3: Mrs. P

Mrs. P and her husband were engaged in drug trafficking, receiving raw drugs from another country, refining them, and exporting them at a huge profit. There was great danger in this work, both from government agents and from competing drug refiners and exporters. An underground war erupted among competitors in which not only dealers themselves but members of their families were assassinated. In fear, Mrs. P takes her five young children and flees to Country A.

Case 4: Ms. F

Ms. F. has been suffering from a serious disease for the past three months. Her doctor believes that she has just a few more months left to live. Her only hope is a new, but very expensive, medical treatment. Unfortunately, Ms. F is very poor. In addition, the government of her country has suspended free health care services. All citizens are now required to pay the full cost of their medical care. Ms. F. will never be able to afford the treatment that she needs to survive. However, health care in Country A is still subsidized by its government. With the help of a friend, Ms. F. travels to the border of Country A and applies for refugee status. She claims that she will not survive if she remains in her home country.

Case 5: Ms. V

Ms. V, a 20-year-old university student, still lives at home with her family, who belong to a very strict orthodox religious sect. Since adolescence, Ms. V's religious beliefs have shifted away from those of her family, becoming increasingly liberal. Her father has responded with escalating violence, beating her, locking her in her room, withholding food, and finally throwing her out of the family home. He and her brothers now stalk her and threaten her with death for "shaming the family." While attending a student conference in Country A, she approaches authorities there and asks for asylum.

Case 6: Ms. R

As a member of a group opposed to the governing regime of her country, Ms. R. secretly distributed pamphlets in the factory where she worked. The pamphlets called for an uprising of the people against the regime. She was discovered, arrested, and sentenced to five years' imprisonment. In prison, she was repeatedly tortured and raped by government agents. After two years, she managed to escape; however, during her escape she wounded and permanently paralyzed a prison guard. After dangerous months in hiding, Ms. R was able to hitchhike to the border of Country A and now asks for asylum.

Answer Key

Case 1: Ms. K

Ms. K should be granted asylum because (1) she is outside her country of origin, (2) she faces great physical harm that can be considered persecution, and (3) she can argue that she falls under the persecution grounds of the 1951 Refugee Convention. Although the Convention does not specifically include gender discrimination as grounds for refugee status, courts have identified women fleeing female genital cutting (FGC) as a dissenting social group. In fact, the United States grants 94 percent of asylum seekers who cite FGC as their reason for application.[39] For example, in 2005 a woman who fled Uganda after being subjected to Type Four FGC (genital stretching) was granted asylum by an immigration judge in Boston, Massachusetts.[40]

Case 2: Dr. Q

Dr. Q should still be granted asylum. UNHCR considers a person who is fleeing severe discrimination or other inhumane treatment amounting to persecution to be eligible for refugee status. Dr. Q is being persecuted for not conforming to strict social codes. And since the government is the source of this discrimination, she has no higher authority to appeal to for protection. In the spirit of the 1951 Refugee Convention, Dr. Q is a refugee.

Case 3: Mrs. P

Although Mrs. P is outside her country of origin and faces danger, as a criminal she is not part of a protected group.

Case 4: Ms. F

Ms. F. should not be recognized as a refugee. Poverty and poor social conditions alone can never be grounds for granting asylum. To be considered a refugee under the 1951 Refugee Convention, two conditions must be met. First, there must be a well-founded fear of persecution for reasons of race, religion, nationality, membership in a particular social group, or political opinion. However, in this case, Ms. F. is not being persecuted for any of these reasons. Although Ms. F. belongs to the lower class, her membership in this social group is not sufficient in itself to accord her the designation of refugee. (There has to be some clear threat of persecution for this designation to be valid.) Second, the individual in question must experience some form of discrimination. In this case, the government health care policy applies to everyone, and no one is being disproportionately mistreated for reasons of race, religion, nationality, membership in a particular social group, or political opinion. However, if the government refused to provide medical treatment to Ms. F because of her ethnicity, then she might be recognized as a refugee.

Case 5: Ms. V

Ms. V is outside her country of origin and faces grave danger because of her political and religious opinions and beliefs. She should be granted asylum.

Case 6: Ms. R

Ms. R should be recognized as a refugee. Her actions were political in nature. However, one must also examine the crime she committed while escaping from prison. Her crime was obviously serious. The next step is to strike a balance between the nature of the offense and the degree of persecution feared. If Ms. R is still to be considered a refugee, the persecution feared must outweigh the seriousness of her offense. It appears that the crime was committed in order to escape persecution. With this in mind, and weighing the offense versus the persecution, the exclusion clause (Article F of the Convention) should not apply. She should be recognized as a refugee.

International Recognition of Wartime Sexual Violence as a Grave Human Rights Abuse

In 1992, for the first time in history, the United Nations Security Council issued a declaration condemning wartime rapes, characterizing those taking place in the former Yugoslavia as "massive, organized and systematic."[41] Under intense public pressure to respond to these atrocities, the Security Council also issued Resolution 808, declaring that "an international tribunal shall be established for the prosecution of persons responsible for serious violations of international humanitarian law committed in the territory of the former Yugoslavia since 1991."[42]

In contrast to previous international tribunal establishment processes, women's human rights advocates were heavily engaged in the formation of the new international tribunal for the former Yugoslavia. Although their approaches varied, the advocates made central to their tribunal advocacy campaign the explicit argument that rape was a violation of international law (and not merely an expected by-product of conflict). In early circulated drafts of the statute for the International Criminal Tribunal for the Former Yugoslavia (ICTY), rape and sexual violence were treated as affronts to personal dignity and honor—a reference to earlier formulations under humanitarian law.[43] Some women's human rights advocates sought to have rape and sexual violence prosecuted as a form of the most serious of crimes such as genocide, torture, enslavement, and mutilation.

Other advocates pushed for a separate section in the ICTY statute that would specify that rape and sexual violence should be prosecuted as serious forms of violence. Still others pursued both tracks simultaneously, to cover all bases and make sure that rape was treated seriously in all scenarios.

The Tribunal's subject-matter jurisdiction is set forth in four articles, giving it jurisdiction over grave breaches of the Geneva Conventions of 1949 (Article 2), violations of the laws or customs of war (Article 3), genocide (Article 4), and crimes against humanity (Article 5). Article 5 defines *crimes against humanity* in armed conflict as "murder, extermination, enslavement, deportation, imprisonment, torture, rape, persecutions on political, racial, and religious grounds, and other inhumane acts."[44] Although the term *rape* does not explicitly appear in Articles 2 and 3 (the provisions relating to grave breaches of the Geneva Conventions and war crimes), sexual violence has been prosecuted under Article 5 (crimes against humanity) as well as other provisions of the statute, including genocide, grave breaches, and violations of the laws and customs of war.[45] This strategy has allowed for more successful sexual violence cases and will undoubtedly open the way for similar cases before the new International Criminal Court,[46] including those having to do with the systematic commission of sexual violence against women in Darfur refugee camps.[47]

The Beijing Platform for Action has also drawn international attention to the particular concerns of war-affected women. Women refugees face increased burdens for caring for their families "as a result of conflict, unexpectedly cast as sole manager of household, sole parent, and caretaker of elder relatives" (paragraph 133). Women are vulnerable to gender-specific violations of human rights while fleeing or relocating across borders, including rape and systematic rape—that is, use of rape by enemy forces as a calculated campaign of terror and destruction (paragraph 135). And women often experience difficulty in countries of asylum with respect to being recognized as refugees when the claim is based on gender-related persecution (paragraph 136).

The Beijing Platform for Action lists six strategic objectives to advance the rights of women in armed conflict:

1. Increase the participation of women in conflict resolution at decision-making levels and protect women living in situations of armed and other conflicts or under foreign occupation.
2. Reduce excessive military expenditures and control the availability of armaments.
3. Promote nonviolent forms of conflict resolution and reduce the incidence of human rights abuse in conflict situations.
4. Promote women's contribution to fostering a culture of peace.
5. Provide protection, assistance, and training to refugee women, other displaced women in need of international protection, and internally displaced women.
6. Provide assistance to the women of colonies and non-self-governing territories.

Since the Beijing Conference in 1995, additional major steps in the increasing recognition of wartime sexual violence as a grave human rights issue have included the following:

- *UN Security Council Resolution 1325.* In October 2000, for the first time in its history, the UN Security Council acknowledged that women have a key role in promoting international stability by passing Resolution 1325 on Women, Peace and Security. It called on all parties to ensure women's participation in peace processes, from the prevention of conflict to negotiations and post-war reconstruction.[48] The resolution emphasizes the responsibility of states and parties to armed conflict to protect women from violence as well as the importance of including women in leadership roles at the national and international levels and of incorporating a gender perspective into international peacekeeping.[49]

- *UNIFEM Women, War and Peace Portal/Campaign.* Following the adoption of Resolution 1325, the United Nations Development Fund for Women (UNIFEM) has become increasingly active on the topic of women, war, and peace. For its 2002 Report on the Status of Women, UNIFEM sponsored *The Independent Experts' Assessment on the Impact of Armed Conflict on Women and Women's Role in Peace-Building,* authored by experienced advocates Elisabeth Rehn and Ellen Johnson Sirleaf.[50] This book brings to life Resolution 1325 with the voices of the world's women, highlights the progress that has been made, identifies the challenges women continue to face, and provides recommendations for how to continue to realize the goals set in Resolution 1325 in bringing peace to the women of the world. Following the publication of the *The Independent Experts' Assessment,* UNIFEM created a web portal on women, war, and peace that provides resources on the topic.[51]

- In 2002 the office of the Secretary-General submitted the study *Women, Peace and Security,* pursuant to Resolution 1325.[52] This study, which examines the role of women in various aspects of armed conflict and the effects of different aspects of armed conflict on women, was an important step in further raising awareness about the need to devote resources and attention to the impact of armed conflict on women and promoting women's role in conflict resolution.

- *UNHCR Publications on Refugee and Displaced Women.* The United Nations High Commissioner for Refugees (UNHCR) has released several publications and guides dealing directly with refugee and displaced women. In 2001, UNHCR released the guide *Good Practices on Gender Equality Mainstreaming: A Practical Guide to Empowerment,*[53] which provides examples of ways to empower refugee and displaced women so that they can rebuild their lives in a sustainable manner. And in May 2003, UNHCR released the publication *Sexual and Gender-Based Violence Against Refugees, Returnees and Internally Displaced Persons: Guidelines for Prevention and Response.*[54] This publication includes discussion of the problem of sexual- and gender-based violence against refugees, returnees, and IDPs; strategies for preventing such violence; appropriate ways to respond to such violence; and strategies for monitoring displaced persons for the occurrence of violence.

- *Beijing +5 Conference.* The final report of the Beijing + 5 Conference, which has assessed progress since the 1995 World Conference on Women, reviews not only the achievements in the area of addressing the effects of armed conflict on women but also the obstacles to further progress. Such obstacles include continued inequality of men and women, high levels of military expenditures, the large percentage of displaced persons who are women, and the violations of women's human rights in armed conflict. The report states that "[i]n situations of armed conflict, there are continued violations of human rights of women, which are violations of fundamental principles of international human rights law and international humanitarian law."[55]

- *The Coalition on Women's Human Rights in Conflict Situations.* This NGO has been active on issues relating to witness protection. Women's advocacy groups have worked to ensure the protection of those who have testified before international tribunals on matters involving sexual violence. Other initiatives have included efforts to preserve the anonymity of witnesses, sometimes even from defense counsel, through darkened glasses and voice-altering devices. In addition, a twenty-four-hour hotline was instituted in conjunction with the Tribunals for witnesses to use if their safety was threatened in any way.[56]

- *The Centre for Women War Victims (CZZZR).* Located in Croatia, this NGO is a feminist, anti-militaristic organization that works to empower women in the region. It was founded in 1992 in reaction to war and the increased violence against women, as well as misogynist and nationalistic policies. CZZZR has established counseling centers, a shelter, and educational programs for women that have experienced violence during conflict.[57]

- *Pro-Femmes Twese Hamwe.* An umbrella organization of Rwandan NGOs, Pro-Femmes is involved in the promotion of women's rights. Within its national program, the Campaign Action for Peace (CAP), Pro-Femmes launched the Pan-African Conference on Peace, Gender and Development. Rwandan women, through a process of appropriate restitution, forgiveness, and healing, provide support to victims of violence, refugees, repatriated people, and fugitives in order to enable them to regain their dignity and rights in a peaceful environment.[58]

⌘ Learning Activity 6: Women as Agents for Peace? ⌘

Objective   To examine the impact of excluding women from decision-making about war and peace

Time   45 minutes

Materials   None

1. Discuss

Lead a discussion on women and conflict, focusing on the following questions:

- What is the impact of excluding women from decision making about war? Would women make a difference? Why or why not? What kind of difference?
- Are there women in your community who have reacted to war, to weapons of mass destruction, or to state violence against women?

Learning Activity 6 Continued

2. Imagine
Read aloud the following scenario:

> It is the year 2090. Half the countries in the world are headed by women; half the cabinet members and leaders are women; half the elected officials are women. Gender equality has been achieved in education and health.

- What is the state of the world? Is it necessarily more peaceful?
- Is the situation regarding peace and conflict the same in societies headed by men as in those headed by women? If yes, why? If no, what are the differences?
- What contribution can leadership, whether male or female, make to peace in the world?

A Concluding Note: Beyond War?

Despite vulnerability to murder, rape, torture, sexual abuse, deprivation, displacement, and psychological trauma in times of conflict, women are usually absent from decision-making positions in the national, regional, and international bodies that make war or negotiate peace. Women can rarely be found in high positions in armies or peace-keeping forces; few women ever sit on the UN Security Council or on regional defense organizations such as NATO. Nonetheless, "[d]uring times of armed conflict and the collapse of communities, the role of women is crucial. . . . Women make an important but often unrecognized contribution as peace educators both in their families and their societies."[59] In the Middle East, for example, despite the stalled peace process, the women of Bat Shalom, an Israeli peace organization, together with a Palestinian women's organization, continue to work toward peace between Israel and its Arab neighbors.[60] The promotion of women's human rights will support their roles in the family and in the larger public sphere and, in so doing, contribute to the peaceful resolution of conflict.

Another historic example of women participating in the peace process is the Northern Ireland Women's Coalition (NIWC). After centuries of fighting in Northern Ireland, the NIWC began in the mid-1990s with only two delegates who represented both nationalist and unionist parties as the only women at the negotiating table. They created an inclusive forum where victims' rights and reconciliation were considered. Their approach to politics was based on cooperation, noncompetitiveness, and a willingness to share ideas. After the Belfast Peace Agreement was reached in 1998, it still needed to be passed by 72 percent of the electorate. The NIWC was crucial in achieving this enormous task. Many in Northern Ireland feel that fewer people would have voted for the Belfast Peace Agreement if not for the public participation that the NIWC brought to the process. Indeed, the NIWC played a key role in increasing the participation both of women and of civil society in the politics of Northern Ireland, and it continues to influence women peacemakers throughout the world by demonstrating women's ability to overcome party lines and create a more inclusive negotiation process.[61]

Remembering Core Concepts

✠ Learning Activity 7 ✠
Speaking Out for the Human Rights of Women in Wartime

Objectives To examine the rights of refugee, displaced, and war-affected women and consider how to take action to improve their lives
Time 60+ minutes
Materials Chart paper and markers

1. Brainstorm

Ask participants to call to mind the refugee, displaced, and war-affected women who reside in their community or country and, using a chart like the one shown in Table 13.1, to list their country of origin and reason for leaving home.

Table 13.1 Speaking Out for the Human Rights of Women in Wartime

Refugee Women		Displaced Women		War-Affected Women	
Country of Origin	Reason for Leaving	Country of Origin	Reason for Leaving	Country of Origin	Reason for Leaving

2. Analyze/Discuss

On the basis of this chart, ask the participants: What patterns emerge regarding the refugee, displaced, and war-affected women in your community?

- Are there numbers of women from the same area? How do you explain this?
- Are many women fleeing similar circumstances? How do you explain this?
- Are there groups about whom you have little or no information? How do you explain this?
- What additional information do you need to evaluate the problems of refugee, displaced, and war-affected women in your community (e.g., are they alone, with children, able to speak the local language, able to read, work, or access services)?
- What kinds of social services and other supports are available to these women in your community?

Note to Facilitator: If the group is well informed about refugee, displaced, and war-affected women in their community, go to Steps 3–5, which address these women's problems directly. If not, go to each step's *Alternative*, which provides suggestions on how to find out more about these groups of women.

✗ Learning Activity 7 Continued ✗

3. List

Ask the full group to list problems faced by refugee, displaced, and war-affected women in their community. Then ask participants, working in small groups, to choose a problem on which they wish to concentrate. Have each group prepare a five-minute presentation to a "panel of community leaders" on their problem. Each presentation should:

- describe the problem, identifying the group(s) of women it impacts and, if possible, the cause(s) of the problem
- relate the problem to women's human rights
- clarify how the problem affects women's lives
- show how addressing the problem can improve their lives
- propose specific actions that should be taken to address the problem
- show how members of the community can get involved in addressing the problem.

Ask each group to choose a spokesperson to make the presentation and a "community leader" to serve on the panel. While the groups plan their presentations, the panel of leaders meets to decide on their roles, representing a variety of differing but typical attitudes within the community leadership, both positive and negative.

Alternative: Challenge the participants by asking them to evaluate their knowledge about refugee, displaced, and war-affected women.

- How can you learn more about refugee, displaced, and war-affected women in your community? About the problems they face?
- Would you personally consult women about the problem and how it affects them? About actions that could improve the problem?
- What obstacles might you face in obtaining information from these women themselves?
- Why is it important in real-life human rights advocacy to include the active participation of those directly involved in and affected by a problem?

4. Present/Role-Play

The spokesperson from each group makes a presentation and members of the panel listen and respond, asking questions and offering comments, objections, or suggestions in keeping with their chosen roles.

Alternative: Divide participants into small groups and ask each group to plan questions to ask in an interview with a group of refugee, displaced, or war-affected women. Each group should choose a group to interview from the list generated in Step 1. The purpose of the interview is to assess the problems and needs of these women; it should not last more than five minutes.

continues

✠ Learning Activity 7 Continued ✠

Participants should keep in mind the kinds of trauma many of these women have experienced and also the probability that the culture in which they are now living is strange to them. While seeking information, the participants should take care not to create offense or additional problems themselves.

5. Discuss
After the presentations and role-play, address these questions:

- How did the spokespersons feel when presenting the problem?
- How did the "community leaders" respond to the presentation? What attitudes in the community were they representing?
- How did the audience, composed of the rest of the group, respond to the presentations?
- Did any spokesperson discuss the problem as a human rights violation? Did putting the problem in a human rights context strengthen the argument? Why or why not?
- Are these ideas for strengthening the human rights of refugee, displaced, and war-affected women feasible in your community? Why or why not?

Alternative: One member from each group conducts the interview. Members of another group represent the refugee, displaced, or war-affected women. The rest of the participants observe the interview.

After each interview, ask both the "interviewees" and the observers to give their impressions and suggestions for improvement.

- How can the interviewer know what questions are painful or inappropriate to someone from another culture?
- How can the interviewer know that the information obtained is representative?

6. Conclude
Challenge the participants by asking them to evaluate their knowledge of the problem and the inclusiveness of their perspective:

- How did you obtain your information about the issues faced by refugee, displaced, or war-affected women in your community? Was it accurate and complete? If not, what additional information do you need and how can you obtain it?
- Did you personally consult women about the problem and how it affects them? About actions that could improve the problem?
- Why is it important in real-life human rights advocacy to include the active participation of those directly involved and affected?

> ### Learning Activity 7 Continued
>
> - How can you apply the example of this learning activity to planning and implementing advocacy for women in your community?
>
> *Alternative:* Discuss these questions with participants:
>
> - Why is accurate and complete information important in real-life human rights advocacy?
> - Why is the inclusion of active participation of those directly involved and affected important in such advocacy?
> - How can you apply the example of this learning activity to planning and implementing advocacy for women in your community?

Notes

1. World Revolution, "Peace, War, and Conflict," *Overview of Global Issues*, available online at http://www.worldrevolution.org/projects/globalissuesoverview/overview2/PeaceNew.htm.

2. UNHCR, "From the Foreign Land," no. 16 (March 2002), available online at http://www.unhcr.pl/english/newsletter/16/world_of_refugee_women.php.

3. Beijing Platform for Action, paragraph 113.

4. "Rape, Sexual Violence Continue in Sudan's Darfur Region," *UN Reports*, July 29, 2005, available online at http://www.un.org/apps/news/story.asp?NewsID=15202&Cr=Darfur&Cr1=.

5. Judy El Bushra and Eugenia Pia Lopes, "The Gender Dimensions of Armed Conflict," in *Development and Conflict: The Gender Dimension* (Oxford: Oxfam, 1994), pp. 18–28.

6. Jeanne Ward, *If Not Now, When? Addressing Gender-Based Violence in Refugee, Internally Displaced, and Post-Conflict Settings: A Global Overview* (Reproductive Health of Refugees Consortium, Women's Committee for Women and Children Refugees), p. 39.

7. Amnesty International, *AI Index*, AMR 23/040/2004, October 13, 2004, available online at http://web.amnesty.org/library/Index/ENGAMR230402004.

8. Colum Lynch, "U.N. Report Details Rampant Sexual Violence in Darfur," *Washington Post*, July 30, 2005, p. A20, available online at http://www.washingtonpost.com/wp-dyn/content/article/2005/07/29/AR2005072901740.html.

9. Jeanne Ward and Mendy Marsh, "Sexual Violence Against Women and Girls in War and Its Aftermath: Realities, Responses, and Required Resources," Briefing Paper Prepared for the Symposium on Sexual Violence in Conflict and Beyond, June 21–23, 2006, Brussels, Belgium, UNFPA, available online at http://www.unfpa.org/emergencies/symposium06/docs/finalbrusselsbriefingpaper.pdf.

10. WomenWarPeace.org, Democratic Republic of the Congo, available online at http://www.womenwarpeace.org/drc/drc.htm.

11. UNICEF, "How Does HIV Affect Young People?" available online at http://www.unicef.org/aids/index_youngpeople.html.

12. Kitty McKinsey, "Mass Rape in Bosnia: 20,000 Women, Mostly Muslim, Have Been Abused by Serb Soldiers," Women's International League for Peace and Freedom, available online at http://www.peacewomen.org/news/BosniaHerzegovina/newsarchive/massrape.html.

13. "Global TV Campaign on Human Trafficking, Fact Sheet on Human Trafficking," United Nations Office on Drugs and Crime (UNODC), available online at http://www.unodc.org/unodc/en/trafficking_tv_campaign_2002_factsheet.html.

14. Shan Women's Action Network (SWAN) and the Shan Human Rights Foundation (SHRF), "License to Rape: The Burmese Military Regime," May 2002, available online at http://www.shanland.org/resources/bookspub/humanrights/LtoR/.

15. Maggie O'Kane, "Return of the Revolutionaries," *The Guardian*, January 15, 2001, available online at http://www.pcug.org.au/~wildwood/JanRev.htm.

16. UNIFEM Women, War and Peace, "Violence Against Women Fact Sheet," available online at http://www.womenwarpeace.org/issues/violence/violence.htm.

17. R. Charli Carpenter, "Assessing and Addressing the Needs of Children Born of Forced Maternity," July 27, 2000, available online at http://www.humanrights-it.org/ing/parttwof.htm.

18. "One Year Follow-Up to MDRI report 'Not on the Agenda: Human Rights of People with Mental Disabilities in Kosovo,'" United Nations Mental Disability Rights International, July 17, 2003, available online at http://www.mdri.org/projects/kosovoinitiative/followup071703.htm.

19. Ustinia Dolgopol and Snhehal Paranjape, "Comfort Women: An Unfinished Ordeal," International Commission of Jurists in Geneva, Switzerland, p. 199, available online at http://www.comfort-women.org/Unfinished.htm.

20. "Gender Roles," Pacific University, available online at http://mcel.pacificu.edu/as/students/korea/gender-comfort.html.

21. IMADR Webmaster, "Seoul Official Urges Japan to Compensate Comfort Women," *Korea Times*, August 8, 2001, International Movement Against All Forms of Discrimination and Racism, available online at http://www.imadr.org.

22. "Recent Policy of the Government of Japan on the Issue Known As 'Wartime Comfort Women,'" Ministry of Foreign Affairs of Japan, May 2004, available online at http://www.mofa.go.jp/policy/women/fund/policy.html.

23. Amnesty International, "Japan Report 2005," available online at http://web.amnesty.org/report2005/jpn-summary-eng.

24. Reproductive Health Response in Conflict (RHRC) Consortium, "General Reproductive Health," available online at http://www.rhrc.org.

25. UNIFEM Women, War and Peace, "Displacement Fact Sheet," available online at http://www.womenwarpeace.org/issues/displacement/displacement.htm.

26. Refugee Health—Immigrant Health, "Women Refugees," available online at http://www3.baylor.edu/~Charles_Kemp/refugee_women.htm.

27. Lydia Bezeruk, "Peace and Mines: Youth Rising to Action," *Respect e-Zine, Refugee Education Sponsorship Program*, no. 40, February 4, 2005, available online at http://www.respectrefugees.org/ezine/ezine20050204_mines.shtml.

28. Patricia Hynes, "War and Women," *ZNet*, March 13, 2003, available online at http://www.zmag.org/content/showarticle.cfm?SectionID=40&ItemID=3229.

29. Megan Mylan and John Shenk, "Lost Boys of Sudan," available online at http://www.lostboysfilm.com/learn.html.

30. Ibid.

31. UNIFEM Women, War and Peace, "Displacement Fact Sheet," available online at http://www.womenwarpeace.org/issues/displacement/displacement.htm.

32. NGO Working Group on Women, Peace, and Security, "International Consultative Meeting on United Nations Resolution 1325, Summary Report," March 25–26, 2002, http://www.peacewomen.org/un/ngo/ngopub/kampala.html.

33. Anastasia Bermudez Torres, "Gender and Forced Migration: Conflict Induced Displacement," *FMO Research Guide*, October 2002, available online at http://www.forcedmigration.org/guides/fmo007/fmo007-3.htm.

34. European Council on Refugees and Exiles, "Position on Asylum Seeking and Refugee Women," December 1997, available online at http://www.ecre.org/positions/women.shtml.

35. Ibid.

36. Julie Mertus, *War's Offensive on Women* (West Hartford, CT: Kumarian Press, 2000). See also the recommendations from UNHCR in "Good Practices on Gender Equality Mainstreaming: A Practical Guide to Empowerment," p. 8, available online at http://www.unhcr.ch/.

37. Adapted from *First Steps—A Manual for Starting Human Rights Education* (Amnesty International, 1996), available online at http://www.hrea.org/.

38. "Plans for Ages 15–18," in UNHCR, *Human Rights and Refugees: The Right to Asylum,* available online at http://www.unhcr.ch.

39. David A. Martin, "Treatment of Gender-Based Asylum Claims in the United States, Memorandum Prepared for the Attorney General of Canada," March 31, 2003, available online at http://www.cic.gc.ca/english/policy/asylum-gender-us.html.

40. World Organization for Human Rights USA, "Asylum Granted to Ugandan Woman Fleeing FGM," available online at http://www.humanrightsusa.org/.

41. S.C. Res. 798, U.N. SCOR, 47th Sess., 3150th mtg., U.N. Doc. S/INF/48 (1992).

42. S.C. Res. 808, U.N. SCOR, 48th Sess., 3175th mtg. at 1, U.N. Doc. S/RES/808, para. 1 (1993).

43. For example, Article 46 of The Hague Regulations of 1899 and 1907 requires respect for "[f]amily honour and rights, the lives of persons, and private property, as well as religious convictions and practice." (See Convention Respecting the Laws and Customs of War on Land, Annex of Regulations, art. 46, 18 Oct. 1907, 36 Stat. 2277, 2306-07, 1 Bevans 631, 651.) The Fourth Geneva Convention of 1949 incorporates these concepts in a provision in Article 27 giving women special protection against rape: "Protected persons are entitled, in all circumstances, to respect for their persons, their honour, their family rights, their religious convictions and practices, and their manners and customs. They shall at all times be humanely treated, and shall be protected especially against all acts of violence or threats thereof and against insults and public curiosity. Women shall be especially protected against any attack on their honour, in particular against rape, enforced prostitution, or any form of indecent assault." (See Geneva Convention Relative to the Protection of Civilian Persons in Time of War, art. 27, opened for signature 12 Aug. 1949, 6 U.S.T. 3516, 3536, 75 U.N.T.S. 287, 306, Geneva Convention IV.)

44. Geneva Convention of 1949, Article 5.

45. ICTY Statute, Article 5.

46. Amnesty International, "The International Criminal Court Fact Sheet 7 Ensuring Justice for Women, *AI Index,* IOR 40/006/2005, April 12, 2005, available online at http://web.amnesty.org/library/Index/ENGIOR400062005?open&of=ENG-385.

47. Lynch, "U.N. Report Details Rampant Sexual Violence in Darfur," p. A20.

48. United Nations Security Council, *Resolution 1325* (New York: UNSC, 2000).

49. The full text of this resolution can be found at available online at http://www.peacewomen.org/un/sc/1325.html.

50. Elisabeth Rehn and Ellen Johnson Sirleaf, *The Independent Experts' Assessment on the Impact of Armed Conflict on Women and Women's Role in Peace* (1992), available online at http://www.reliefweb.int/rw/lib.nsf/AllDocsByUNID/3f71081ff391653dc1256c69003170e9.

51. UNIFEM, "A Portal on Women, Peace and Security," available online at http://www.womenwarpeace.org/.

52. UN Division for the Advancement of Women, available online at http://www.unifem.org/gender_issues/governance_peace_security/.

53. See the website of the UN Refugee Agency at http://www.unhcr.ch.

54. Ibid.

55. United Nations General Assembly, "Report of the Ad Hoc Committee of the Whole of the Twenty-Third Special Session of the General Assembly" (A/S-23/10/Rev.1), paragraph 19, available online at http://www.un.org/womenwatch/daw/followup/as2310rev1.pdf.

56. Frances T. Pilch, "Sexual Violence During Armed Conflict: Institutional and Judicial Responses," *GSC Quarterly* (summer 2002), available online at http://www.ssrc.org/programs/gsc/gsc_quarterly/newsletter5/content/pilch.page.

57. See the website of the Centre for Women War Victims at http://www.czzzr.hr/eng/index.html.

58. More details on Pro-Femmes Twese Hamwe can be found at http://translate.google.com/translate?hl=en&sl=fr&u=http://www.profemmes.org/1337.html&prev=/search%3Fq%3DPro-Femmes%26hl%3Den%26lr%3D%26sa%3DG.

59. Beijing Platform for Action, paragraph 140.

60. Chris Patten, "The Role of Women in Conflict Resolution," speech given at the World Women Lawyers Conference, June 30, 2003, available online at http://europa.eu.int/comm/external_relations/news/patten/wwl.htm.

61. Kate Fearon, "Northern Ireland Women's Coalition: Institutionalizing a Political Voice and Ensuring Representation," Conciliation Resources (2002), available online at http://www.c-r.org/our-work/accord/public-participation/ni-womens-coalition.php.

14

The Road Ahead:
Local Action and Global Change

The field of human rights appears to have come full circle. Human rights began as a localized phenomenon, embodied in religious and spiritual teachings, highly particularized communal practices, and ethical codes of conduct directed at recognizing and protecting the dignity of humanity.

Human rights gradually became internationalized through a series of international treaties, offering protections first in particular periods of war and crisis and, then, with a particular emphasis on certain groups, such as religious minorities and ethnic and national minorities. Some provisions from these early treaties found their way into the complex systems for minority rights protections fashioned by the League of Nations in 1919 following World War I. These "minority treaties" sought to achieve the twin aims of granting legal equality to individual members of particular minority groups and preserving the groups' characteristics and traditions.

After these efforts failed to prevent the atrocities of World War II, the focus of advocacy shifted from group rights to individual rights and emphasis was placed on universalizing human rights guarantees through a series of new international instruments, beginning with the UN Charter and the Universal Declaration of Human Rights. Human rights enforcement efforts were impaired by the ideological and political tensions of colonialism, which solidified north/south divides, and of the Cold War, which exploited east/west divisions. However, human rights standard-setting limped along in the 1950s and 1960s, emerging as a viable political force in the 1970s and 1980s amid a proliferation of international human rights conferences, human rights treaties and declarations, and local, national, and international organizations dedicated to promoting and protecting human rights. The cessation of colonialist rule in several parts of the world, along with the end of the Cold War, fostered a sudden growth spurt in the number and capacity of governmental and nongovernmental human rights organizations interested in rights promotion in newly emerging democracies. The percentage of these projects addressing women's human rights issues soared and, with rapid improvements in the Internet and other communications technology, local activists, in unprecedented numbers, finally had a voice in global human rights debates.

Does this mean that we are back where we started from? No, too much has changed in the intervening years. A host of domestic and international human rights systems and mechanisms for protecting human rights now exist, staff working on human rights concerns in governmental and nongovernmental offices have become better trained and more professional, and, although still in need of improvement, public awareness about human rights has improved greatly. The expansion in the number and variety of actors involved in human rights work can be seen as occurring in three directions: vertically, horizontally, and diagonally.

The image of "vertical growth" refers to the way in which the same human rights issue may now be addressed on at least three levels: local, national (also termed *state* or *domestic*), and international (or *trans-state*). Today, almost without exception, advocates working at all three of these levels articulate their demands for social justice, environmental responsibility, cultural recognition, economic security, and civil rights using the moral, legal, and political language of human rights. To cite an example from the field of women's human rights, activists concerned with violence against women can participate in local police training activities, monitor state commitments to address violence against women as set forth in country-specific action plans, and prepare reports on this issue for UN Special Rapporteurs concerned with the topic, or for international treaty-monitoring bodies.

Expansion has also occurred in a "horizontal" manner in that the kinds of human rights work accomplished at the same level has expanded dramatically, in terms of both subject matter and impact. Extending upon the example of violence against women, we find that organizations working on this issue at any level are increasingly making links with activists focusing on a range of complementary issues. In particular, activists previously concerned with a single aspect of the problem of violence against women, such as domestic abuse, are joining efforts with activists working on related topics, including human trafficking, globalization and workplace exploitation, health care, and poverty.

Closely related to these "horizontal" changes are developments of a "diagonal" nature, as witnessed by the growth of transnational advocacy networks and the accompanying increased ability of human rights staff working on one level to voice their concerns in new ways, with new allies working on another level (on the same or different issue). Again, the example of violence against women is instructive. "Diagonal" movement on this topic occurred in the late 1980s and early 1990s, when nonstate actors, faced with blockage to local efforts to improve law enforcement responses to domestic violence, sought out state and nonstate allies in the international arena. Their efforts culminated in the explicit recognition, by state representatives at the 1993 United Nations World Conference on Human Rights, that women have a right to nonviolence. Since then, activists have been able to work together to build on this achievement and expand the benefits of recognition of the right to nonviolence to other fields, including immigration, housing, and workplace standards.

What is the road ahead for human rights? Although the exact path cannot be charted, one thing is for sure: Local action is increasingly being linked to global change, and global change is relying more and more on local action.

Appendix I

Analytical Tables:
Analyzing Human Rights Problems,
Implementing Human Rights Strategies

The following two tables may be used to analyze human rights problems and to work toward solutions. Here are three ways to use them in conjunction with this book:

1. Individuals reading the book alone may refer to them at the conclusion of every chapter.
2. Facilitators and teachers may incorporate them in their training.
3. Anyone concerned with a human rights problem may use them to analyze the problem and design an action* plan.

To use the tables with a group, reproduce them as overheads or copy them on large sheets of paper.

Table A.1 links responsibilities to action plans. Use it by answering the numbered questions in order:

- Fill in Question 1 at the top, identifying the human rights violation(s).
- For Questions 2–4, check the boxes that apply, locating all actors that contribute both to the violation, either by their actions or their inaction, and to potential solutions. You will see that you are being asked to consider whether actors contribute to human rights problems through both their actions and their failure to act.
- For Question 5, list all the strategies that may be undertaken for the actors listed across the top of the chart.

Table A.2 lists horizontally the variety of actors that may play a role in creating and implementing human rights strategies and vertically some of the various types of strategies that could be used to address a specific human rights problem. Use Table A.2 by filling in specific actions that different actors (as listed across the top) can take with regard to each strategy. You may make additions to it if other actors and strategies come to mind.

*Action means those cases where the violator did something; inaction is where the violator could be responsible for failing to do something.

Table A.1   Analyzing Human Rights Problems

1. What is the violation?									
	Family	Religious/ Media Institutions	Business Interests	Other Commu- nity Actors	State Authority	Regional Authority	Inter- national Authority	Para- military/ Military	Other
2. Who or what is the violator?									
3. How is the violator responsible?									
4. Where can resources be found for solutions or remedies?									
5. List all the strategies** you can take under each category.									

**These strategies can be expanded to include specific actions and steps using Table A.2, "Implementing Human Rights Strategies."

Table A.2   Implementing Human Rights Strategies

	Family	Religious/ Media Institutions	Business Interests	Other Commu- nity Actors	State Authority	Regional Authority	Inter- national Authority	Para- military/ Military	Other
Education									
Policy/ Education									
Litigation/ Legal									
Organizing/ Networking									
Service Delivery									
Protest/ Public Action									
NGO Tribunals/ Hearings									
Mobilization Petition Campaigns									

Appendix II

Participatory Methodologies for Educators and Facilitators

Participatory Methodologies[1]

Human rights education needs facilitators, not teachers. A teacher stands at the front of a class and does most of the talking. Learners mostly sit quietly, speaking only when called on to ask or answer questions. However, adult learners (and children too) need to be actively engaged in their own learning. They need to be able to bring their experience of life into the learning and have it respected.

The facilitator and participants should feel as equals, engaged in a common effort toward a shared goal. Together they examine their own experiences and seek to come to individual conclusions. This relationship is important when the subject matter is emotional and sensitive. Because people cannot be told what to think, the goal is not some right answer or even agreement but, rather, a co-operative exploration of ideas and issues.

For more on facilitating human rights education, see the University of Minnesota's Human Rights Library, *The Human Rights Education Handbook: Part 2: Effective Practices for Learning, Action, and Change.*[2]

Icebreakers and Introductions

The following are suggestions for short and simple ways to introduce participants to each other.

Group Still Life. All participants bring a meaningful object from home to contribute to an opening display. Each in turn explains why she or he chose that object. Alternatively, participants find some symbolic object in the workshop area to represent themselves; then explain and contribute that object to the group still life.

Interviews. Each person pairs off with another and asks several questions. Then each partner introduces the other to the whole group. Some questions might be:

- What makes you unique?
- What person in your life has helped to make you the strong leader you are?
- When you hear the phrase *human right*, what do you think about?
- What event in your life has most affected your worldview?
- What brought you here?

In the Same Boat. Participants locate others who share the same characteristic, then call out some categories (e.g., those born in the same decade or month, those with the same number of children or siblings, those who speak the same language at home or the same number of languages). Under the right circumstances, more sensitive categories might be used (e.g., those whose skin tone is the same, number of times arrested).

Musical Chairs. Arrange chairs in a close circle and ask participants to sit down in them. Stand in the middle of the circle and explain that you are going to state your name and make a statement about yourself. When you do, everyone for whom that statement is also true must change chairs (e.g., "I am X and I am left-handed," "I am X and I have three daughters," "I am X and I dislike eating ___"). Try to get a chair for yourself. The person left without a chair then makes a similar statement about herself or himself. Continue until most participants have had a chance to introduce themselves in this way.

Portraits. Provide participants with plain paper and a pen. Participants find a partner they don't know, draw a quick sketch of her or him, and ask questions (e.g., name, hobby, a surprising fact) that will be incorporated into the portrait. Allow only a short time for this exercise, and encourage the participants to make their portraits and names as large as possible. Then ask each participant to show his or her portrait and introduce the "original" to the group. To facilitate learning names, hang the portraits where everyone can see them.

Teamwork. Divide participants into small teams and allow them time to discover the characteristics they have in common (e.g., culture, appearance, personal tastes, hobbies). Ask each team to choose a name for itself, and to make sure it can explain this name. Teams then introduce themselves to the whole group, naming team members and explaining their name.

Brainstorming

Brainstorming encourages creativity and generates ideas quickly. It can be used for solving a problem, answering a question, introducing a new subject, raising interest, or surveying knowledge and attitudes. Most brainstorming sessions follow this procedure:

- Introduce a question, problem, or topic both orally and in writing on chart paper.
- Invite participants to respond with as many ideas as possible, in single words or short phrases. Encourage everyone to participate, but do not proceed in any set order.
- Explain that until the brainstorm is complete, no one may repeat or comment on any response.
- Record every response on chart paper. Often the most creative or outrageous suggestions are the most useful and interesting.
- Afterward, prioritize, analyze, or use the list to generate discussion or problem solving.

Timelines

Overview Participants create symbolic representations of life experiences.
Time 60 minutes.
Materials For each small group, a piece of yarn or string about three meters long, ten small pieces of brightly colored yarn, several small pieces of paper (ideally in three colors), and tape or paperclips.

Note: This activity can be used for many purposes (e.g., to illustrate times of violence in a lifetime, periods of particular need for support, joyful times). The example below serves to illustrate human rights in a woman's life.

Procedure Divide participants into groups of three or four and give each a set of materials. Provide these instructions and demonstrate as you describe:

- Tie up the string at both ends. This will represent a typical woman's life in the community today. Attach the colored yarn at even intervals to represent decades of her life.
- On the slips of paper draw the important events of a typical woman's life. (e.g., physical maturity, marriage, birth of children).

Variation: Use one color for positive events, a second one for negative events, and a third one for neutral events. Attach them at the appropriate place on the line.

When everyone is finished, invite participants to walk around and look at other group's work. Then reassemble and discuss what they observed:

- What events were common to all the timelines? (List these on chart paper as they are mentioned.)
- Were there important differences between them? (List additional events mentioned.)
- If different colored slips were used: Were there differences in whether events were considered positive or negative?
- During what period of life did the most important events occur?

- During what periods of life did most females need particular support and protection?
- Who is responsible for providing that support and protection?

Ask participants to look back at the lifelines and identify examples reflecting events in which women exercised/enjoyed a human right and in which a human right was violated or denied. List these under columns labeled "Rights Enjoyed" and "Rights Denied."

Variations: (1) This activity can be changed to focus on a particular period of life (e.g., years of girlhood), a particular aspect of life (e.g., health, exposure to violence, education, economic activity), or women in varying circumstances (e.g., living in rural area, married). (2) To emphasize differences in gender perspectives, divide participants into all-female and all-male groups. When you discuss, ask how male and females differed in terms of what they thought were important events and whether certain events were viewed as positive, negative, or neutral.

Case Studies

Give small groups of participants case studies to respond to as primary data for learning. Cases can encourage analysis, critical thinking, problem solving, and planning skills, as well as cooperation and team building. They can be used to set up effective debates (e.g., with groups arguing assigned positions on an issue) and comparisons (e.g., different analyses or solutions of problems in the case). Many different kinds of cases can make effective studies:

- *Real cases* can be drawn from historical or current events. Participants can supply cases from their own experience.
- *Fictional* or *hypothetical cases* can be developed to address issues or workshop topics. Fictional situations can help the group to address locally sensitive issues without evoking responses to particular individuals, organizations, social groups, or geographic regions.

Debates

Debates help to clarify different positions on a controversial issue. They usually involve two or several small groups whose members present arguments on different sides of an issue, which may not necessarily represent their views. Debates develop logic, understanding of an issue, and listening and speaking skills. Ideally, a debate will conclude with all participants able to vote for or against the proposition and to discuss their positions.

Formal Debates. Usually some version of formal debating techniques are used, including a proposition, preparation of positions, statements and rebuttals, summaries, and voting.

Informal Debates. Informal debates can take many forms. Two examples follow.

- Ask participants to literally "take a position" on an issue and then to explain this position (e.g., see "Voting with Your Feet" below).
- Divide participants into two groups, each with an assigned position on an issue. The two groups prepare their arguments, with each person in the group making one point for that side. Then the two sides present their arguments, with all participants speaking. Afterward, participants indicate their personal positions, perhaps including "undecided."

Active Listening. Working in pairs or in groups of four, Person A gives one reason for support of an issue. Person B listens and then summarizes or restates A's reason. Person B then gives one reason opposing the statement. Person A (or Person C in a group of four) listens and summarizes B's reason and so forth, until each person has had a chance to express at least two reasons. This method might be preceded or concluded with the activity described in the section below headed "Voting with Your Feet," to determine whether or not people have changed their positions after hearing the arguments.

Discussion

To keep discussion focused, you might initially pose several key questions. The larger the group, the more likely that some participants will dominate and others will remain silent. To ensure that everyone has the opportunity to speak, you may want to divide participants into small groups. The more sensitive the subject, the smaller the group should be, including pairs for the most sensitive topics. When any discussion concludes, summarize the main points orally and in writing.

Small Groups. Size will depend on time constraints as well as on the sensitivity or complexity of the subject. In most cases, each group chooses a reporter to summarize its discussion.

Buzz Group. Participants discuss in pairs for a limited period. This method is especially effective for articulating ideas in preparation for a general discussion or for giving expression to personal responses to a film, presentation, or experience. After talking in pairs, couples might be asked to combine in groups of four and compare their opinions.

Leading Qusetions. Facilitators need to develop the skills of keeping the goal of discussion clearly in mind and of asking questions that encourage participation and analysis. Following are some typical leading questions:

- "What would you do if . . . ?"
- "How might we solve this problem?"
- "Can you say more about how that idea would work?"
- "Why do you think that?"
- "Am I right to say that you think . . . ?"

Open-Ended Stimulus. This method requires each participant to respond individually, supplying opinions, words, or information in response to a common question or task. It resembles the discussion method known as "Talk Around/ Go Around," which is described below.

- Check-In. A good way to start a session, especially in a workshop that lasts several days, is to ask a question as general as "How are you feeling this morning?" or as focused as "How has this work on children's rights affected you so far?" No one should comment on any statement made in a Check-In.
- Finishing Sentences. Start sentences in a way similar to this: "When I imagine soldiers, I think of . . ." or "If I could change one thing to improve my community, it would be. . . ."
- Supplying Titles or Labels. Show an illustration or cartoon and ask participants to give it a title or caption.
- Supplying a Solution. Read an article or tell a story and then ask a question similar to this: "What are her options in this situation?" or "If you were a leader in that community, what would you do?"

Rules for Discussion. One way to help create an environment of trust and mutual respect is to have participants develop "rules for discussion":

1. Write suggestions, combining and simplifying where necessary. You might want to suggest some of the following principles:

- Listen to the person who is speaking.
- Only one person speaks at a time.
- Raise your hand to be recognized if you want to say something.
- Don't interrupt when someone is speaking.
- When you disagree with someone, make sure that you make a difference between criticizing someone's idea and criticizing the person.
- Don't laugh when someone is speaking (unless she or he makes a joke).
- Encourage everyone to participate.

2. If many people in the group are literate, copy the list of rules neatly and hang it where participants can refer, add, or make changes to it as necessary.

Talk Around/Go Around. The facilitator sets a topic or asks a question, and everyone in turns responds, usually within a set time. Limit the time consistently. Make clear that anyone who doesn't wish to speak may pass.

Talking Circles/Word Wheels. Participants are divided in two groups, one sitting in a circle facing outward and the other facing inward so that each person faces someone else. These pairs then exchange views on an announced topic. After a set period, the facilitator asks everyone on the inside to move one seat to the right and discuss with the new person sitting opposite. This process continues until each person has exchanged views with several others.

Talking Stick. In this method, derived from a Native American tradition, anyone who speaks must be holding a designated object, which could literally be a stick or anything else easily visible and portable. The "talking stick" method builds awareness of how long and how often one speaks.

Talking Tickets. To provide everyone an equal opportunity to speak, give each participant three "talking tickets." Each ticket represents a certain amount of time to hold the floor. Once someone has used all of her or his tickets, that person has no further opportunities to speak. This method encourages thoughtful and concise discussion and discourages repetition and rambling speeches.

Think-Pair-Share. Participants are given time to write or simply to think on their own about a critical question; they then join with one other person to discuss their opinions. Finally the entire group re-forms and discusses the question. This method helps to raise the level of discussion, inasmuch as participants have already reflected and articulated their views.

Dramatizations

Dramatic techniques can enhance learning. Some dramatizations help participants to "experience" an unfamiliar situation or identity (e.g., being a refugee, being disabled) and develop empathy and appreciation for different points of view (e.g., acting the role of a perpetrator, a witness, an advocate). Other dramatizations may serve to concretize concepts (e.g., acting out articles of the Universal Declaration of Human Rights) or to analyze conflict (e.g., acting out confrontations between soldiers and villagers).

Act/Guess. Working in several teams, participants act out articles of human rights documents, which others must guess. These charades might illustrate rights denied, rights enjoyed, or rights defended.

Image Theater. Ask a volunteer to name a human rights problem from her or his own experience. The volunteer then uses the other participants like statues to build an image of this problem, asking people to stand or look in a particular way (e.g., a child might create a playground scene of bullying). Everyone must agree that the image accurately represents the problem. Then ask the volunteer to slowly change the "actual" image into an ideal one—that is, an example of the situation as she or he would like to see it (e.g., a safe play environment at school). Discuss possible agents of change relating to the situation.

Role-Play. This well-known method can take many forms, but in all such cases participants act out little dramas. Give clear instructions and ensure time for full development and discussion of the role-play, concluding with an explicit restatement of its purpose and learning points. Be sensitive to feelings that the drama may evoke in the actors and the audience. Allow sufficient time in which to discuss the role-play and to ask both actors and audience how they felt. Encourage evaluation of what took place and analysis of its relevance to human rights.

In some cases participants make up role-plays; in others the facilitator assigns a "plot." Participants may either take on roles spontaneously or be given specific roles, sometimes with assigned attitudes and behaviors (e.g., "You are a witness of domestic violence but don't want to get involved"). Elaboration of the role-play can include some of the following methods:

- Freeze. Call out "Freeze" during a moment of intense action and ask actors to describe their emotions at that moment or invite participants to analyze what is happening.
- Role Reversal. Without warning, stop the action, ask actors to exchange roles (e.g., gender switch, oppressor becomes victim), and continue the action from that point. Debrief thoroughly.
- Replay. After a role-play, change the situation (e.g., " . . . except this time you cannot read" or "You are gay") and ask the actors to replay the same scene with this change incorporated.
- Shadow. Have participants stand, in turn, behind each actor. Halt the action midway and ask the "shadows" what they think their character is feeling and thinking and why.

Street Theater. To raise public awareness, especially among limited-literacy audiences, participants can perform human rights plays in public places, sometimes inviting onlookers to take part.

Effects Webs

The following suggestions encourage participants to think about the effects of both real and imagined situations.

1. Start by writing a clear question or statement at the top of a sheet of paper (e.g., "What if women controlled as much wealth as men?") and circle it.
2. Next, draw three arrows from this statement and write three effects that would result from the statement (e.g., "Improved ability to provide for family," "More responsibility outside the home," "More involvement in business").
3. Then draw two arrows from these three effects and write two more effects that would result from each (e.g., "Better health for children," "More independence").

Variations: (1) Two small groups work on the same statement and compare their results. (2) The facilitator prepares a list of relevant questions or statements and lets each group choose one to work on.

Energizers

The following can help raise group spirits, create solidarity, and refocus energy.

The Chain. Ask participants to stand in a circle with their eyes closed. Move them around, attaching their hands to each other so that they make a knot. Then tell participants to open their eyes and try to untangle themselves without letting go of their hands.

Fireworks. Assign small groups to make sounds and gestures representing different fireworks. Some are bombs that hiss and explode. Others are firecrackers imitated by handclaps. Still others are Catherine Wheels that spin. Call on each group to perform separately, and then ask the whole group to make a grand display.

Group Sit. Ask participants to stand in a circle toe-to-toe. Then ask them to sit down without breaking the connection of their toes. Avoid this activity if members of the group are disabled or elderly or if the physical contact is culturally inappropriate.

The Rain Forest. Stand in the center of a circle of participants, who mimic your movements, making different sounds and gestures representing aspects of the forest (e.g., birds, insects, leaves rustling, wind blowing, animals calling) by snapping fingers, slapping sides, clapping hands, and imitating animals. The resulting sound is like a rain forest.

Silent Calendar. Explain that the whole group must line up in order of the day and month they were born, but they cannot use words to accomplish this.

The Storm. Assign different sounds and gestures to small groups of participants (e.g., wind, rain, lightning, thunder, etc.) and then narrate the soft beginnings of the storm, conducting the various sounds like an orchestra (e.g., "And then the lightning flashes! And the thunder roars!") through to the conclusion of the storm.

To the Lifeboats! First demonstrate a "lifeboat." Ask two people to hold hands to form the boat, and have passengers stand inside the circle formed by their hands. Then explain that everyone is going on a voyage: "At first the sea is calm and everyone is enjoying the trip. Then, suddenly, the ship hits a rock. Everyone must get into a lifeboat in groups of two." Participants then scramble to form "lifeboats" and take in the proper number of passengers. Usually someone "drowns." Then take up the narrative again. "Now the ship continues peacefully . . . but suddenly a hurricane begins. The ship is sinking. Everyone to the lifeboats in groups of two!" Continue this process through several "shipwrecks."

Storytelling

Both personal and traditional stories can be a rich source of relating human rights themes to lived experience. Participants need a receptive audience (often a small group works best) as well as control over how much they wish to reveal about themselves. Stories can be retold from a human rights perspective, dramatized, or analyzed in relation to human rights issues and documents.

To stimulate narratives, ask "Is this an issue in our community?" and encourage participants to offer illustrative stories from their experience. These stories need not be personal; encourage stories drawn from legend, literature, films, television, or local history. Invite historical perspective (e.g., "How was domestic violence handled in your grandmother's day?") and analysis of these stories (e.g., "How might the story be different if told by the police?").

Voting with Your Feet

Ask participants to literally "take a position" according to their degree of agreement or disagreement with a statement:

1. Designate areas in the room that represent positions on a continuum (e.g., "Strongly Agree," "Generally Agree," "Don't Know," "Generally Disagree," "Strongly Disagree").
2. Read a statement on a controversial issue (e.g., "I would never interfere in a situation of domestic violence") and allow time for reflection.
3. Then ask participants to "take a position."
4. When groups have formed, ask the participants to explain their position or discuss with others who hold the opposite position. Encourage those who are undecided to ask questions.
5. After discussion, invite anyone who wishes to change places to do so.

Closings

The method for closing depends greatly on the goals of the workshop or presentation. Following are a few ideas:

Ball Toss. Participants toss a ball from one to another. Each person who catches the ball states one thing she or he has learned or can use from the workshop.

Calling in the Names. Ask the group to stand in a large circle and think of people who support, inspire, or guide them in their work. Invite these people to be present by calling their names, one by one. This is also a good activity to use as an opening.

Collective Summary. Pose a summarizing question (e.g., "What remarks that you have heard here today will you especially remember as meaningful?" or "What idea can you take home to use in your community?") or an open-ended statement (e.g., "Try to think of a word or phrase that sums up your feelings at the end of today's session" or "I still wonder . . ."). Ask participants to respond in turn.

Group Still Life. Each participant in turn adds one object to a group display and explains why it represents something important about the workshop. The objects could be articles brought to the workshop for this purpose or simply symbolic items found at the site.

Releasing the Dove of Peace. The facilitator holds an imaginary object that has meaning to participants (e.g., bird, newborn baby) and invites each participant to say something to it as it is passed from one participant to another. After the "object" has been passed to everyone, they draw into a tight circle and collectively let it go.

Notes

1. This section was adapted from Nancy Flowers, *The Human Rights Education Handbook*, University of Minnesota Human Rights Center (2000), available online at http://www1.umn.edu/humanrts/edumat/hreduseries/hrhandbook/aboutseries.html.

2. Ibid.

Appendix III

Using Human Rights Systems and Mechanisms

Questions and Answers

Question: Where do I go with my human rights claim?
Answer: Three levels.

Human rights can be heard at three levels: (a) at the national or domestic level, such as a country's own judicial system and special commission set up to deal with human rights; (b) at the regional level (e.g., Africa, the Americas, and Europe all have formalized judicial systems and human rights organs, whereas the Asian system is developing at a more subregional level); and (c) at the international level, such as the organs of the United Nations, affiliated bodies, and other international courts and commissions.

Start in you own country. Under most circumstances, you cannot bring your case to an international level until you have exhausted every possibility at the national level.

Find out whether your country is part of a regional system. You must also ask whether individuals and NGOs can bring claims before that particular system or mechanism. Determine whether your country has ratified relevant human rights treaties. You may also be able to access the international system if you bring your claim under customary international law or some other grounds that do not require a written state agreement. Again, as at the regional level, you should ask whether individuals can bring cases.

Question: Where can I look for the law to apply to my case?
Answer: Three sources.

There are three main sources of international law: treaties, international customary law, and general principles of law. Consider whether you can bring a claim under any or all of the three.

The key to treaties is that they usually apply only to states that voluntarily agree to them. International customary law provides another source of law. Not all laws are written down in a clear and organized fashion, however. Sometimes laws develop over time and these norms gain the status of customary international law.

A third source of international law has grown out of the general principles of law followed by state courts. This source sounds very much like customary law. However, to find general principles one looks for agreement among the unwritten laws of states. To find customary law, one looks at what states do on a regular basis.

The ABCs of Treaties

- Treaties are also called conventions, covenants, charters, and protocols.
- Treaties between two countries are bilateral treaties; those among more than two, multilateral treaties.
- What distinguishes a treaty from other kinds of law is that it does not work unless it is ratified (signed and officially adopted). This happens through a process of ratification.
- The process of ratification differs from country to country. In the United States, for example, the president signs an international treaty, but the Senate must then agree by a two-thirds vote.
- When ratifying a treaty, a country can make reservations (exceptions) to parts with which it disagrees. This is known as "ratifying with reservations."
- Countries are not supposed to make reservations to key sections of a treaty that would undercut the main purpose of the treaty.
- Usually states must comply only with the treaties that they sign. However, if the ideas in the treaty have become almost universally followed, a state may be held responsible whether it has signed or not. In these cases, we say the treaty has become a part of "customary law."

Question: How do the systems work?
Answer: Through treaty- and non-treaty-based mechanisms.

The main difference is whether the mechanism is treaty-based or non-treaty based.

Treaty-Based Mechanisms

International human rights treaties have their roots in the Charter of the United Nations and the Universal Declaration of Human Rights (UDHR), adopted by the UN General Assembly on December 10, 1948. Countries never signed the UDHR as they would a formal treaty. Most commentators now agree that the Declaration has become binding as part of customary international law. In other words, countries do, in fact, act as if the provisions of the UDHR were law.

The other main human rights documents are divided between civil and political rights, on the one hand, and economic, social, and cultural rights, on the other. The International Covenant on Economic, Social, and Cultural Rights and the International Covenant on Civil and Political Rights (with an Optional Protocol to permit citizens to lodge complaints against their own governments), together with the Universal Declaration of Human Rights, are collectively known as the International Bill of Rights. They took effect in 1976. Other major international human rights treaties are divided into topical areas. Some address egregious acts, such as torture and genocide; others promote the rights of especially vulnerable populations, such as children and refugees. The main conventions include the Convention on the Prevention and Punishment of Genocide (1951), the Convention on the Elimination of All Forms of Racial Discrimination (1969), the Convention on the Elimination of All Forms of Discrimination Against Women (CEDAW) (1981), the Convention on the Rights of the Child (1990), the Convention Relating to the Status of Refugees (1951), and the Convention Against Torture and Other Cruel and Unusual Punishment (1987). Regional treaties relating to human rights include the American Convention on Human Rights (1978), the African Charter on Human and People's Rights (1981), and the European Convention for the Protection of Human Rights and Fundamental Freedoms (1953).

A particular treaty on human rights is almost always paired with a committee that has a name similar to that of the treaty. The committee is the body that actually gives effect to the words of the Convention. Each has a "secretariat" that usually coordinates and considers reports about adherence to its particular convention.

Non-Treaty-Based Mechanisms

In addition to treaty-monitoring bodies, avenues for enforcing human rights include the complaint and/or monitoring procedures of various United Nations bodies and associated agencies, such as the United Nations High Commissioner on Human Rights (UNCHR), the International Labour Organisation (ILO), and the World Health Organization (WHO).

Gross violations of human rights can be brought to the Commission on Human Rights under the Resolution 1503 procedure. Information can be sent to the Commission's various topical and geographical working groups, subcommissions, and special investigators, including the Special Rapporteur on Violence Against Women. And advocates can submit individual communications to the Commission on the Status of Women.

Advocates can also bring information to the attention of other UN bodies that deal partially or incidentally with human rights, such as the General Assembly, the Security Council, and the Economic and Social Council (ECOSOC). The General Assembly, in particular, may issue declarations that guide state policy, although such declarations lack power as binding law and enforcement mechanisms. One important example is the Declaration on the Elimination of Violence Against Women, adopted by the General Assembly in 1993.

The structure of the procedures under non-treaty-based mechanisms varies from the more formal (such as ILO procedures) to the less formal (such as letter writing to the Commission on the Status of Women).

Question: What kind of role can I play?
Answer: It will be based on the human rights procedure in question.

You have to determine first what types of human rights procedures are available. All procedures usually fit within the following two types: (1) complaint mechanisms, and (2) monitoring and reporting mechanisms.

Complaint Mechanisms

In many countries, these procedures often resemble court procedures. An individual, NGO, or state body submits a paper—the complaint or petition—(a) stating what happened and to whom, (b) explaining how the human rights violation occurred, who is responsible, and why, and (c) specifying which rights under which specific documents were violated. Sometimes only states and not individuals can make complaints. This section discusses only the possible types of complaints that could be made by individuals.

There are two types of complaint procedures: complaint-recourse and complaint-information procedures.

Under *complaint-recourse procedures*, you make a complaint for remedies for a grievance. For example, you could demand compensation for a human rights violation committed against you, such as torture in prison. You deliver the complaint to the appropriate body, which depends on what level you approach and what type of claim you are making. You continue to participate in the process, much as you would in a court. The state may respond to your complaint, and the commission or court may undertake its own independent investigation of your claim. The complaint you make is extremely important as the commission or court relies heavily upon it in considering the case. Even if you are not the one bringing the case, as part of an NGO you may participate by monitoring and publicizing the proceedings.

Under *complaint-information procedures*, you can make a complaint for violations affecting a large population and deliver it to the appropriate body. You cannot demand specific remedies, but you can demand that the state change its practices. You could demand that the state change its treatment of all women prisoners. Once you deliver your communication, your participation in the case stops. The proceedings then continue largely in secret, with the commission possibly contacting the state for information and conducting its own investigation. Your complaint is important as it could help trigger an investigation, but it is only part of the information before the commission on that particular issue.

Monitoring and Reporting Mechanisms

Monitoring and reporting procedures do not resemble court cases. Many regional and international agreements require states to submit periodic reports on their own behavior, explaining whether they are complying with the obligations they willingly undertook. This is like a student reporting on herself. When she is a good student, the self-criticism works; when she is not so good, problems may ensue. Often the monitoring proceeds according to a regularly scheduled plan of inspection; or, much more rarely, the process may be triggered by advocates who point out a particularly pressing problem. Individuals and NGOs can usually review the state reports—which must be made public—and issue the NGO version of reality. In recent years, some NGOs working on women's human rights have issued "alternative reports" to the reports that their countries must submit on their implementation of CEDAW.

A successful complaint procedure usually means "winning" a claim. On the other hand, monitoring and reporting procedures are successful if they bring publicity to human rights abuses and shame governments and other human rights violators into changing their behavior.

Glossary

adoption   Usually refers to the initial diplomatic stage at which the official text of a **treaty** is accepted, in the case of a treaty by the UN General Assembly. After adoption a treaty must usually be **ratified** by individual governments.

affirmative action (also positive discrimination, reverse discrimination)   Action taken by a government or private institution to make up for past discrimination in education, employment, or promotion on the basis of gender, race, ethnic origin, religion, or disability.

African Charter on Human and People's Rights (African Charter)   A regional human rights treaty for the African continent adopted by the Organization of Africa Unity (OAU) in 1981.

American Convention on Human Rights (American Convention)   A human rights treaty adopted by the Organisation for American States (OAS) in 1969. It covers North, Central, and South America.

Beijing Declaration and Platform for Action   Consensus document emerging from the 1995 **Fourth World Conference on Women**, reviewing and reaffirming women's human rights in all aspects of life. As a **declaration** it is morally but not legally binding.

Beijing+5 (2000) and Bejing+10 (2005) Conferences   Conferences held five and ten years after the 1995 **Fourth World Conference on Women**; these follow-up conferences provided states with an opportunity to justify their actions.

"best interest of the child" standard   This fundamental principle of the **Convention on the Rights of the Child** affirms that the best interest of the child shall be a primary consideration in all actions concerning children. Article 3 of the Children's Convention emphasizes that governments and public and private bodies must ascertain the impact on children of their actions and give proper priority to children and to building child-friendly societies.

Convention on the Rights of the Child (Children's Convention, CRC) (adopted 1989; entered into force 1990)   **Treaty** setting forth a full spectrum of civil, cultural, economic, social, and political rights for children. It also monitors implementation of two optional protocols to the convention, on involvement of children in armed conflict and on the sale of children, child prostitution, and child pornography.

Committee on Economic, Social and Cultural Rights   The body of independent experts that monitors implementation of the **International Covenant on Economic, Social, and Cultural Rights** (ICESCR) by its states parties.

convention   Binding agreement between states; used synonymously with **treaty** and **covenant**. Conventions are stronger than **declarations** because they are legally binding for governments that have signed them. When the UN General Assembly adopts a convention, it creates international norms and standards. Once a convention is adopted by the UN General Assembly, **member states** can then **ratify** the convention, promising to uphold it. Governments that violate the standards set forth in a convention can then be censured by the UN.

Convention Against Torture and Other Cruel, Inhumane or Degrading Treatment or Punishment (CAT Torture Convention) (adopted 1984; entered into force 1987) **Treaty** defining and prohibiting torture.

Convention on the Elimination of All Forms of Discrimination Against Women (CEDAW, Women's Convention) (adopted 1979; entered into force 1981) The first legally binding international document prohibiting discrimination against women and obligating governments to take **affirmative action** to advance the equality of women.

Convention on the Elimination of All Forms of Racial Discrimination (CERD, Race Convention) (adopted 1965; entered into force 1969) **Treaty** defining and prohibiting racial discrimination.

Convention on the Protection of the Rights of All Migrant Workers and Members of Their Families (ICRMW) (adopted 1990; entered into force 1998) **Treaty** defining the rights of migrant workers and their families.

Convention on the Rights of the Child (CRC, Children's Convention) (adopted 1989; entered into force 1990) **Treaty** setting forth a full spectrum of civil, cultural, economic, social, and political rights for children.

covenant Binding agreement between states; used synonymously with **convention** and **treaty**. The major international human rights covenants, both passed in 1966, are the **International Covenant on Civil and Political Rights** (ICCPR) and the **International Covenant on Economic, Social and Cultural Rights** (ICESCR). Both were adopted in 1966 and entered into force in 1976.

declaration Document stating agreed-upon standards that is not legally binding. UN conferences (e.g., the 1993 UN Conference on Human Rights in Vienna, the **Fourth World Conference on Women**) usually produce two sets of declarations: one written by government representatives and one by nongovernmental organizations (NGOs). The UN General Assembly often issues influential but legally **nonbinding** declarations.

Earth Summit The UN Conference on Environment and Development held in Rio in 1992 to help governments rethink economic development and find ways to halt the destruction of irreplaceable natural resources and pollution of the planet, resulting in the **Rio Declaration on Environment and Development**.

entry into force The process through which a **treaty** becomes fully binding on the states that have **ratified** it. This happens when the minimum number of **ratifications** called for by the treaty has been achieved.

environmental justice The fair treatment and meaningful involvement of all people regardless of race, color, national origin, or income with respect to the development, implementation, and enforcement of environmental laws, regulations, and policies.

environmental racism Racial bias that puts minority groups at greater risk to environmental threats, such as housing near polluting facilities, contaminated food, and risky occupations.

European Convention for the Protection of Human Rights and Fundamental Freedoms (European Convention, European Convention on Human Rights, ECHR) A regional human rights treaty adopted in 1950 by the Council of Europe. All Council of Europe **member states** are party to the ECHR, and new members are expected to ratify the convention at the earliest opportunity.

export processing zones (EPZ)   Industrial zones set up to attract foreign investors or delineated industrial estates, which constitute a free trade enclave in the customs and trade regime of the country.

female genital cutting (FGC)   Also called female genital mutilation or FGM.

food security   Term used broadly to describe a situation in which people have continuity of food of adequate quantity and quality and cultural appropirateness, or the methods by which this aim is achieved.

Fourth World Conference on Women   Held in Beijing in 1995, this conference was attended by representatives of over 180 countries, including more than forty thousand who attended the NGO Forum. Resulted in the **Beijing Declaration and Platform for Action**.

functional illiteracy   The inability of an individual to use reading, speaking, writing, and computational skills in everyday life situations. For example, a functionally illiterate adult is unable to fill out an employment application, follow written instructions, or read a newspaper.

gender   A social construct that informs roles, attitudes, values, and relationships regarding women and men. While sex is determined by biology, gender is determined by society, almost always functioning to subordinate women to men.

gender analysis   A diagnostic tool that focuses on the key differences between the incentives and constraints under which men and women work, highlighting gender differences in access to and control over income and resources and considering the implications of these divisions and differences for project design.

"gender and development"   An approach to development planning and assessment that holds that the **gender** roles of men and women lead to differences in needs, skills, and access to resources and must be taken into account.

gender budgets   Initiatives to make budget policy and decisions more accountable from a **gender** perspective and to ensure policies on gender equality are matched with adequate resource allocations.

gender mainstreaming   A strategy for promoting gender equality, involving ensuring that gender perspectives and attention to the goal of gender equality are central to all activities (e.g., policy development; research; advocacy; legislation; resource allocation; and planning, implementing, and monitoring programs and projects).

gender perspective   An approach that seeks to expose the ways in which roles, attitudes, and relationships between women and men are constructed in a society and to challenge assumptions that exclude women's experience and capacities.

general comment   A written statement by the committee monitoring a UN **treaty** (e.g., **Committee on Economic, Social and Cultural Rights**) that advises states how best to fulfill their obligations under that treaty. They also analyze and interpret the meaning, content, and scope of a treaty.

Geneva Conventions   Four treaties adopted in 1949 under the International Committee of the Red Cross (ICRC) in Geneva, Switzerland. These treaties revised and expanded original treaties adopted in 1864 and 1929. They address the treatment of sick and wounded soldiers and sailors, prisoners of war, and civilians under enemy control.

genocide   Acts committed with intent to destroy, in whole or in part, a national, ethnical, racial, or religious group.

globalization   An increased connectivity among societies due to transculturation and the explosive evolution of transportation and communication technologies to facilitate international cultural and economic exchange.

The Habitat Agenda   The main political document resulting from the 1996 Habitat II Conference in Istanbul (or "City Summit). It addressed two main themes: that a large segment of the world's population lacks shelter and sanitation and that sustainable development of human settlements combines economic development, social development, and environmental protection, with full respect for all human rights and fundamental freedoms.

humanitarian law   the body of law, mainly based on the **Geneva Conventions**, that protects certain persons in times of armed conflict, helps victims, and limits the methods and means of combat in order to minimize destruction, loss of life, and unnecessary human suffering.

Human Rights Committee   The body of independent experts that monitored implementation of the **International Covenant on Civil and Political Rights** by its states parties; replaced by the **Human Rights Council** in 2006.

Human Rights Council   The body of independent experts that monitored implementation of the **International Covenant on Civil and Political Rights** by its states parties; replaced the **Human Rights Committee** in 2006.

inalienable   Refers to the principle that human rights belong to every person and cannot be taken from a person under any circumstances. Human rights automatically belong to each human being. They are not given to people by their government or any other authority, nor can they can be taken away.

indivisible   Refers to the principle that each human right is of equal importance. A person cannot be denied a right because someone decides it is "less important" or "nonessential."

inherent   Principle that human rights are a natural part of who you are. The text of Article 1 of the **Universal Declaration of Human Rights** (UDHR) begins "All human beings are born free and equal in dignity and rights."

Inter-American Convention on the Prevention, Punishment and Eradication Of Violence Against Women ("Convention of Belem do Para")   A 1994 regional treaty recognizing that "violence against women constitutes a violation of their human rights," that this violence is pervasive, and that in order to eliminate violence against women, states parties agree to pursue policies to prevent and punish violence against women.

interconnectedness   A fundamental principle that affirms the interdependence of all human rights.

interdependent   Refers to the complementary framework of human rights law. For example, your ability to participate in your government is directly affected by your right to express yourself, to get an education, and even to obtain the necessities of life.

internally displaced persons (IDPs)   Persons or groups of persons who have been forced or obliged to leave their homes or places of habitual residence, in particular as a result of or in order to avoid the effects of armed conflict, situations of generalized violence, violations of human rights, or other natural or human-made disasters and who have not crossed an internationally recognized state border.

intergovernmental organizations (IGOs)   Organizations sponsored by several governments that seek to coordinate their efforts; some are regional (e.g., the Council of Europe, the Organisation of American States), some are alliances (e.g., the North Atlantic Treaty Organization); and some are dedicated to a specific purpose (e.g., the **World Health Organization, International Labour Organization**).

International Bill of Human Rights   The combination of the **Universal Declaration of Human Rights** (UDHR), the **International Covenant on Civil and Political Rights** (ICCPR) and its **optional protocol**, and the **International Covenant on Economic, Social, and Cultural Rights** (ICESCR).

International Conference on Population and Development   1994 conference convened in Cairo under the auspices of the United Nations with over 11,000 participants from 180 countries; resulted in a program of action in the area of population and development for the next twenty years.

International Covenant on Civil and Political Rights (ICCPR) (adopted 1966; entered into force 1976)   The ICCPR declares that all people have a broad range of civil and political rights. One of the components of the **International Bill of Human Rights**.

International Covenant on Economic, Social, and Cultural Rights (ICESCR) (adopted 1966; entered into force 1976)   The ICESCR declares that all people have a broad range of economic, social, and cultural rights. One of the components of the **International Bill of Human Rights**.

International Criminal Court (ICC)   Established by the Rome State, which entered into force in 2002, the ICC was the first permanent, treaty-based international criminal court to promote the rule of law and ensure that the gravest international crimes do not go unpunished.

International Criminal Tribunal for Rwanda (ICTR)   Created in 1994 by the UN Security Council, the ICTR contributes to the process of national reconciliation in Rwanda and prosecutes persons responsible for genocide and other serious violations of international humanitarian law committed in Rwanda and neighboring states during 1994.

International Criminal Tribunal for the Former Yugoslavia (ICTY)   Located at the Hague, the ICTY was established by the UN Security Council in 1993 to address serious violations of international humanitarian law committed in the territory of the former Yugoslavia since 1991.

international humanitarian law   the body of law, mainly based on the **Geneva Conventions**, that protects certain persons in times of armed conflict, helps victims, and limits the methods and means of combat in order to minimize destruction, loss of life, and unnecessary human suffering.

International Labour Organization (ILO)   An **intergovernmental organization** established in 1919 as part of the Versailles Peace Treaty to improve working conditions and promote social justice; the ILO became a specialized agency of the UN in 1946.

member states   Countries that are members an **intergovernmental organization** (e.g., the United Nations, the Council of Europe).

nongovernmental organizations (NGOs)   Organizations formed by people outside of government. NGOs monitor the proceedings of human rights bodies such as the Human Rights Council of the United Nations and are the "watchdogs" of the human rights that fall within their mandate. Some are large and international (e.g., the Red Cross, Amnesty International, the scouts); others may be small and local (e.g., an organization to advocate for people with disabilities in a particular city, a coalition to promote women's rights in one refugee camp). NGOs play a major role in influencing UN policy, and many have official consultative status at the UN.

nonbinding   A document, like a **declaration**, that carries no formal legal obligations. It may, however, carry moral obligations or attain the force of law as customary international law.

Office of the High Commissioner for Human Rights (OHCHR)   Established in 1993, the OHCHR has formal responsibility for UN human rights activities. It serves as the Secretariat of the Human Rights Council, the committees that monitor human rights treaties, and other UN human rights organs.

optional protocol   A **treaty** that modifies another treaty (e.g., adding additional procedures or provisions). It is called *optional* because a government that has ratified the original treaty can choose whether or not to ratify the changes made in the protocol.

Optional Protocol to CEDAW (entered into force in December 2000)   States that ratify this **optional protocol** recognize the competence of the Committee on the Elimination of Discrimination against Women to receive and consider complaints from individuals or groups within its jurisdiction.

ratification, ratify   Process by which the legislative body of a state confirms a government's action in signing a treaty; formal procedure by which a state becomes bound to a treaty after acceptance.

reservation   The exceptions that states parties make to a **treaty** (e.g., provisions that they do not agree to follow). Reservations, however, may not undermine the fundamental meaning of the treaty.

Rio Declaration on Environment and Development   A document produced at the 1992 United Nations Conference on Environment and Development, informally known as the **Earth Summit,** consisting of twenty-seven principles intended to guide future sustainable development around the world.

Rome Statute of the International Criminal Court   The treaty establishing the **International Criminal Court** (ICC) that sets out its jurisdiction, structure, and functions. Entered into force in 2002.

sexual harassment   Threatening or disturbing behaviors of a sexual nature or persistent and unwanted sexual advances, typically in the workplace, where the consequences of refusing are potentially very disadvantaging to the victim.

shadow report   An unofficial report prepared by institutes or individuals representing civil society submitted to a committee monitoring a human rights **treaty**. Such reports usually contradict or add to the official report on treaty compliance and implementation submitted by a government as part of its treaty obligations.

special rapporteur   A person chosen by a UN human rights body to report on a particular theme (e.g., on the sale of children, child prostitution and child pornography, or violence against women) or on the human rights situation in a particular country.

Special Rapporteur on Torture   An independent expert first appointed in 1985 by the UN Commission on Human Rights to report on the situation of torture in the world, including transmitting urgent appeals to states regarding individuals reportedly at risk of torture, communicating on past alleged cases of torture, and undertaking fact-finding country visits.

structural violence   Institutionalized patterns of social, political, or economic domination; subordination; or exploitation that result in physical and psychological harm.

treaty   Formal agreement between states that defines and modifies their mutual duties and obligations; used synonymously with **convention** and **covenant**. When conventions are adopted by the UN General Assembly, they create legally binding international obligations for the **member states** who have signed the treaty. When a national government **ratifies** a treaty, the articles of that treaty become part of its domestic legal obligations.

United Nations Charter   Initial document of the UN setting forth its goals, functions, and responsibilities; adopted in San Francisco in 1945.

United Nations Conference on Environment and Development   See **Earth Summit.**

United Nations Development Programme (UNDP)   Formed by the UN General Assembly in 1965, this body administers and coordinates most of the technical assistance provided through the UN system to help countries achieve sustainable human development, especially poverty eradication.

United Nations Educational, Scientific and Cultural Organization (UNESCO)   Created in 1945, UNESCO included human rights in its mandate to promote international cooperation in the fields of education, science, and culture, while seeking to forge universal agreements on emerging ethical issues and to serve as a clearinghouse for the dissemination and sharing of information and knowledge.

United Nations Millennium Declaration In September 2000, the UN General Assembly adopted this global agenda for the twenty-first century, defining values, thematic issues, and goals to guide the daily activities of the UN and its programs.

United Nations Development Fund for Women (UNIFEM) Created in 1976 by the UN General Assembly, INIFEM promotes the human rights of women and ensures their participation in all levels of development planning and practice.

Universal Declaration of Human Rights (UDHR) (adopted by the UN General Assembly on December 10, 1948) Primary UN document establishing human rights standards and norms. All UN member states have agreed to uphold the UDHR. Although the UDHR was intended to be **nonbinding**, through time its various provisions have become so respected by states that it can now be said to be customary international law. One component of the **International Bill of Human Rights**.

universality A principle that all human rights are held by all persons in all states and societies in the world.

Women in Development (WID) Approach to development that attempts to address women's interests and concerns; criticized as "add woman and stir" approach; generally replaced with a **gender and development** approach that more explicitly addresses women's and men's socially constructed roles.

Women's Convention See **Convention on the Elimination of all Forms of Discrimination Against Women**

World Conference Against Racism Held in South Africa, this 2001 conference addressed the following issues: sources, causes, forms and contemporary manifestations of racism, racial discrimination, and related intolerance and measures of prevention, education, and protection aimed at the eradication of racism.

World Conference on Human Rights At this 1993 conference in Vienna representatives of 171 states and over 800 NGOs adopted the Vienna Declaration and Programme of Action, a common plan for the strengthening of human rights work around the world.

World Conference on Women See **Fourth World Conference on Women**

World Food Summit A 1996 conference in which over 10,000 participants debated the imperative of eradicating hunger and malnutrition and achieving sustainable **food security**; the Rome Declaration on World Food Security and the World Food Summit Plan of Action were adopted at the summit.

World Health Organization (WHO) Created in 1946, this UN agency works for "the attainment by all people of the highest possible level of health" by coordinating international action and technical assistance and training health providers.

Bibliography

Abdellefatah Amor, Special Rapporteur on Religious Freedom or Belief, Report on Religious Freedom or Belief to UN Commission on Human Rights, E/CN.4/1999/58.

Action Canada for Population and Development, "Trafficking and Girls," 2001, Ontario, available online at http://www.crlp.org/pdf/pub_fac_adoles_trafficking.pdf.

Alyek, Helen, "Harmful Cultural Practices Against Women and Children (Girl Child) in Uganda and Africa," conference paper for the Australian Government Institute of Criminology, October 2002, available online at http://www.aic.gov.au.

American Association of University Women, "Hostile Hallways: Bullying, Teasing, and Sexual Harassment in School," New York, 2001, available online at http://www.aauw.org.

Amnesty International Canada, "Canada: Stolen Sisters: A Human Rights Response to Discrimination and Violence Against Indigenous Women In Canada," October 4, 2004, available online at http://www.amnesty.ca/resource_centre/reports/view.php?load=arcview&article=1895&c=Resource+Centre+Reports.

Amnesty International, *Women in China*, AI Index ASA 17/29/95, London, 1995.

Anderson, Shelley, "More Training Towards Gender-Sensitive Non-Violence Training," International Fellowship for Reconciliation Women Peacemakers Program, The Netherlands, available online at http://www.ifor.org/WPP/TOT%20report%202002.pdf.

Australian Government Family Assistant Office, "Large Family Supplement," available online at http://www.familyassist.gov.au/Internet/FAO/FAO1.nsf/content/payments-large_family_supp.

Bannon, Ian, and Maria C. Correia, eds., *The Other Half of Gender: Men's Issues in Development*, The World Bank, 2006.

Beijing Declaration and Platform for Action, Fourth World Conference on Women, September 15, 1995, A/CONF. 177/20 (1995) and A/CONF. 177/20/Add. 1 (1995).

Buhler, Rich, "Women and Children in Portions of Africa Are Being Sexually Violated by Men Who Believe That Sex with a Virgin Will Cure Their AIDS," *Truth or Fiction*, available online at http://www.truthorfiction.com/rumors/a/aids-virgins.htm.

Canadian International Development Agency, "Child Labour," January 23, 2004, Quebec, available online at http://www.acdi-cida.gc.ca/index.htm.

Center for Reproductive Rights, *Ensuring the Reproductive Rights of Adolescents*, February 1999, New York, available online at http://www.crlp.org.

Chelala, Cesar, "The Unrelenting Scourge of Child Prostitution," November 28, 2000, Portland, Maine: Common Dreams News Center, available online at http://www.commondreams.org/views/112800-104.htm.

Commission for Racial Equality, "Statistics: Housing," available online at http://www.cre.gov.uk/research/statistics_housing.html.

Commission for Racial Equality, "Statistics: Labour Market," available online at http://www.cre.gov.uk/research/statistics_labour.html.

Consulate General of the United States, Dhahran, Saudhi Arabia, "Public Services, International Parental Child Abduction," U.S. Department of State, January 16, 2002, available online at http://dhahran.usconsulate.gov/dhahran/custody.html.

Disability Awareness in Action, *Disabled Women*, vol. 5, 1997, http://www.daa.org.uk/index.htm.

Doi, Abdur Rahman, "Women in Society," USC-MSA Compendium of Muslim Texts, available online at http://www.usc.edu/dept/MSA/humanrelations/womeninislam/womeninsociety.html.

Earl-Taylor, Mike, "HIV/AIDS, the Stats, the Virgin Cure and Infant Rape," *Science in Africa*, 2002, available online at http://www.scienceinafrica.co.za/2002/april/virgin.htm.

Eide, Asbjørn, "Economic and Social Rights," in *Human Rights: Concepts and Standards*, edited by Janusz Symonides (UNESCO, 2000).

Ennew, Judith, "Outside Childhood: Street Children's Rights," in *The Handbook of Children's Rights*, edited by Bob Franklin (London: Routledge, 1995).

Evans, Andrea, "Group Warns of Risks to Teenage Mothers and Their Babies," *San Francisco Chronicle*, May 3, 2004.

Flowers, Nancy, *Human Rights Here and Now: Celebrating the Universal Declaration of Human Rights*, Human Rights Resource Center, Minneapolis, Minnesota, 1998, available online at http://www.hrusa.org.

Flowers, Nancy, *The Human Rights Education Handbook: Effective Practices for Learning, Action, and Change,* Human Rights Resource Center, 2000, Index of Methods, Techniques, and Activities, University of Minnesota Human Rights Library, available online at http://www1.umn.edu/humanrts/edumat/hreduseries/hrhandbook/aboutseries.html.

Global Fund for Women, available online at http://www.globalfundforwomen.org/.

Guerin, Philippe J., et al., "Malaria: Current Status of Control, Diagnosis, Treatment, and a Proposed Agenda for Research and Development," *The Lancet Infectious Diseases*, vol. 2, September 2002, London: The Lancet Publishing Group, available online at http://www.accessmed-msf.org/upload/ReportsandPublications/25920021619148/malaria.pdf.

Hernandez-Truyol, Berta Esperanza, "Women's Rights as Human Rights—Rules, Realities and the Role of Culture: A Formula for Reform," *Brooklyn Journal of International Law*, vol. 21 (1996), p. 605.

Hosken, Fran, *The Hosken Report: Genital and Sexual Mutilation of Females*, Fourth Revised Edition, Women's International Network News, Lexington, Massachusetts, 1993.

Human Rights House Network, "Roma Still Suffer Discrimination," available online at http://www.humanrightshouse.org/.

Human Rights Watch, "Children's Rights: Child Soldiers," 2007, New York: Human Rights Watch, available online at http://www.hrw.org/campaigns/crp/index.htm.

Human Rights Watch, "Women and Girls with Disabilities," 2004, New York: Human Rights Watch, available online at http://www.hrw.org/women/disabled.html.

Human Rights Watch, Women's Division, *Background Paper on Abuses of Disabled Women's and Girls' Rights*, New York: Human Rights Watch, available online at http://www.hrw.org/women/disabled.html.

Human Rights Watch Press Backgrounder, "Race and Incarceration in the United States," February 27, 2002, New York: Human Rights Watch, available online at http://www.hrw.org/backgrounder/usa/race/.

Indian and Northern Affairs of Canada, Government of Canada, "Backgrounder: The Residential School System," available online at http://www.ainc-inac.gc.ca/gs/schl_e.html.

International Center for Research on Women, "Property and Inheritance Rights for Women," 2005, available online at http://www.icrw.org/html/projects/projects_property%20rights.htm#context.

International Covenant on Economic, Social and Cultural Rights (ICESR) in *Human Rights: A Compilation of International Instruments*, ST/HR/1/Rev.5, Vol. 1. Pt. 1.

International Labour Organisation, "Child Labour Risks Growing in Africa: Organization of African Unity and International Labour Organisation, Convene Tripartite Meeting," Geneva, 1998, available online at http://www.ilo.org/public/english/bureau/inf/pr/1998/4.htm.

International Women's Health Coalition, "Nigeria: Challenging a Culture of Silence: A Conversation with Dorothy Aken'Ova," available online at http://www.iwhc.org/programs/africa/nigeria/index.cfm.

Japan-National Assembly of Disabled Peoples International, *Counter Report of the Report of the Japanese Government Made at the 26th Session of the Extraordinary Session of the Committee on Economic, Social and Cultural Rights*, Geneva, August 13–31, 2001.

Kebebew, Ashagric, "Statistics on Working Children and Hazardous Child Labour in Brief," International Labour Organisation, Geneva, 1998.

Kennedy, Margaret, "Rights for Children Who are Disabled," in *The Handbook of Children's Rights*, edited Bob Franklin (London: Routledge, 1995).

Leony, Grich, "WUNRN and the UN Study," Human Rights Education Associates, available online at http://www.wunrn.com/anthology/anthology.htm.

Mental Disability Rights International, *Not on the Agenda: Human Rights of People with Mental Disabilities in Kosovo* (2002).

Mertus, Julie, "State Discriminatory Family Law and Customary Abuses," *Women's Rights, Human Rights: International Feminist Perspectives*, edited by Julie Peters and Andrea Wolper (New York: Routledge, 1995).

Mertus, J., N. Flowers, and M. Dutt, *Local Action, Global Change: Learning About the Human Rights of Women and Girls*, 1st ed. (New York: UNIFEM and the Center for Women's Global Leadership, 1999).

Metts, Robert L. *Disability Issues, Trends and Recommendations for the World Bank*, Discussion Paper No. 0007, 29, February 2000.

Ms. Foundation report, citing Lyn Brown, "Narratives of Relationship: The Development of the Care Voice in Girls Age 7–16." Ph.D. dissertation, Harvard, 1989, in *Women, Girls, and Psychotherapy: Reframing Resistance*, edited by C. Gilligan, A. Rogers, and D. Jolman (New York: Hayworth Press, 1991).

Muntarbhorn, Vitit, "International Perspectives on Child Prostitution in Asia," in *Forced Labour: The Prostitution of Children* (Washington, DC: U.S. Department of Labor, 1996).

National Center for Education Statistics, *Family Characteristics of 6- to 12-Year Olds*, January 2000, available online at http://nces.ed.gov/pubs2000/2000004.pdf.

National Coalition for the Homeless, "Who Is Homeless?" Fact Sheet #3, available online at http://www.nationalhomeless.org/publications/facts/Whois.pdf.

National Council on Disability, *From Privileges to Rights: People Labeled with Psychiatric Disabilities Speak for Themselves*, vol. 12, January 20, 2000.

News India, "World Health Day 2005," available online at http://www.healthinitiative.org/html/whd/2k5/.

Niaz, Dr. Unaiza, "Overview of Women's Mental health in Pakistan," *Pakistan Journal of Medical Sciences*, vol. 17, no. 4 (December 2001), available online at http://www.pjms.com.pk/issues/octdec01/article3.html.

Parry, John W., *1999 Employment Decisions Under the ADA Title I—Survey Update*, 24 *Mental and Physical Disability Law Reporter*, vol. 24 May–June 2000, pp. 348, 349.

Progressive Policy Institute, "Worldwide Child Labor Rates Have Fallen by Half Since 1980," May 8, 2002, Washington, DC, available online at http://www.ppionline.org/ppi_ci.cfm?knlgAreaID=108&subsecID=900003&contentID=250458.

Psychology: An International Perspective, "Approaches to Abnormality, Eating Disorders," London: Psychology Press, available online at http://www.psypress.co.uk/pip/resources/slp/topic.asp?chapter=ch22&topic=ch22-sc-07.

Population Council Media Center, "The Risks of Early Marriage," June 17, 2004, New York: Population Council, available online at http://www.popcouncil.org/mediacenter/newsreleases/early_marriageJB.html.

Population Council, "Married Adolescent Girls: Human Rights, Health, and Development Needs of a Neglected Majority," Working Group on Girls Steering Committee, September 6, 2001, New York: Population Council.

Population Reference Bureau and Centre for Population Options, "The World's Youth 1994: A Special Focus on Reproductive Health," Washington DC, March 1994.

Sadgopal, Mira, *Na Shariram Nadhi: My Body is Mine*, Sabala and Kranti (Mumbai, 1996).

Siddiqi, Faraaz, and Harry Anthony Patrinos, "Child Labor: Issues, Causes and Interventions," Human Capital Development and Operations Policy, World Bank, Washington, DC, available online at http://www.worldbank.org/html/extdr/hnp/hddflash/workp/wp_00056.html.

Singh, S., et al., "Gender Differences in the Timing of First Intercourse; Data from 14 Countries," *International Family Planning Perspectives*, vol. 26, no. 1 (2000), pp. 28, 43.

Smyke, Patricia, *Women and Health* (London: Zed Books, Ltd., 1991).

Sindelar, Daisy, "China: Population May Peak Under 'One-Child' Policy," *Radio Free Europe, Radio Liberty*, January 6, 2005, available online at http://www.rferl.org/features article/2005/01/5c329a6d-0678-4be8-b651-b198e1565b94.html.

Sindelar, Daisy, "China: A Future with a Shortage of Brides, an Abundance of Elderly," *Radio Free Europe, Radio Liberty*, January 7, 2005, available online at http://www.rferl.org/featuresarticle/2005/01/ae9008d3-263c-4cc8-8047-2a23f5085b22.html.

Singleton, Tina, et al., *Gender and Disability: A Survey of InterAction Member Agencies*, Mobility International USA, 2001.

Sisodia, Rajeshree, "'Honor' Most Foul," *Indianest*, November 28, 2004, available online at http://www.boloji.com/wfs3/wfs312.htm.

Sohoni, Neera Kuckreja, *The Burden of Childhood: A Global Inquiry into the Status of Girls* (Oakland, CA: Third Party Publishers, 1995).

Stavenhagen, Rodolfo, "Information Note on the Mandate of the Special Rapporteur on the Situation of Human Rights and Fundamental Freedoms of Indigenous Peoples," June 2004, available online at http://www.unhchr.ch/indigenous/rapporteur.htm.

The Hindu, "Status of the World Population Report 2005, Gender Violence," October 15, 2005.

Toubia, Nahid. *Female Genital Mutilation: A Call for Global Action* (New York: Women, Ink., 1993).

United Nations, "Looking Back Moving Forward: Second Review and Appraisal of the Implementation Strategies of the Nairobi Forward-Looking Strategies for the Advancement of Women," February 13, 1995. New York: United Nations.

United Nations, *The Study on Freedom of Religion or Belief and the Status of Women from the Viewpoint of Religion and Traditions*, Unofficial Summary in English, E/CN.4/2002/73/add.2, available online at http://www.wunrn.com/un_study/english.pdf.

United Nations, *The World's Women 1995: Trends and Statistics*, New York: United Nations.

United Nations, *The World's Women 2000: Trends and Statistics*, New York: United Nations.

United Nations, "Widowhood: Invisible Women Secluded or Excluded," *The World's Women 2000*, December 2001. New York: United Nations, available online at http://64.233.161.104/search?q=cache:JlTkYCEHXNIJ:www.un.org/womenwatch/daw/public/wom_Dec%252001%2520single%2520pg.pdf+Widows+comprise+a+significant+proportion+of+all+women+worldwide,&hl=en&gl=us&ct=clnk&cd=6.

United Nations, *World Youth Report 2003*, New York: United Nations.

United Nations Children's Fund (UNICEF), "Education of the Girl Child, Her Right, Society's Gain," Report of the NGO Conference, Educational Working Group, NGO Committee on UNICEF, New York, April 2122, 1992.

United Nations Convention on Consent to Marriage, Minimum Age for Marriage and the Registration of Marriages, 1964, New York: United Nations.

United Nations Convention on the Elimination of All Forms of Discrimination Against Women, 1981, New York: United Nations.

United Nations Convention on the Rights of the Child, 1990, New York: United Nations.

United Nations Department of Economic and Social Affairs, Population Division, "Living Arrangements of Older Persons Around the World," New York: United Nations, available online at http://www.un.org/esa/population/publications/livingarrangement/report.htm.

United Nations Development Fund for Women (UNIFEM), Rwanda: Country Page, available online at http://www.womenwarpeace.org/rwanda/rwanda.htm.

United Nations Development Fund for Women (UNIFEM), *Securing Indigenous Rights and Participation*, available online at http://www.unifem.org/filesconfirmed/2/355_at_a_glance_indigenous_women.pdf# search='Key%20issues%20raised%20by%20indigenous%20women%20at%20various%20regional%20and%20international%20forums%20have%20included%20the%20need%20for%20protection%20of%20their.

United Nations Economic and Social Development in Asia and the Pacific (ESCAP), *Hidden Sisters: Women and Girls with Disabilities in the Asian and Pacific Region*, UN Doc. ST/ESCAP/1548 (1995).

United Nations General Assembly Resolution 10/2018, November 1, 1965. New York: United Nations.

United Nations Population Division, "2000 Report on Replacement Migration," New York: United Nations, available online at http://www.un.org/esa/population/publications/migration/chap5.pdf.

United Nations Population Division Press Release, DEV/2234, POP/735, "New Report on Replacement Migration," March 17, 2000, New York: United Nations, available online at http://www.un.org/News/Press/docs/2000/20000317.dev2234.doc.html.

United Nations Population Fund (UNFPA), New York: United Nations.

United Nations Report for the United Nations Special Rapporteur on Violence Against Women, February 5, 1996, E/CN.4/1996/53, New York: United Nations.

United Nations Statistics Division, Department of Economic and Social Affairs, "Statistics and Indicators on Women and Men 2005," New York: United Nations, available online at http://unstats.un.org/unsd/demographic/products/indwm/ww2005/tab1a.htm.

United Nations Sustainable Networking Development Programme (SNDP), New York: United Nations, available online at http://www.sdnpbd.org.

United States Agency for International Development Health Overview, Washington, DC, available online at http://www.usaid.gov/our_work/global_health.

United States Census Bureau, "Overview of Race and Hispanic Origin 2000," Washington, DC, available online at http://www.census.gov/prod/2001pubs/c2kbr01-1.pdf.

United States Department of Health and Human Services Office on Women's Health, "Eating Disorders Information Sheet," February 2000, Washington, DC, available online at http://www.4woman.gov/owh/pub/factsheets/eatingdis.htm.

United States Department of State Human Rights Report, February 2000, Washington, DC, available online at http://www.state.gov.

United States National Institute of Allergy and Infectious Diseases, National Institute of Health, U.S. Department of Health and Human Services, "HIV Infection in Infants and Children," July 2004, Bethesda, Maryland, available online at http://www .niaid.nih.gov/factsheets/hivchildren.htm.

Von Struensee, Vanessa, "Reports and Analyses: Widows, AIDS, Health and Human Rights in Africa," Association of Women's Rights in Development, February 10, 2005, available online at http://www.awid.org/members/reports.php?id=13.

Williams, Suzanne, Janet Seet, and Adelina Mwau, *Oxfam Gender Training Manual*, Oxfam, Publishing 1995, Oxford, United Kingdom.

Women's Environment and Development Organization (WEDO), New York, available online at http://www.wedo.org/.

Women's Human Rights Step by Step, Women, Law & Development International, 2007, available online at http://www.unhchr.ch/hredu.nsf/.

Wonacott, Peter, "India's Skewed Sex Ratio Puts GE Sales in Spotlight," *Wall Street Journal*, April 18, 2007, p. A1.

World Bank, *Voices of the Poor*, Case Study 9: Widows, Washington DC, 2000.

World Bank Group Regional Activities Latin America and the Caribbean, "Child Labor," Washington, DC, available online at http://www1.worldbank.org/sp/childlabor/lac.asp.

World Health Organization, "The Health of Youth, Facts for Action: Youth and Reproductive Health," A42/Technical Discussions/5, Geneva 1989.

Youth Advocate Program, "Street Children and Homelessness," March 17, 2004, Washington, DC, available online at http://www.yapi.org/street/.

Index

abortion: legalizing, 142; right to, 132, 156;
 safe *v.* unsafe, 135, 142; selective, 90–91,
 130, 148; WHO facts on, 135
abuse: domestic workers in United
 Kingdom, 151; dowry-related, 149–150,
 151, 274; emotional, 98; physical *v.*
 psychological, 160; protection against,
 237
activism, women's: aims of, 25; collective,
 200, 209; in formal labor sector, 220;
 social role of women and, 13
adolescents, 101, 140, 141. *See also* girls
advocacy, 1, 7, 13; affirmative action, 80,
 225, 265–266; challenges for, xiv, 25–26;
 groups for change, 269–270; human
 trafficking and, 197; strategies, 209–210,
 309–310; within UN human rights
 system, 22–23
affirmative action, 34, 39, 80. *See also*
 discrimination, affirmative
Afghanistan, 257, 266
Africa: education in, 241–242; media in,
 275; user fees in, 202–203; women-
 headed households in, 63, 64t. *See also*
 specific countries
African Charter on Human and Peoples'
 Rights, 93, 132, 156
age: discrimination based on, 54–55; for
 marriage, 45, 75, 76; reproductive, of
 world's female population, 128
American Convention on Human Rights, 93
Amnesty International: founding of, 13; on
 indigenous people, 40; support from, xv,
 xvi; on women prisoners, 263
Australia, 77
Austria, 259

Bangladesh, 69, 151, 179, 197

basic needs: adequate standard of living
 and, 173; fulfillment of/access to, 115,
 259, 288; housing and, 181
Beijing+5 Conference, 23, 194, 299–300
Beijing+10 Conference, 23
Beijing Platform for Action, xiii, 192, 194;
 education and, 245, 252; on
 empowerment, 266; media and, 271–272;
 on rights, 81, 83, 88–89, 92, 115–116,
 127, 128, 132; on violence, 74, 95–96,
 156; on war, 280, 281, 298
bisexuals, 140
Bosnia, 266, 282
Britain: laws in, 209; media in, 273
Burma, 186, 282

Cambodia, 96
Canada: indigenous women in, 40–41;
 White Ribbon Campaign, 270
child labor, 102–103, 225
children: as prostitutes, 96, 97, 103; as
 soldiers, 99; born of rape/sexual
 exploitation, 282; rights to parental care,
 67; street, 99; UNICEF on, 99, 103, 119,
 236; unmarried women giving away, 130;
 without parents, 67
Chile: Latin American and Caribbean
 Women's Health Network of, 167; politics
 in, 257
China: family restrictions in, 77; infanticide
 in, 91; politics in, 263; son
 preference/sex selection in, 91, 105
Colombia: domestic violence in, 282;
 indigenous women in, 40; legal abortions
 in, 142
colonialism, 13, 309
"comfort women," 186, 283

contraception, 23, 93–94, 209; in Japan, 142; sex education and, 101, 135

Convention Against Torture and Other Cruel, Inhumane, or Degrading Treatment, 154, 291

Convention and Recommendation on Workers with Family Responsibilities, 228

Convention on Consent to Marriage, Minimum Age for Marriage and Registration of Marriages, 68, 75–76

Convention on the Elimination of All Forms of Discrimination Against Women (CEDAW), 8, 88, 92, 267; Committee on, 118, 122–123; on discrimination, 34, 71, 80, 155, 172, 224, 225, 251, 256; on family and marriage, 67, 68, 78, 80; on health, 112, 115, 121–122; on right to participation, 258; Optional Protocol to, xvii–xviii, 22; ratification of, 31, 267

Convention on the Elimination of All Forms of Racial Discrimination (CERD), 34, 38–39

Convention on the Rights of Persons with Disabilities (CRPD), xviii, 34–35; Optional Protocol, 34–35

Convention on the Rights of the Child (CRC), 36, 67, 68, 87–88, 92–93; on culture, 43; on education, 251; on health, 101, 112, 122; Somalia and U.S. refusal to ratify, 88, 105; violence in home and, 73, 98

Convention Relating to the Status of Refugees, 68, 286, 290

Coomaraswamy, Radhika, 91, 156, 164

Costa Rica, 274

Council of Europe, 156; on discrimination types in workplace, 221–222; on gender budgeting, 206

crimes against humanity, xiii, 156, 298

culture: cultural adequacy, of housing, 182; cultural diversity, 41–42; discrimination based on, 41–43, 71, 179; identity, right to, 42–43; cultural practices, harmful, 43, 119; and gender-based violence, 162; and gender roles, 14, 206; international cultural cooperation, right to, 43; and political participation, 261–262; right to, 12, 41, 42–43; strategies for analyzing, 42; traditions and, 118–120, 248

Darfur: genocide in, 31; rape in, 282, 298

decision making: conflict resolution and, 6; in governments, trade and economic bodies, 209; politics and, 257–258, 266; power and, in family, 62–64; reproductive, 128–130; right to, 137

Declaration on the Elimination of Violence Against Women: adoption of, 22, 73; Articles 1–3, 153; on violence against women, 153, 155

Democratic Republic of Congo, 282

development: economic, underdevelopment and, 13; empowerment through, 207; gender, women and, 205–207

dignity, 6; equality and, xi, 3, 13; as principle for women's human rights, xiii, 4, 8

disability: charity/medical/social models of, 47; defined, 46; discrimination based on, 46–49, 222, 239; and education, 47–48; and employment, 47–48; girls with, 100; and health care, 48, 100, 114, 117, 118; hidden, 47; human rights related to, 8; and reasonable accommodation, 34, 48; and reproductive choices, 130

discrimination: affirmative, 265; class, xii, 52; defined, 38; direct/indirect, 33–34; differential treatment and, 34; in family, 70–71; positive, 225; workplace, 173, 179, 221–223; race and ethnicity, xii, 34, 38–39, 239; reverse, 34, 39, 80; types of, 34, 38–55

disease, 117–118; malaria, 118, 275; media and, 275; sexually transmitted, 93, 98, 99, 117, 140. *See also* HIV/AIDS

displaced women: defining, 285–286; human rights concerns of, 287–291; rights of, 179

divorce: property ownership and, 83, 183; right to, 45

domestic violence, 159–162; during wartime, 281–282; incest and, 97–98; myths *v.* facts about, 159–161; preventing, 162; protective orders for, 166; shelters and, 184

domestic workers, 217; abuse in United Kingdom, 151

dowry-related abuse, 149–150, 151, 274

economy: advocacy strategies and, 209–210; globalization and, 193–195, 200–203, 230; informal, 216

education: in Africa, 241–242; in Beijing Platform for Action and, 245, 252; of disabled people, 47–48; discrimination and, 39, 222; about health care, 114; about human rights, 5–7 251-2; for action, 7–8; and GDP, 238; gender-role stereotypes in, 244–245, 249; importance of, 1, 2, 166–167; productivity and, 237; right to, 3, 36, 43, 93, 248; social benefits of, 237–238; stereotypes, in, 244–245, 249; strategies for, 249, 252. *See also* schools; sex education

elderly people: rights of, 55; as widows, 82

employment: disabled people and, 47–48; diversification of women's opportunities, 195; education and, 237; full employment, 218–219; gender inequality in, 219–220; hostile work environment sexual harassment, 226–227; laws on corporations and, 209; reasonable accommodation in, 34, 48; and wages, 231. *See also* work

empowerment: through culture, 41; through development, 207; as outcome of human rights education, xiv, 5, 6, 74; politics and, 266

environment: World Conference on Environment and Development, Rio de Janeiro, 22

equality, 32–33; as principle for women's human rights, 4; dignity and, xi, 3, 13; formal, 32, 33; gender and, 14, 33, 205–206; of opportunity, 33; in family, 67, 80; health care and, 122–123; substantive, 32–33, 34. *See also* employment; gender

Ethiopia, 251

family: breakdown of, 195–196, 287–288; businesses, work in, 71, 216, 217, 219; defined, 63; discrimination within, 67–7, 80; human rights in, 3, 66–69; power and decision making in, 62–64; and kinship networks, 195–196; reunification, right to, 66, 67; status of women in, 73, 78, 119; women's roles in, 63, 70, 77, 26

family planning: and decision making, 128–130; and forced sterilization, 138; impacts of, 137–138, 140, 237; right to, 67, 68; U.S. policies on, 143

female genital cutting (FGC), 88, 94, 95; banning/prohibition of, 105, 132, 148–149, 156; legislative efforts to eliminate, 157t; occurrence of, 149t; types of, 119–120; women who believe in, 150t

female genital mutilation (FGM), *See* female genital cutting

food: access to, 178; availability of, 178; free from adverse substances, 178; free programs, 205; gender discrimination in, 179–180; insecurity, 178–180; minimum requirement for, 178; right to, 177–180

Fourth World Conference on Women, Beijing: on family planning, 68; People's Decade for Human Rights Education and, xv, xvi–xvii; on violence against women, 150; on women's rights, 137, 225. *See also* Beijing Platform for Action

France, 259, 266

gender: defined, 14; equality and, 14, 33, 205–206; human rights violations and, xii, 1; identity and, xii, 7; mainstreaming, 206, 267; sex *v.*, 14; socialization, 162, 245; stereotypes, in education, 244–245, 249; theory, 14; women, development and, 14, 205–207; women's roles and, 14, 180, 205

gender-based budgeting, 206–207, 267; steps to create sensitive, 207

Geneva Conventions, 283, 298

genocide, 30, 31, 38, 282

Ghana, 167, 202

girls: boys *v.*, 91, 92, 117, 118; health care, 91, 92, 100, 101; HIV/AIDS and, 93, 96t, 100, 140; right to food and water, 179; sexual and reproductive health of, 93–94; in schools, 96, 102, 105; socialization of, 88–89; status of, 89, 93; violence against, 95–100; vulnerable groups of, 99–100; young women and, at risk, 102. *See also* education, schools

globalization, economy and, 193–195, 200–203, 230; impact on women, 194–197;

government: corruption in, 257, 263; economic decision making, 209; oppression by, 32; on public-private split, xii, 15; spending cuts, 201–202; women's human rights and, xii, xiv, 5, 25

Guatemala: intimate surgery in, 94; politics in, 257

health: for all, 117–118; education and, 237; facts about, 118; long-term problems, 117; right to, defining, 115–116; role of authorities in, 121–122

health care, 23; access to, 115–116, 117, 118, 123, 133, 288; cultural barriers to, 114, 117; disability and, 48, 100, 114, 117, 118; girls', 91, 92, 117, 100, 101, 118; harmful traditional practices and, 118–120; mental, mental disorders, 118, 161; right to, 55, 113–114, 179. *See also* reproductive health care, reproductive and sexual health rights

HIV/AIDS: girls and, 93, 96t, 100, 140; media and, 275; money to fight, 203; percent of women with, 118; resistance against, 237; ritual "cleansing" of widows and, 51; screening for, 117; sex with virgins as cure for, 48, 96; young people with, 96t, 140, 141

honor killings, 100

housing: affordability of, 182; availability of, 182; denial of, xi, 36; eviction, forced, 181, 183–184, 186; gender-biased financing policies for, 184–185; habitability of, 182, 184; and homelessness, 177, location of, 182; minimum requirements of, 182; right to adequate, 181–186; violence, poverty and, 184–185

human rights: defined, 8, 12, 32; individual responsibility for, 5; monitoring and enforcing, 12, 25; in public *v.* private sphere, 15; at stake, 50; universality and, 31; vertical/horizontal/diagonal changes for work on, 310. *See also* specific groups/rights

human rights education: empowerment as outcome of, xiv, 5, 6, 74; goals, xi, 5–7; media for, 275. *See also* education

human rights violations: causes of/ education about, 6; gender and, xii, 1; identifying, 7; monitoring, 13; violence against women as, xii, 25, 73–74, 156, 310

Human Rights Watch: on child soldiers, 99; on disabled people, 48; founding of, 13; on genocide in Sudan and Darfur, 31

India: abortions and sex selection in, 90, 91, 105, 148; AIDS in, 96; dowry-related abuse in, 149–150, 151, 274; politics in, 265, 266; SEWA in, 218–219; slum eviction in, 186

indigenous people: discrimination against, 29, 40–41; human rights related to, 8

indivisibility of human rights, 3, 4, 36

infanticide, female, 91, 130, 148

inheritance: marriage and, 51, 82, 91; sex trafficking and, 97; widowhood and, 82, 183

Inter-American Convention on the Prevention, Punishment and Eradication of Violence Against Women, 156, 167

interconnectedness of human rights, 3; of discriminatory factors, 29; as principle for women's human rights, 5; of public and private spheres, 15

interdependence of human rights, 36

internally displaced persons (IDPs), 285–286

International Conference on Population and Development, Cairo (ICPD), xiii, 22–23, 67; on girls' rights, 88; on needs of young people, 139; Program of Action, 68, 127, 132

International Covenant on Civil and Political Rights (ICCPR), 8, 12, 154, 258; on children's rights, 92; on family, 68; on indigenous people, 41; on prisons, 154

International Covenant on Economic Social and Cultural Rights (ICESCR), 8, 12, 36, 172; on adequate standard of living, 174–175; on culture, 43; on education, 251; on family, 67–68; on health, 121

International Criminal Court, xiii, 156, 298

International Criminal Tribunal for Rwanda, 156

International Criminal Tribunal for the Former Yugoslavia (ICTY), 156, 297–298

International Labour Organisation (ILO): on child labor, 102; Declaration Concerning the Aims and Purposes of, 93; on health, 113, 195; on women and work, 221–222, 224, 228

International Monetary Fund (IMF), 200–203

Iran, 94

Iraq, 266

Ireland, 142, 160, 167; Northern, 301

Islam, 71, 94

Israel, Palestine and, 301

Japan: Action Plan to Combat Trafficking, 198; "comfort women" and, 283; contraception in, 142; sterilization of disabled people in, 48; women in politics in, 259

Jordan, 251, 266

Kenya: inheritance in, 51; refugees in, 286; SAPs and, 200

Kosovo, 283

labor, freedom from forced, 224; labor laws, 220, 224–225, 228

land ownership, 13, 51, 222. *See also* property ownership

land tenure, secure, 173, 182–183

law: education for human rights and, 6, 7; on employment and corporations, 209; human trafficking and, 197; immigration, 63; Islamic religion and, 71, 94; labor, 220, 224–225, 228; nationality, 63, 77–78; property ownership, 82–84; right to education in, 250–251; violence against women and, 162, 164, 166, 263

lesbians, 81, 140

Liberia, 257

literacy: beyond, educating for needs of girls/women, 241–242; lack of , 239, 251–252; programs, 241

Malaysia, 167

malnutrition, 91, 119, 173, 178, 179. *See also* food

marriage: age for, 45, 75, 76t; death by, 149–150; direct and indirect restrictions on, 78; early, 95, 99, 119, 241; forced, 67, 70, 95; harmful traditional practices and, 94; HIV/AIDS risk for unmarried *v.* married girls, 140; human rights and, 75–76; sexual assault in, 164

marriage rights: full and free consent to marriage, 67; right to marry and

establish family, 67, 70; role of
authorities in promoting, 79–80; role of
authorities in restricting, 77–78
media: access to, 273; alternative, 274;
community leaders, violence and, 167;
politics, public life and, 257; role of,
271–275
Mexico: legal abortions in, 142; maquila
program in, 220
Millennium Development Goals, 187–188,
203
Mongolia, 185
Morocco: family code in, 45, 71; politics in,
257, 267
mortality rate: infant/child, 137; maternal,
for girls and women, 75, 94, 117, 119,
128, 135; morbidity and, for female
infants/girls, 91; reproductive health
and, 128
Mozambique, 251, 259
multinational corporations (MNCs), 199–200

Namibia, 251, 259
nationality, laws, 63, 77–78; national origin
v., 38
Nepal, 142, 263
Nigeria, 51, 209
non-discrimination, 4, 33–35; as core
human right, 30–36; five types of conduct
and, 33–34
nongovernmental organizations (NGOs), 22,
155; forum, 23; politics and, 266–267;
privatization and, 201. *See also specific
NGOs*
Norway, 266

older women, problems of, 54–55; rights of,
55; support ratio, 54

Pakistan, 167, 263
Palestine, Israel and, 301
parents: abusive, 73; children's rights to
parental care, 67; rights of children
without, 67; single, 51
participation: political, 256–270; public,
256–259, 261; right to, 55, 88, 93,
258–259
patriarchy, 70–71, 150
peace, 6, 299, 301
Poland, 142
political participation, 256–270; barriers to,
261–262; and gender quotas in electoral
systems, 265–266; and right to vote, 36,
257, 258; strategies to increase, 265–267;
women, violence and, 263
politics: beyond traditional, 266–267;
gender-based violence and, 162; human
rights activism and, 13–14; quotas in,
265–266

population: control, reproductive rights *v.*,
137–138; and fertility rates, impacts of,
137–138; growth, 23, 132. *See also*
International Conference on Population
and Development, Cairo
poverty: adequate standard of living and,
173; class and, 52; disabilities and, 46,
48; education and, 242; food security
and, 178; infant mortality and, 137;
reduction strategies, 200–203; violence
and, 150, 161, 184–185; in women-
headed households, 64; work and, 217,
219–220, 231
power: decision making and, in family,
62–64; sexual harassment as, 227;
universality and, 31, 32
pregnancy: early, health dangers of, 140;
malaria and, 118; rights regarding, 67;
violence during, 148. *See also* teenage
mothers
prisons: international standards on,
154–155; women in, 153–155, 179, 263
property ownership, 82–84, 183, 186
Protocol on the African Charter on Human
and Peoples' Rights on the Rights of
Women in Africa, 132, 156
Protocol to Prevent, Suppress and Punish
Trafficking in Persons (UN), 31, 196
public-private split, xii, 12, 15, 25; human
rights in family and, 73–74

race and ethnicity, discrimination based on,
xii, 34, 38–39, 239
rape: and ethnic cleansing, 282; burden of
proof and public shame for, 96; children
born of, 282; as crime against humanity,
156, 298; legal disputes about, 164; as
torture, 291; war and, 156, 281,
282–283, 288, 297–298. *See also specific
countries*
refugees: defining, 285–286, 290–291;
human rights concerns of, 287–291;
rights of, 66, 68, 179–180, 283; scenarios
of hope for, 289–290; on Thai-Burmese
border, xvii
religion: discrimination based on, 44–45;
and extremism, 262; freedom of, 44;
Islamic religion and law, 71, 94; political
participation and, 261–262
reproductive age, of world's female
population, 128
reproductive and sexual health: defined,
116, 132; facing facts on, 128; girls',
93–94; information on adolescence and,
141
reproductive and sexual health rights:
actions to promote, 142–143; as
composite of several separate human
rights, 133; as human rights, 131–133;

racism, forced sterilization and, 138; thinking about, 128; population control, reproductive rights *v.*, 137–138
reproductive health care: defined, 48; for disabled people, 48; needs of young people, 139–140
reproductive rights, xiii; "naming and shaming" for, 209; population control *v.*, 137–138; role of authorities: in education, 248; in promoting/restricting marriage rights, 79–80; in rights of young women and girls, 105; in violence against women, 166; in women and work, 224–225; in women's health, 121–122
roles, women's, 13, 41; in family, 63, 70, 77, 261; gender and, 14, 180, 205; population control and, 138; stereotypes of, 222
Rwanda, 156, 209, 259, 300

Saudi Arabia, 257
Scandinavian countries, 257
schools: dropping out of, 241–242; girls in, 96, 102, 105; residential, in Canada, 41; sexual harassment in, 96, 105, 246–247
Scotland, 154
secure land tenure, 173, 182–183
sex education: contraception and, 101, 135; for girls, 93–94; reproduction, sexuality and, 101, 135, 137, 140
sex selection, 90–91, 105, 119; and misuse of, 90–91, 148
sex trade, 97
sexual abuse, 98
sexual and reproductive health, of girls, 93–94
sexual assaults, 163–164; of girls, 93, 96; legal disputes about, 164
sexual characteristics, of women, 14
sexual exploitation, 93, 97, 282
sexual harassment: defined/examples of, 226, 247; of girls, 96, 105; in schools, 96, 105, 246–247; in workplace, 34, 222–223, 226–227
sexual health. *See* reproductive and sexual health; reproductive and sexual health rights
sexual health care needs, of young people, 139–140
sexual health rights. *See* reproductive and sexual health rights
sexuality: adolescent, 101; reproduction, social conventions and, 137; reproduction, son preference and, 130
sexual rights, 81
sexually transmitted diseases, 117; girls and, 93, 98, 99; treatment for, 140. *See also* HIV/AIDS

sexual violence: girls and, 96; incest, 97–98; war and, 282–283, 297–300. *See also* rape
sex *v.* gender, 14
shelter, obstacles to right to, 185–186
skin color, cosmetics for, 94–95
slavery, 30–31, 39. *See also* trafficking, human
Slovakia, forced sterilization in, 138
socialization: gender-specific, 162, 245; of girls, 88–89
son preference, 119; examining, 91–92; reproduction, sexuality and, 130; right to survival and, 90–92
South Africa: education in, 242; politics in, 266
Special Rapporteur on Violence Against Women, xiii, xvii, 22, 156
standard of living, right to adequate, xviii; facts relating to, 177; as human right, 174–175; other rights related to, 175; thinking about, 173
status of girls: boys' status *v.*, 89; facing facts on, 93
status of women, 14; in family, 73, 78, 119; impacts on, 137; legal status of men *v.*, 162; minority, 185; public *v.* private spheres and, xi–xii, 73
status, refugee, inability to prove, 288
stereotypes: of elderly people, 55; gender-role, in education, 244–245, 249; of women's roles, 222
sterilization, forced, xii, 48, 138
street children, 99
street crime, 99
Structural Adjustment Participatory Review Initiative (SAPRI), 201
structural adjustment programs (SAPs), 200–202
structural violence, 150
Study on Freedom of Religion or Belief and the Status of Women from the Viewpoint of Religion and Traditions, 44
subordination, emancipation *v.*, 14
substantive equality, 32–33, 34
suicide, 140
survival, right to, 90–92
Sweatshop Watch, 231–232
Sweden, 259, 265

Tanzania, 201, 266, 275
tariff protections, 202
tax benefits, for large families, 77
teachers, female, 244–245
teenage mothers, 75, 93, 101
tenure, insecurity of, 182–183
Third World Network, 200–201
34 Million Friends for the UNFPA, 142
torture, 291

trade liberalization, exports and, 202

traditional practices, harmful, 94–95; health care and, 118–120

traditions, culture and, 118–120, 248

trafficking, human, 31, 97, 196–198, 282

training sessions: facilitators in, 7; gender-sensitive, 290

transgendered adolescents, 140

treaties: discrimination and, 34, 39; on family, 68; on harmful cultural practices, 43; minority, 309. *See also specific treaties*

tribunals, 39, 156, 297–298

Trinidad and Tobago, 251

Uganda: female genital cutting in, 43; user fees in, 203

UN Basic Principles for the Treatment of Prisoners, 154

UN Commission on Human Rights, xiii

UN Committee on the Status of Women, xvii

UN Conference on Human Settlement (Habitat II), 185

UN Declaration on the Protection of Women and Children in Armed Conflict, 283

UNIFEM Women, War and Peace Portal/Campaign, 299

unions, 218–219, 223, 231

United Kingdom: domestic worker abuse in, 151; forced marriages of Indian women in, 70. *See also* Britain

United Nations (UN): conferences, xiii, 22–23, 39, 67, 88; "development decades" of, 13; Program on Disabilities, 46. *See also* Universal Declaration of Human Rights; *specific covenants/conventions*

United Nations Body of Principles for the Protection of All Persons Under Any Form of Detention or Imprisonment, 154

United Nations Charter, 309; on health, 121; human rights principles in, 12; on rights of elderly, 55

United Nations Convention Against Transnational Organized Crime, 31

United Nations Development Fund for Women (UNIFEM), xv, 94, 167; globalization and, 200, 201; on work and poverty, 217, 219–220, 231

United Nations Development Program, 216

United Nations Educational, Scientific and Cultural Organization (UNESCO), 43; on literacy rate for disabled people, 48; on television, 271

United Nations High Commissioner for Refugees (UNHCR), 68, 283, 286; publications, 299

United Nations Human Rights Committee (UNHRC): on family definition, 63; General Comment 28, 133; on indigenous women, 40–41; on women in workplace, 225

United Nations Office on Drugs and Crime, 282

United Nations Population Fund (UNFPA), 119, 133, 142

United Nations Standard Minimum Rules for the Administration of Juvenile Justice, 154

United Nations Standard of Minimum Rules for the Treatment of Prisoners, 154

United States (U.S.): disabilities in, 47, 49; health care costs in, 55; rape in, 163–164; reproductive and sexual rights in, 142–143; segregation in, 38; sexual harassment in, 96; street children in, 99; violence in, 151, 167; women in politics in, 259

Universal Declaration of Human Rights (UDHR), xii, 12, 147, 309; on adequate standard of living, 174; on children's rights, 92; on cultural rights, 36; on education, 235; on equality and non-discrimination, 4, 33–35; on family, 62, 67; on motherhood, 68; on prisons, 154; on religion, 44; on rights of elderly, 55

universal health care, 55

universality of human rights, 3, 30–31; challenges to, 32; as principle for women's human rights, 4, 25

unmarried women: giving children away, 130; property ownership and, 83–84

Vienna Declaration: Program of Action: xiii, 28, 155; on violence against women, 22, 155

Vietnam, 259

violence: during forced eviction, 184; gender-based, factors that perpetuate, 162; partner, lifetime prevalence of, 159t; poverty, housing and, 184–185; structural, 150

violence against women: dehumanization and, xi; with disabilities, 48; within family, 70; female infanticide, 91; against girls, 95–100; domestic violence, 97–98, 159–162, 281–282; as human rights violation, xii, 25, 73–74, 156, 310; laws and, 162, 164, 166, 263; by partners, 159t; recognizing, 147–150, 155–157; by states, 263; strategies to combat, 167; types of, 151

virgins: intimate surgery and, 94; sex with, as HIV/AIDS cure, 48, 96

wage gap, 219–220, 222, 231

war: child soldiers and, 99; food security and, 178; human rights abuses as part of, xviii, 282–283, 297–300; impact of, on

women, 281–283; rape and, 156, 281, 282–283, 288, 297–298; and sexual violence, xviii, 282–283, 297–300
widowhood, 82, 83t; housing and, 183
women-headed households, 80, 177, 195, 236; in Africa, 63, 64t
women living apart, from men, 80–81
women's human rights, 1; achievements of, 22–23; action for improving, 5; defined, 8; development of, xvii–xviii, 12–15; key concepts for, 14–15; obstacles and challenges, 25–26; political struggles and, 13–14; recognition of, 25–26
work, 215; discrimination and, 173, 179, 221–223; health problems and, 117; inability to find meaningful, 287; in formal sector, 219–220; in informal sector 173, 217–219, 225, 23; protectionism and, 68–69; right to, 33, 36; sexual harassment at, 34, 222–223, 226–227; "women's work," 173, 205, 215–216, 217, 220
World Bank, 209; debt, global economy and, 201–202; on gender, 206; on health, 113, 118; on sexual assault, 163
World Conference on Environment and Development, Rio de Janeiro, 22
World Conference on Human Rights, Vienna, xiii, xvi, 22, 28, 73, 310. *See also* Vienna Declaration
World Health Organization (WHO): on defining right to health, 115; facts on abortion, 135; on FGC, 119; on maternal mortality, 94

Zimbabwe, 251

About the Authors

Julie Mertus is an Associate Professor and Codirector of the MA program in Ethics, Peace, and Global Affairs at American University. A graduate of Yale Law School, Professor Mertus has twenty years of experience working for a wide range of nongovernmental and governmental human rights organizations. Her prior appointments include: Senior Fellow, U.S. Institute of Peace; Human Rights Fellow, Harvard Law School; Writing Fellow, MacArthur Foundation; Fulbright Fellow (Romania 1995; Denmark 2006); and Counsel, Human Rights Watch. Her book *Bait and Switch: Human Rights and U.S. Foreign Policy* (2004) was named "human rights book of the year" by the American Political Science Association Human Rights Section. Her other books include: *Human Rights and Conflict* (2006)(editor, with Jeffrey Helsing); *The United Nations and Human Rights* (2005); *Kosovo: How Myths and Truths Started a War* (1999); and *The Suitcase: Refugees' Voices from Bosnia and Croatia* (1999). Professor Mertus has won several awards for her innovative curriculum design and teaching. In 2005, she was named the School of International Service Scholar/Teacher of the Year.

Nancy Flowers serves as a consultant to governments, nongovernmental organizations, and UN agencies on human rights education. She has trained activists, educators, lawyers, police, journalists, and parliamentarians in Europe, Asia, Africa, and the Middle East. Her publications include articles, books, and manuals on human rights education, most recently *Compasito*, a manual for children's rights education (2007); *Enabling Rights*, a manual on the human rights of people with disabilities (2007); and The Human Rights Education Series (2007). She is the editor of the Human Rights Education Series for the University of Minnesota's Human Rights Center. She makes her home in Menlo Park, California.